The Burroughs-Warhol Connection

by Victor Bockris

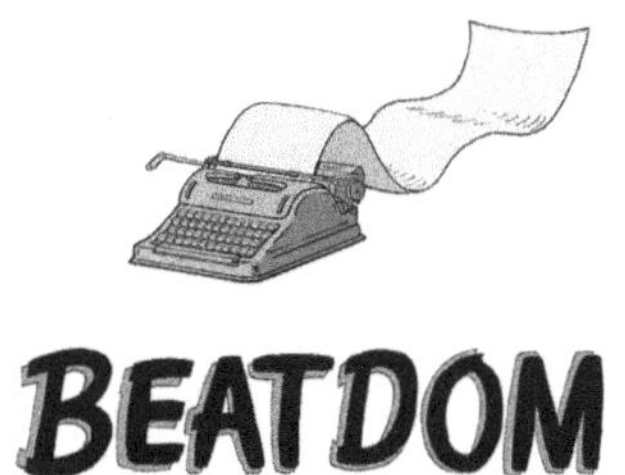

BEATDOM

This book is dedicated to the songwriter, musician, photographer, and author, Chris Stein.

Published by Beatdom Books

View the publisher's website:
www.beatdom.com

Printed in the United Kingdom
First Print Edition
ISBN 978-1-0686980-0-2

The Burroughs-Warhol Connection

by Victor Bockris

What are writers trying to do? They are trying to create a universe in which they would like to live. Sometimes the effect produced by a writer is immediate, as if a generation were waiting to be written… Writers are very powerful indeed. They write the script for the reality film.

William Burroughs

Very few people have seen my films or paintings. But perhaps those few will become more aware of living by being made to think about themselves. People need to be made more aware of the need to work at learning how to live, because life is so quick and sometimes it goes away too quickly.

Andy Warhol

WILLIAM BURROUGHS: I think I'll have a gin and tonic. How about you?

VICTOR BOCKRIS: A gin and tonic?

BURROUGHS: Oh no, excuse me, a vodka and tonic.

BOCKRIS: A vodka and tonic. Yeah, I'll have a vodka and tonic.

ANDY WARHOL: A vodka martini.

BOCKRIS: Oh, a vodka martini! Yeah, I'll have a vodka martini.

BURROUGHS: I'll stick with the vodka and tonic.

WARHOL: Oh, when are you going off to Europe?

BURROUGHS: Tomorrow.

OH ANDY

Across the span of 1980, I tape-recorded four meetings between William S. Burroughs and Andy Warhol. It all began when I was under a stiff deadline to finish my book, *With William Burroughs: A Report from the Bunker* [Seaver Books: New York, 1981]. After several years of contributing to Warhol's *Interview* magazine, I had picked up on his idea of introducing two celebrities and taping their conversation. For my book, I recorded William in conversation with some fifteen figures including Mick Jagger, Lou Reed, Christopher Isherwood, and Allen Ginsberg. I had just added Susan Sontag and Debbie Harry, but I felt Warhol and Burroughs would prove to be the ultimate combination.

Burroughs first met Warhol when Allen Ginsberg took him to a party at the Silver Factory with Tennessee Williams and Judy Garland in the summer of 1965. That fall, socialite Panna Grady set up a dinner for Burroughs and Warhol at a Chinese restaurant. Andy was happy to meet Bill, but when one of Warhol's friends plunked his unfinished plate of food on a table where Chinese people were still eating, Burroughs walked out.

Ten years later over another dinner, Burroughs told David Bowie, "I'd seen Andy Warhol in all light and still have no idea as to what is going on, except that it is something quite purposeful. It's not energetic, but quite insidious, completely asexual."

"I don't think there is any person there," he added. "It's a very alien thing, completely and totally unemotional. He's really a science fiction character."

By 1980, I had a good working relationship with both men, so it wasn't hard to get Bill to accept an invitation to cocktails with Andy. It was Andy who had initially appeared apprehensive. When I suggested we could tape the meeting for my book, he responded, "Oh, yeah! That would be great! But I never know what to say to him. I mean, does he talk?" Both men thought they were going to meet the other man's image.

After two meetings at the Factory, Andy invited us to dinner. This transcript of the first dinner party, "Oh Andy!" was recorded on February 4, 1980, at Warhol's favorite restaurant, called 65 Irving, near his Union Square Factory. It is quite different from the official transcript, "Dinner with Andy and Bill," published in the 5th anniversary edition of *Blueboy*, September 1980. The *Blueboy* edition was organized around big topics you might expect Burroughs and Warhol to discuss, while this recently discovered transcript attempts to capture the affectionate, playful atmosphere of the evening and shows the flowers of friendship blooming. That night, Andy and Bill became friends and remained so for the rest of Warhol's life, which would end in 1987.

Apart from the three of us, the party included the charming fashion consultant and writer, Andre Leon Talley, who helped considerably in spreading the conversation between Andy and Bill. He had recently left *Woman's Wear Daily* and was just beginning to consult for *Vogue*. We sat at Warhol's favorite table in the far-left-hand corner as you came into the room. Andy sat with his back to the wall, which gave him the best available view of the whole room. Bill sat to his right, Andre to his left, with me opposite, in the best position from which to capture the sound and take photographs.

WARHOL: Did you see that commercial for a roach motel? I mean that's a great movie title: *Roach Motel.*

BURROUGHS: Yes, those are good, those are good.

BOCKRIS: You mean [singing] "The roaches check in and the roaches check out?"

BURROUGHS: Er, excuse me, they *don't* check out.

WARHOL: We're trying to get Andre a new boyfriend.

BOCKRIS: Oh really, well what kind of guys do you like?

WARHOL: He likes older guys. Intellectuals.

BOCKRIS: Christopher Isherwood[1] would be good.

WARHOL: He has a boyfriend.

BOCKRIS: I know, but he must want a little action. On the side.

BURROUGHS: I think on the side.

BOCKRIS: Charles Henri Ford[2] would be good, wouldn't he?

ANDRE LEON TALLEY: Who?

BOCKRIS: Charles Henri Ford! Let's get Charles Henri Ford down here right now! He called me today. He invited me to his movie and he gave me six different days to go... so... six!

WARHOL: Oh, really?

BOCKRIS: 'Cos I said, "Well I really don't..." He said, "Well you can come on this, this, or this date." So basically...

BURROUGHS: He pinned you down. Did you see his thing?

WARHOL: No, the *Minotaur*?[3]

BURROUGHS: It was terrible.

WARHOL: Oh, uh...

TALLEY: The film? I think I saw it.

WARHOL: We have to say it was wonderful!

TALLEY: Does he have good stories about Edith Sitwell?[4]

BOCKRIS: Well, he has good stories I'm sure because they date back so... You like Edith Sitwell? Allen Ginsberg has good stories about Edith Sitwell. Ask him, she went to his...

TALLEY: I love Allen Ginsberg.

BURROUGHS: That story is a fabrication. He asked her if she tried

---

1   Anglo-American novelist, 1904-1986.
2   American poet and filmmaker, 1908-2002.
3   *Johnny Minotaur* (1971)
4   British poet, 1887-1964.

heroin. She said, "Oh my dear it brings me all out in spots!"

WARHOL: You know those English girls take… took everything…

BOCKRIS: Those rich English girls…

WARHOL: Yeah, they took, take…

BOCKRIS: They're the ones who come over here and get the American boys into trouble.

WARHOL: Yeah.

BOCKRIS: That's what happened to a lot of boys.

WARHOL: Oh really?

BOCKRIS: Yes.

WARHOL: But English girls are funny. They always do things just to write a book. Get involved with different things and invite the wrong people just so they can write a book…

BURROUGHS: Like Nancy Mitford.[5]

BOCKRIS: Like the Mitford sisters, who got involved with Hitler.[6]

WARHOL: Those are Catherine Guinness's cousins.[7]

BOCKRIS: What was the party you went to last night?

WARHOL: It was great. Bobby DeNiro was there. Al Pacino, Scorsese, Susan Sontag… Diane von Furstenberg[8] and Barry Diller[9] gave it for Richard Gere and Lauren Hutton and the director Paul Schrader.

TALLEY: For the new film, *American Gigolo*.[10]

WARHOL: *American Gigolo*. Oh, it's really good, it's really great! Oh yeah, you'd love it. He's so sexy in it. She's really good in it too. It's really sexy. It's good, it's a movie about a hustler. It's really, really good.

BURROUGHS: Hustling women or hustling men?

TALLEY: He doesn't do fags.

WARHOL: Hustling women. Well, he did fags, but he…

TALLEY: No! He would, he…

WARHOL: He did do fags. He said, "I'll go back and do fags if you do this one thing and get me out of…" He did.

TALLEY: "I'll do fags…"

WARHOL: He said, "I'll go back and do them."

TALLEY: No!

WARHOL: Yes, he did.

BURROUGHS: I've been told that hustling women is a hell of a lot more profitable.

BOCKRIS: I should think so.

TALLEY: More uncomfortable?

BOCKRIS: More profitable.

WARHOL: Yeah, but in this one scene they have, the husband calls the hustler and then he says, you know, "Burn her, beat her, hit her over the head and tie her up and fuck her in the ass, and I'll watch." And then the next day she was murdered, and he was…

TALLEY: …framed.

WARHOL: Framed.

BURROUGHS: The hustler was framed?

WARHOL: Yeah.

---

5   Novelist and biographer, 1904-1973.
6   Unity Mitford (1914-1948) was a British aristocrat who was close friends with Adolf Hitler.
7   British aristocrat and friend of Warhol's, b.1952.
8   Belgian fashion designed, b.1946.
9   American businessman, b.1942.
10   This 1980 film was directed by Paul Schrader and starred Richard Gere and Lauren Hutton.

TALLEY: And the hustler is Richard Gere. But John Travolta was originally to play the part, and he gave it up because of his nervous breakdown, and you always imagine John Travolta being in Richard Gere's pants and walking like Mae West, and that's the best part of the whole movie.

BOCKRIS: When I saw the big ad in the *New York Times* I thought it was John Travolta.

WARHOL: Richard Gere has a new look, I mean a new walk, a new…

TALLEY: What new look?

WARHOL: Oh, it is…

TALLEY: A new look!

WARHOL: What look? I mean, he does…

TALLEY: What's the new look? .

WARHOL: Well, I mean, it's a new walk.

BOCKRIS: How does he walk? Go ahead and show us!

TALLEY: Yes! Show us the new walk and the new look. I want to know.

WARHOL: You don't think he has… he doesn't walk like John Travolta?

TALLEY: No! John Travolta has a good walk.

WARHOL: Oh no, no, no! Richard Gere has a better walk!

TALLEY: Oh, I think John Travolta is the sexiest.

WARHOL: Who do you think has a good walk?

BURROUGHS: I got a pretty good walk. Yeah, you see one foot goes right in front of the other. They don't turn out.

TALLEY: John Travolta is a male Mae West the way he walks, and Richard Gere, you would think he can walk like that, but he can't.

BOCKRIS: So how was Debbie [Harry]?[11]

WARHOL: Oh yeah, she was really cute. Diane von Furstenberg fell madly in love with her and said, "I've got to have her."

BOCKRIS: Really! She said that?

WARHOL: Yes!

BOCKRIS: That's just girl talk, right?

WARHOL: No, no. She said, "She's so wonderful, we have to do something with her! And I've got to introduce her to Barry Diller, because he's going to put her in movies."

BOCKRIS: I can't believe that you haven't put her in a movie, because it's going to be… she definitely could be…

WARHOL: Oh, she's the best, yeah! She's so cute and so smart and sweet…

TALLEY: Very charming.

BOCKRIS: She's very together too. I mean, you know, she's working very well now.

WARHOL: Diane von Furstenberg called us, sitting together on the couch, The Glamourettes. What does that mean?

BOCKRIS: That's like the Interviewettes.

WARHOL: I'm not young.

BOCKRIS: How was Felicity's[12] tea party? She's Anne Cumming, who wrote a book about having sex in her sixties.

WARHOL: Oh, the one who Peter Hujar[13]

---

11   Lead singer of Blondie, b.1945.

12   Felicity Mason was an English woman who befriended Gysin and Burroughs at the Beat Hotel in Paris in the 1950s. She wrote *Love Habit: The Sexual Confessions of an Older Woman* (1978).

13   American photographer, 1934-1987.

says is his mother? Why does he say that's his mother?

BURROUGHS: Oh, she's always…. She's Brion Gysin's[14] sister and Peter's mother and….

WARHOL: Oh really? See, but I don't believe people over twenty-one should have sex.

BOCKRIS: She showed me a photograph of herself being fucked by a porn star on a billiard table at Plato's Retreat. She gives really nice teas at the Alden, up the street from where Charles Henri gives teas. You probably haven't been to tea at his place for some time.

WARHOL: Oh, I mean, I know. The last time I went, he opened a can of Spam for about forty people, I mean it's so true.

BURROUGHS: Did you get any drinks?

WARHOL: No! We didn't get any drinks.

BOCKRIS: He doesn't drink.

WARHOL: No, no, he just doesn't serve drinks. People don't know how to give teas here.

BOCKRIS: But here they give you big fat cakes and you don't want a big fat chocolate cake.

WARHOL: I've never been to a tea where they had fat cakes.

BOCKRIS: She told me she had this nineteen-year-old lover, and then this young guy came in and sat beside her and she said, "That's right dear, then I can just push you over when I feel like it."

WARHOL: Well, I don't even have experiences like that. Nobody ever, gee, nothing ever happens to me.

BOCKRIS: Well, everyone is too nervous.

WARHOL: What?

BOCKRIS: Everyone is too nervous to approach you. They don't know how you would react. You always say you don't want anyone to touch you, so how can people rush up and grab you? I mean…

TALLEY: You reject them, and they don't want to be rejected.

WARHOL: Oh really. Oh that's… oh that's a good line. OK. I must remember that.

BOCKRIS: So, was Truman surprised by his big success with *Hand Carved Coffins*?[15]

WARHOL: No.

BOCKRIS: He just thought it would happen. You said it wasn't that…

TALLEY: Oh, it was fabulous.

WARHOL: No, I thought it was greaaaat!

TALLEY: Oh Andy! Admit it! You probably said that.

WARHOL: No, I didn't!

BURROUGHS: I started to read it. I was getting to the bit with all the snakes. Is this a true story?

WARHOL: I don't know. He said it was.

BURROUGHS: I never read about it in the papers.

BOCKRIS: That's what he said. It's so strange there was no publicity.

TALLEY: Do you believe he went to bed with Errol Flynn?

BURROUGHS: No.

WARHOL: Oh yeah, gee!

---

14   English artist, 1916-1986. Close friend of Burroughs.

15   A novella by Truman Capote, published in Warhol's *Interview* magazine.

BURROUGHS: I just got as far as the snakes.

TALLEY: The snakes part is the best part.

BURROUGHS: Is that true? He injected the snakes with amphetamine and they're all…

TALLEY: And then there's more about the snakes being hung on the wire like laundry when they kill the snakes. It's a good story. You don't like it?

WARHOL: Yes, it was good, no I did. I thought it was greeeaaat!

BOCKRIS: How come he didn't have anything in the last issue?

TALLEY: But nothing was so funny as when Truman went out with the maid and got stoned all day.

BURROUGHS: I haven't finished it yet.

WARHOL: That was another column. Truman's been writing for us for a whole year. Don't you [to Bill] want to write for us for a whole year?

TALLEY: He's not even reading them!

BOCKRIS: No, I've shown him.

WARHOL: I mean Victor could be the editor for you.

BOCKRIS: I have a great idea, we… Bill and I… should do something together.

WARHOL: I think you should have an affair with Victor. He's so cute, isn't he adorable? I… I fell in love with him when he was in love with Andrew Wylie.[16]

BURROUGHS: What happened to Andrew?

BOCKRIS: He's a big shot now.

WARHOL: He's a… [with contempt]

literary agent.

BOCKRIS: He was supposed to have lunch with Liz Ray[17] at the Russian Tea Room.

WARHOL: Liz Ray!

BOCKRIS: And this big fat businessman kept saying, "Andrew Wylie will be here at any minute!" I was having lunch with a girl who was so distraught over her boyfriend not fucking her anymore that she suddenly grabbed an ashtray off of Liz Ray's table. And then Liz Ray turned around and took another ashtray and sort of viciously tossed it across the two inches between the tables. And she said, "Have another one why don't'cha!" But she wrote a great book about blowing all the senators in Washington. What was that called?

WARHOL: *Suck It!* Oh, that's a great title for the next book. *Suck It!*

TALLEY: You know the best thing I heard about Ahmet Ertegun?[18] When he has girls in his limousine, he says, "If you want cocaine, you'll have to take it off my cock!"

WARHOL: And he puts it on his cock?

TALLEY: You know that?

WARHOL: No Andre!

BOCKRIS: Well, my new girlfriend, Damita Richter, called me right in the middle of a dinner I was giving for her to meet the photographer, Gerard Malanga, and said she had to rush uptown with her lesbian girlfriend Mary to have sex in front of

---

16   American literary agent, b.1947.

17   Elizabeth Ray, b.1943. Washington Playgirl who wrote a 1974 exposé of her sex life with famous politicians.

18   American-Turkish songwriter, 1923-2006.

Huntington Hartford[19] for $50.

TALLEY: *Fifty dollars!*

BOCKRIS: I said, "Forget it! That's ridiculous!" Anyway, she started screaming, "You don't love me!" Then she hung up. When she got there, it turned out she had to have sex with Mary in front of him, and then he fucked her too. She claimed she didn't know about that bit. So she got $25 per scene. I thought that was too cheap.

WARHOL: What do you give?

BOCKRIS: Chris Makos[20] said, "You should have doubled it."

BURROUGHS: Well, I should think a hundred.

TALLEY: No! Not even a hundred, more! With Huntington Hartford, she should get $500.

BURROUGHS: Yes well…

BOCKRIS: This was two weeks ago…

WARHOL: It's your new girlfriend? You're still seeing her?

BOCKRIS: Well, it's strained, but she's so cute.

WARHOL: What's wrong with you, Victor? You could get all this free sex from the most beautiful boys and you have to get all these girls to do it to you. Oooooh, come on! The boys who are in love with you are really great, but the girls are so funny. Why is that?

BURROUGHS: You and your Lolitas!

TALLEY: Shall we ask the waiter for refills?

WARHOL: Oh, we want four more drinks! Can we have the Russian vodka?

FABRIZIO [owner]: We're trying to do without [because of the Russian invasion of Afghanistan].

WARHOL: Fabrizio did the funniest thing. I never tell this story but this time I will tell this story. We ordered a birthday cake here because his cakes are so great, and the cake arrived. It was Truman's birthday. So we got him this big cake and everything like that. So the bill hadn't come yet and here we were having another birthday. Fred [Hughes][21] just happened to walk by Côte Basque[22] and he ordered up a cake. And the cake arrived and it looked just like the cake that Fabrizio, this guy, [standing right there] said he makes with his own hands down in the basement! And then Brigid [Polk][23]… I photographed that cake because I photograph every birthday cake, and it was the *same* cake! So, Brigid called up and said, "Your cake looks exactly like the birthday cake we just got from Côte Basque." And he just got so embarrassed. He had gone to Côte Basque and just gotten it, and after telling us, you know, telling me how he makes the best cakes, and just works so hard in the kitchen and stuff like that. It was so cute.

BOCKRIS: Andy, you'd be interested, William met Truman in… When did you meet him? 19…

BURROUGHS: I met him before… he still worked for the *New Yorker*.

BOCKRIS: He met him!

WARHOL: Really!

---

19 American businessman, 1911-2008.
20 American photographer, b.1948.
21 Warhol's manager, 1943-2001.
22 La Côte Basque was a New York City restaurant. It closed in 2004.
23 One of Warhol's Superstars, 1939-2020.

BURROUGHS: Yeah, he worked for the *New Yorker.*

WARHOL: Did you go to bed with him?

BURROUGHS: No, I did not.

WARHOL: Did you think he was cute?

BURROUGHS: No, I did not.

BOCKRIS: You had dinner with him in Washington Square right?

BURROUGHS: I had dinner with him at Margaret Young's.

WARHOL: And you didn't think he was cute? You didn't make a come-on or uh…

BURROUGHS: No, I didn't think he was cute.

BOCKRIS: When was this, in the thirties?

WARHOL: No, no it wasn't in the thirties. It was *the fifties!*

BURROUGHS: It was in the forties. Just got an acceptance of a story, "Miriam."[24]

WARHOL: 1948.

BURROUGHS: I think it was published in the *Atlantic Monthly.* Yeah, yes. That was when it was. So how long ago…? I was around thirty. I'm sixty-five now. And how old is he? Fifty-five. So ten years I was around thirty, he was about twenty.

WARHOL: Was he cute? Because you know I made him get a hair transplant, get a facelift, and lose like one hundred pounds. He looks so good you can't believe it.

BURROUGHS: He does now?

WARHOL: Oh yeah, you can't believe it.

BURROUGHS: He lost a lot of weight.

WARHOL: He gave up drinking and he doesn't drink anymore.

BOCKRIS: He doesn't drink anything?

WARHOL: *No!*

BURROUGHS: Well, he was really bad.

WARHOL: He was really bad, but for the whole year he worked for us, he didn't drink at all, he was so great. And, uh, he looks really terrific! I mean he looks like what maybe the early Truman really looked like. Because Truman had gotten…

BURROUGHS: Well, you know the famous picture of him lying on the couch?

WARHOL: Oh yeah! He looks the same way now.

BURROUGHS: [skeptical] Really…

BOCKRIS: Well not exactly!

WARHOL: Oh yes he does!

TALLEY: Andy!

WARHOL: Listen, he had a facelift, he looks great, come on…

BURROUGHS: Had a hair transplant? There was something aged about him…

WARHOL: Was he cute? Was he cute? But he would be your type wasn't he, I mean, at all?

BURROUGHS: Oh Andy…

---

24   Short story published in *Mademoiselle*, June 1945.

CONTENTS

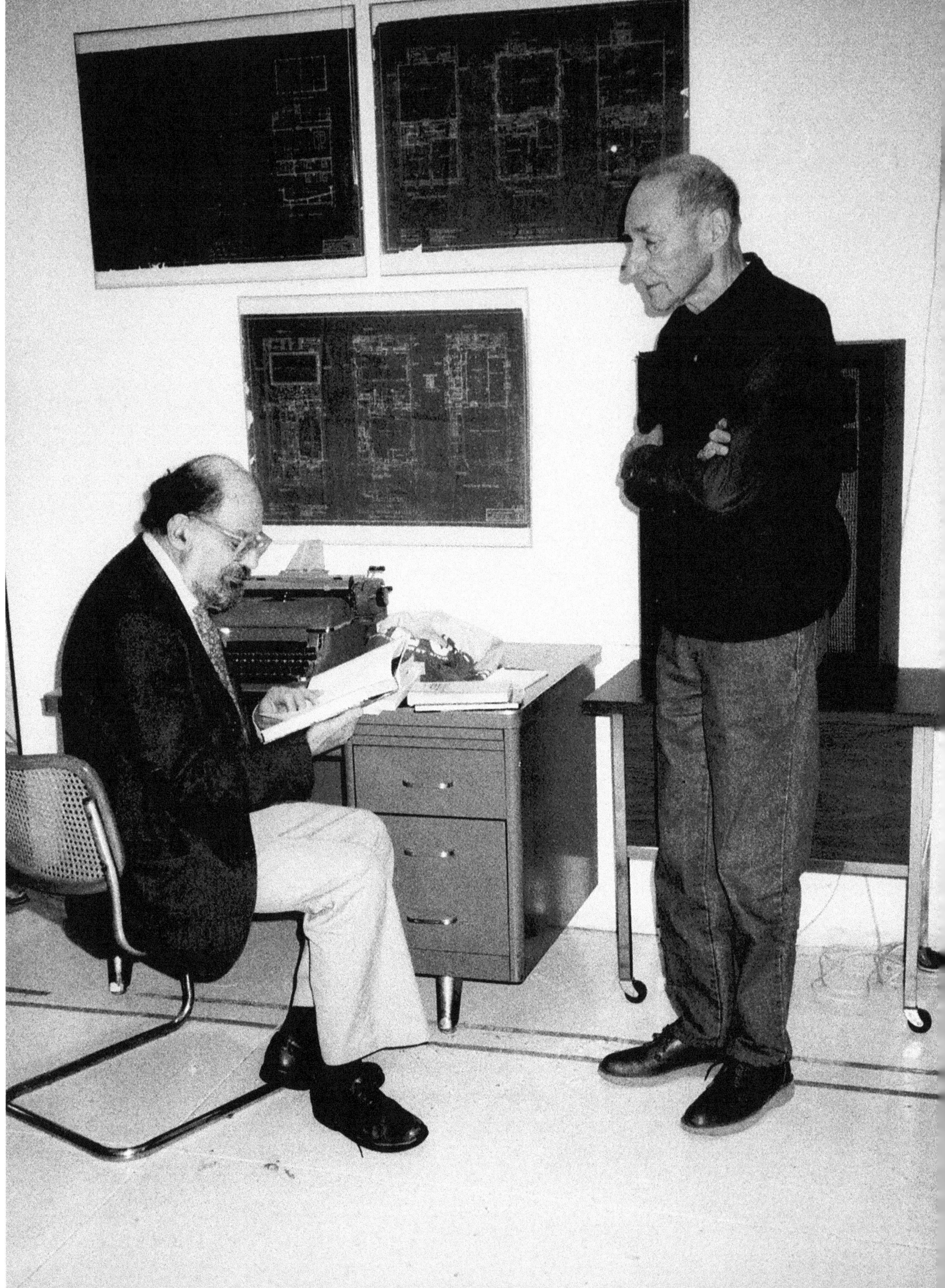

Preface by Allen Ginsberg

Heroes are okay if you learn from them. I have learnt a lot from Jack Kerouac, who was a hero to me, and I learnt a tremendous amount from Burroughs. From Kerouac, spontaneous mind and Buddhism; from Burroughs, blank mind and wiping out the word, unconfusing and disentangling semantic difficulties. Everything Andy Warhol's done has been very useful. I am beginning to appreciate his personality. The very emptiness of his nature and the fact that things pass in and out of his person without him getting hung up is almost Zen, really. His laconism is mistaken for some mysteriousness, but I think he's just very often completely straight. It is really mindfulness of a kind: the mindfulness of the strangeness of our lives and the ordinariness of the strangeness of his contributions. So, I don't see why he was so constantly attacked in that sense as a leader. All he was doing was making people more aware of who they are.

It was an enormous effort to capture that era and aura of the counterculture in the 1960s. I don't think he invented anything there. I just think he'd be the last person to say he invented it, it's just that he noticed it and saw it as art, saw it as art material.

Everyone is boring. Heroes are boring, and the acceptance of their boringness is something significant and useful. Disillusionment is a great therapy. It would be interesting to see Warhol get a little lyrical. It seems to me that he sacrificed a great deal of his ego in a way to allow himself to be the transmitter of the news and to be a mirror, but it also seems to some extent an honorable artistic gesture, that's why it had such an impact.

I think the problem was that the intervention of the media diluted the transmission. I don't think it's the nature of the media, I think it's the nature of the non-learning cynics behind the media. In other words, whatever image of myself or Kerouac or Burroughs or Warhol was spread in the sixties began with a smelly inarticulate image passed through the hands of the CIA and transformed to become a sort of bum kick, originally. So, I think the problem is not heroes, it's the medium. So the problem then is to make use of the media for transmissions of the spark of intelligence, of awareness and awakedness. The person who does it has to be very straightforward.

New York, March 1977

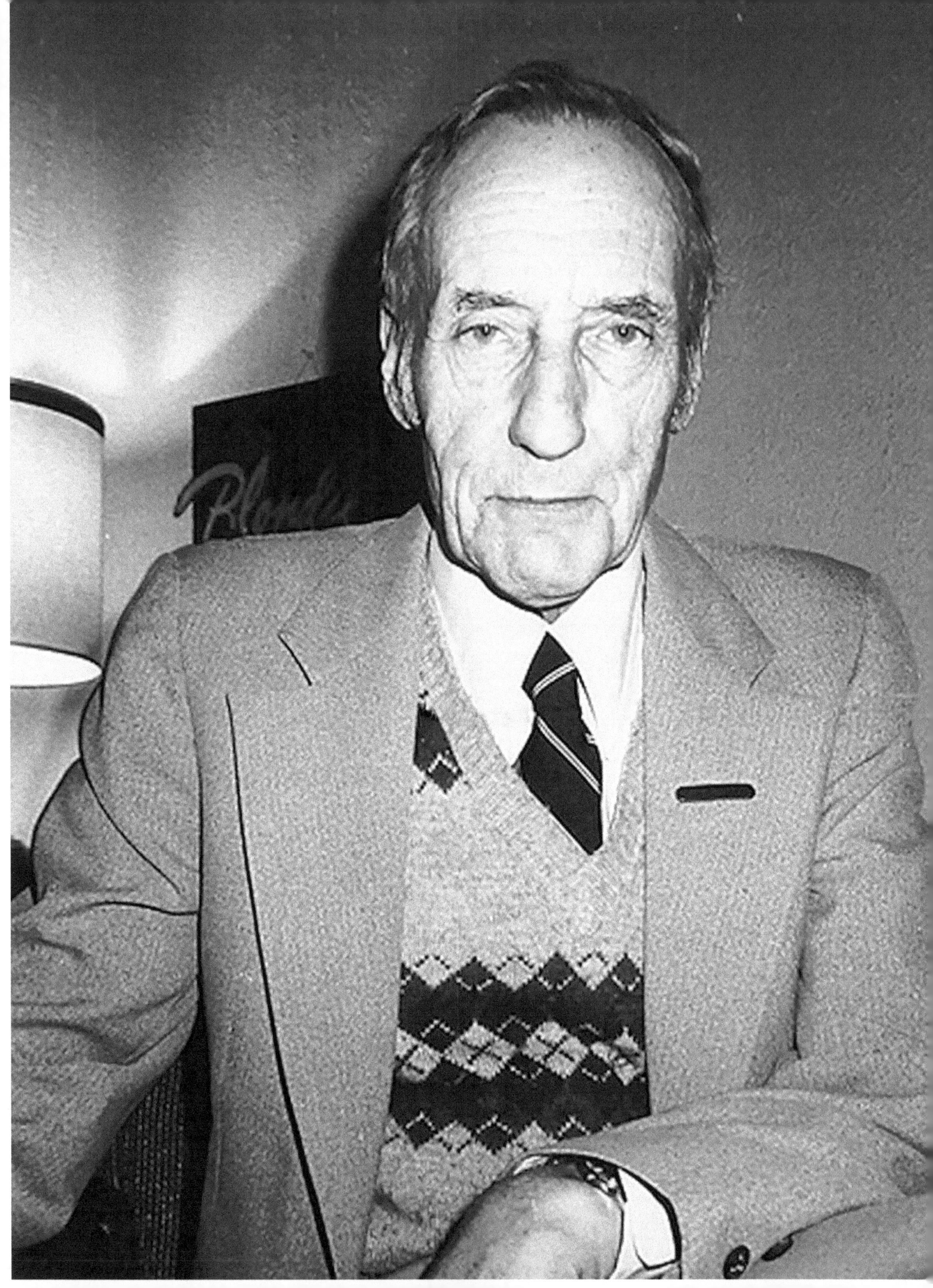

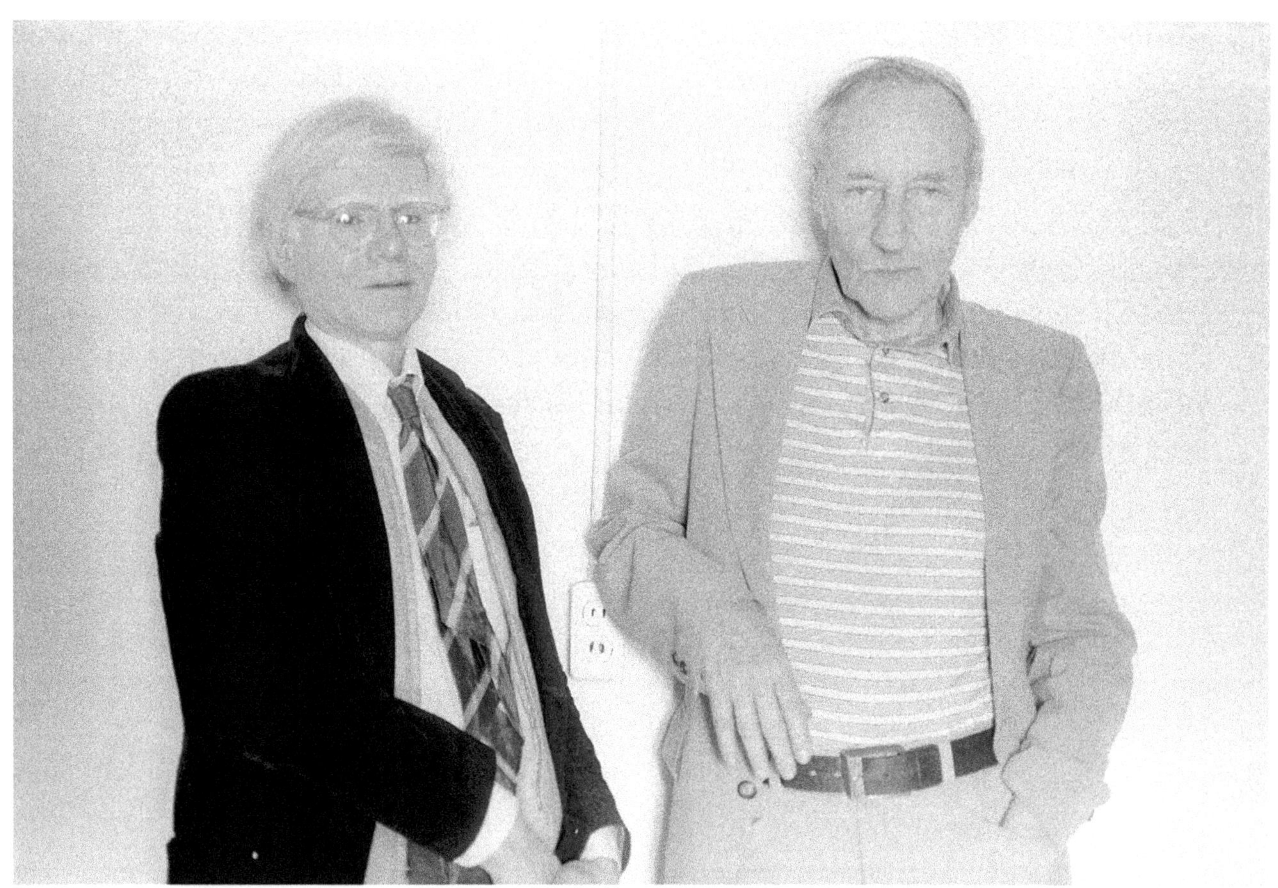

CHAPTER ONE
THE BURROUGHS-WARHOL DIARIES

It was a very literary scene. Burroughs wrote the script and we all adhered to it and attempted to create Interzone.

Mick Farren[1]

I thought of Manhattan as my graduate school, with William Burroughs as the principal and Andy Warhol as the vice-principal. Allen Ginsberg, Terry Southern, and Lou Reed were among the professors.

Sunday, September 14, 1975

William Burroughs and his amanuensis, James Grauerholz, invited me to dinner at William's New York apartment, the 77 Franklin Street 4th-floor walk-up, floor through loft. I had an assignment to do a profile of Burroughs for a prestigious British literary magazine, *The New*

1   English journalist, 1943-2013. Farren was the lead singer in The Deviants (late sixties and early seventies) and a prolific science fiction novelist.

Review, edited by the poet and biographer Ian Hamilton. I'll never forget walking up those stairs one Thursday evening, two chilled bottles of white wine clinking in the crook of my arm. It was one of those rare moments when you are going to step into a room and your life is going to change forever. I was filled with the glow of wonder.

James opened the door and invited me in, taking my coat with a large welcoming grin. William had positioned himself in the middle of the shiny wooden floor. Dressed in cavalry twill trousers, black boots, a British sports jacket, shirt, and tie, he looked a little bit like a military man. I walked over, we shook hands, and he was immediately affable going into his *what-I-know-but-don't-know-I-know* William Burroughs act.

Within five minutes, as James was making me a vodka and tonic and William was passing me a joint, we were talking about venomous snakes. After ten minutes, I was flying by the seat of my pants. I don't think I had ever been so high. I was flying so high I thought maybe they put acid in the grass! Luckily I didn't get paranoid, but I was finding it hard to focus on everything William was saying about the recent assassination of some sheik by his bodyguard. Then he offered to take me on a tour of the loft and show me the desk where he worked.

I accepted the offer with a weak smile, which I suddenly thought he might misinterpret for some terrible attempt to sort of leeringly come on to him. I hoped not. Next thing, I found myself leaning over his typewriter as he pointed out—*my God*—his famous cut-up process! He had four pieces of paper which had been cut up and reassembled so you could read right across them. This was what he was working on at the moment, he told me. At that precise second, I dropped my glass of vodka and tonic with ice on the cut-up pages. The glass shattered, vodka soaking the pages. The ink ran, making them unreadable, and they were covered in splintered glass. This happened in two seconds of silent horror and then the soundtrack came back on. Bill is saying, "Don't worry, don't worry! Do not worry, my dear. I have a lot of paper towels. Paper towels! Paper towels! You always need a lot of paper towels." He sort of sang, dancing back and forth from the kitchen counter to the desk, mopping up the mess. He almost seemed to be laughing.

Friday, October 7, 1977

Last night, Andy, Victor Hugo,[2] Marcia Resnick[3] and I walked from Radio City Music Hall to Studio 54. On the way, we passed a record store window full of the Rolling Stones' new double album, *Love You Live*. Andy had done the cover. It was a collage of his polaroid portraits of each member of the band biting somebody else. Mick was biting his daughter, Jade Jagger. Keith was biting Ronnie. We oohed and aahed. It was like living in history to be standing in the street with Andy Warhol looking at his cover of the Rolling Stones album. I cannot wait to hear the songs.

---

2   Venezuelan-born American artist, 1948-1994. Collaborator with fashion designer Halston and Andy Warhol on his *Sex Parts* series.

3   American photographer, b.1950. Author of *Punks, Poets and Provocateurs*.

Studio 54 was virtually empty. Marcia and I were in awe. Kneeling on the floor as she rummaged through her bag of tricks, she told me how she'd always wanted to hang out with Andy just like this. I was like all smug and *yeah that's cool*. We danced. I threw her on the floor and sort of kicked her around. It was punk, I guess; everybody was impressed. There was hardly anybody there 'cos we were so early. I was just panting in between songs to Andy, "Why don't they play some punk music?"

"Oh, I know," he said when suddenly the Talking Heads' "Psycho Killer" came blistering out of the speakers like a weapon of mass destruction. And we all started dancing again like crazy, cavorting around and waving our spidery arms in spastic gestures of uptight contempt. By the time Marcia and I left Studio 54, the place was packed. I looked back and saw Andy in the midst of a crowd surging around him. His face looked like a slab of stone, his mouth slightly ajar, his tie slightly askew. He was standing there like a sculpture or an oracle.

Monday, November 21, 1977

My face got sliced up in a nightclub brawl with the ex-Warhol Superstar, poet, and artist, Rene Ricard, which left a pretty photogenic scar on my left cheekbone. We used to call scars punk jewelry. Six photographers had already taken my portrait. Yesterday, I was stepping through the tall double glass doors into the kidney-shaped reception room at the Factory when Andy appeared all lit up and whispered, "Oh, uh, gee, let's take that picture now!" As we started to stride side-by-side across the room heading for the windows overlooking Union Square, a massive jolt of energy swept through my body like some miracle drug. I shot a glance sideways and glimpsed the manner in which Andy, like the modern dancer he was, had adopted the exact rhythm in which I was walking. I felt as if he had unzipped my side and climbed in. It was so sudden and such a shocking transformation. He gave me a five-second shot of his exhilaration and amazing energy.

After Andy took the picture, he started joking about how crazily I had been acting since I had started going to Studio 54.

"This is you!" he said, throwing his hands up in the air and dancing around in a little circle.

"It is not!" I chortled.

"You were!" he said. "Listen, I… I warned you. I told you not to have anything to do with Rene! I mean God, aaaaahhh…"

"Andy, you never said anything!" Everybody standing around tittered.

The Factory was throbbing with people waiting for his attention. He was the president of his world, and he drifted off to sign checks and issue orders for the day, dropping jokes, smiles, and pokes in the ribs along the way, playing his workers with his personality. The royal court of the Factory was by far the most exciting place I had ever been.

Wednesday, February 1, 1978

I was standing around the Factory at 860 Broadway with Andy, his florist Tommy Pashun, his photographer Chris Makos, and his painting assistant Ronnie Cutrone, exchanging witticisms about going to the gym. I held my swimming trunks in front of me and did the can-can. Andy mimicked doing pushups with a grimace. Then Lou Reed walked in. I had not seen him for a year, having graduated from the University of Manhattan and commenced graduate studies at the Factory. Andy was cold to Lou. On the other hand, Lou was doing a little bit more than ignoring the convention of dress and comportment on a visit to Warhol in the late seventies. He was wearing ass-grabbing blue jeans, chic shiny high-heel Italian boots, and a skimpy leather jacket over his skinny torso; but he had neglected to don a shirt. Consequently, his black wiry-haired concave chest was quite visible through the half-zipped up jacket.

"Where, ah, what, who… happ… how come you're not wearing a shirt?" Andy asked tersely. Vincent Fremont, the head of Warhol's video department, was filming this for his *Factory Diaries* video.

As Lou cut out after hanging around for twenty minutes, he motioned to me to join him. Andy nodded imperceptibly. In London, they called me Mr. Interview. In *Interview*, Bob Colacello[4] called me Sictor Bockris. I figured I could find out what Lou was thinking about and tell Andy. We got into a Checker cab.

"What's the matter with you, Victor?" Lou hissed, "When did you turn into a monster?"

Sunday, March 5, 1978

Yesterday morning, I started working in the dining room at the Factory tape-recording the text to Andy's second book of black and white photographs, *Exposures*. I was wearing a tight beige rockstar's jacket that Bill Wyman had had designed, but when it didn't fit, he gave it to Keith Richards. When I interviewed Keith at Frog Hollow, their house in South Salem, Anita Pallenberg had traded it for a beautiful white jacket I'd inherited from Richard Pryor's fiancé. I was also wearing a pair of brand new shiny red plastic high-heel shoes I'd bought the day before for $8 on 8th Street. As soon as I got there and he spotted the shoes, Andy came running out from behind Bridget's desk with quick little steps like an eight-year-old kid. Seeing this great artist transform into a child was beautiful and intimate.

Andy is so cute. He had just seen the famous tightrope walker, Mr. Wallenda, drop to his death off the high wire on the TV news and had to tell me all about it. "Mr. Wallenda was walking on the tightrope between two buildings on the 12th floor," he began in a breathless voice. "You could see the wind was blowing extra hard up there, but Mr. Wallenda had… aaahhh… his pole and he was I mean he he… [the hesitation perfectly reflected the feeling of the event] was halfway across the tightrope but then he stopped and suddenly I mean

---

aaah… [he was almost bursting into laughter] a big, a big, uh, the big wind came and Mr. Wallenda was trying to balance with the big stick, you could sort of see on his face that he knew he was going to… And he really tried to balance… But then Mr. Wallenda sort of he slowly fell [we all looked down], but I mean it was so great because Mr. Wallenda's face didn't change at all as he fell. He just… aahh he fell without changing his expression which I thought was really great, so great. I mean he…he…"

Deep down inside, his voice contained a gale of laughter at the human comedy cut by the memory of his father, Mr. Warhola, who died in 1942—the great turning point in Warhol's childhood. Almost everything Andy said was funny because of the way he said it, in that hesitating voice of a lunatic child. It perfectly pinned the hesitating inner voice of America during the Carter administration. Andy's the sort of person that, as soon as you see him, you start laughing and he starts laughing too.

Monday, August 7, 1978

I flew out to Boulder, Colorado, to conduct the *High Times* interview with William Burroughs. For the first time, I had the opportunity to record it over two days. I stayed at the Lazy L Motel. I first visited him in his small apartment at 1155 Marine Drive during the afternoon and evening. His apartment building was mostly inhabited by students, and as I rode up in the elevator, I reflected that whenever I encountered William, he always seemed to be surrounded by young people.

During the first session, we were interrupted by a small boy selling subscriptions to the daily newspaper. William, amused and charmed by the kid's openhearted eagerness, signed up for it, chuckling. A second interruption was not as amusing. William Burroughs Jr., who is about my age, knocked on the door. From where I was sitting at a table facing the door, I could quite clearly see how needy he was to come in and how equally determined William was that he not interrupt the work, which was indeed going well. Bill literally body-blocked his son, revealing after a couple of minutes a testiness. Then, quickly pulling out his wallet, he handed his son $5 and definitively closed the door. Nothing was mentioned of this incident.

The interview went well. When we completed the first session at around 5:30 p.m., Bill announced he was going to collect some supplies and invited me to accompany him. This was the first time I had done anything with Burroughs outside of the structure of interview activities. I was giddy with the whole experience, which was leant further color by the fact that, unlike the other citizens, I was wearing exceedingly tight fake black leather pants, high-heeled Beatle boots, white shirt, a thin black tie, and long black coat. Walking along the street to Bill's running commentary on the neighborhood, I felt, for the first time, like I was inside his magic universe.

He seemed particularly keen to show me the liquor store. As soon as we walked in, I saw why. It was a liquor supermarket. I had never seen such a vast space stacked from floor to ceiling and end to end with alcohol. The experience was further burned into my memory by a third encounter. As we strolled down a wide aisle pushing a supermarket cart—into which Bill was vigorously loading supplies for what looked like a siege—I once again spotted the form of William Burroughs Jr. He had established a campsite on the ground next to a series of shelves. His coat was spread out on the floor like a blanket. I do not recall if he was drinking, but he was undoubtedly consuming something while writing in a notebook or squinting at the pages of some text. Despite William's cart passing within one foot of his son's recumbent frame, neither father nor son acknowledged the other's presence. There was only the inescapable fact that Billy was haunting his father and that Bill had only discovered one way to respond.

We exited the store in silence, but it did not take Bill long to discover some junk jewelry in the street. He picked it up and toyed with taking it to a pawn shop before shrugging his shoulders and muttering like a character out of *Junkie* that it was "Strictly from Walgreens, my dear."

On the second afternoon, after recording the interview, he took me swimming in the apartment building's pool. After I dived in and cut a few vigorous capers in the water, Bill jumped in and swam up and down. "Victor," he called out, "can you do this? Look." And Burroughs relaxed, lying on his back in the water as if he were sitting in an armchair. "I can just float like this without any effort," he said. "Can you do it?" I tried and could not. "Yes," he said, "it's interesting. Few people seem to be able to do it, but I have always had the ability. I just sit here you see, and… float."

On the second day, we completed the interview at around 6:30 p.m. Now two young men, including his new amigo, Cabell Hardy, appeared with food and wine. Soon we had drinks. Bill stuck strictly to vodka and pot. That night, aged sixty-four and wearing a short sleeve jungle-green shirt and brown slacks, he looked trim, healthy, handsome and right there. He reminded me in turn of Noël Coward, Jimmy Stewart, W.C. Fields, and Graham Greene. It was the first time I had really seen William outside of his image. During dinner, in between hugging himself and laughing gleefully, he spoke brilliantly and hilariously about many topics, but mainly the location of the "I," which he said does not exist. Half an hour into this verbal gallop, he caught me looking at him with a mixture of awe and a regret he recognized, commenting, "The best stuff often gets left off tape." It was at this moment I decided that in the future, I would only tape record Burroughs during cocktails and dinner.

Saturday, December 2, 1978

"The Nova Convention, three days and nights of readings, panel discussions, film showings and various sorts of performances that sought to grapple with some of the implications of the writing of William S. Burroughs, concluded Saturday night with a program at the Entermedia theater. Actually, the convention was not entirely over; there was a midnight rock concert featuring

Robert Fripp, Blondie, and other rock performers. But it was over for Mr. Burroughs and his inner circle, who all went immediately to a private party."

Robert Palmer

The private party was at Mickey Ruskin's One University Place.[5] At the height of it, a cute waitress whispered in my ear, "Victor, there's been a bomb scare."

"There ain't no bomb," Burroughs sniffed, "And we're not moving. It's just some jerk who can't get in and wants the place to empty out." And he stared down his long aquiline hooter like Sherlock Holmes' older brother, Mycroft. "Let's forget about it."

Bill spent the balance of the evening talking with Allen Ginsberg, Carl Solomon, and Terry Southern, surrounded by a *Who's Who* of the counterculture. I stood guard behind his chair. To our left, Timothy Leary entertained his entourage with a western rap on André Gide. Across from the Beat High Command, rock's avant-garde composer, Frank Zappa, discussed his reading of the "Talking Asshole" sequence from *Naked Lunch* under the watchful eye of his man mountain of a bodyguard.

"No hard feelings, Tim!" whispered Aron Kay as he lunged from behind the Acid King and jammed a Boston cream pie into his visionary face, massaging the gooey mulch deep into the eyes, mouth, and ears of the great man. Assaulting celebrities with a pie in the face is an accepted practice in New York City, courtesy of the late Tom Forcade, who had committed suicide two weeks earlier. It was Forcade, owner and publisher of *High Times* magazine, who created Aron Kay as Manhattan's Official Pie Thrower, aka "The Pie Man," paying him $50 per delivery. Tom had also put up the seed money for the Nova Convention.

We had just witnessed the first gathering of a new tribe. This combination of the Beats, the Warhol Generation and the current Punk Rock Movement would come to be called the Beat Punk Generation. Among the audience were the radiant artists, Jean-Michel Basquiat and Keith Haring. Both men were awed to see El Hombre Invisible, the author of *Junkie* and *Naked Lunch*, whose 1974 return to New York after twenty-five years of self-imposed exile coincided with the fall of Nixon and the birth of punk. I vividly recall the night at St. Mark's Poetry Project back in 1974 when Patti Smith announced, "Guess who's moved back to the city? William Burroughs! Isn't that great!" It was one of her finest moments and the beginning of punk's call to recognize and illuminate our forefathers instead of destroying them.

By December 1978, William Burroughs was the Godfather of Punk. I was exhilarated to be in the honor guard who surrounded him that night as he left the restaurant like, according to Kerouac, "A Zenzi witch king in his dragoon."

---

5   A New York bar and restaurant run by Mickey Ruskin, who opened Max's Kansas City in the sixties, popular with artists and musicians, including Andy Warhol.

Tuesday, January 2, 1979

I met Andy at the Factory in the afternoon. He was playful, tickling my stomach as he walked by. That evening Tom Sullivan,[6] his wife Winnie, Andy, and I were going to film the scene I wrote for *Cocaine Cowboys* on the Upper East Side. After visiting Muhammad Ali, co-starring in this movie was the second biggest thing I ever did with Andy. Before we left, Andy asked me if he could bring Henry Post, who worked at *New York* magazine. I told him he could not because it was a closed set.

When we arrived at the designated building on 65th Street just off Central Park, the cheery red-cheeked Irish elevator operator out of central casting kept asking me for a name. "Warhol!" I kept saying, "Warhol!" When we got up there, we discovered that, although the producer Franz-Christoph Giercke had insisted this be a closed set, there were about thirty people milling about, eating, chatting, taking drugs, having a cocktail party—all waiting to see Andy. "I could have asked Henry Post to come to this," Andy snapped and promptly called him. Consequently, in between takes, Andy and Henry sat on a couch eating potato chips and whispering. I stomped around feeling uptight.

All the scene required was Andy, Tom, Winnie, and I to sit around a coffee table talking. Andy and I were interviewing Tom about a plane crash that changed his life. Every time Gierke screamed "Ruhe! Ruhe!" [Silence! Silence!] before a take, Andy muttered "So German." But Andy was incredibly nice, patting my face as we ended the scene. He was praising me for doing nothing, but I was too uptight to enjoy myself most of the time and this was no exception. I guess that was true of everyone. Everybody was scared of Andy in a ridiculous way but understandably. You could get cross-eyed trying to figure it out. It was an uptight scene.

When Henry kissed him at the end of the evening, Andy quipped, "Wow! A potato chip kiss!" I got the sense he had not changed since the fifties. As everyone who acted in the scene left together walking east on 65th to Madison Avenue, Andy told us who lived in every single mansion we passed. He described every piece of furniture they had and where it stood in their living rooms in incredible, animated detail, his rich proud face glowing in the night. It was an extraordinary display of obsessive memory.

Thursday, February 1, 1979

I gave Andy the first copy of my self-published limited edition xerox book, *The Burroughs File*, which I made for Bill's sixty-fifth birthday on February 5th. "You did all of this by yourself!?" Andy exclaimed, bright-eyed, shooting his enthusiasm into my brain. He was so ebullient and effervescent it gave me the biggest boost. At the time, I didn't know he had made books just like this when he was my age. He went and stuck it in one of his *Time Capsule* boxes. I was often struck by how incredulous people were when I started turning

---

6   Co-writer and actor in *Cocaine Cowboys*.

out books: "You did this all by yourself!?" I guess I didn't appreciate just how much work was involved, or how much of an idiot I appeared to be. After years of magazine work, I love making books so much.

Tuesday, August 21, 1979

Lou Reed was passing through New York on a world tour, so I arranged for him to visit William for cocktails. Burroughs was a stickler for punctuality, so I headed over to the Bottom Line where Lou was doing a sound check. When I got there, I discovered he was freaking out because his bass player, the Moose, was missing and the gig was in jeopardy. He couldn't rock without a solid bass to ground the beat. "Who saw him last, man?" Lou was asking every member of his band. "Maybe he got mugged… maybe he's lying in a gutter bleeding to death." Lou loved the Moose.

After much phone calling, hair pulling, and hand ringing, the Moose thundered into the club, bug-eyed, sweating profusely, and grasping in one large paw a guitar case. It transpired that he had overslept.

No sooner had Lewis received this information than he went berserk. Ordering everybody out of the dressing room, he proceeded to pound the Moose with a long, loud, blistering dressing down—interspersed with many threats about never working or traveling around the world first class again—that could be heard out on the street. Then, abruptly turning to his trembling entourage, Reed ordered his wife, two guitar players and myself to follow him out of the club and into his limousine.

I had called Burroughs and explained that we were going to be a little late. Instead of arriving at 6:30 p.m., we got there at 7:15 p.m., which was not too bad. However, as soon as we walked into the room it became obvious that, whereas Bill was fully aware of what was going on, he had not prepared his other guests—the biographer Ted Morgan[7] with a female companion (a college girl), and the writers John Giorno and Stewart Meyer—for the impending invasion. There was a sudden impasse. Lou, who was adept at picking up on what was going on and turning it to his advantage, suddenly snapped, "Well, are there any extra chairs or are we all going to sit on the floor?"

"Lou! Please!" I hissed, wanting to fall through the floor but to no avail. Only then did it occur to me that, since he was amid a world tour, Reed was in full confrontational mode. He had already consumed more whisky than the body requires and had brought along a pint, from which he continued to nip throughout the ensuing discourse.

As soon as we sat down, Lou seized control. First, he went around the table requesting of each guest their name and then marveling over their response. For example, when Ted Morgan answered "Ted Morgan," Lou repeated incredulously "Ted?" as if it were the most ridiculous name he had ever heard. The funny thing was, he was actually addressing Count Sanche Charles Armand Gabriel de Gramont, a French aristocrat who had moved

---

7   Author of Burroughs' biography, *Literary Outlaw*.

to America where, in an attempt to blend in, he chose to rename himself like a character out of Hemingway. Now, much to Lou's amusement, "Ted" was going into a slow boil.

By the time Lou completed his rapid-fire consensus, everyone at the table—except Bill and I—had been laid out before him. Now, Lou laid into the real thrust of his visit. He started firing off a series of hilarious questions that many people may have wanted but would never have had the gall to ask William Burroughs: Was it true, for example, that Bill had cut off his toe to avoid the draft? And had he needed to go to bed with his publisher in order to get his books published?

While Burroughs' guests stiffened at every turn, Bill took it all in stride, responding with equivalent humor. In fact, as he told me afterwards, he could tell from his references that Lou was well informed and this was in fact an honorable Dadaist exchange between two artists of equal caliber. There was more: Was it true that he was a very cold person? Had he shot a passing Paris clochard while walking with Beckett by the banks of the river Seine? And finally, would he please sign and give Lou a rare first edition of Burroughs' *Last Words of Dutch Schultz*? Bill gracefully complied.

As the twenty-eight-minute *tour de force* reached its climax, a grinning Lou gleefully announced, "We who play cannot stay!" and thanked the company as if they were an audience, "It's been a pleasure… etc." Burroughs, in turn, showed his respect by doing something I had never seen him do before: he walked Reed down the stairs and out into the street. As we stood on the Bowery in an intimate group, shaking hands and saying good-byes, Lou asked Bill if he could have his phone number so they could get together and talk. Bill happily agreed. When I suggested that we should all get together and have dinner soon, Lou replied, "What's this 'we'? I just want to have a quiet dinner with Bill and talk!"

Tuesday, January 1, 1980

I suppose I am one of the ten to twelve people who ever got close enough to Bill professionally to see into his writing center. Working on *With William Burroughs* was fun. Working on *The Adding Machine* was inspiring. I'll never forget the first day.

I sat down at the conference table in the Bunker. Bill sat at the head of the table; I was sitting two seats down to his left with a stack of pages between us. As I looked up to begin, he gave me the most enchanting smile I had ever seen from him. Once in 1978, when I was first getting to know him over a joyful dinner in his Boulder, Colorado digs, he had started smiling at me across the table while batting his eyes and flapping his ears, creating a goofy come-on. We were both quite drunk and I could not understand what the strange smiles portended. Later I realized they were an invitation to the ultimate schlup. The enchanting smile was neither a smile of humor nor a smile of seduction. It was the smile of collaboration.

I think one of the reasons Burroughs and I got along as well as we did was because we shared a boarding-school background. In that context, he was the headmaster and I

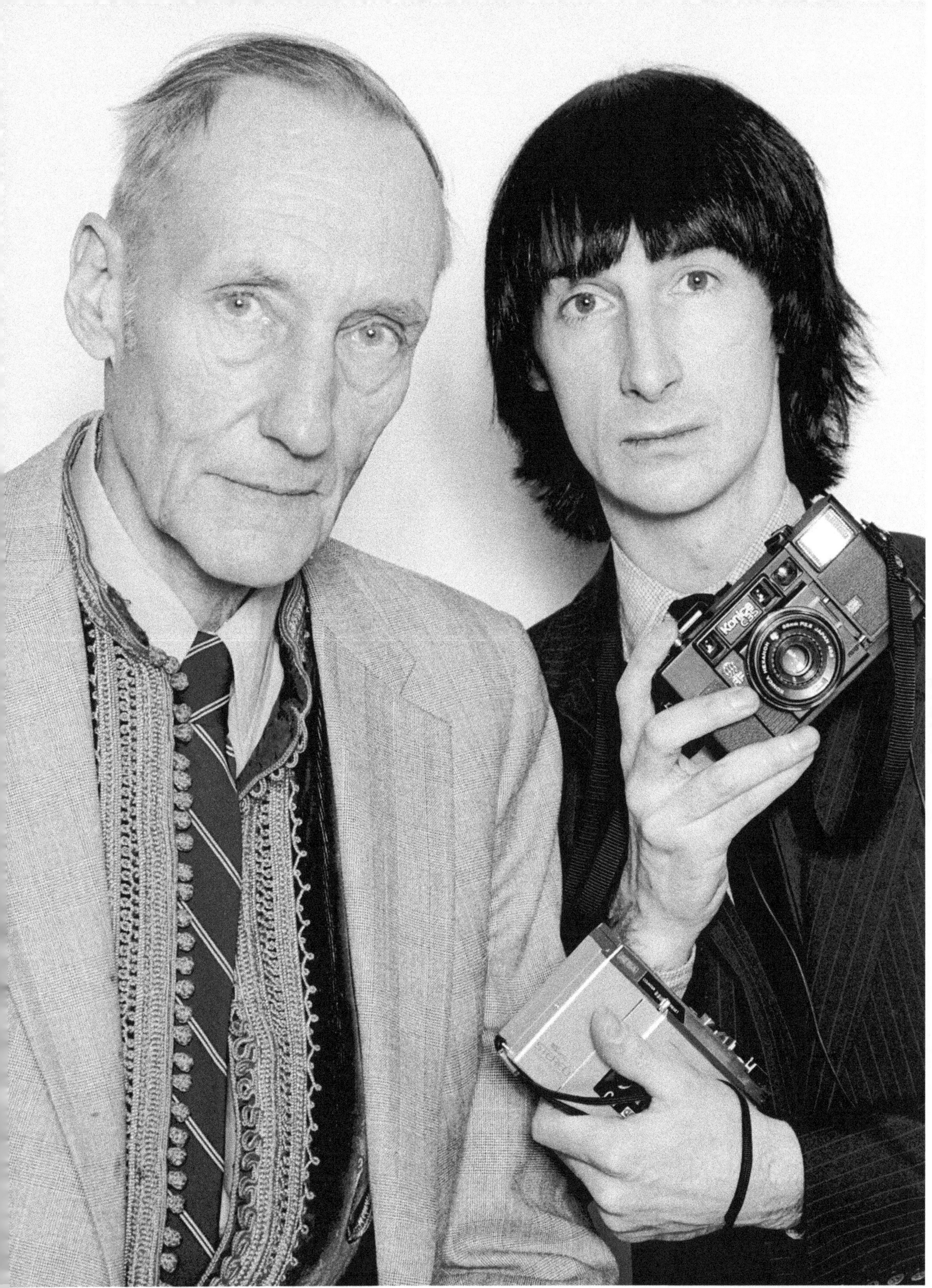

was the head boy. This was a relationship we both cherished. In 1939, aged twenty-five, Burroughs took part in a weeklong seminar with Count Alfred Korzybski at the professor's Institute of General Semantics in Chicago. I was stunned when I saw a photograph of Bill with the other students because I looked so similar to the way he looked then. We were dressed the same way and held ourselves in the same way.

At the end of the first session, I poured drinks while William smoked a joint provided by Stew, who was cooking some dinner on the small beat stove. I walked up and down past William's chair, picking up and returning the joint as we kicked ideas for a title back and forth. It didn't take us ten minutes to hit it. I kept saying, "It's light reading… light reading…" over and over again until Bill gave me that wonderful smile again and chimed in, "for light years. *Light Reading for Light Years*." Stew was applauding from the stove. That was the book's working title. (Years later it was changed to *The Adding Machine*).

We met once or twice a week over a three-month period and collected some forty essays. My work entailed collecting fugitive pieces, typing up material that was being transformed from a speech into an essay, tape-recording inserts and cutting in the results, thus bringing the book to fruition.

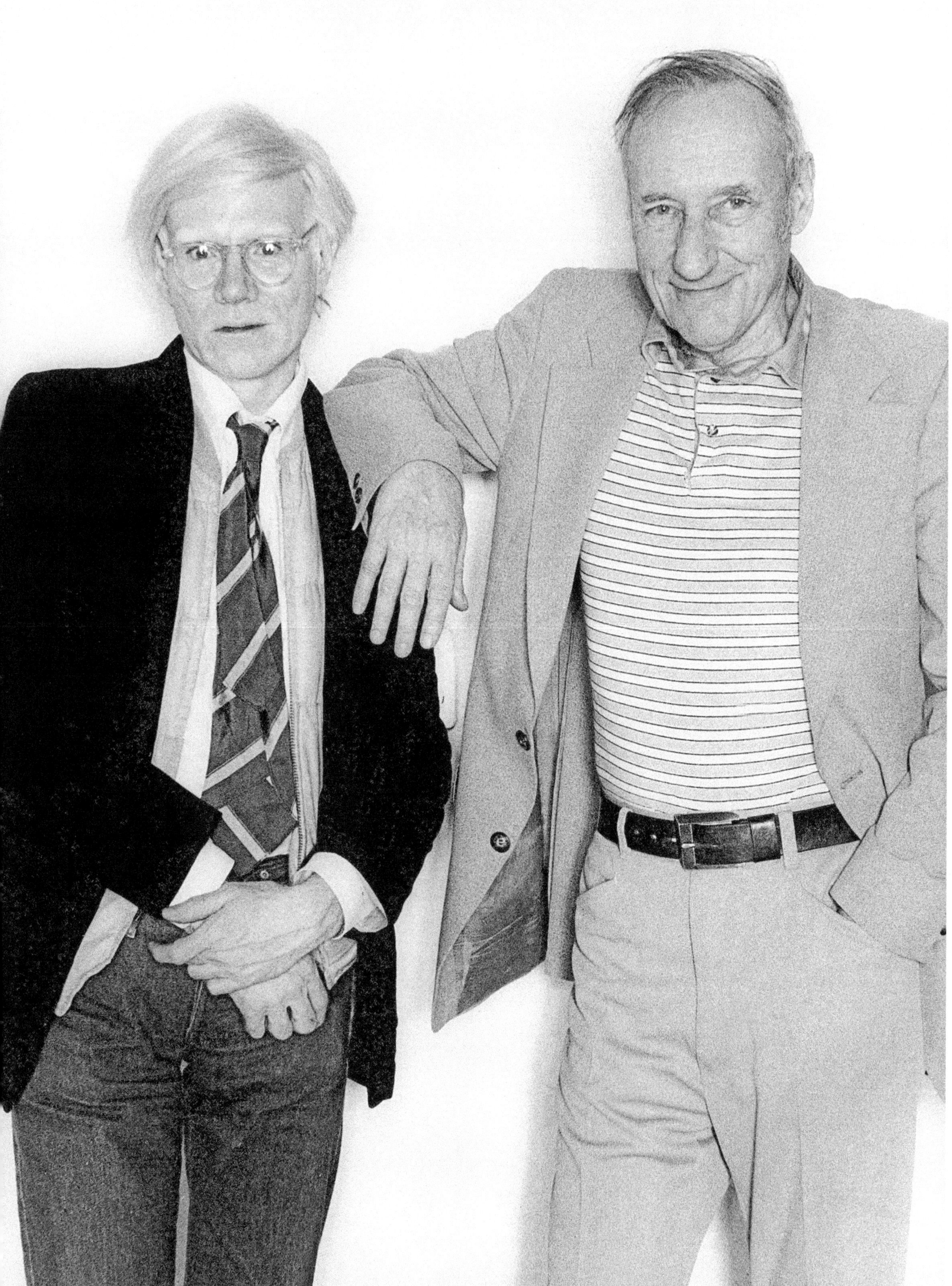

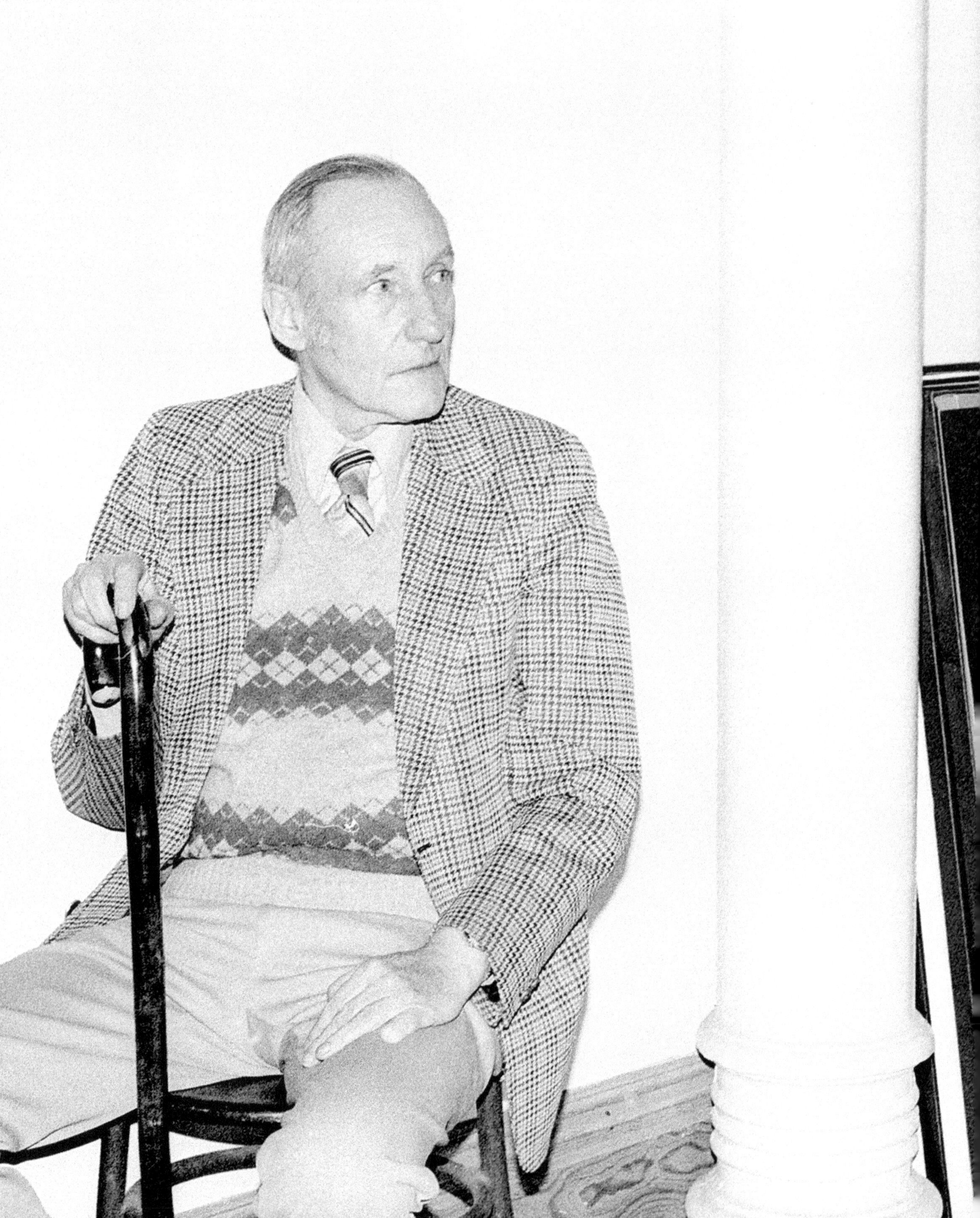

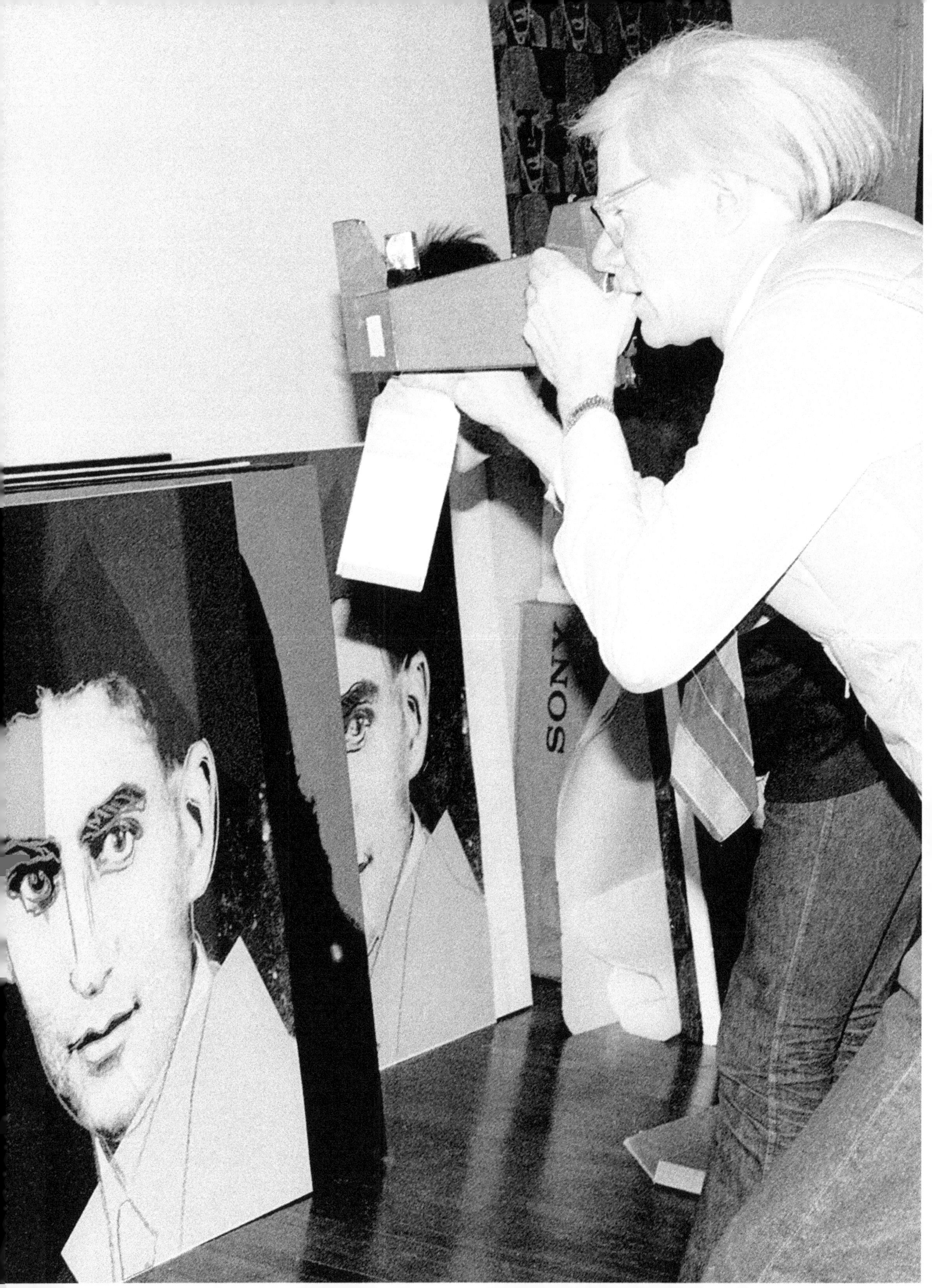

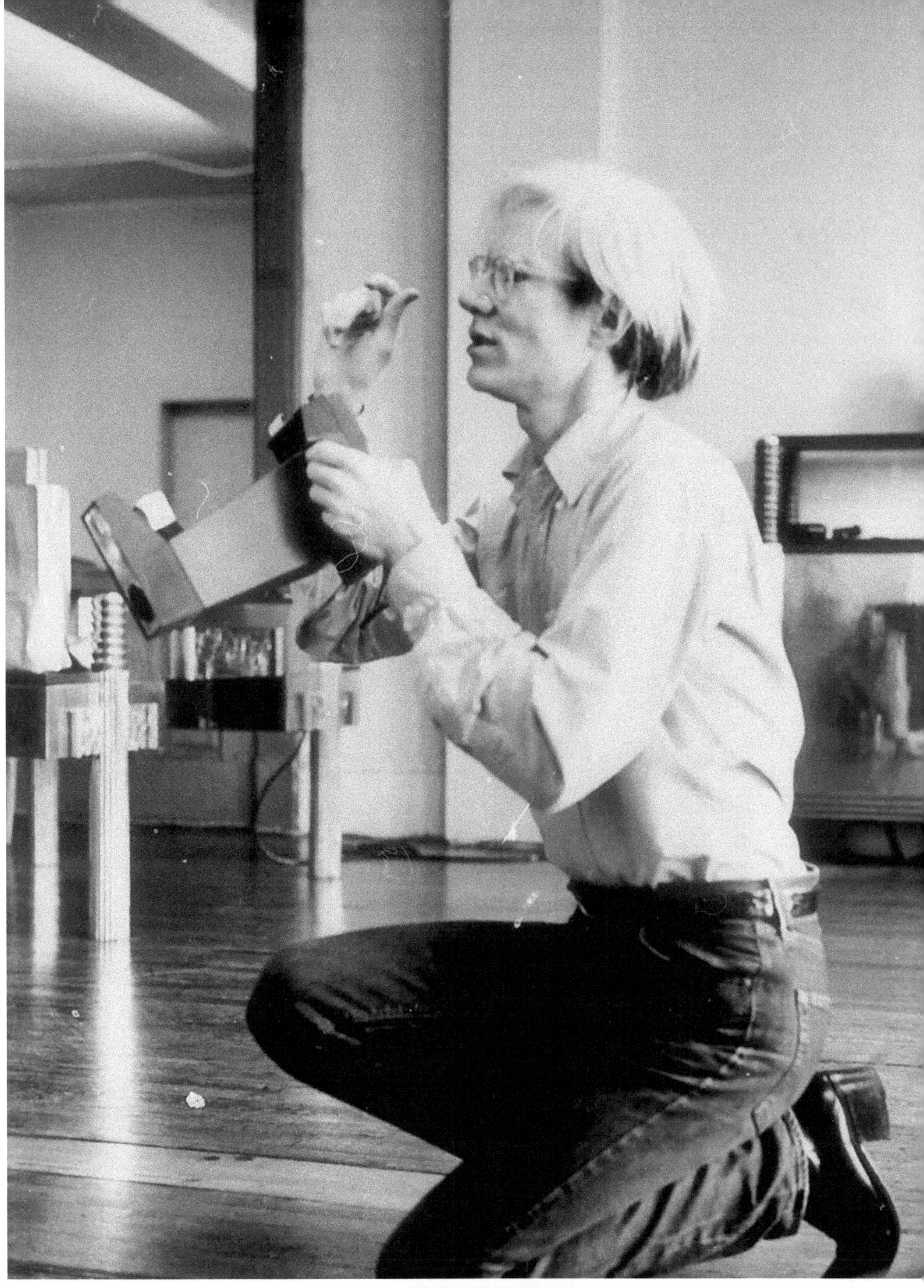

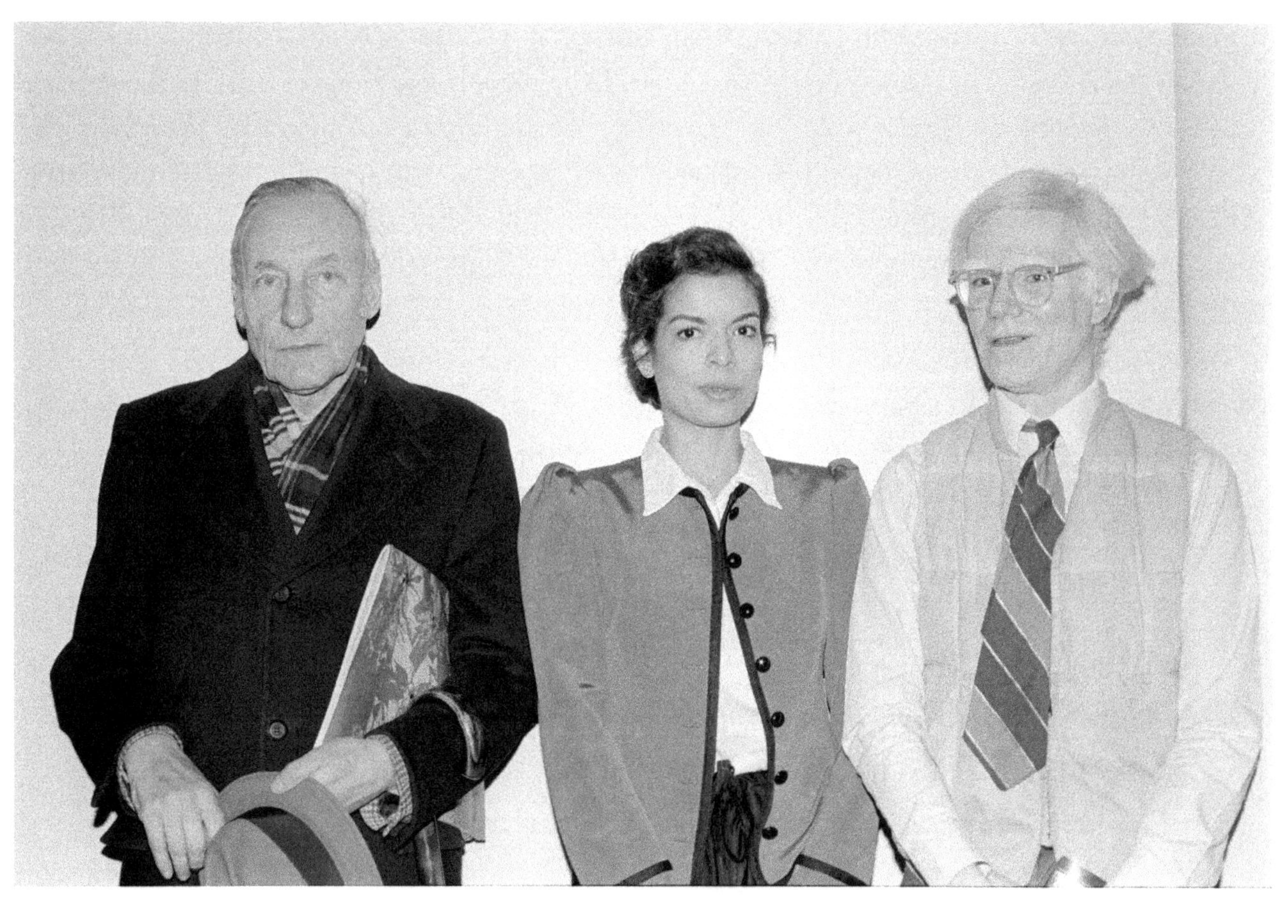

CHAPTER TWO
BURROUGHS AT THE WARHOL FACTORY

Friday, January 18, 1980—Cocktails at the Factory, New York

If William Burroughs is the best talker I ever met, Andy Warhol has got to be a close second, so I was amazed to discover that they had never talked to each other and I immediately took steps to rectify the situation by taking Bill over to the Factory for a brief chat early one evening.

We arrived at the Factory at precisely 6 p.m. A young man wearing a red shirt and blonde mustache, whom I recognized as one of Andy's part-time painting assistants but whose name I didn't know, answered the door and we walked in. I was going to introduce William to Andy and tape-record a conversation between them for my book, *With William Burroughs: A Report from the Bunker.*

Warhol's famous Factory was no longer the fiercely lit silver room full of freaks it had

29

been in the 1960s. In this third Factory, on the third floor at 860 Broadway, the polished wooden floors reflected the sunlight that sparkled through the long row of large spotless windows overlooking Union Square. Professional arrangements of beautiful flowers mixed with designer colognes and Paris perfumes created an enchanting, slightly seductive aroma. William immediately commented on how large the place was. He was at a very different speed than I was, having evidently had a smooth day; I, meanwhile, had had a rough and rumpled one.

A beautiful girl was slouching behind Ronnie Cutrone's desk. We walked in. I crossed to the windows and took off my coat and put my briefcase on the radiator. William followed, taking off his coat. I turned, took it from him, and placed it with his hat and cane on a chair, then walked into Vincent's office. He was on the telephone.

"I'm here with Mr. Burroughs," I said.

"Who are you?" he asked, "Do I know you from somewhere?"

I gave him the finger and he said, "I'll go find the boss."

"Could you turn the lights on in the conference room?"

"No, we're cutting down on electricity," he said.

I motioned to Bill and he followed us into the conference room.

A series of tall, wooden totem figures from Kenya stood guard. A stuffed antelope head peered down at us from wood-paneled walls. A large, rectangular art deco conference table

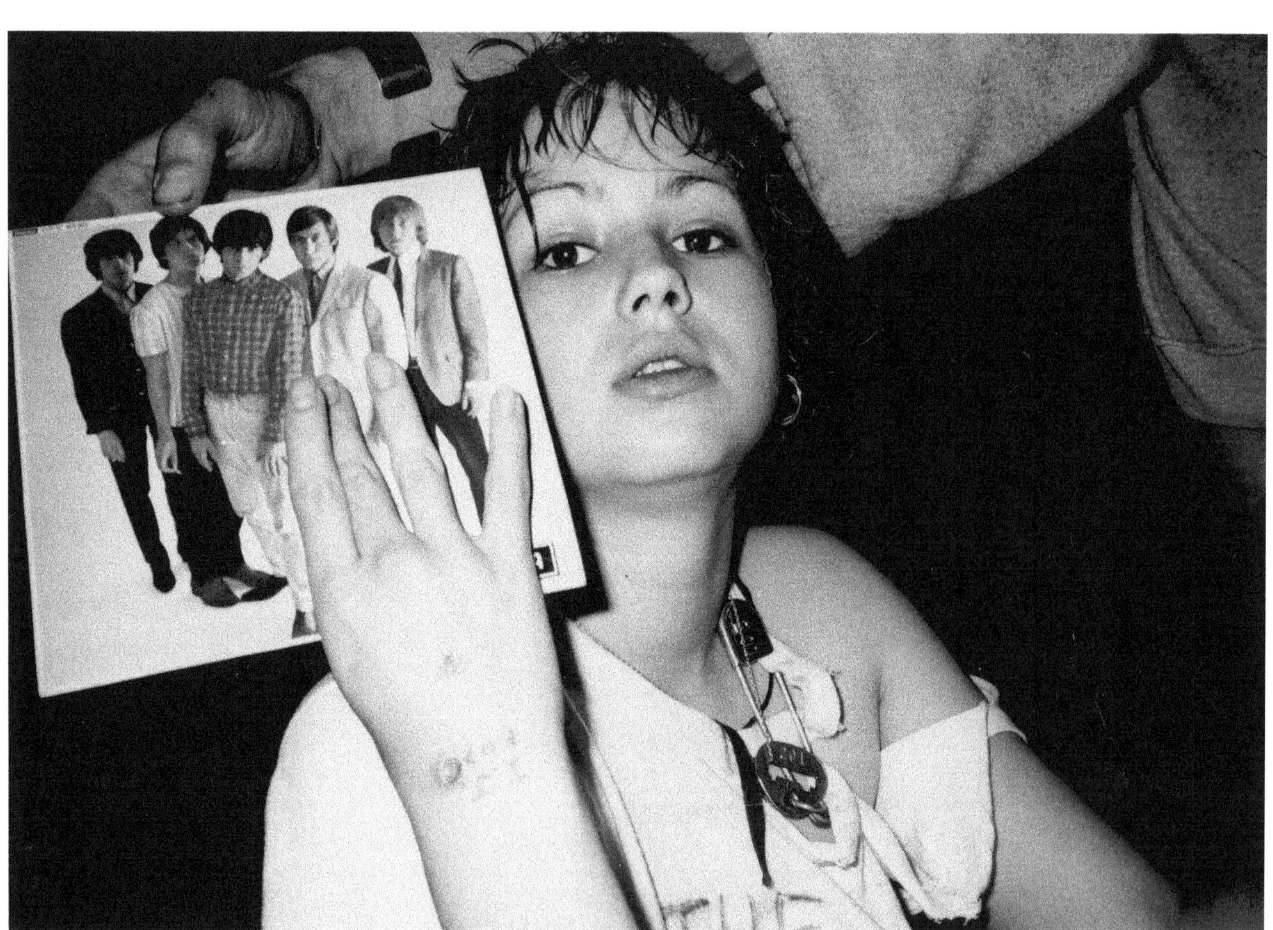

dominated the space. "Ronnie's got that music on too loud again! Tell him to turn it down," I demanded, thinking about my recording. Vincent went down the corridor. I ran back into the main office to get my tape recorder. When I returned, William was pouring himself a Smirnoff. We'd looked through the bottles on entering and he'd conservatively chosen to stick with the Smirnoff instead of trying out the Wyborowa, which I'd recommended.

Andy entered the room. He was dressed in slim-cut pressed blue jeans, grey elephant skin cowboy boots (a gift from a flamboyant drug smuggler) and an open-neck yellow and black plaid shirt. A blonde wig sat slightly askew atop cut-glass Slavic cheekbones, a bulbous red nose, and pockmarked skin—the ruins of angelic features. His charismatic presence was so empowering that he glowed like a great beauty. Everything he did was work. In one hand, he carried a small switched-on Sony cassette recorder; in the other, a tiny Minox camera with the flash attachment on. William wore his customary suit and tie. He had just finished his novel *Cities of the Red Night* and was feeling no pain. We had been discussing its cover.

BOCKRIS: Andy, do you remember when you and William last met?

WARHOL: Oh yeah, it was just recently.

BOCKRIS: It was just yesterday?

WARHOL: Yeah, just yesterday. [Andy is always willing to go into a complete fictionalization if that's what you suggest.]

BOCKRIS: Really? No, you haven't seen each other for a long time, have you?

WARHOL: Aaaaahhhh, no, but I mean the best times were with Jerome Hill.[1] Remember when Jerome Hill brought us to the Algonquin Hotel?

BURROUGHS: Oh yes. Oh, yes, yes. That was when they were really into making a film about *Junkie*.

WARHOL: I'm surprised they have not done that movie yet. It is a good idea.

BURROUGHS: Right and it was kind of… were you at Jacques Stern's party on Gramercy Park at more or less the same time?

WARHOL: Oh yeah, I think so. [He wasn't there.]

BURROUGHS: Jacques was magnificent zipping around in his electrified wheelchair.

BOCKRIS: He's really good looking, isn't he?

BURROUGHS: Not really.

BOCKRIS: How old is he?

BURROUGHS: About forty-eight. I don't know what the hell is happening because he was sort of flipping out and I got called from Bellevue…

BOCKRIS: They threw him out of the Chelsea Hotel.

BURROUGHS: And then they wouldn't take him at the Earl… When the Earl won't let you in… hmmmph hmmph hmmph. They didn't want him there at any price. So that's when I lost track of him. He left all his gear at my place and it's still there. What am I going to do with it? He said he was going back to Europe. It's been a good six months since I've

---

1   American filmmaker, 1905-1972.

seen him.

BOCKRIS: Bill was telling me that some publishers go out and buy a lot of their own books…

WARHOL: Well listen, we just bought three hundred…

BOCKRIS: I'm talking like 25,000 or something!

WARHOL: [excited] Oh really? Ooooohh that's wonderful! 25,000. God…

BOCKRIS: Well, you just resell them again.

BURROUGHS: Oh well yeah, if you can.

WARHOL: We should buy 25,000. I mean we were buying…

BURROUGHS: They did that on *Valley of the Dolls*, but I mean ok the book goes out, so there are people who rush out and buy them.

WARHOL: No, but Jennifer Susann[2] had to go and visit all these little towns. I mean you have to buy them from these little towns.

BURROUGHS: I think they probably concentrate on the big cities so you… Here the bookseller is sold out so he has to reorder and this sort of gets a flow going. $25,000 worth of priming the pump.

WARHOL: But they've done that with records too. They aaahhh… sell all these, no but people with… the record business is really terrible because the stores don't have to buy them and they just return them. So I mean, if this store takes a hundred million copies of a record that's a big hit, so it becomes a gold record

overnight, then they get all these returns back, but they don't take the gold record away. [Resentment lurks.]

BURROUGHS: Well that happens with books too! Oh yes. Because, oh yes, you think you're doing fine and then all of a sudden—the returns!

BOCKRIS: William and I are going to do a big interview with Jerry Brown.

WARHOL: You are! Every time I see him, he's with either Shirley McClaine[3] or Bella Abzug.[4]

BOCKRIS: We met him once but only briefly. What's he like?

WARHOL: Really er well he's uummm… Great! He's wonderful.

BOCKRIS: Are you supporting him?

WARHOL: Well, I support them all. As Sylvia Miles[5] says, "We go to every party!"

BOCKRIS: Are you doing any posters for the Presidents?

WARHOL: I'm doing one for Ted Kennedy.

BOCKRIS: Did you read in the newspapers about the heroin from Iran and Afghanistan?

WARHOL: Oh really.

BOCKRIS: I heard about this person who took some Iranian heroin and they took a third of the amount they would normally take and immediately barfed. It's just so strong in comparison I guess to whatever's been around.

WARHOL: I don't know anybody who takes it. [At least two members of his current staff are regular users.] No, I

---

2   Warhol is talking about Jacqueline Susann, author of *Valley of the Dolls*.

3   American actress, b.1934.

4   Member of the US House of Representatives, 1920-1998.

5   American actress, 1929-2019.

don't know anybody that takes it. Do you ever see…

BOCKRIS: No, I haven't. Bill, do you know anybody who takes it? [Bill is on heroin during this taping.] But I think it's going to spread and I keep telling the people at *High Times* that they should publish some kind of article warning people about it.

WARHOL: [revealing his knowledge] Oh really, because it's so cheap?

BURROUGHS: It's going to become a recreational drug.

BOCKRIS: But no one admits to it anyway. They say they'll take anything else, but when it comes to heroin…

WARHOL: Yeah, I know, they don't, but most people never do so… Let's go next door.

BURROUGHS: Can I, er, help myself to another vodka…?

WARHOL: Oh yeah, do.

BOCKRIS: Oh wow, can we look at this? [walking over to an unfinished Kafka portrait] This is what it's finally like, or…

WARHOL: Oh no it's really different. That was just one working.

BURROUGHS: Yeah, he had an extraordinary face with these big ears sticking out. He died at quite a young age. Wasn't he about forty?

BOCKRIS: What is this for?

WARHOL: It's called aaahhh, the ten eeeeeerrrrr the famous Jews or something like that.

BURROUGHS: Ten famous Jews? Oh oh uhm.

BOCKRIS: Whose idea was that? Was that your idea?

WARHOL: Well, no it wasn't mine it wasn't…

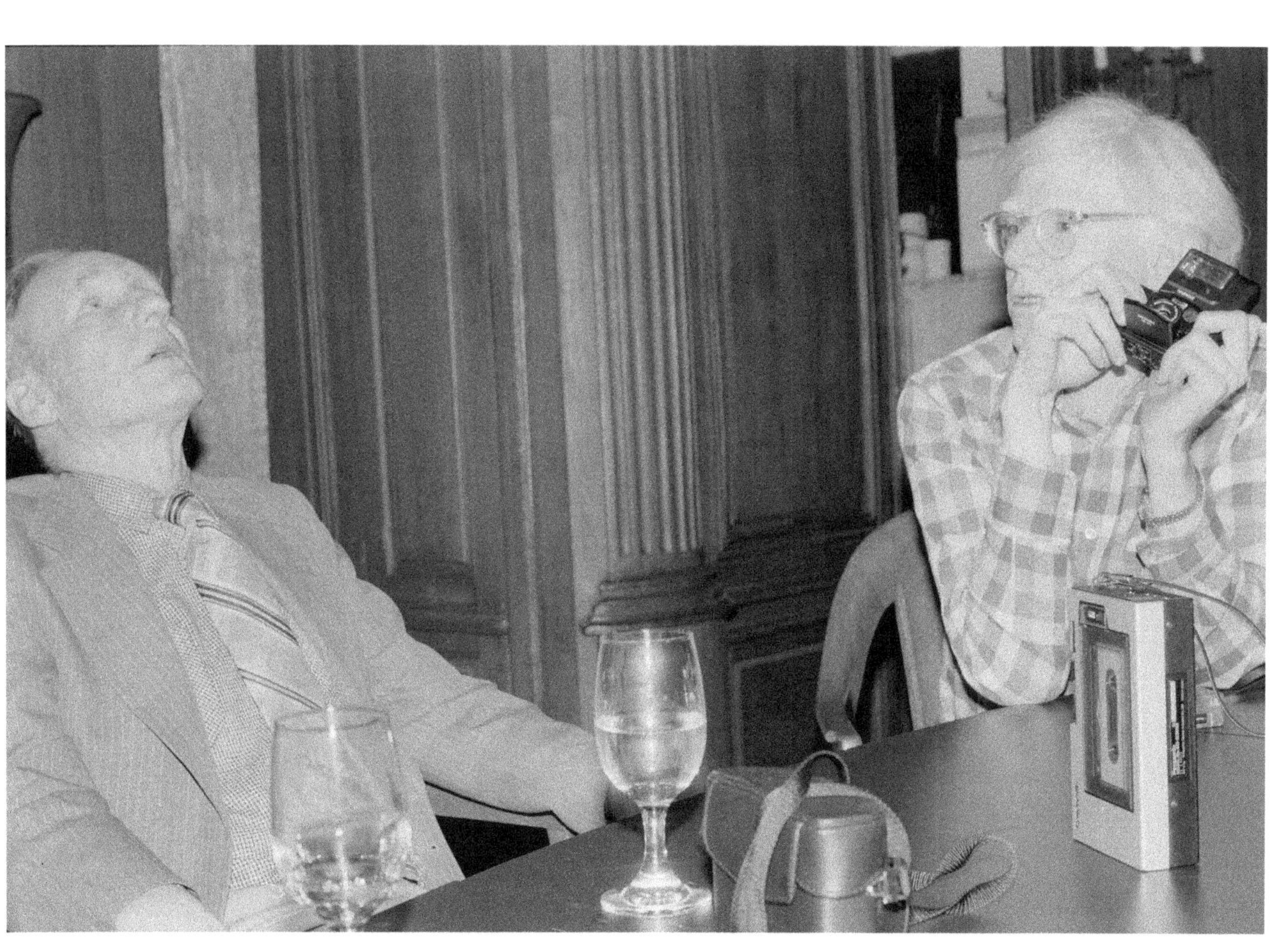

BURROUGHS: Well, who are they, who are the ten famous Jews? Kafka, Einstein?

WARHOL: Kafka, Einstein.

BURROUGHS: Freud.

WARHOL: Freud.

BURROUGHS: Marx.

WARHOL: Well, we wanted him but it was like of the 20th century or something.

BURROUGHS: Oh, I see.

WARHOL: Gertrude Stein.

BURROUGHS: Gertrude Stein.

WARHOL: And, er, Sarah Bernhardt[6] and Golda Meir[7] and the Marx Brothers and one more person. Burpie? Not Burpie.

BOCKRIS: Well, that's only…

WARHOL: No that was…

BOCKRIS: That was it?

WARHOL: *Yeah.*

BURROUGHS: Who's this over here?

WARHOL: That's Joseph Beuys.[8]

BURROUGHS: That's an extraordinary picture.

BOCKRIS: [aside to Andy in separate room] You know, I really wanted to take a picture of William with your Kafka portrait and use it in my book.

WARHOL: Oh really, oh I didn't know that. You never told me. Well, why don't you wait? He's going to have the finished ones and it'll be great because I want to do a Polaroid of Bill and we could do a… a… a portrait of him, just for fun. Ok? So why don't we make it for another day next week?

---

6   French stage actress, 1844-1923.

7   Israel's fourth prime minister, 1898-1978.

8   German artist, 1921-1986.

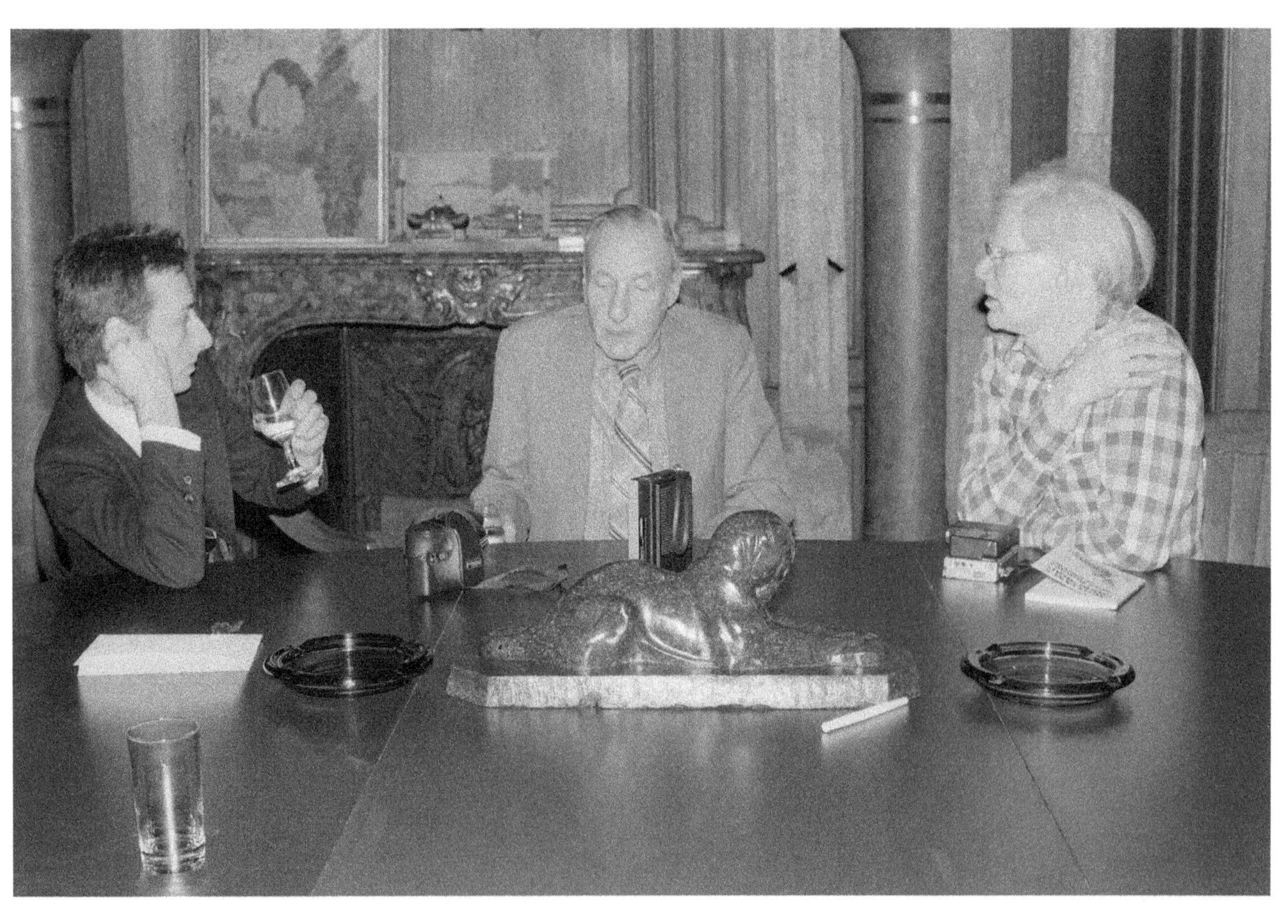

Thursday, January 24, 1980

"Victor Bockris came over with William Burroughs. I introduced Bianca to William Burroughs. Bianca's hair is really short now, like a crewcut, it looks terrible."

The Andy Warhol Diaries

I picked Bill up at his place at 3:30 p.m. Thanked him for coming to dinner last night with Susan Sontag and said I hoped it hadn't been any kind of an imposition. He said no and he'd enjoyed it. Bill was talking about the time it takes between an idea and its development, where you get the Wright Brothers inventing an airplane and forty years later the airplane is a flying hotel, whereas in the history of weaponry it took hundreds of years after the invention of the cannonball for people to realize that it could explode on impact, creating a much greater effect. I told him a little bit about the material I was reading from his *Time-Life* files and we headed downstairs to get a cab. On the way over, we discussed Charles Henri Ford's movie *Johnny Minotaur*, which Bill hadn't seen but had heard about, and Bush's chances in running for the presidency.

At the Factory, Bill relaxed in the conference room talking with Bianca Jagger, whom he had first met through Mick in the early 1970s. The subject turned to the interview and they sat around denigrating the whole concept as ridiculous and of little merit. Bill had the sense to say he thought what I was doing was interesting. Bianca said she hoped we

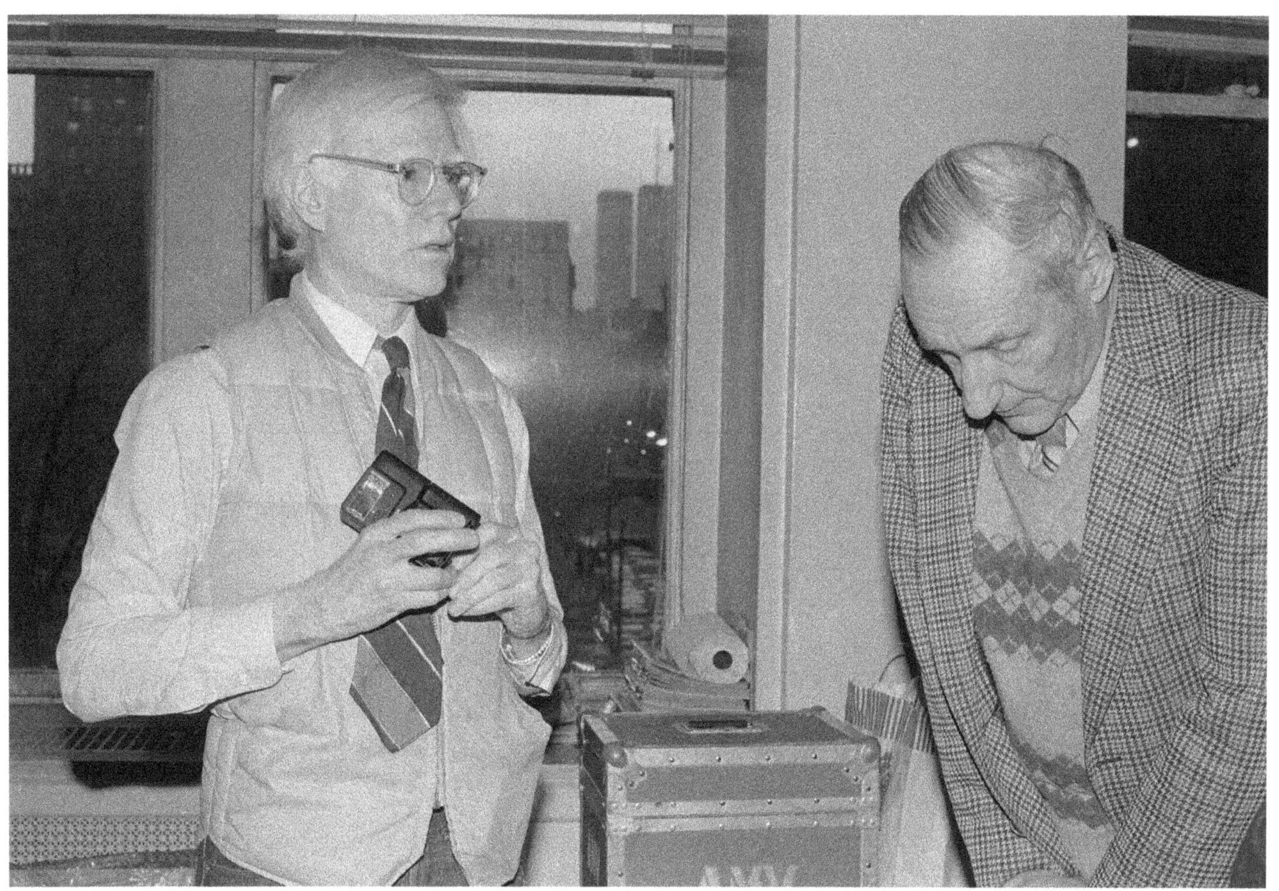

weren't interviewing her. Unbelievably, I had neglected to bring a tape recorder or a camera, but I had summoned one of Andy's favorite young photographers, Bobby Grossman, to document the event. Andy's tape recorder was grinding away interviewing Bianca unnoticed on the large table in front of us.

Burroughs did a lot of tape-recording experiments in the 1960s, but I think Warhol is the only artist who has changed language with the tape recorder. What am I talking about? Andy called his cassette recorder his wife! He loved the machine unconditionally. All he had to do was turn it on in the right place at the right time and it produced a real-life drama. His tape-recorded *a, A Novel* (Grove Press, 1968) is one of the key texts of the sixties. This overlooked work of genius consists of twenty-four hours of recorded conversations between Andy, Ondine, and their friends running around New York. It created a new American language. Andy's *Interview* magazine, started in 1969, introduced the notion of recording informal conversations as opposed to Q&As with celebrities. *Interview* changed journalism. By 1972, it led to *People* magazine, which became the most successful magazine in the world. One of the finest examples of his inventive recording style is "Sundays with Mr. C: An Audio-Visual Documentary," a conversation with Truman Capote about the Rolling Stones' 1972 tour of America, which was published as the cover story of *Rolling Stone*'s April 1973 issue.

Andy floated into the conference room and greeted Bill warmly. Everything was warm and cool. He took Bill next door and sat him on a hardback chair just a little to the left of where his Kafka portrait was leaning up against the white wall. Andy started moving back and forth in front of and to the side of Bill, snapping some thirty head and shoulders portraits with Polaroid's 1972 Big Shot camera. Bill was not normally comfortable being photographed for more than a few minutes, but Andy identified so intimately with his subject that he infused his energy into them by finding a common rhythm as if breathing with them, and Bill relaxed, leaning into rather than shying away from the camera. The pictures captured the writer at the triumphant moment when he had just finished his novel, *Cities of The Red Night*. It had been six years in the making.

Andy laid the Polaroids across Ronnie's desk in grids. Bill lingered over the pictures. He indicated his favorite shot, choosing the one in which his fingers strayed across the bottom of his chin. Bill said, "I like it because it makes me look like a French intellectual."

This was special treatment. As we started putting on our coats, wrapped in the enthusiasm of the Warhol effect, Andy rushed Bill once again, saying, "Oh, oh, let's do some more! More! When can we meet again? Oh, let's have dinner. I'll take you out to dinner!"

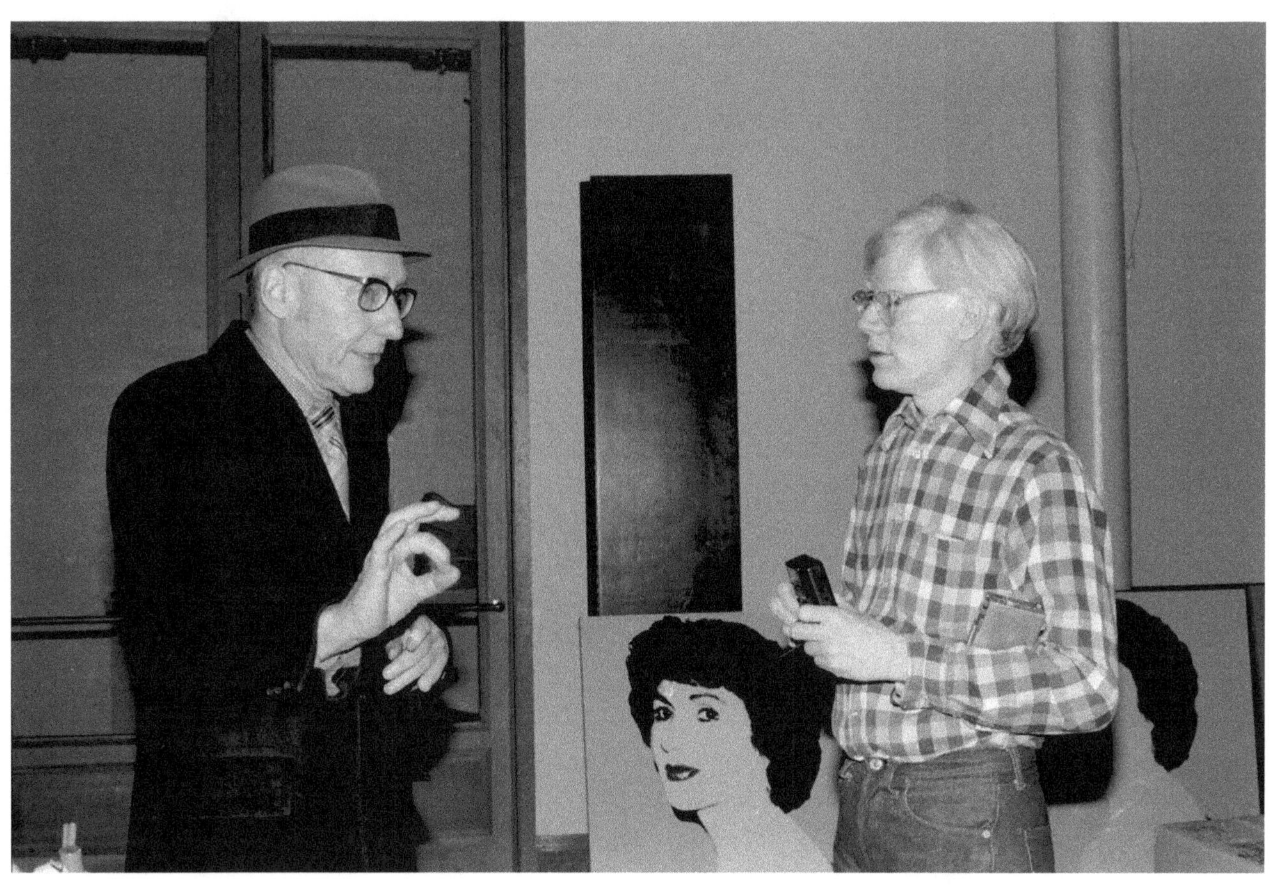

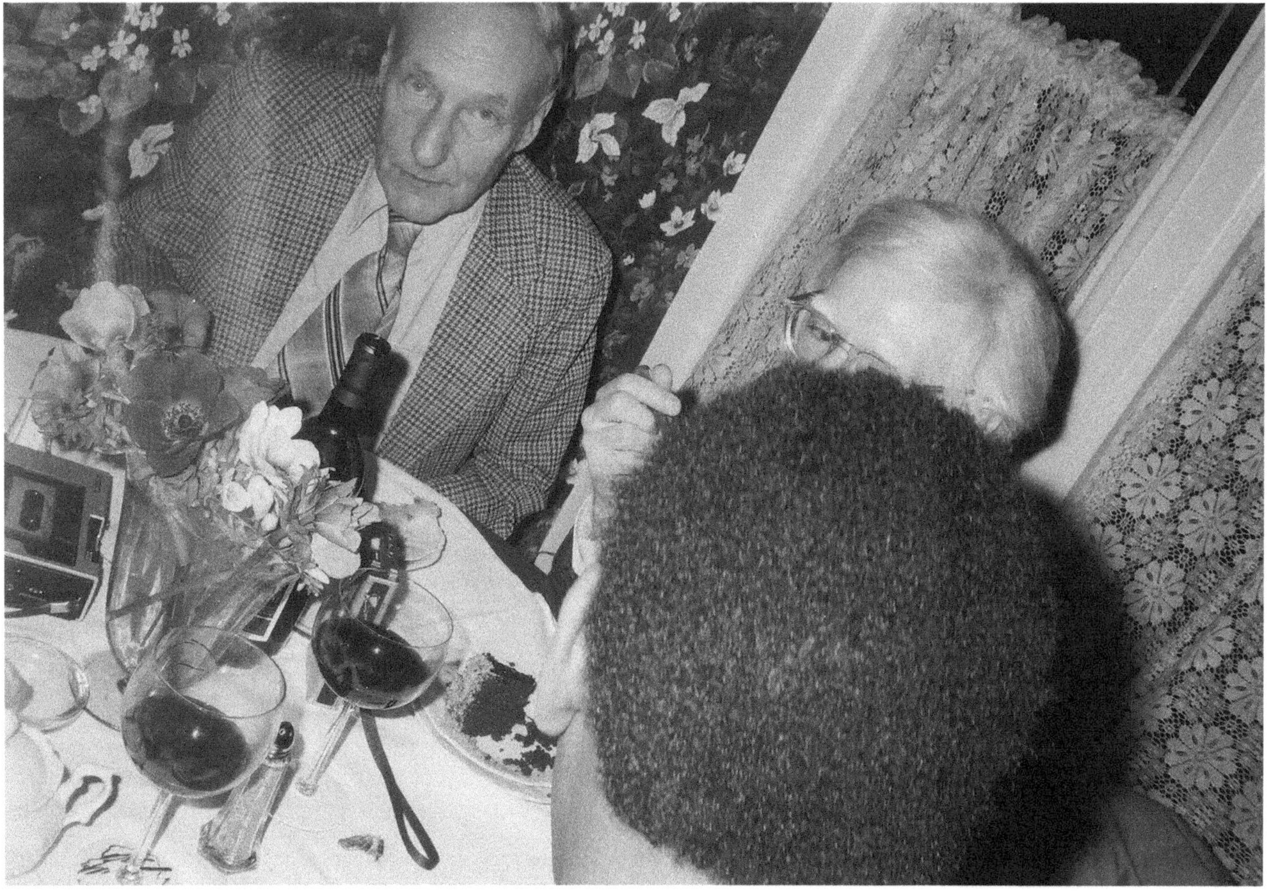

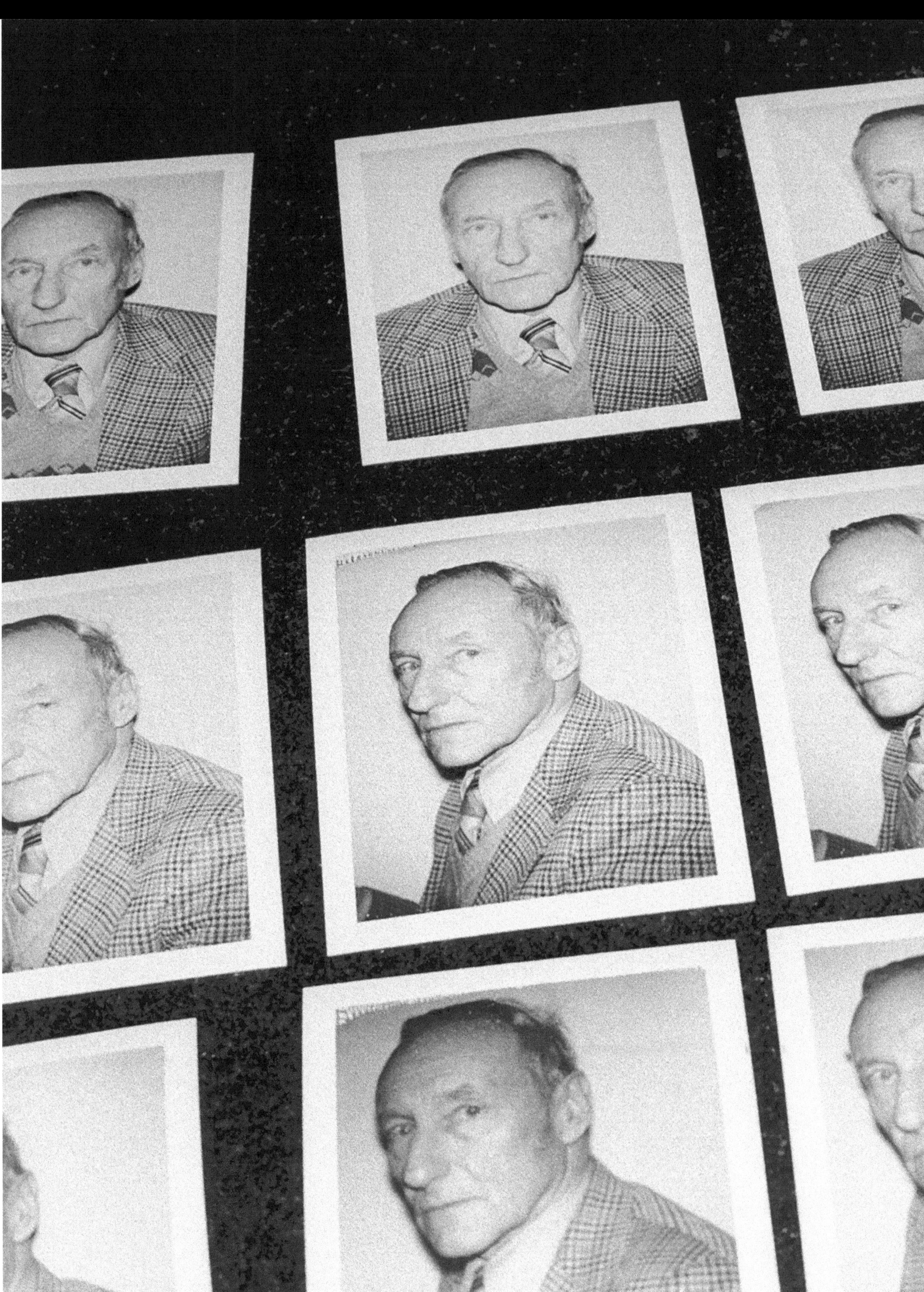

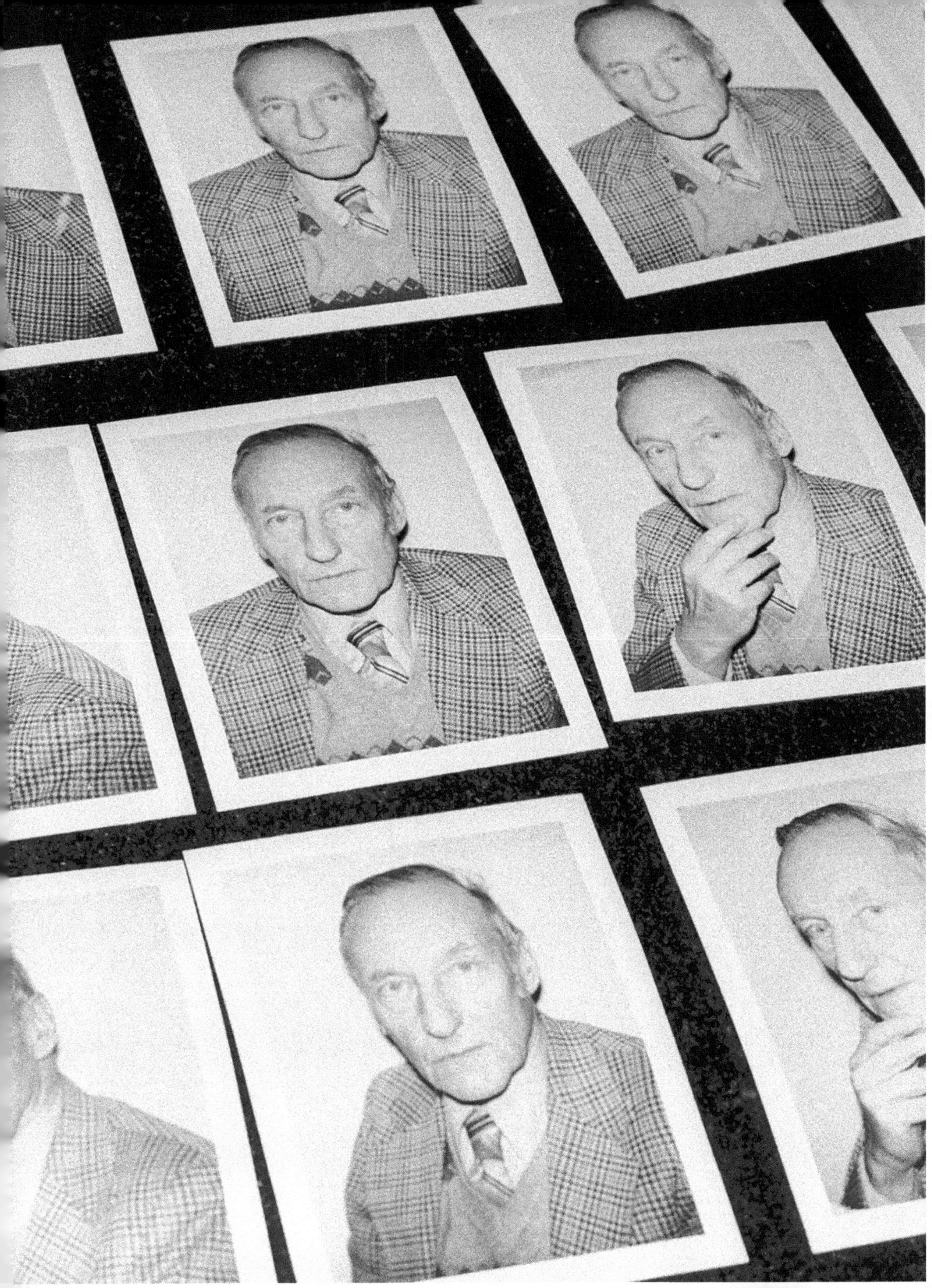

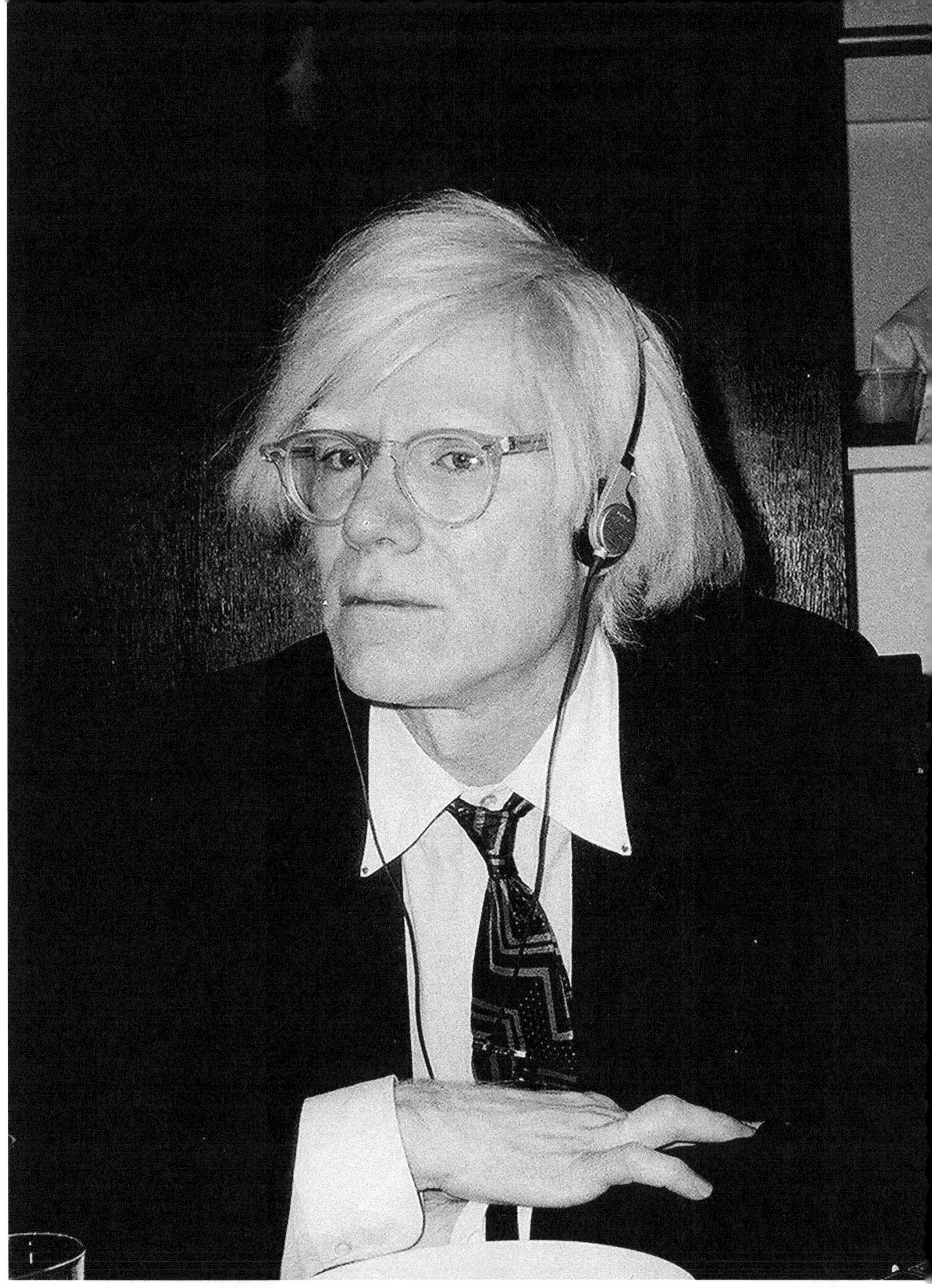

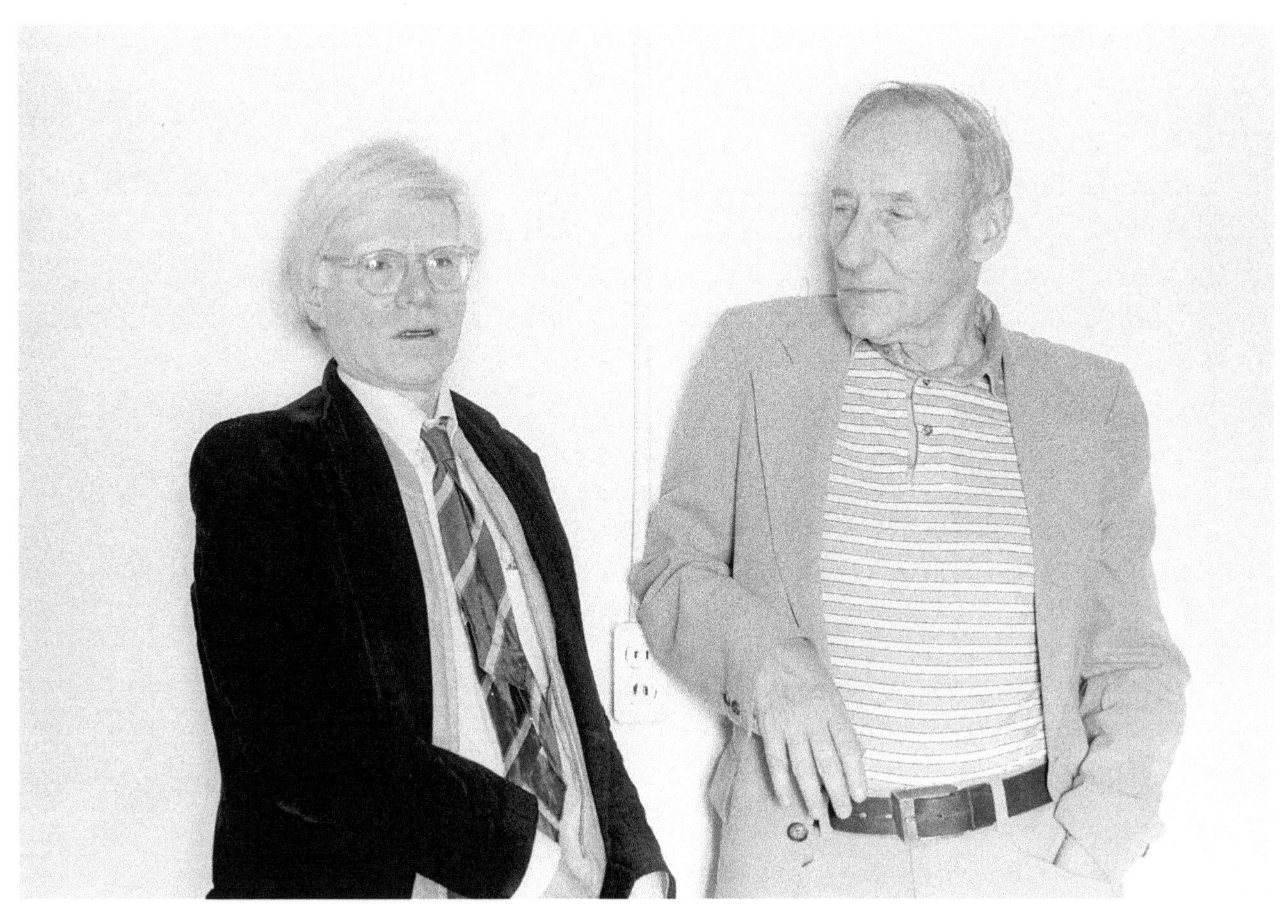

CHAPTER THREE
DINNER WITH BURROUGHS
AND WARHOL

Monday, January 28, 1980—65 Irving Restaurant, New York

When I introduced Bill to Andy, they were both thriving, but they were both also suffering from loss. Andy's boyfriend, Jed Johnson, had been a force in the Warhol films of the 1970s, but traveling with Andy had taken him into many of the best-designed houses in the world and Jed had developed a successful career as an interior designer. Now he was in the process of leaving Andy and Andy started drinking heavily. He could hold his liquor like a stevedore.

Meanwhile, Bill's son, William Burroughs Jr., was suffering through a long series of humiliating mental and physical disasters caused in part by drug and alcohol abuse. He had led a tragic life and now he was dying. William had two other problems. He had been, at times, suffering from writer's block and grinding poverty. As a result, for the last year and a quarter, he had been using heroin and opium again. It helped him complete *Cities of the Red Night*.

I like to believe their friendship really began the night Andy took us out to dinner at his favorite restaurant near the Factory. 65 Irving Place is two blocks south of Gramercy Park. William and I arrived in a cab at 7:00 p.m. We were discussing the non-existence of the unconscious: "It's like Voltaire said about the Holy Roman Empire: 'it was neither Holy, Roman, nor an Empire,'" Bill sniffed. "There is no such thing as the unconscious any longer."

Andre Leon Talley, who had just resigned from *Women's Wear*, sat at the bar sipping a Scotch. He smiled engagingly.

The owner, Fabrizio, shook hands and asked, "How many?"

"Four with Mr. Warhol," I told him.

"Yes, I have the table but Andy isn't here yet."

"Hurry up and wait," muttered William behind my back as we followed Andre and Fabrizio into the dining room.

"He usually likes to sit here." The patron indicated a table in the left-hand corner of the room and a chair with its back to the window, which afforded Mr. Warhol the best view of the room. Before we sat down, Andy materialized like a ghost from a crowd of waiters. Coming into sharper focus, he slipped out of an almost comically enormous parka, palming a tape recorder, which he placed onto the table in front of Bill's plate, and slid into his seat. Andy sat with his back to the wall. Bill sat to his right, Andre to his left, with me opposite

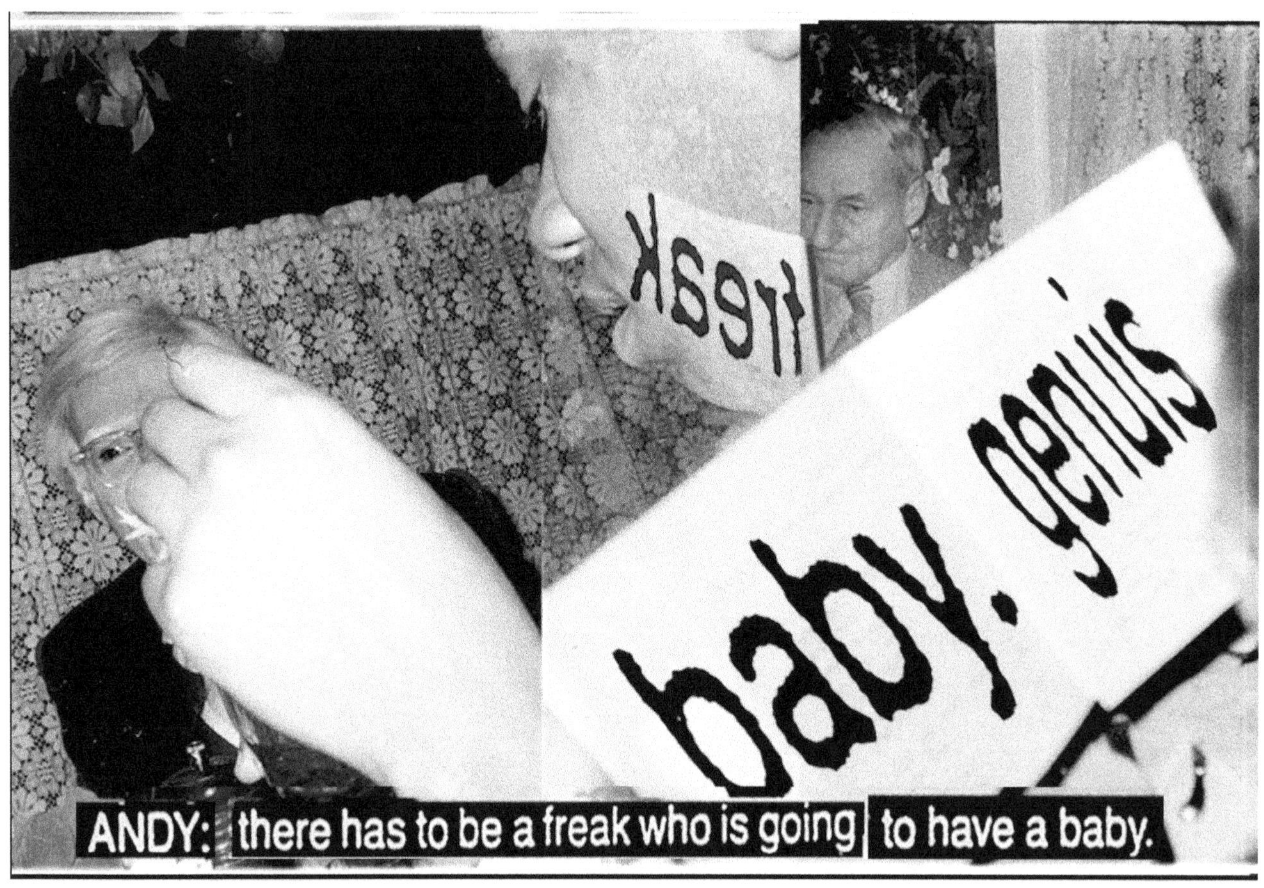

Andy, in the best position from which to capture the sound and take photographs. As he turned to Bill, Andy pulled the tiny 35mm Minox out of his jacket pocket and immediately began a rapid conversation.

ANDY: How old were you the first time you had sex?

BILL: Sixteen.

ANDY: What did you do?

BILL: Not very much, just mutual masturbation. It wasn't until years later I first got fucked in 1938 in Cambridge. It was the year of the great hurricane. I remember now. It was very funny. I was sleeping in my room and this snippy faggot that I was sharing it with… this is when I was doing graduate work… I'm in my room and I hear these sorts of buzzes and I'm sleeping see, he knocks on the door, he says, "Well, Bill, I think the house is being blown down in case you're interested." So I said, "Well okay… I'll put on a coat." We put on our clothes and walk out on the street and I suddenly saw the wind disintegrate a plate glass window and blow a great cloud of glass down the street. So I said, "Well, I guess it's time to go back inside." So we went back inside. That was the 1938 hurricane. I don't know, about four hundred people were killed.

ANDY: So in the middle of all this you made it with him?

BILL: I never made it with him no. He was fucking 'orrible! But I did make it with this other guy who I had known before, when we sort of jerked off together and on this particular occasion, he fucked me.

ANDY: But you know what I really don't understand is when white guys have these really great dark cocks.

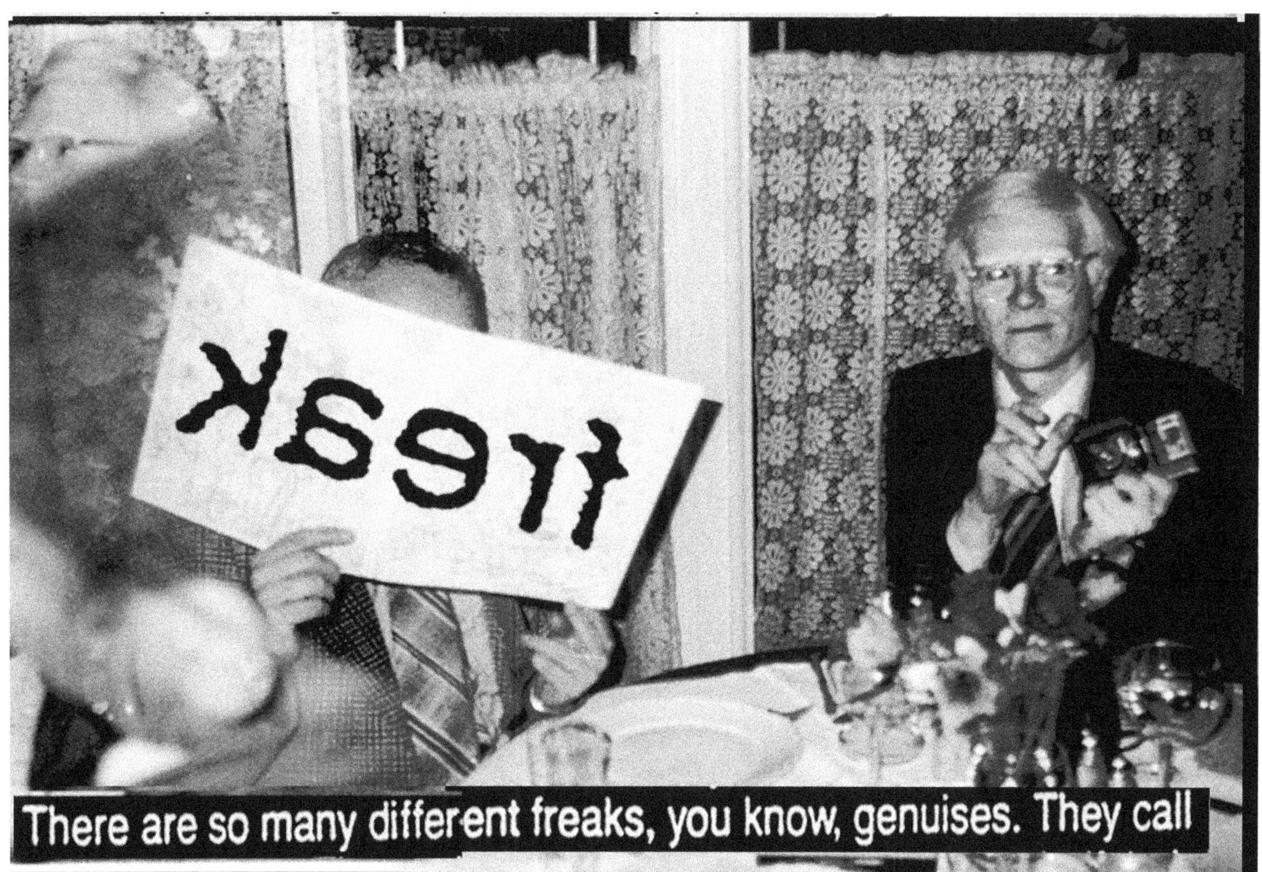

VICTOR: The cock is darker than the rest of the skin?

ANDY: Oh, really dark sometimes.

VICTOR: Well, Bill said Arabic boys have wedge-shaped cocks.

ANDY: Wedge-shaped? What do you mean wedge-shaped?

BILL: Well, yeah. There's a sort of wider wedge-shaped, but it isn't at all uniform. My dear, it's not all that different. Some of them tend to be a little bit, ah, you know, shaped wide.

ANDRE: The tip? The head?

ANDY: It's hard to get the head in then, isn't it? Here, draw it.

BILL: My dear, I can't. It's not so well defined. Victor has misled you to think that there's anything very special about this. Actually, it has nothing to do with the nationality. There are a lot of people like that.

ANDY: Well, Bill has a big cock.

ANDRE: How do you know?

ANDY: Well, he does. Huh?

BILL: Average, average.

VICTOR: Average.

ANDRE: Average, average.

VICTOR: Do you have an average…

ANDY: Yeah.

BILL: Everybody's got an average cock.

ANDY: Andre's got a really big cock.

ANDRE: Andy's so sure that I have a big cock! It's not true. [Andre is a black man.]

ANDY: Oh, come on.

BILL: He said he had an average, average.

ANDRE: It's all right to be average.

ANDY: I only fall in love with kids who have what's-it-called ejaculation.

ANDRE: You mean premature ejaculation?

ANDY: Yeah. That's my favorite trick. Are you one?

BILL: What?

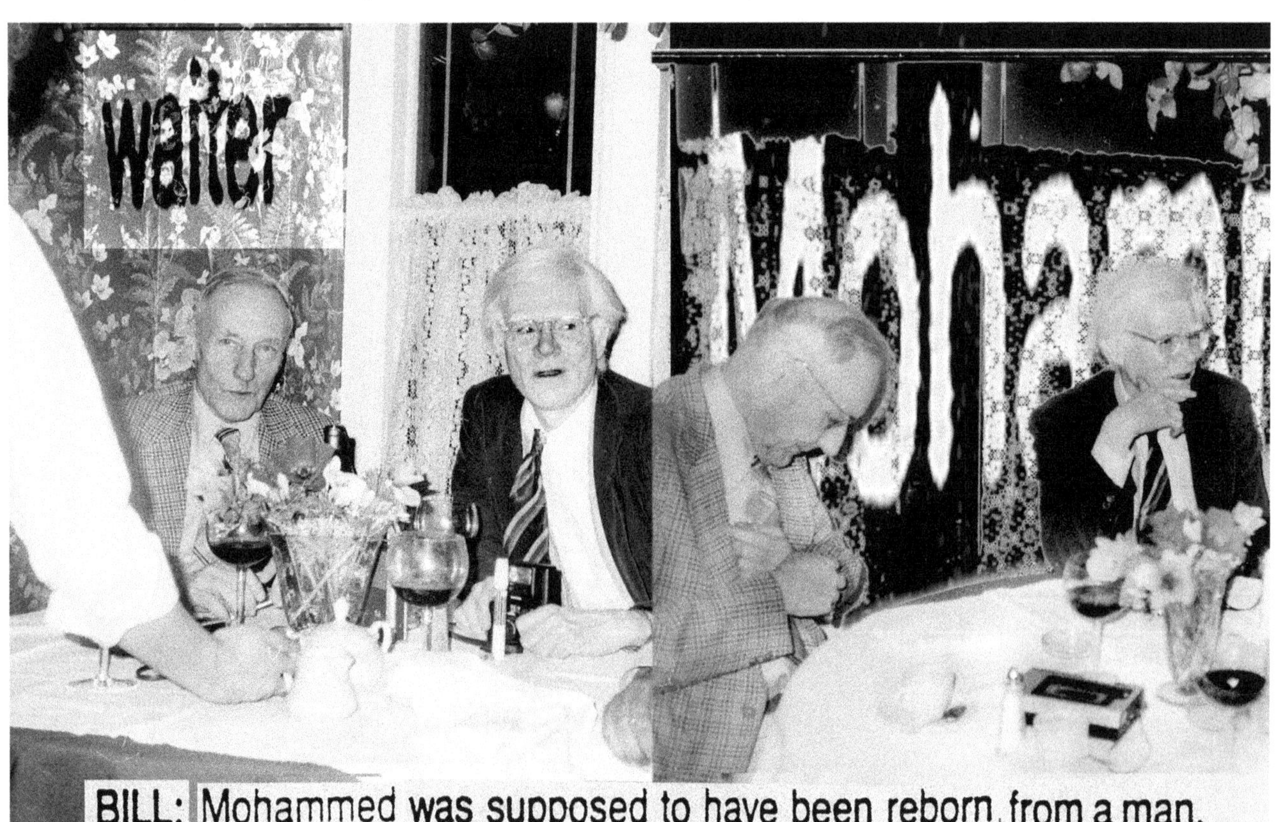

ANDY: Are you a premature ejaculator?

BILL: Uhmmm, pretty quick, pretty quick!

ANDY: Really?

VICTOR: I figure sex should be right away.

BILL: I do too, but see, women have different cycles.

ANDY: Bill is not a premature ejaculator!

BILL: Well certainly I am.

ANDY: Are you really? What do you mean—seconds?

BILL: Nnnnoooooo. Twenty seconds, twenty seconds…

ANDY: What, just petting?

BILL: Well, no no no you have to get a little beyond that.

VICTOR: Petting and then ah…

ANDY: Oh, no no no. I…

VICTOR: No, but once it's in…

ANDY: No no no not in. I mean, it's premature!

VICTOR: Before it gets in?

ANDY: Yeah, you just sort of go like this and…

ANDRE: I know somebody who's thirty-seven and still has wet dreams. Does that mean he has a strong sex drive?

ANDY: I don't have any sex dreams.

VICTOR: You mean wet dreams where you come all over your pants and then in the morning you're embarrassed?

ANDY: Are you kidding? Come on! That's stupid.

BILL: These phenomena are generally associated with adolescence but can occur at any age.

VICTOR: But seriously. I think Bill's career is in acting because he's written so much and now he needs a change. Do you know he didn't start writing until he was thirty-five?

ANDY: What were you doing before?

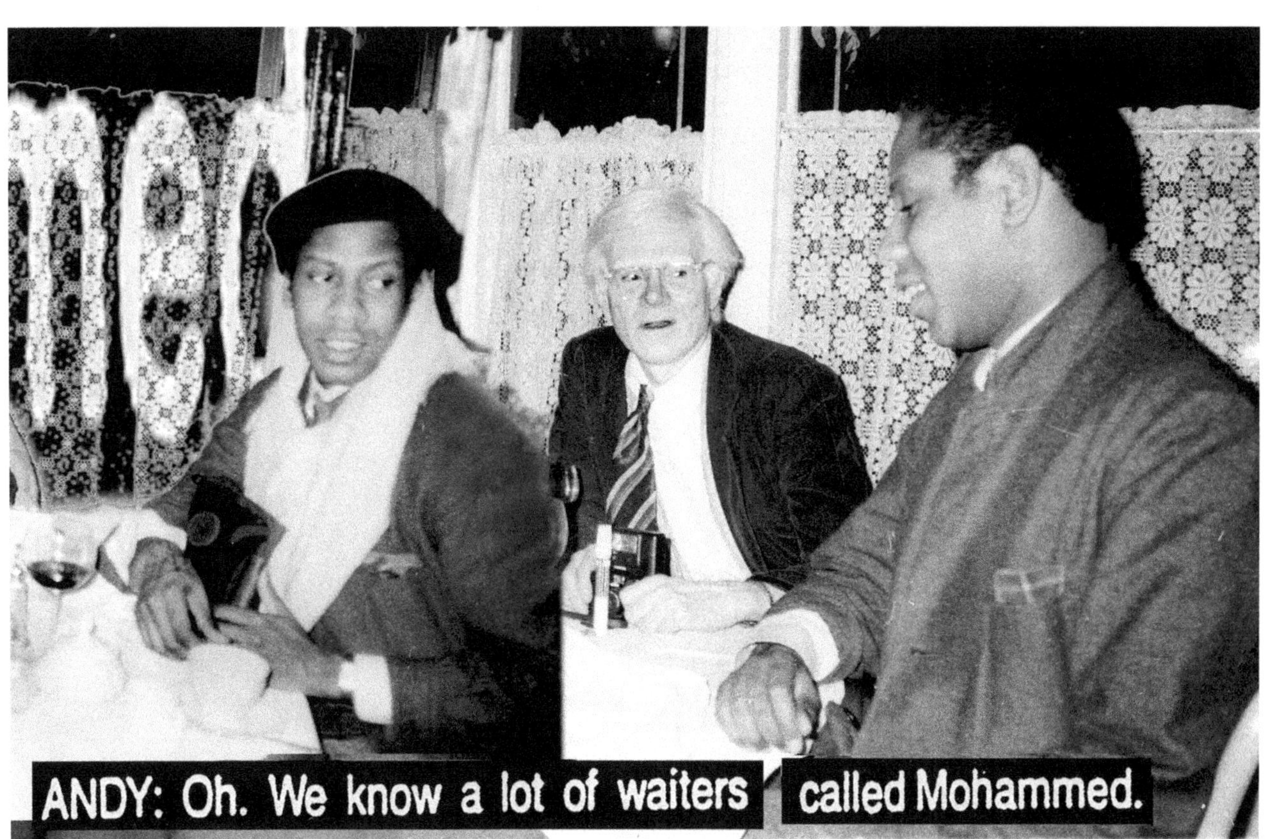

BILL: I was just fooling around. Very marginal.

ANDY: Just bumming around? Working at an office?

ANDRE: You were killing roaches! He was killing roaches in Chicago! He was an exterminator!

ANDY: No! You owned the company?

BILL: No, no.

ANDRE: He killed the roaches.

BILL: It was the best job I ever had. It was so easy. I enjoyed it. To this day, I know all about roaches.

ANDY: God, I had bedbugs. I… only last year…

ANDRE: Andy please!

ANDY: [to Bill] What's your last novel about?

VICTOR: *Cities of the Red Night.* It's about brain transplants. It's a very interesting book. It's a fascinating book.

These hardy Transmigrants, in the full vigor of maturity, after rigorous training in concentration and astral projection, would select two death guides to kill them in front of the copulating parents. The methods of death most commonly employed were hanging and strangulation, the Transmigrant dying in orgasm, which was considered the most reliable method of ensuring a successful transfer.

Cities of the Red Night Review
by Thomas M. Disch, *New York Times*
March 15, 1981

BILL: It's very complicated and tricky.

VICTOR: It's a detective story but it's fabulously complicated, but it's a story… and it ends up in South America with some very rich people who are developing the possibility of brain transplants.

ANDY: You mean they transplant their brain to a younger person?

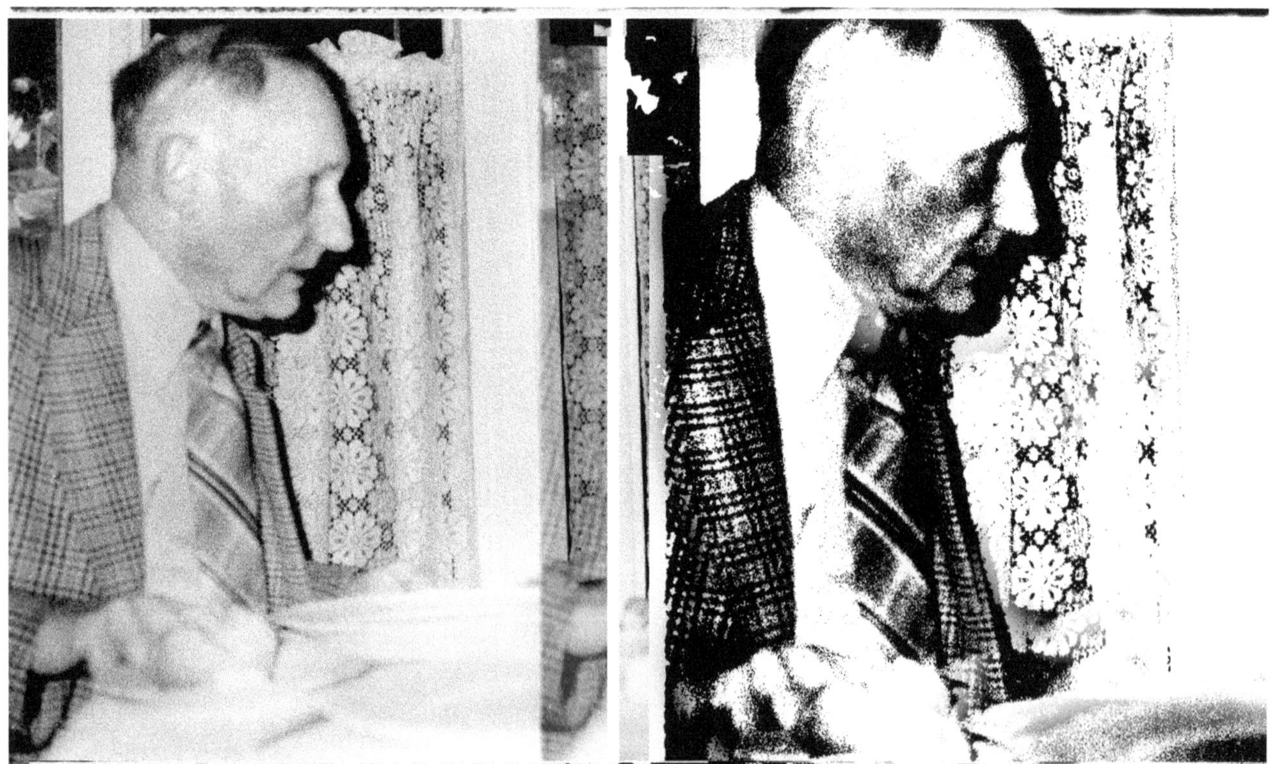

VICTOR: Well, the thing is, you can transplant the "I" from a younger person into another person, correct?

BILL: Yes, presuming you knew where it was located, just as you can transplant a liver. Dr. Starzl[1] is working on the idea of brain transplants now.

ANDY: A lot of people don't want to be transferred though.

BILL: Well, that's true. It isn't compulsory.

ANDY: Oh well, that's fascinating. Would you want to be, Victor?

VICTOR: Transplanted?

BILL: Transplanted into what?

VICTOR: Well, what do you want to do?

ANDY: No, I don't want to be transplanted.

VICTOR: What do you want to do when you die?

ANDY: Oh, er… nothing.

We laughed our way through the meal and completed it with wonderful desserts. By the time Andy paid the bill, we were enveloped in an affectionate bonhomie. I was so elated that—as Bill and I stood facing Andy and Andre saying goodnight on the pavement outside the restaurant—I ran over and laid a kiss on Andy Warhol's plastic cheek.

Udo Breger[2] told me that on the way out to Kennedy airport the following morning William expressed surprise and delight at how open and funny Andy had been. A week later, when I showed Andy the transcript to get permission to publish it in *Blueboy* magazine, he said, "Gee, this certainly isn't an intellectual conversation. Take out some of that stuff about shit and piss, I mean…"

---

1 American physician, researcher, and expert on organ transplants, 1926-2017.

2 Writer and publisher. Friend of Burroughs and Brion Gysin. b.1941.

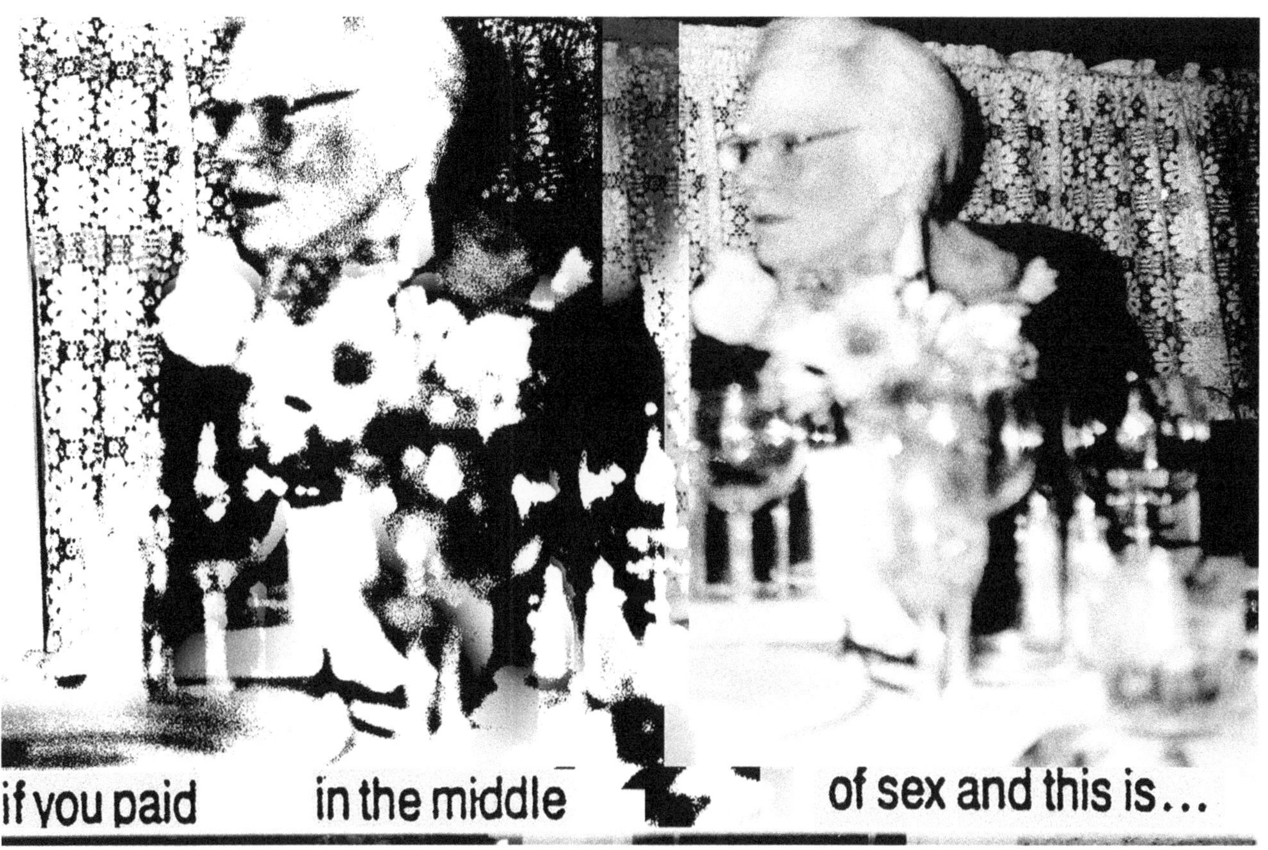

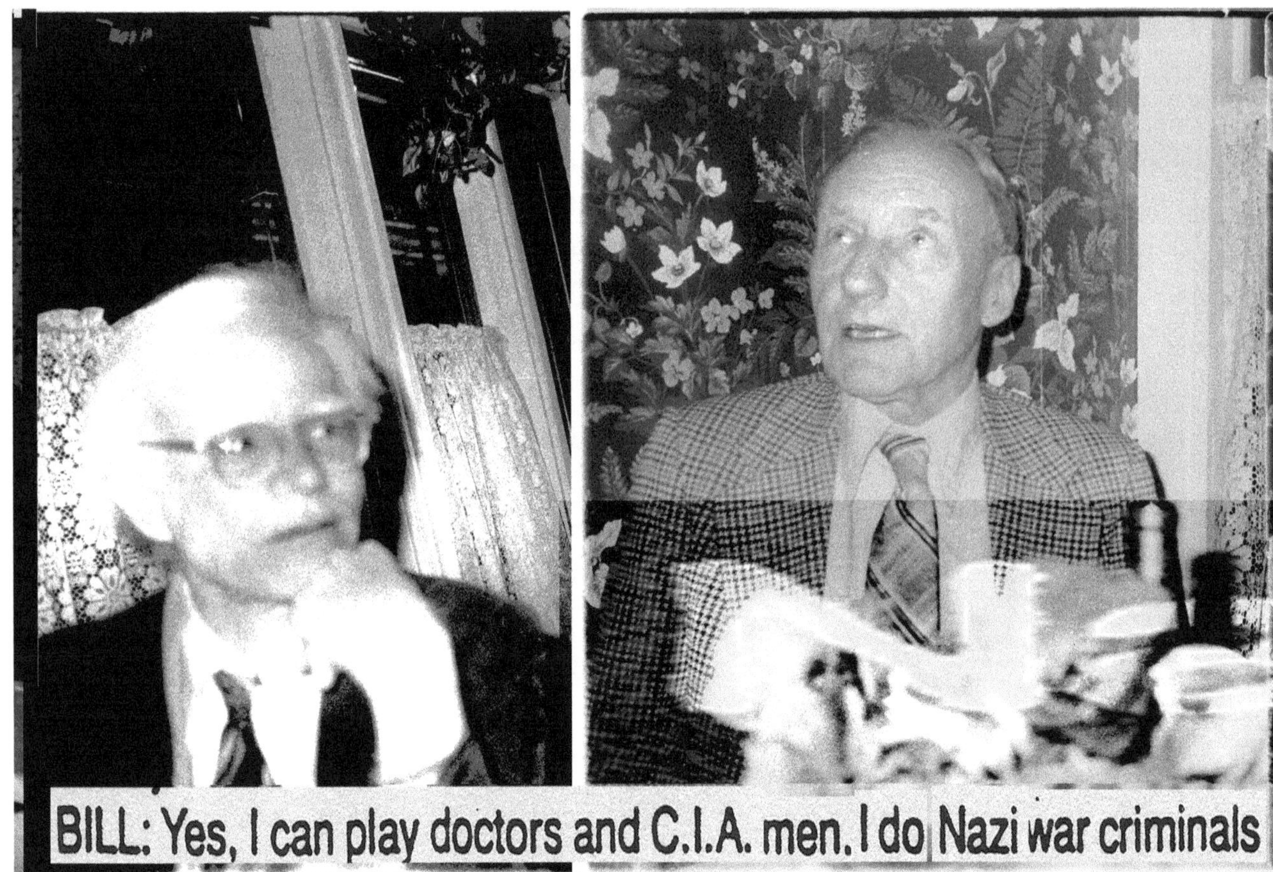

BILL: Yes, I can play doctors and C.I.A. men. I do Nazi war criminals

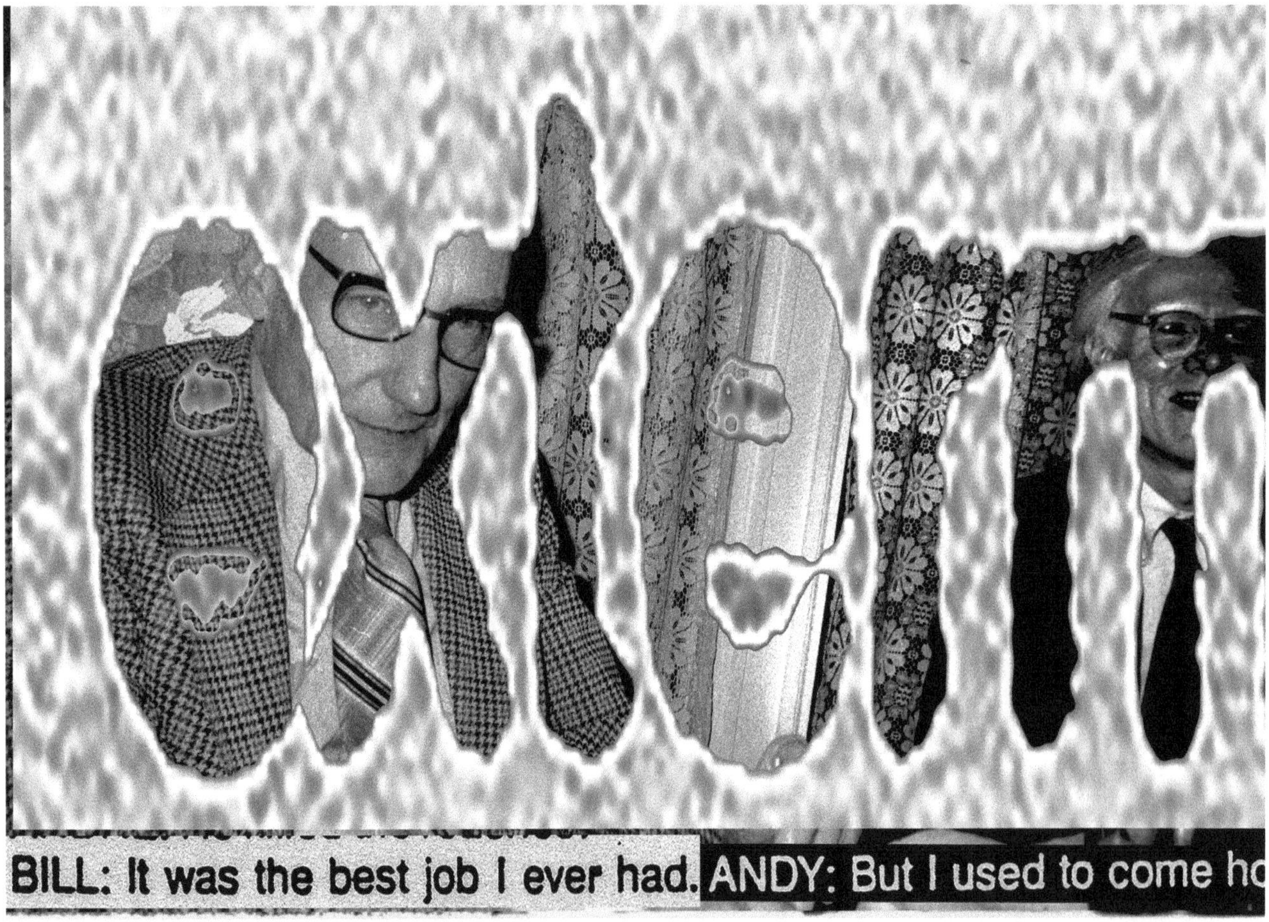

BILL: It was the best job I ever had. ANDY: But I used to come ho

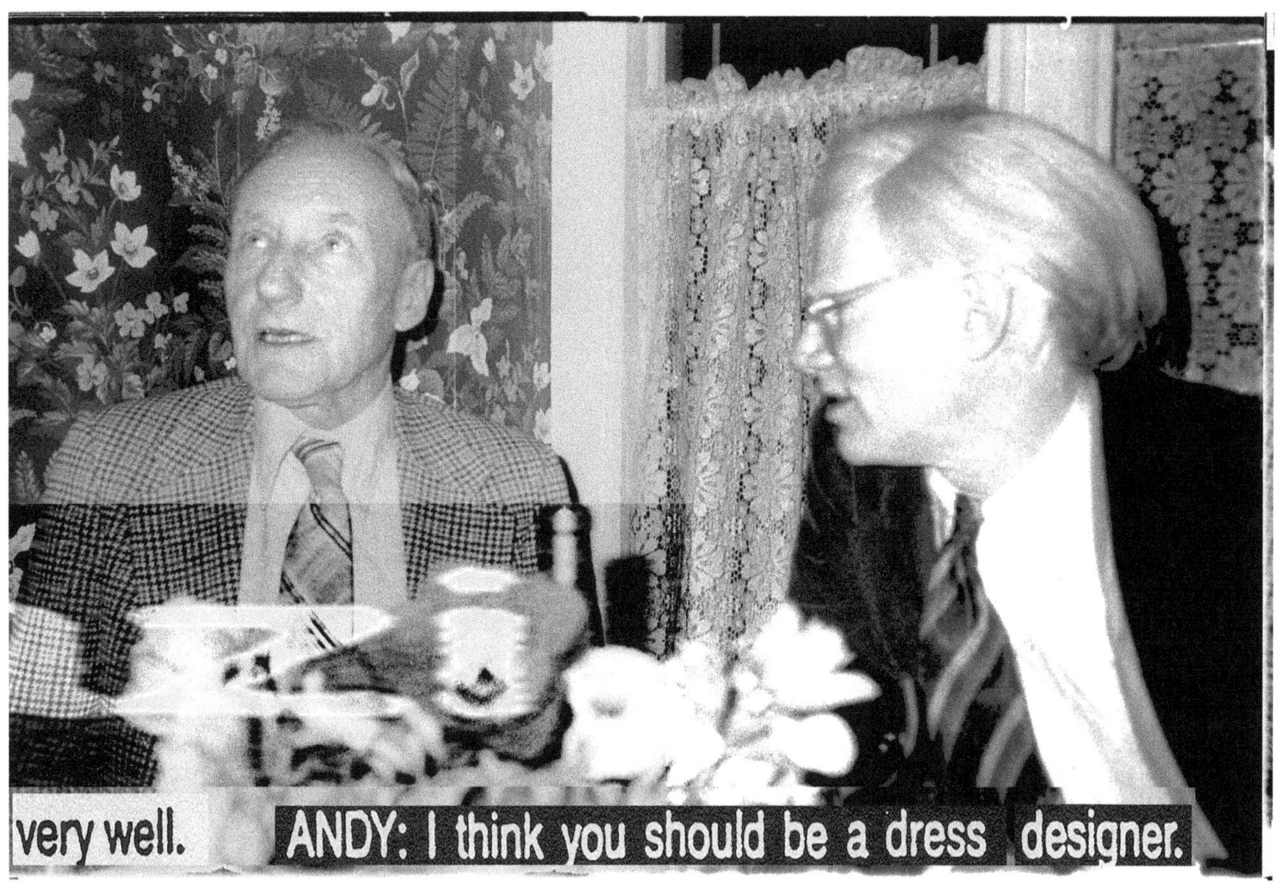
very well.   ANDY: I think you should be a dress designer.

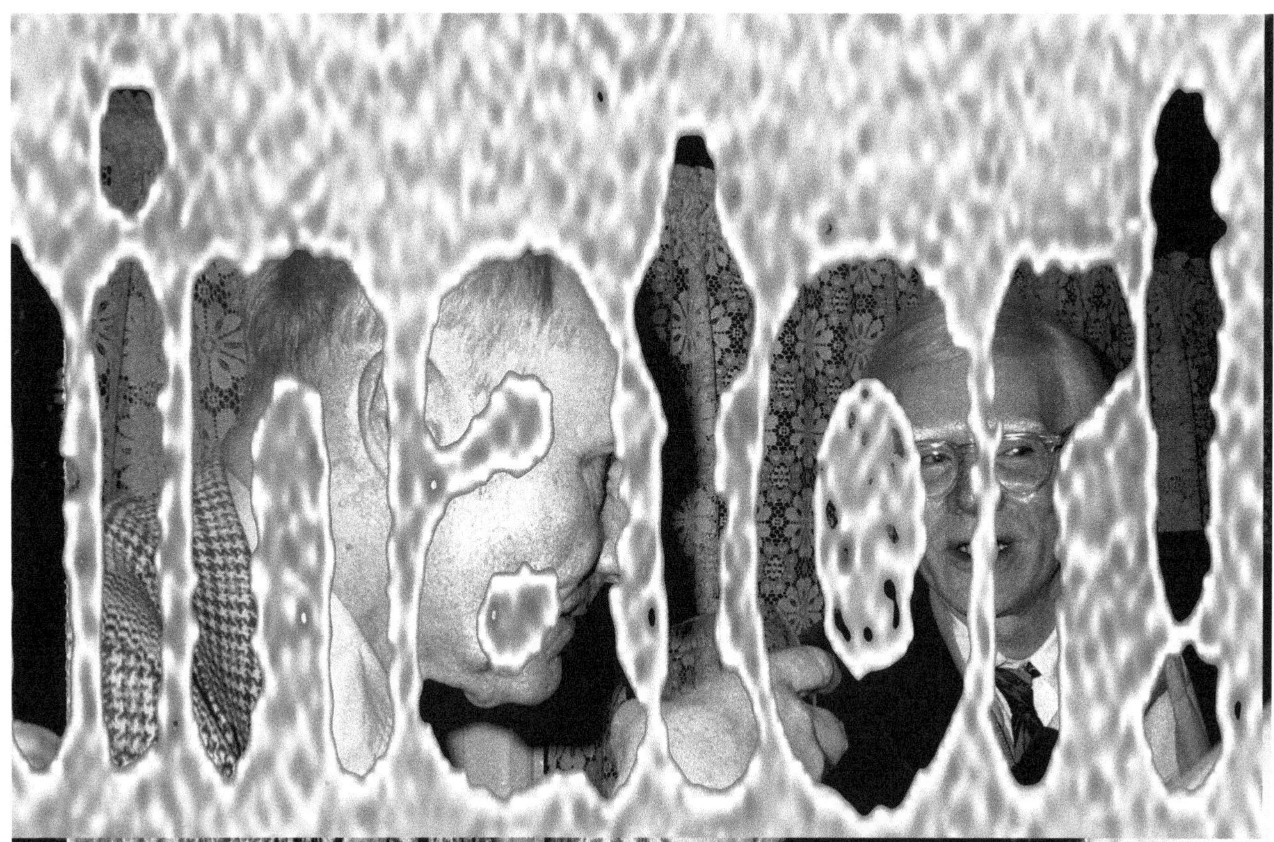
ome and I used to be so glad to find a little roach there to talk to,

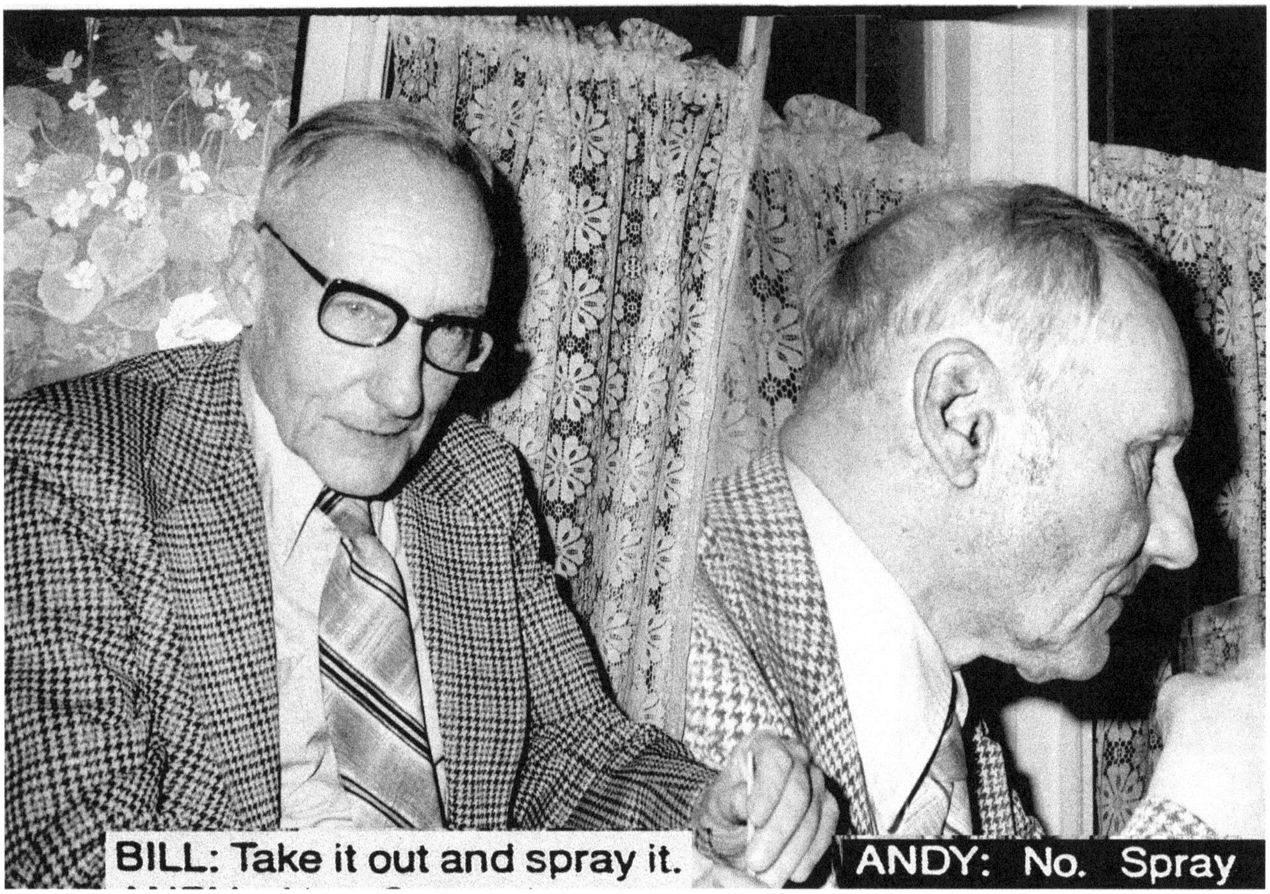

BILL: Take it out and spray it.

ANDY: No.   Spray

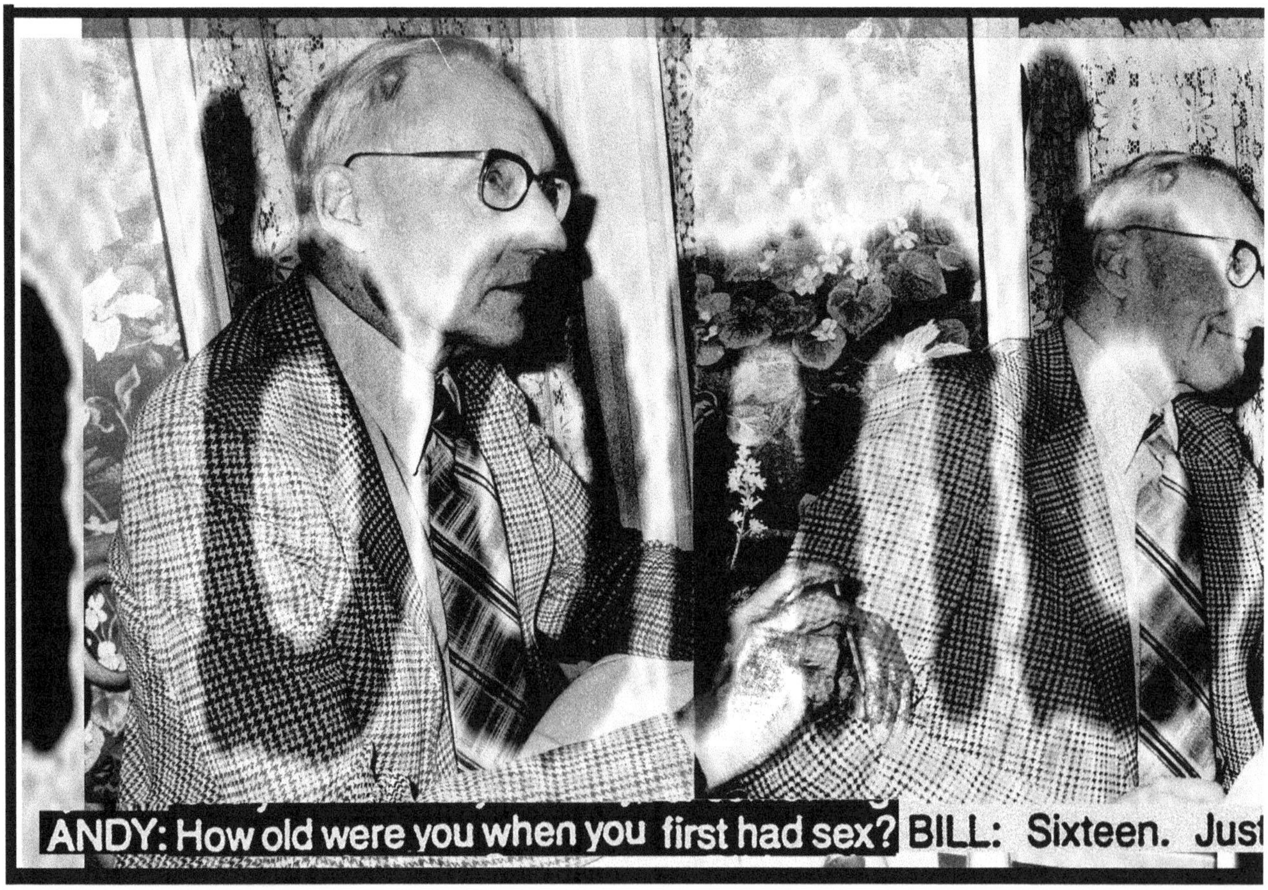

ANDY: How old were you when you first had sex? BILL: Sixteen.   Just

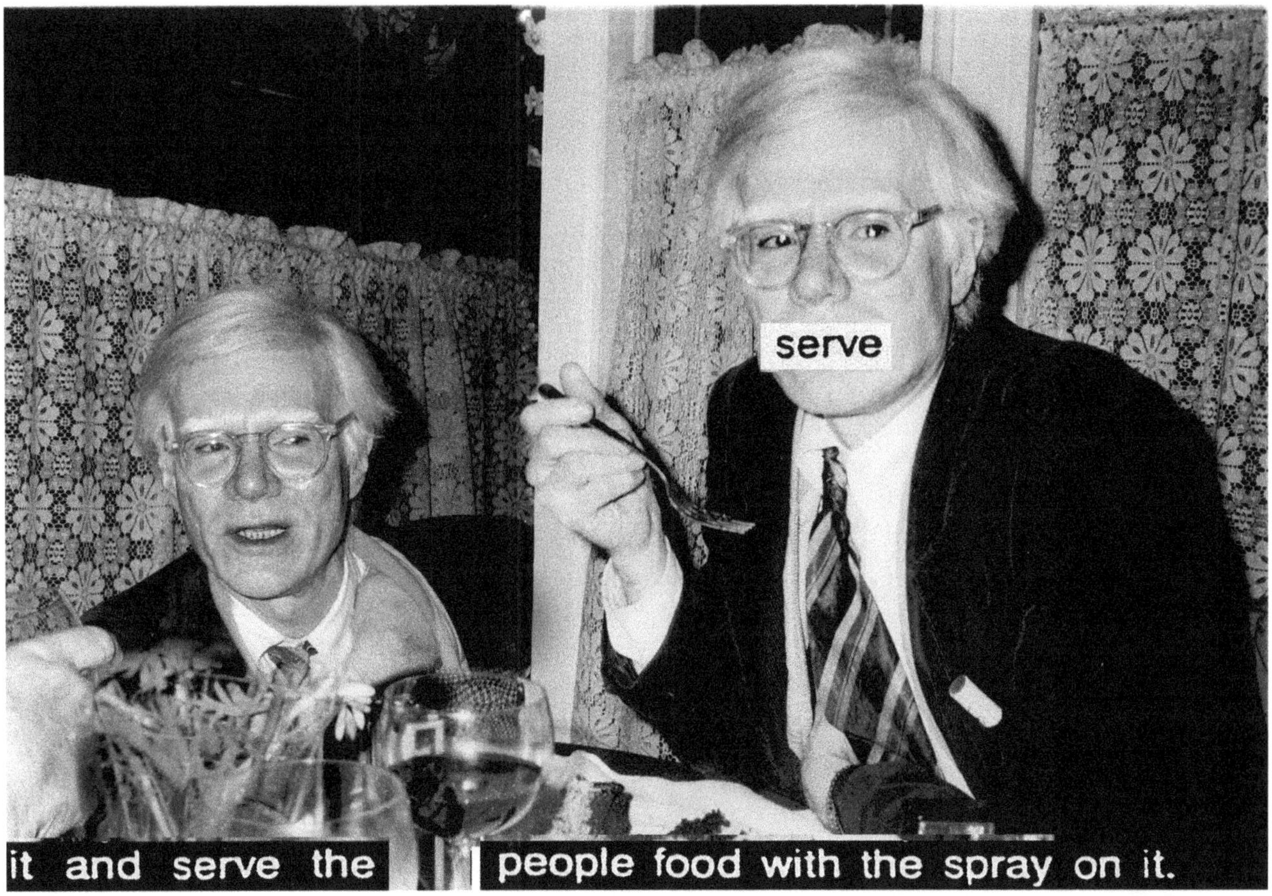

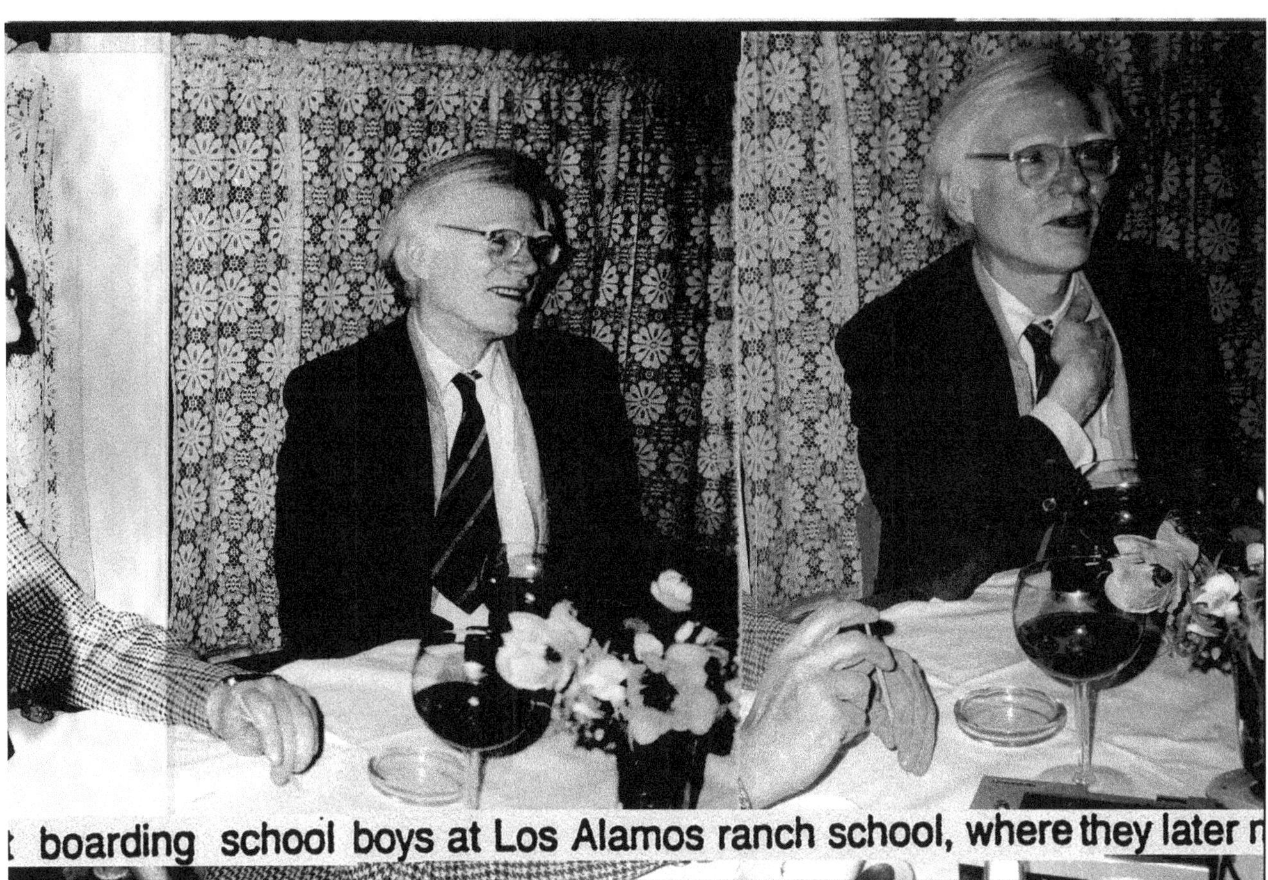
serve
it and serve the   people food with the spray on it.
boarding school boys at Los Alamos ranch school, where they later

FLOW-CHART OF CONVERSATIONAL CATASTROPHES

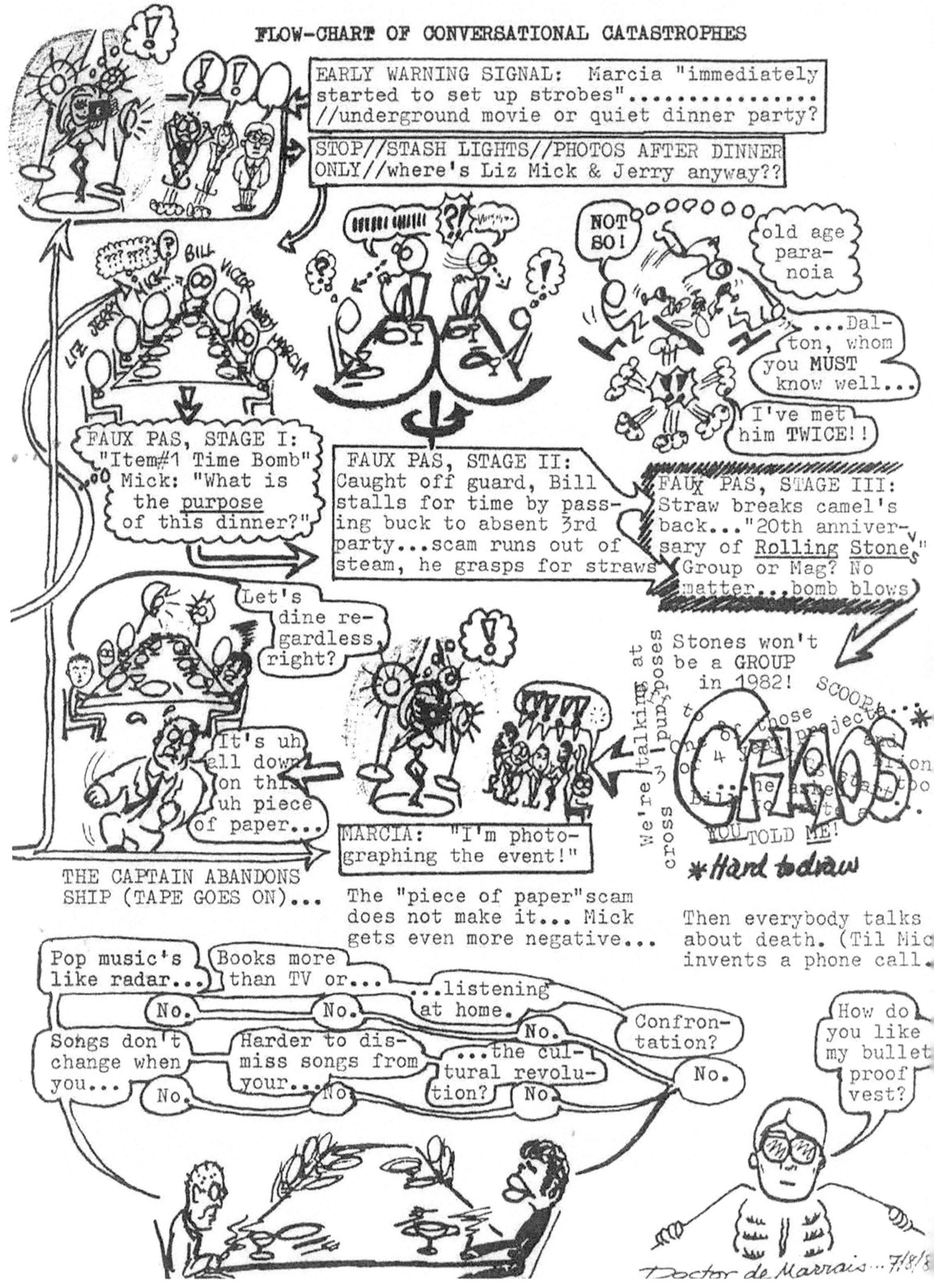

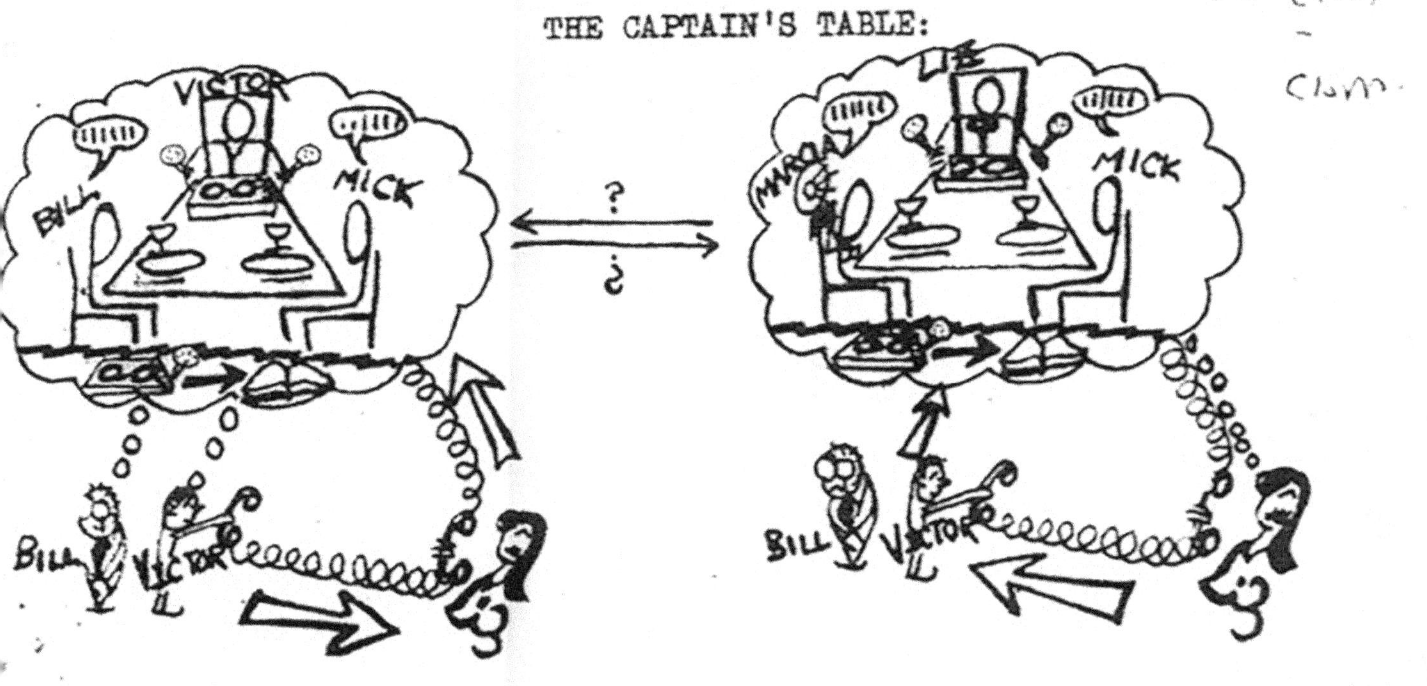

.....CRITICAL TRADE-OFF: To fulfill HIS balloon (Get Mick to Bill's)
Victor buys the analogy to LIZ's balloon (& Marcia enters in).....:

* * *

"TELEPHONE GAME" INSTABILITY BEGINS.
(A tells B; B tells C what A said; C tells D what B said A
 said; D tells E what C said B said A said;...HOW LONG CAN
 THE CHAIN GET BEFORE DEFORM MESSAGE? Answer: NOT VERY!)

* * *

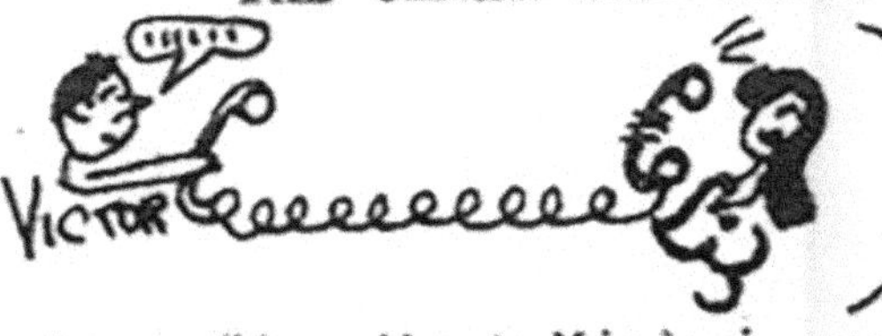

Item #1: Want Mick in on
ONE CHAPTER of our project
(which = OUR BOOK)

Item #1 (After critical defor-
mation to MAKE MICK BITE):
Want YOU in on (delete qualifier)
their project (which = ??? ???)

Item #2: LESS like an
interview; MORE like
informal chat

Item #2 (After MARCIA inter-
prets LIZ's version of VICTOR's
message with sufficient distor-
tion to INVERT it): LESS like
informal chat, MORE like interview

Item #3: Dinner has
expanded from Bill + Mick
(& Jerry) + Victor... to
Bill + Mick (& Jerry) + Victor
+ Liz + Marcia ... CRITICAL MASS?!
SO: Victor adds ballast - calls ANDY
(EVERYBODY knows ANDY WARHOL - right?)

Meanwhile...
What's BILL
up to?

* The Doctors mark... see recto →

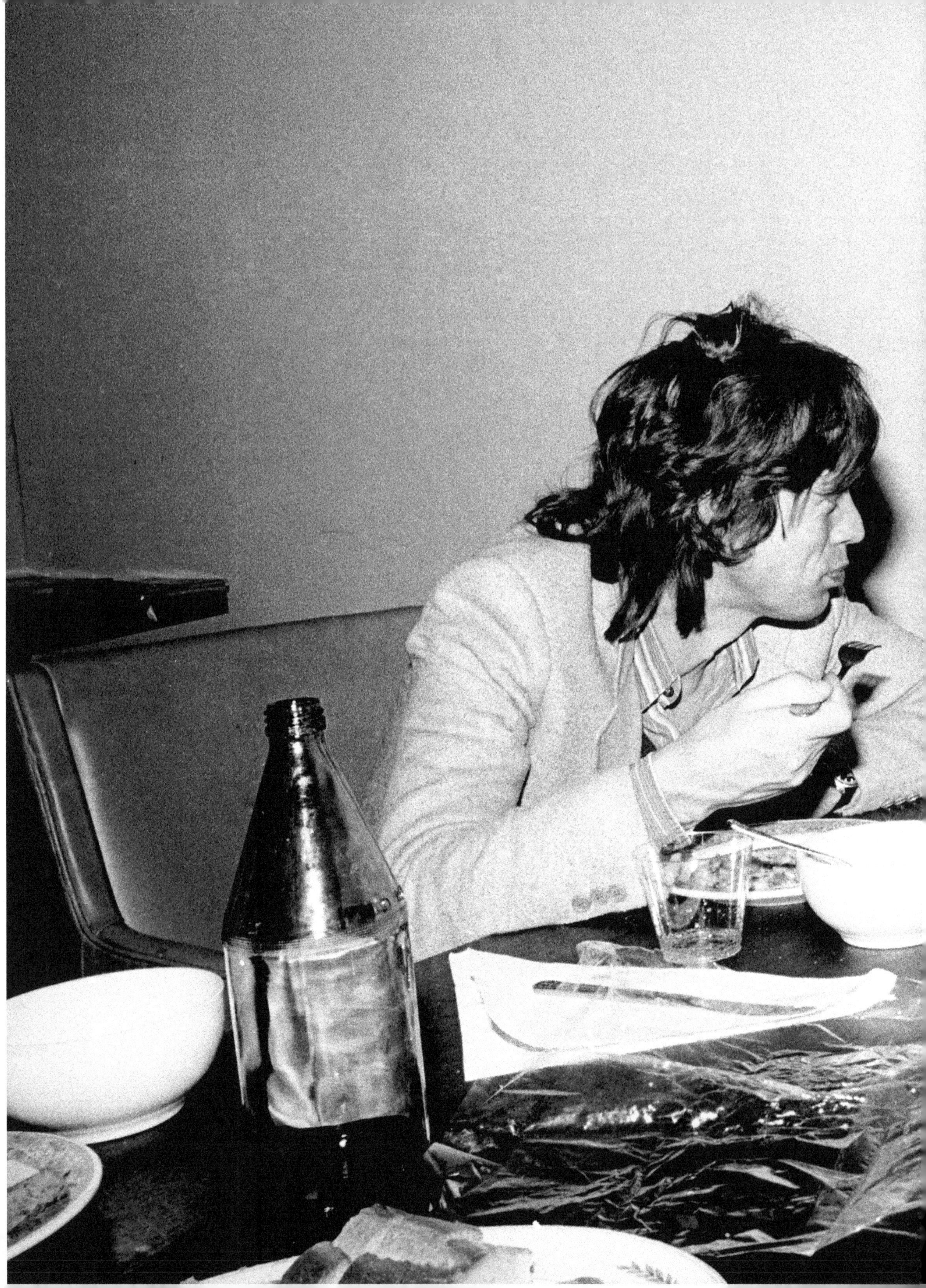

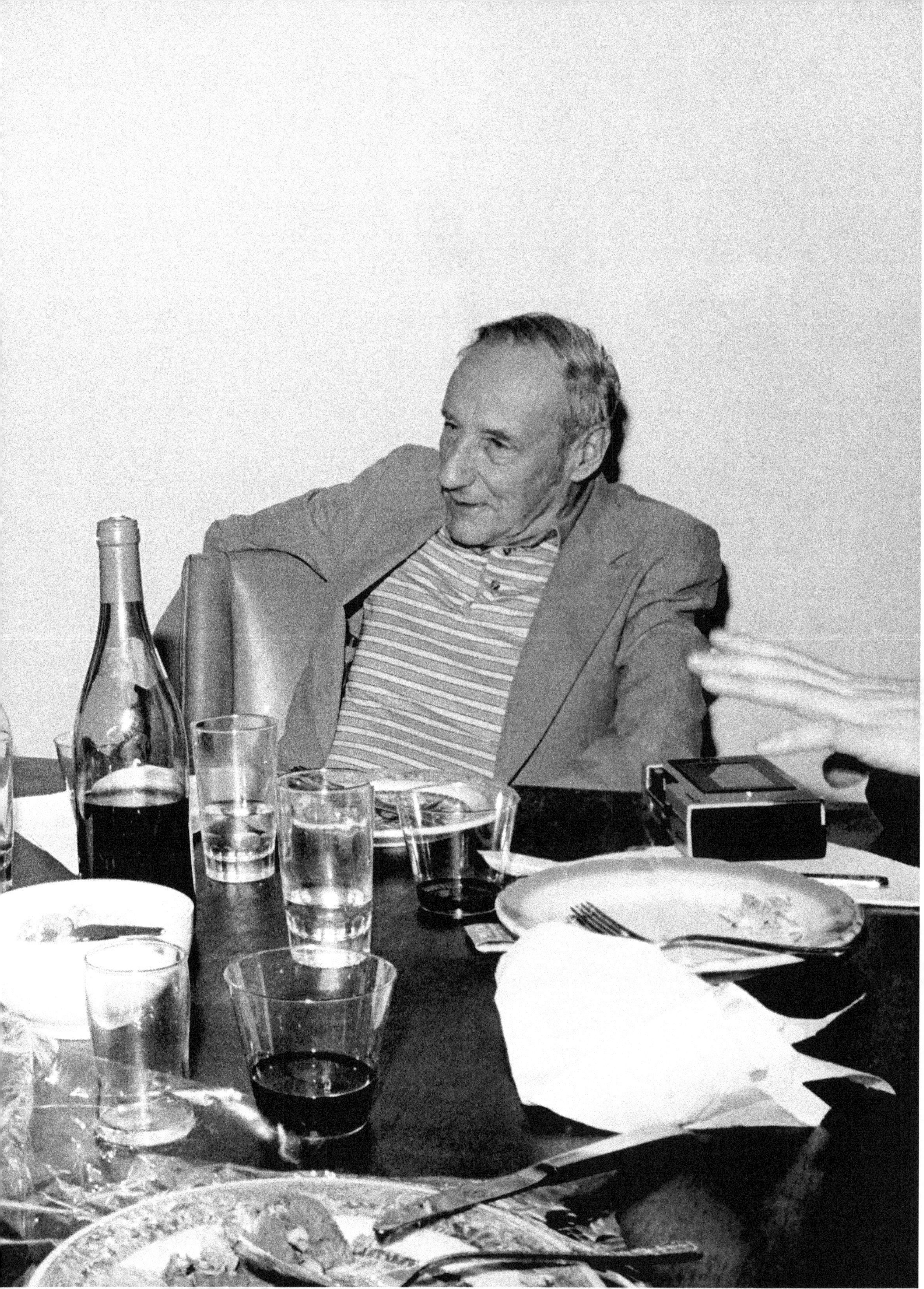

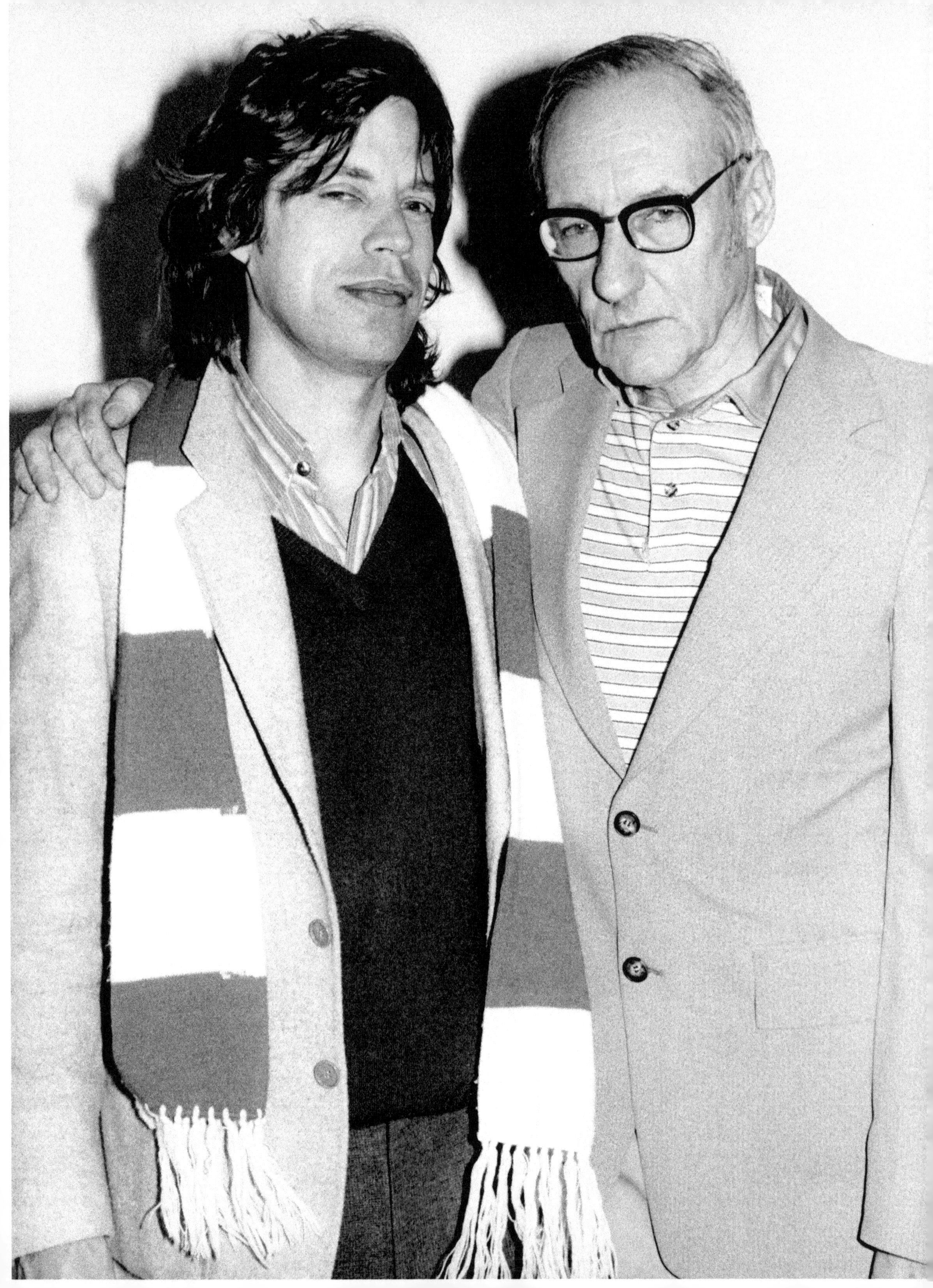

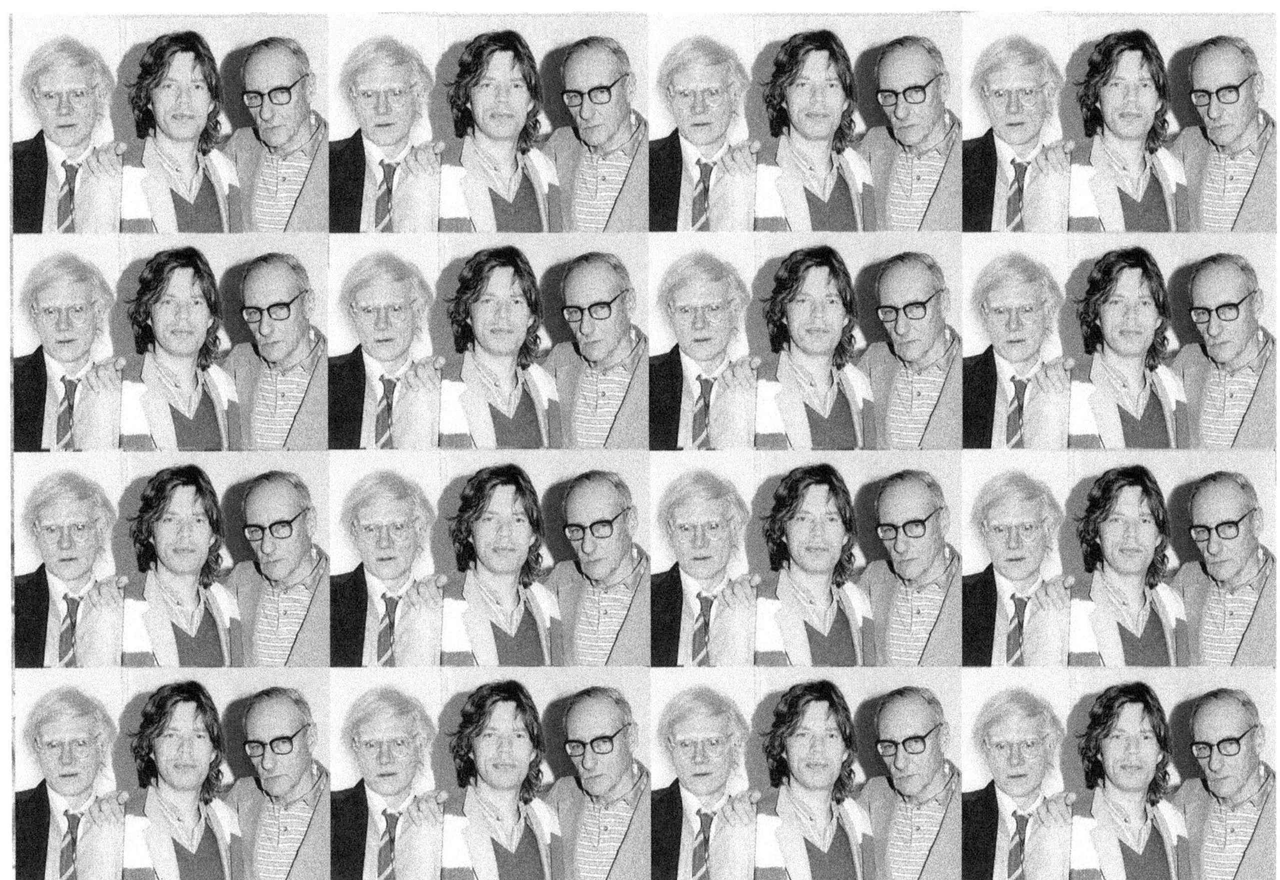

CHAPTER FOUR
BURROUGHS, WARHOL, AND JAGGER

William Burroughs and Andy Warhol had such a profound influence on rock 'n' roll that they should both be in the Rock & Roll Hall of Fame. It was there at the very beginning. Warhol's *Red Elvis* painting appeared in his first one-man show in New York, November 1962. This vision of the spirit of rock 'n' roll is from Burroughs' famous novel, *Naked Lunch*, published in the U.S. that same month:

Rock & Roll hoodlums storm the streets of all nations. They rush into the Louvre and throw acid in the Mona Lisa's face. They open zoos, insane asylums, prisons, burst water mains with air hammers, chop the floor out of passenger plane lavatories, shoot out lighthouses, file elevator cables to one thin wire, turn sewers into the water supply, throw sharks and sting rays, electric eels and candiru into swimming pools… in nautical costumes ram the Queen Mary full speed into New York harbor, play chicken with passenger planes and busses, rush into hospitals in white coats carrying saws and axes and scalpels three feet long, throw paralytics out of iron lungs (mimic their suffocations flopping about on the floor and rolling their eyes up), administer injections with bicycle pumps, disconnect artificial kidneys, saw a woman in half with a two-man surgical saw, they drive herds of squealing pigs into the curb, they shit on the floor of the United Nations and wipe their asses with treaties.

In 1965, Burroughs' boyfriend, Ian Summerville, produced an album of Bill reading *Naked Lunch* called, *Call Me Burroughs*. It became a hip item in the underground. Burroughs' books became a treasure trove from which rock bands like Steely Dan and Soft Machine took their names and rock critics invented genres. "In America (in 1969), 'Whole Lotta Love' and 'Led Zeppelin II' had changed the sound of rock," wrote Stephen Davis in *Hammer of the Gods*.[1] "The old terms—'white blues, heavy music'—didn't fit Zeppelin. A new term was coined: 'heavy metal.' It had first been used by the writer, William S. Burroughs."

In the 1960s, Warhol's Factory became rock central for the hipper bands passing through New York: the Rolling Stones, Bob Dylan, and the Byrds. Dylan acknowledged Burroughs' influence but, in my opinion, no rockstar paid homage on the level Dylan did when he made Warhol the antagonist of his signature anthem, "Like A Rolling Stone."

In terms of changing rock 'n' roll, Warhol played a more hands-on role than Bill. In 1966, he discovered and managed the Velvet Underground. Within months, he produced one of the greatest albums in rock, *The Velvet Underground and Nico*. At the same time, Andy invented the first multimedia rock performance, *Andy Warhol Exploding Plastic Inevitable*. He placed the Velvet Underground in front of a white wall on which he projected his films. Warhol Superstars Gerard Malanga and Mary Woronov danced in front of the band. Andy projected strobe lights and colored gels on the ensemble.

Across the ocean in London, Paul McCartney was playing Bill Burroughs the first acetate of the Beatles' latest album, *Rubber Soul*. McCartney rented a flat for musicians to make informal recordings. He hired Ian Somerville to take care of the technology and oversee the recording sessions. Somerville moved into the flat. Burroughs started visiting to work on his own aural experiments. At the same time, Paul McCartney was using the studio to work up a new song, "Eleanor Rigby." Paul and Bill spent many an evening discussing the future possibilities of electronic recordings with Paul's friend, Barry Miles.[2]

In the early seventies, Warhol's influence on David Bowie transformed him from an everyday rocker to the Christ-like crossover, Ziggy Stardust. Bowie's "Andy Warhol" was among a rash of early seventies rock tributes to the artist, including Lou Reed's "Walk on the Wild Side" and "Andy's Chest." Bowie started using Burroughs' cut-up techniques to write the lyrics for his 1974 album *Diamond Dogs*. The same year, *Rolling Stone* published a conversation between Burroughs and Bowie: "Beat Godfather Meets Glitter Mainman."

1   *Hammer of the Gods: The Led Zeppelin Saga* (1985)
2   Beat Generation biographer, b.1943.

In 1975, Dylan invited Burroughs to accompany him on his legendary *Rolling Thunder Revue* tour. Burroughs and Warhol's dual influences continued to spread through the seventies, from Iggy and the Stooges to Patti Smith, Richard Hell and Blondie.

> **BURROUGHS:** I think the so-called punk movement is indeed a media creation. I have, however, sent a letter of support to The Sex Pistols in England because I've always said that the country doesn't stand a chance until you have 20,000 people saying, "Bugger the Queen!" And I support The Sex Pistols "God Save The Queen" and "Anarchy in the U.K." because this is a constructive, necessary criticism of a country, which is bankrupt.
>
> Ray Rumor (Raymond Foye), *Search and Destroy*, 1977

But since the mid-sixties, the band Andy and William had been most associated with in the media was the Rolling Stones. Indeed, Mick Jagger's relations with Burroughs and Warhol had always been productive. After meeting Warhol on the Stones' first U.S. tour in 1964, Mick adopted Andy's hesitant way of handling interviewers. I saw him do it on an early documentary and noted how effective it was. He soon dropped the more extreme aspects—the Brando mumble, the whispering voice, and the body language, but he kept the core—be polite, seem interested, but keep them at bay with layers of covers. Jagger also started collecting Warhol paintings in the sixties.

According to Barry Miles in his authoritative history of the British Underground, *London Calling*, not only was the Burroughs cut-up technique used in the 1968 cult classic film *Performance*, directed by Nicholas Roeg and starring Mick Jagger, but "William Burroughs is continually referenced and casts his presence over the film. Jagger uses the title of Burroughs' novel, *The Soft Machine*, in his soundtrack song, 'Memo to Turner.' When Mick and Anita find how badly injured James Fox is, Anita suggests they call 'Dr. Burroughs to give him a shot.' Hasan-I-Sabbah's maxim, 'Nothing is true, everything is permitted' is used in numerous Burroughs texts, beginning with *Minutes to Go* (1960), and is quoted in the film along with the story of the Old Man of the Mountain himself."

In the late sixties in Tangier, Burroughs ran into the Stones' brilliant founder and bad boy icon, Brian Jones, right after he had recorded the trance music of the local Joujouka musicians. William and Brion Gysin were impressed by the results, which were not released until after Jones' tragic death in 1969. When William lived in New York in the 1970s, the only music he played regularly in the Bunker was the Joujouka album *Brian Jones Plays with The Pipes of Pan*.

The voices of William Burroughs, Mick Jagger and Andy Warhol entered the American conversation in the 1960s. As a new generation tried to put WWII behind them and make their own culture, these three artists found themselves confronting the emotional turmoil of their audiences. Between 1968 and 1973, when the counterculture was under severe attack from the Nixon administration and the happy hippie world went up in flames, William Burroughs, the Rolling Stones, and Andy Warhol played strong creative roles in keeping the tribes of the counterculture enlightened and connected.

The Stones rose to the occasion by setting new attitudes and styles with their albums, *Beggar's Banquet, Let it Bleed, Sticky Fingers,* and *Exile on Main Street.* Burroughs did it with his books, *The Wild Boys, The Last Words of Dutch Schultz, The Job, Port of Saints,* and *Exterminator.* After being shot and almost killed in 1968, Andy Warhol published four books: *Andy Warhol's Index Book, The Flowers Catalogue* (Stockholm), *a, A Novel,* and *Blue Movie.* Started *Interview* magazine. Released six films: *Lonesome Cowboys, Blue Movie,* his trilogy *Flesh, Trash,* and *Heat,* and *Women in Revolt.* Painted his series of *Mao* portraits.

All these works fit into each other. You could listen to *Sticky Fingers,* read *The Wild Boys,* and look through the photographs in *The Flowers Catalogue* at the same time. The same people who watched *Trash* listened to "Gimme Shelter." It's no coincidence that the crotch shot on the cover of *Sticky Fingers* was created by Andy Warhol. Or that Bill had written the Brian Jones liner notes.

Burroughs, Warhol, and Jagger were among the first rank of artists whose images became more well-known than their work. Their images were repeatedly interviewed by the underground and mainstream press. Many people developed their look and way of life by combining bits and pieces from all the works, words and photographs of these three counterculture figureheads.

I thought Keith would connect with Bill more than Mick, but it was Jagger who brought Burroughs into the Stones' orbit. Mick asked Bill to write the liner notes for *Brian Jones Plays with The Pipes of Pan* album, a very cool project. Burroughs also inspired the "Casino Boogie" cut-up lyric on the Stones' 1972 album, *Exile on Main Street.* That was all through Jagger. Around the same time, Mick met with Bill in Burroughs' London flat and discussed starring in a film of *Naked Lunch.* For his part Bill admired Jagger. He thought Mick was very cool.

BURROUGHS: Mick gave off the impression of great energy and intelligence and a sort of special cool of knowing where his connections are going. I had admired his work, what I'd heard of it, and also I admired him because of the pressure he was under. There's someone who is idolized and yet receives shockingly rude treatment. Six cabdrivers refused to have him in the cab when he and Marianne Faithful arrived at Heathrow airport. There's something about Mick that arouses great antagonism in a certain kind of person, the cabdriver-hardhat-redneck strata throughout the world, and to be able to stand up to that and be able to maintain his equilibrium and cool, as he certainly has, is quite something.

Interview by Bockris National Screw, 1977

In 1975, Burroughs wrote in one of his *Crawdaddy* magazine columns, *Time of the Assassins*, "The essential ingredient for any successful rock group is energy—the ability to give out energy, to receive energy from the audience, and give it back to the audience. A rock concert is in fact a rite involving the evocation and transmutation of energy. Rock stars may be compared to priests." And as recently as six months before Mick Jagger came to dinner at the Bunker, Bill had told Debbie Harry, "I would take the approach that the two most far-reaching developments in the last thirty years were the use of the atom bomb at Hiroshima and rock music. It's true because the whole cultural-revolution would never have been possible without this rock music, which translated it into mass media."

In 1971, Andy Warhol designed the historic crotch cover of the Rolling Stones' album, *Sticky Fingers*. He frequently featured Mick and Bianca in his *Interview* magazine. In 1975, he painted a portrait of Jagger which was later released as a portfolio of prints signed by artist and subject. That summer, the Rolling Stones rented Warhol's Montauk Estate to rehearse for their upcoming US tour. In 1977, Andy designed another Stones cover for their double album, *Love You Live*. Throughout the seventies, he maintained social relationships with Mick and Bianca and later, Mick and Jerry Hall. However, his attempts to star Mick in a film came to nothing. Six months before our dinner, Andy wrote this about Jagger:

> I think it's really a shame that Mick and Bianca have drifted apart. I guess it's difficult being married to a man that all the women and half the men in the world want. Mick brings out the bisexuality in men who normally would not be like that. He's androgynous enough for almost anyone. That's always been his basic appeal, mixed with the facts that: 1) He's very talented; 2) He's very intelligent; 3) He's very handsome; 4) He's very adorable; 5) He's a great business person; 6) He's a great movie star; 7) I like his fake Cockney accent.
>
> I think Bianca was good for Mick's career when they first married. Just the idea of Mick Jagger married changed the whole idea of Mick Jagger. That kind of change is good for anyone whose work is really being an idea.
>
> *Exposures*, Andy Warhol and Bob Colacello, 1979

By the time I tried to bring Bill and the Stones together for *With William Burroughs: A Report from the Bunker*, Burroughs and Keith Richards were the coolest guys in New York. But if you want to immerse yourself in "Gimme Shelter" or *Naked Lunch*, you have to have a strong constitution and mind. Lou Reed put it well when he said in defense of Andy Warhol in the 1960s, "The Factory was not a mental hospital."

New Year's Eve, Monday, December 31, 1979

We were sitting up in John Giorno's loft above Bill's Bunker in their landmark building at 222 Bowery. It was two blocks south of Blondie's Bowery loft and three blocks south of CBGB. I had just recounted how our favorite photographer, Marcia Resnick, had called that morning to report that she could not, under any circumstances, see me that night because she was sick in bed. Then she had called back in the afternoon to explain that the incredible Liz Derringer[3] had summoned her to Mick Jagger's apartment. It was vital! They had to discuss Marcia's *High Times* cover shoot for Liz D's interview with the biggest rock star in the world. Marcia jumped out of bed, took an extra dose of medicine and glued herself together. She had to go, she told me. She knew I would understand.

"Little Marcia, she never hesitates," Bill chuckled as he made sure I was taking a correctly measured dose of the powerful fudge-like concoction of marijuana called majoun. The drug takes an hour to come on, but then it hits you with the effect of smoking twenty joints at the same time. I had no idea this was going to happen.

Monday, January 7, 1980

David Dalton had asked Bill to write an essay about the Rolling Stones for his book on their 20th anniversary. The $500 fee did not attract Burroughs to the project but because it was the Stones, he tried to do it anyway. A few days later, he told me he was having trouble getting anything good down on paper and that he really did not want to do it. I suggested that we solve the problem by inviting Keith Richards to the Bunker for drinks and dinner. Bill liked that idea so I decided to call Keith's manager, Jane Rose. The band was in the throes of completing their album *Emotional Rescue*.

She indicated that Keith definitely wanted to do this and seemed eager to put it together. I interviewed Keith in 1977 and asked whether he had read Burroughs' statement in *Junky*: "I think I am in better health now as a result of using junk at intervals than I would have been if I had never been an addict."

KEITH RICHARDS: Yeah, I agree with that. Actually, I once took that apomorphine cure that Burroughs swears by. Dr. Dent was dead, but his assistant, whom he trained, this lovely old dear called Smitty who is like a mother hen, still runs the clinic. I had her down to my place for five days, and she just sort of comes in and says, "Here's your shot, dear, there's a good boy." Or, "You've been a naughty boy, you've taken something, yes you have, I can tell." But it's a pretty medieval cure. You just vomit all the time.

Interview by Bockris *High Times*, 1978

---

3   Music journalist. Liz Derringer was the wife of guitar player songwriter and producer Rick Derringer.

Monday, January 14, 1980

I called Jane back but it soon became evident that I would not be able to pin Keith down to a date before the deadline for the interview. So I mentioned to Liz Derringer that I was having a problem getting Keith to a dinner at the Bunker. She said she thought she could get Mick to do it.

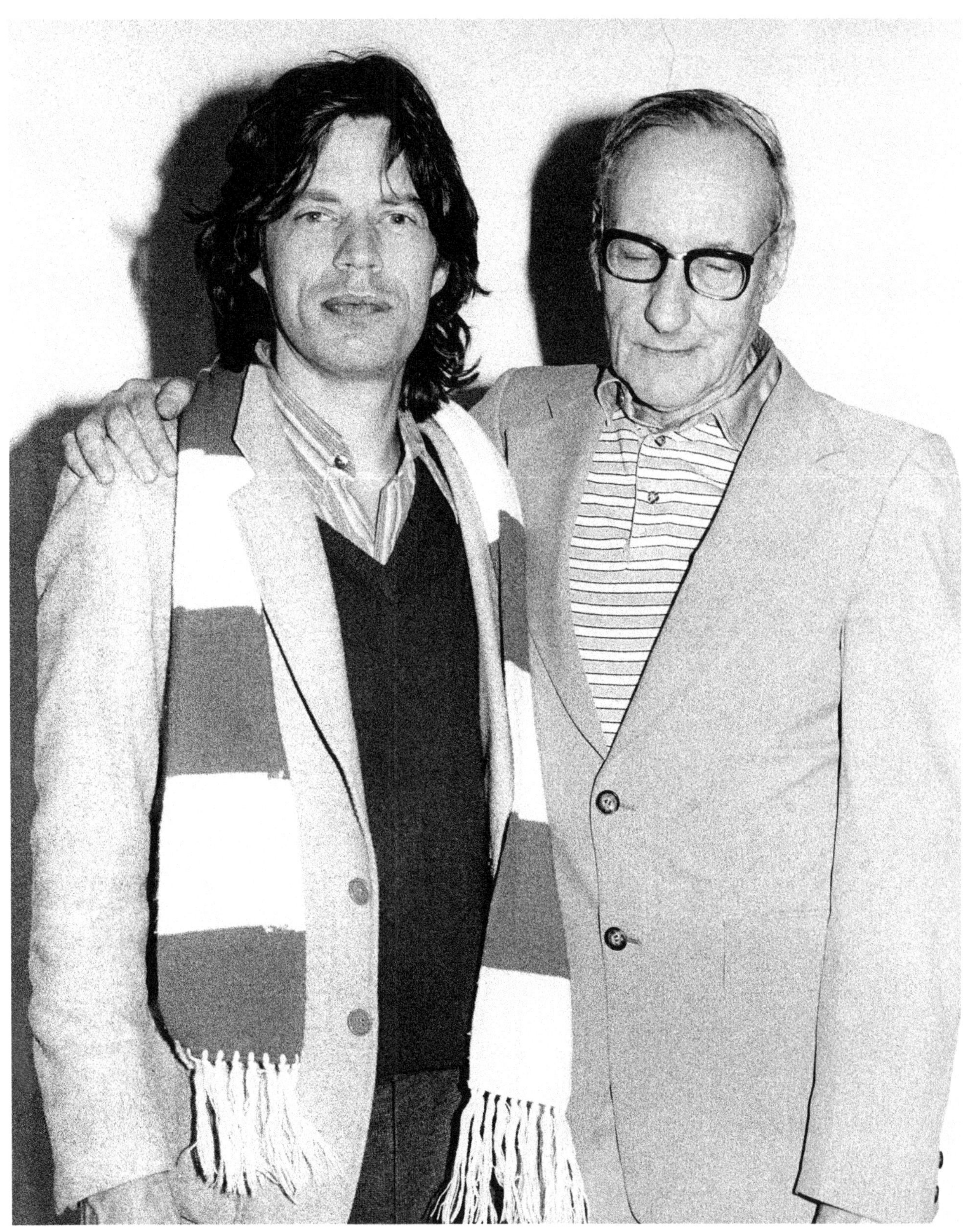

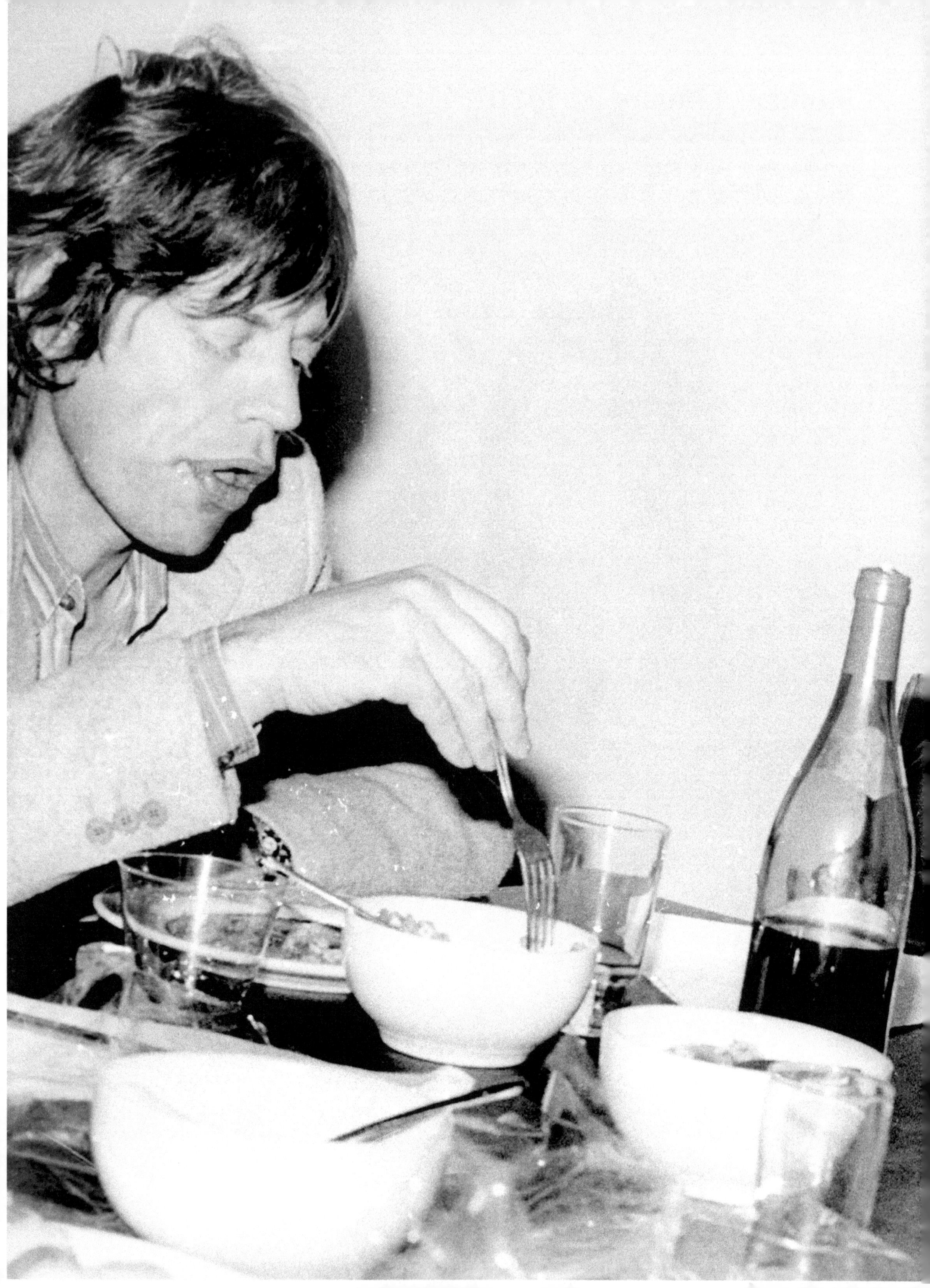

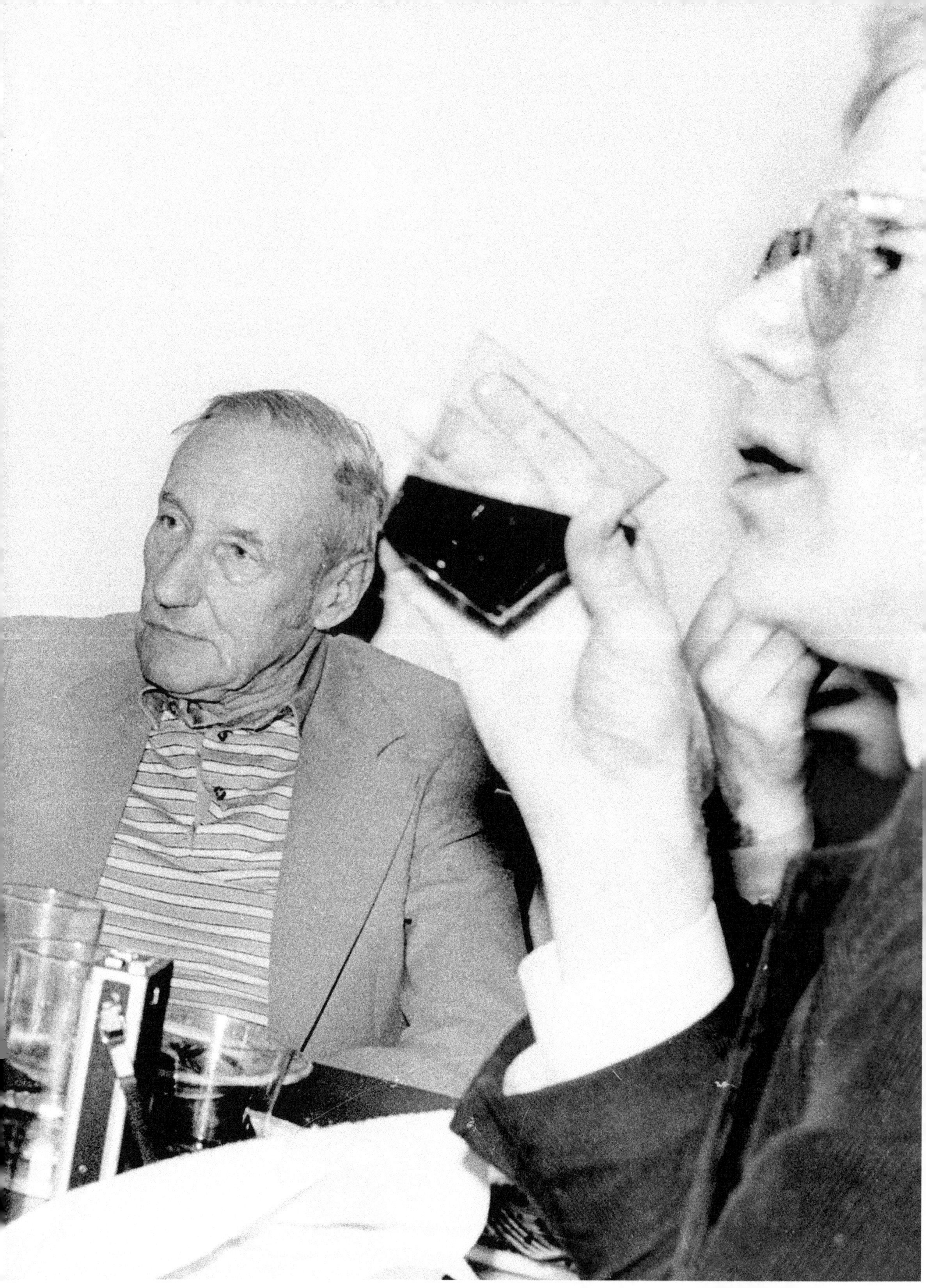

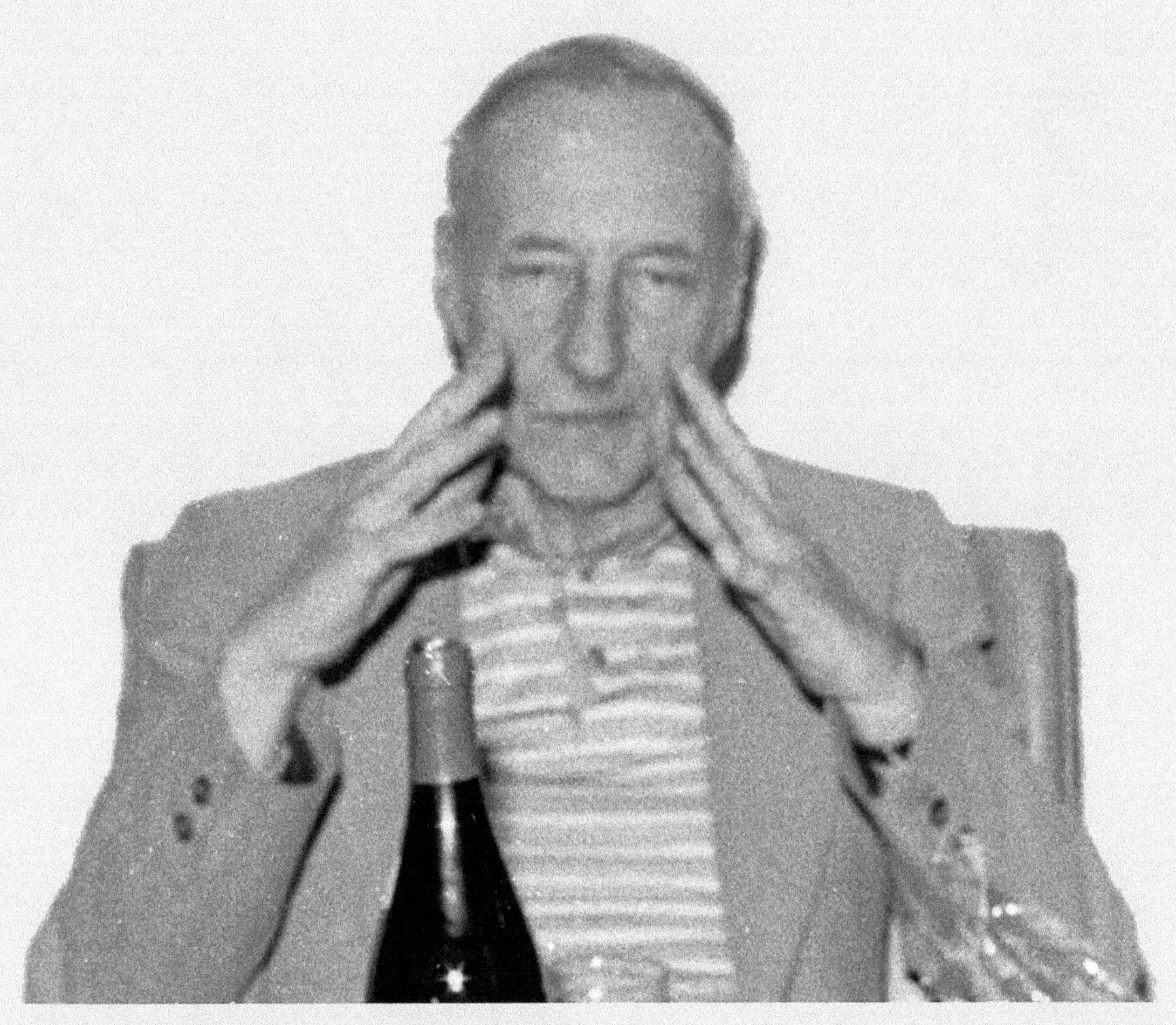

The Captain's Cocktail Party:
Dinner with
William Burroughs,
Mick Jagger, and Andy Warhol
New York City, 1980
Victor Bockris

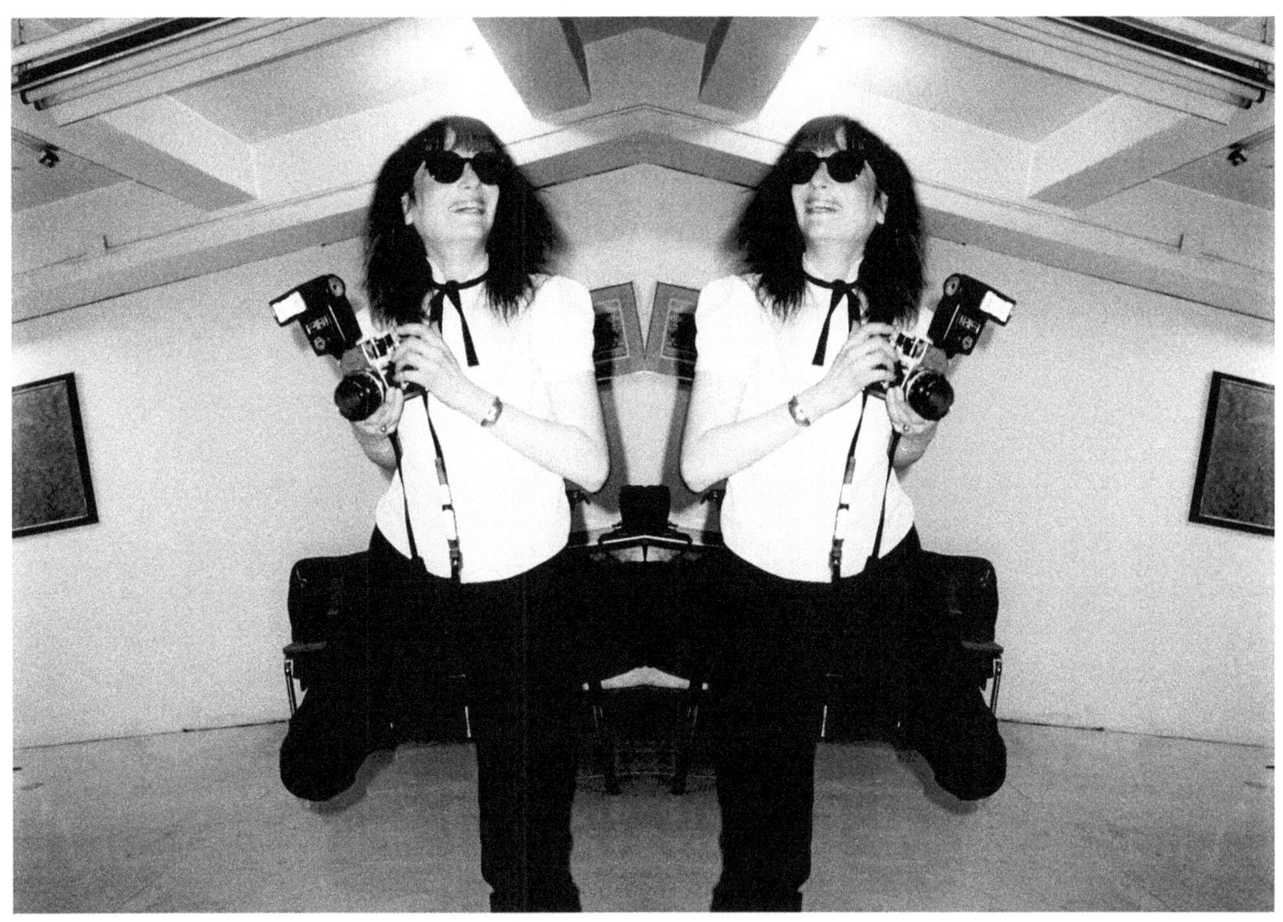

CHAPTER FIVE
JAGGER AT THE BURROUGHS BUNKER

Saturday, March 1, 1980—Dinner with Mick Jagger, Jerry Hall, Andy Warhol, Liz Derringer, and Marcia Resnick at The Bunker, 222 Bowery, New York

By the second month of 1980, my delightful girlfriend was dealing hard drugs out of my apartment, so I told her she had to leave. A couple of days later, I found out she "borrowed" my bank card to withdraw most of the money from my account. The day before the dinner, she asked if she could come back home. When I said no, she said she was going to blow my head off with her shotgun. This image haunted me as I prepared to host the biggest dinner of my life.

The goal was to have William Burroughs interview Mick Jagger about the twentieth anniversary of the Rolling Stones for a book edited by the well-known rock writer, David

Dalton, whose book marking the band's tenth anniversary in 1972 had been a fan favorite.[1] This new book, *The Rolling Stones: The First Twenty Years*, had a lot of potential.

I think Bill was expecting the same pleasant conversational-style interview he had done with Bowie and Jimmy Page. Rock star pays homage and they chat. Bill and I had never made any preparations for these dinners. Only this one was different. Instead of me mentoring a conversation between Bill and one guest, Bill was going to interview Mick.

The doorbell rang and I raced down the stairs and opened the three locks that guarded the interior of 222 Bowery. I greeted Andy Warhol, who was wearing the same enormous parka he had worn at our first dinner. Andy walked into the Bunker for the first time. Andy loved homes that were unusual. His enthusiasm for Bill's living quarters, which in the 1880s had been a YMCA gymnasium, kicked off the evening. He ran around the windowless white-walled rooms with the excitement of a child. He thought the pipes running along the ceilings looked like sculpture. He liked Brion Gysin's painting of people in Morocco. The urinals gave pause for speculation.

As soon as they sat down, Andy and Bill made up a story about an advert for artificial insemination called Sell your Sperm. "You should sell yours right now," Andy laughed.

"I bet Mick Jagger could name his own price!" crowed Bill.

I never saw them so at ease with each other. They were like old friends. Imagine what could have happened if this had just been the two of them. The conversation was flowing

---

1   *Rolling Stones: An Unauthorized Biography in Words, Photographs, and Music* (Amsco: New York, 1972)

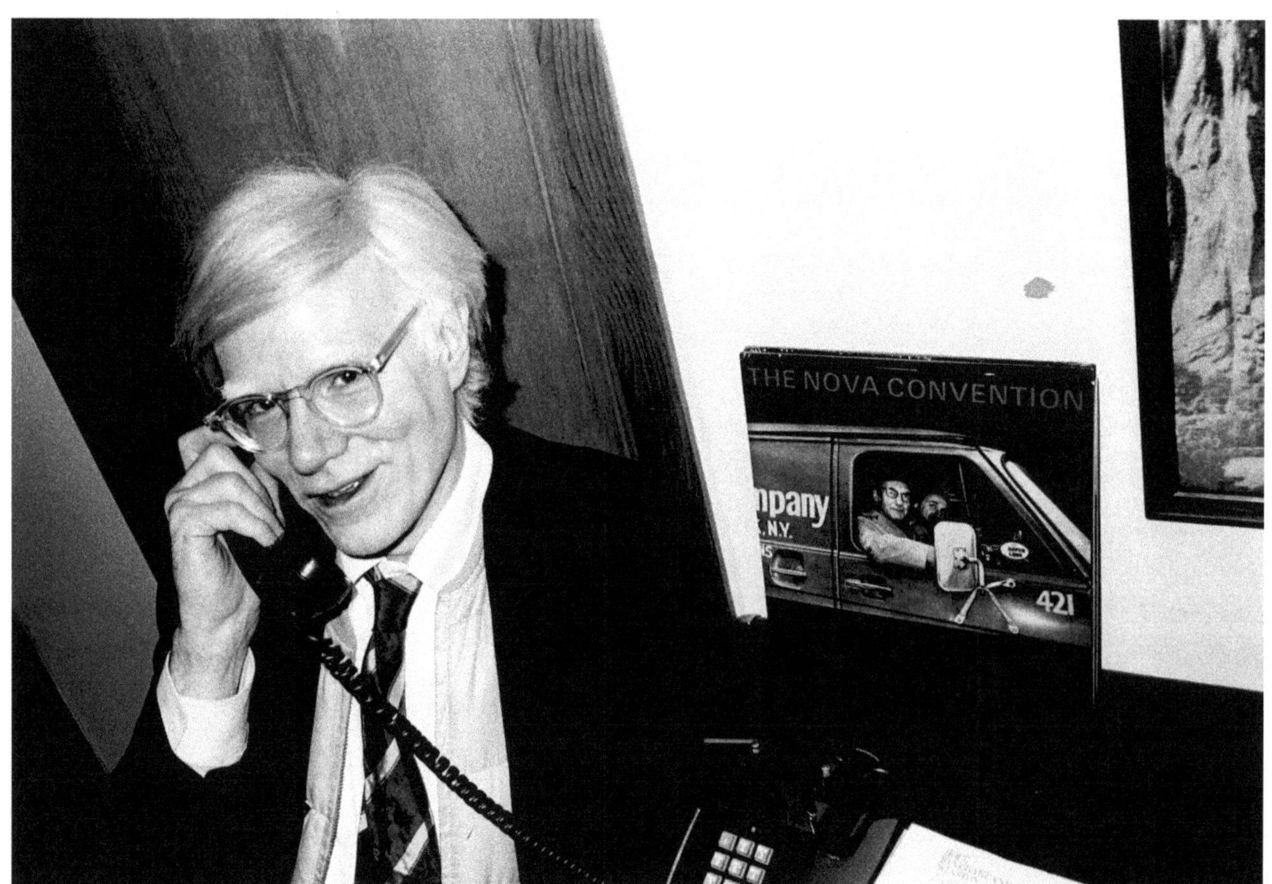

when the doorbell rang for the second time. Heart pounding in my chest, I went downstairs to let in the photographer, Marcia Resnick. She knew everybody at the table that night. Her job was to photograph this unique combination of people talking to each other.

The first thing Marcia did was set up some extremely bright photo lights. I panicked at the set-up, picturing Mick Jagger walking in on a barrage of lights thinking we just wanted his photograph. Bill and I told Marcia to turn them off. Marcia gave all three of us angry glances, which radically changed the atmosphere in the room. Now, instead of talking animatedly, Bill and Andy sat in frozen silence.

Ten minutes after Marcia arrived, the doorbell rang for the third time, and I hurried downstairs to reopen the three locks. A man who looked very much like Mick Jagger stood outside with his girlfriend Jerry Hall. Liz Derringer stood behind him. As I followed him up the long flight of wooden stairs to the front door, I noticed Mick was dragging his feet and worried that he was too tired for the rapier-like questions Burroughs was going to throw at him.

Everybody greeted each other in a low-key way. We headed to the dining table with three chairs on each side. Bill sat at the head of the table, and I put Mick on his right with Jerry and Liz. I put myself on his left next to Andy then Marcia.

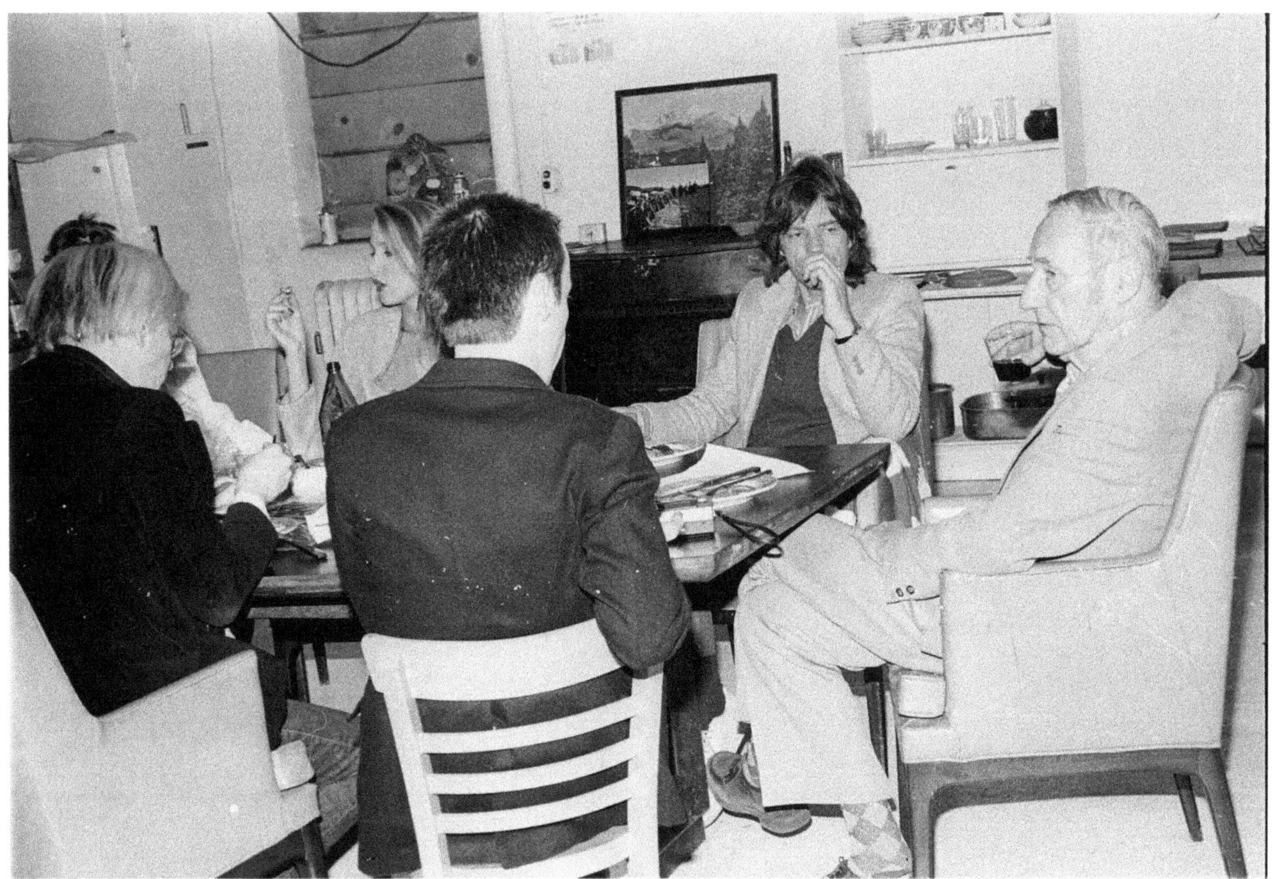

JAGGER: [coming straight to the point] What are you doing here? What is the purpose of the dinner?

BOCKRIS: Well, you should tell him Bill because I don't know. [What an incredibly stupid thing to say!]

BURROUGHS: The purpose is very simple. David Dalton is getting together—what is this—the twentieth anniversary of the Rolling Stones?

DERRINGER: *It is?*

JAGGER: What? That's not been going for twenty years! They're making it up.

Mick's attitude about the twentieth anniversary of the Stones, coming up in 1982, was suddenly like a wall between us. It was like he had been insulted! I knew exactly what the dinner was about. But when Bill asked me, my mind went blank. It quickly became clear no one knew why they were there. Mick's doubt of our intentions threw a cloud over the dinner from which it never really escaped. A nightmare of misunderstanding began to envelope the Bunker.

Bill gave it another try. David Dalton, he explained, was editing a book about the twentieth anniversary of the Rolling Stones. But then I got Bill confused about whether it was the twentieth anniversary of the Rolling Stones or *Rolling Stone* magazine. Suddenly everybody was wondering and we started retreating remarkably quickly.

BOCKRIS: So, this is just a completely mistaken occasion?

BURROUGHS: Well, it seems to be a mistake all round. This David Dalton is talking about the twentieth anniversary of *something*. Don't put it on me, man.

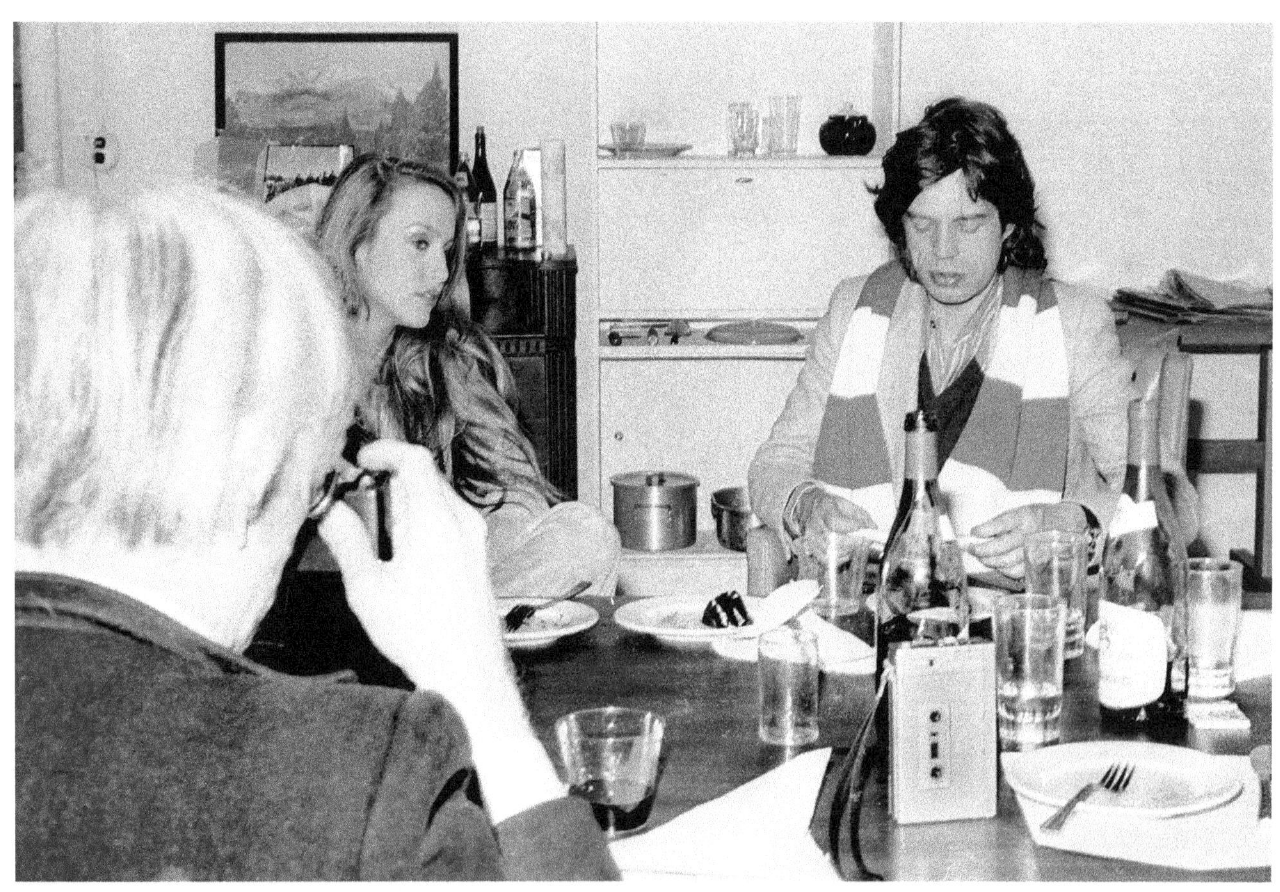

Marcia Resnick jumped up and started dancing around the table taking pictures.

JAGGER: Why is Marcia Resnick taking pictures?

RESNICK: Oh, I don't know.

BURROUGHS: On the twentieth anniversary of the…

RESNICK: I'm documenting the event.

JAGGER: Oh, you're documenting… We're trying to work out *what* you're documenting…

That was a hot stage to be sitting on, trapped in a Burroughs-Jagger nightmare. Resnick did a great session. She knew she was getting something unique. The most important thing for me was what she was recording. In one image Mick toys with his fork, while Bill looks at him askance and Andy holds a glass of wine in his hand looking for an escape.

Bill grabs his head. I am bursting at the seams. Grasping for a diversion to give me time to regroup, I followed up the opening scenes of the worst interview of my life by placing on the table the worst dinner I've ever fed anyone. I laid out some helpful looking plates and cutlery along with two bottles of red wine, giving the impression that I intended to serve a meal. Then I placed two white dinner plates at intervals on the table with some slices of French bread and a single piece of pâté wrapped in saran wrap on each plate. Next to them I placed a small container of cold string beans. Then I skulked back to my seat with my eyes fixed on my shoes. The meagerness of the meal did not go unnoticed by Jagger and Warhol, thus delivering a second sledgehammer blow to the crumbling negotiations. Both William and I were flat broke.

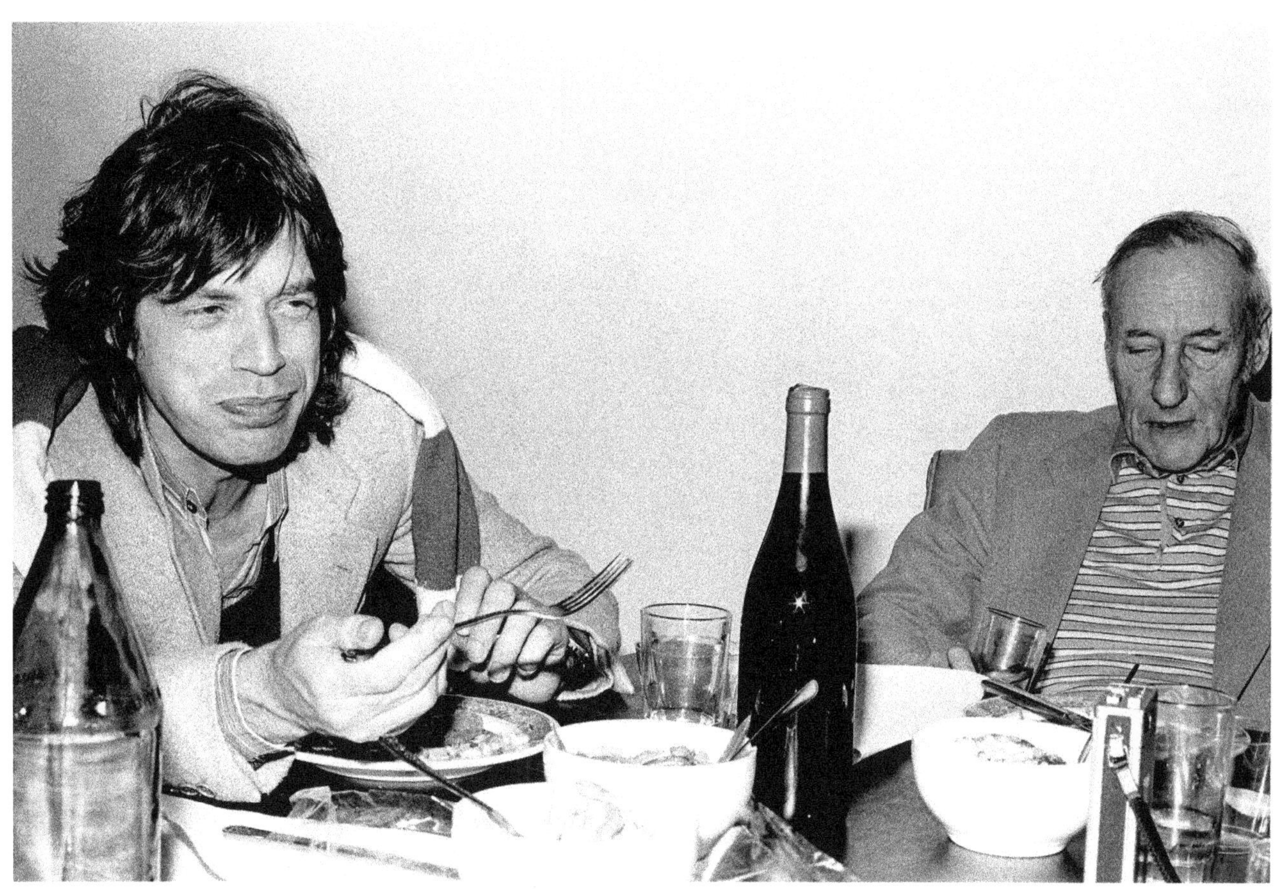

JAGGER: Who sent the food over? Did *Rolling Stone* send the food over?

WARHOL: No. Isn't that great? It's all different kinds of pâté. What are the different kinds?

BOCKRIS: Uh, I don't know. It's different. Yeah, really different.

WARHOL: Are they each one different?

BOCKRIS: Yeah.

DERRINGER: [The astonishing realization that *this* was the dinner began to sink in.] You take a whole packet?

BOCKRIS: Yeah, you take a little package and then uh eat it.

BURROUGHS: Is there any pheasant here?

BOCKRIS: Yes, man, that looks like a piece of pheasant.

BURROUGHS: I think so.

Jagger now started cutting into Andy and Bill.

JAGGER: Couldn't it be your twentieth anniversary or something, Andy? I mean Bill you've been doing something for twenty years. [Shit! I thought we'd put aside this stinking subject.]

BURROUGHS: Um, well yes, I know. If only I could find that piece of paper where I've got it written down.

BOCKRIS: I know where that piece of paper is!

I leaped up and rushed into the other room frantically looking for the piece of paper on which Bill had written David Dalton's instructions regarding what we were supposed to be asking Mick about.

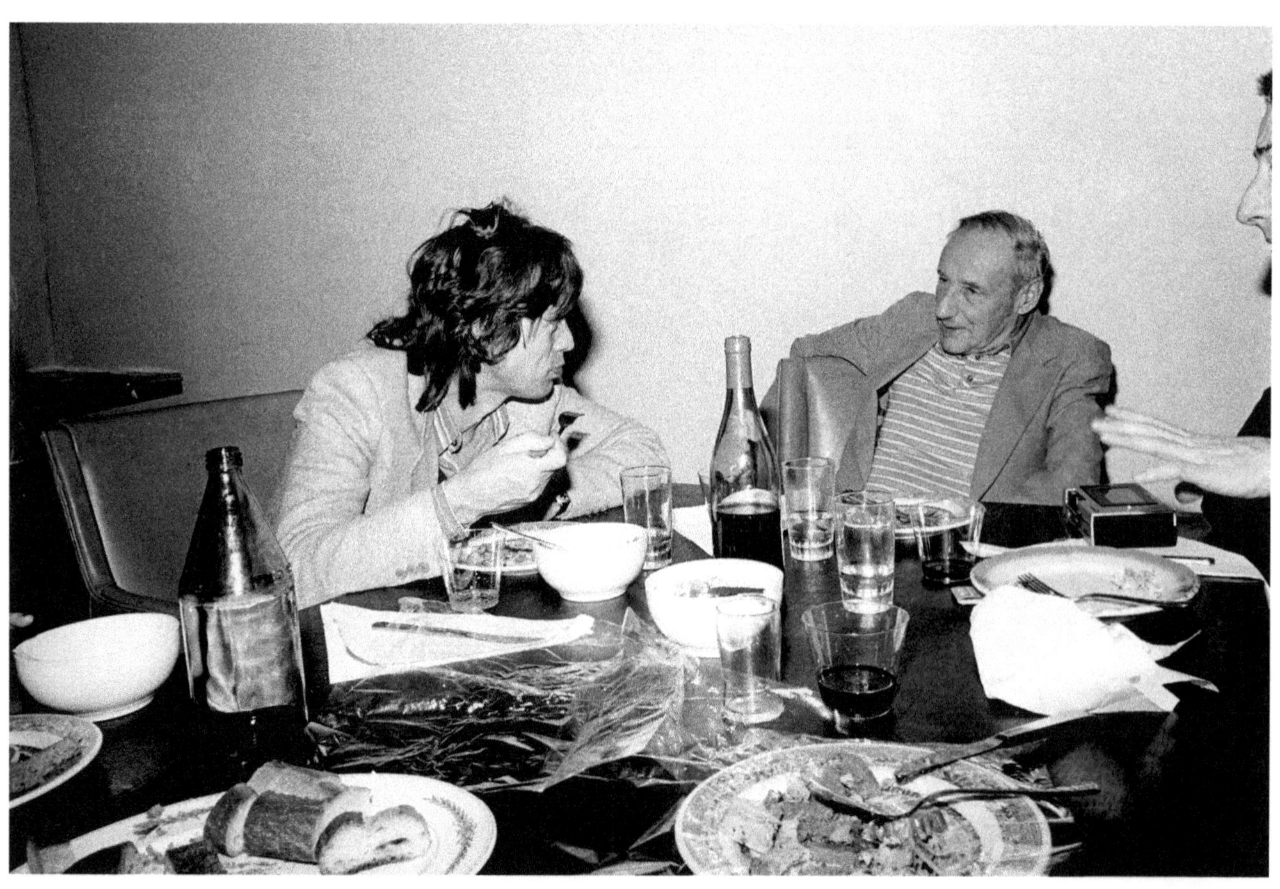

WARHOL: I just thought it was for the twentieth anniversary of *Rolling Stone* and then I was trying to figure out…

BURROUGHS: That's what I thought. I thought it was the twentieth anniversary of *Rolling Stone*, which they were devoting to the Rolling Stones.

WARHOL: No, but I thought *Rolling Stone* magazine so it just made sense, but could it be twenty years for the Rolling Stones?

JAGGER: No, that isn't going to come up for a few years I'm afraid.

This leads them back into the labyrinth of the Rolling Stones versus *Rolling Stone* magazine conundrum. Suddenly, Bill remembers where his notes are and hustles off to the Bunker's office to retrieve them. He strides back to the table with the notes in hand and starts all over again.

BURROUGHS: Here it is! Right here.

WARHOL: [cheerleading] Oh, you've got the note!

BURROUGHS: Yes. [reading aloud] *The Twentieth Anniversary Issue…* uuummm…

WARHOL: Hopefully of the Rolling Stones.

BURROUGHS: [uncertainly, wavering] … which presumably would be devoted to the Rolling Stones' music.

BOCKRIS: Well, the point is they asked Bill to write something and…

WARHOL: Maybe this is one of those things that's going to take three or four years to do, so I mean...

JAGGER: It's taking off to a racing start.

I suggest with unmatchable gall that we forget about the interview and just have a good dinner—despite there being nothing but limited hors d'oeuvres to consume.

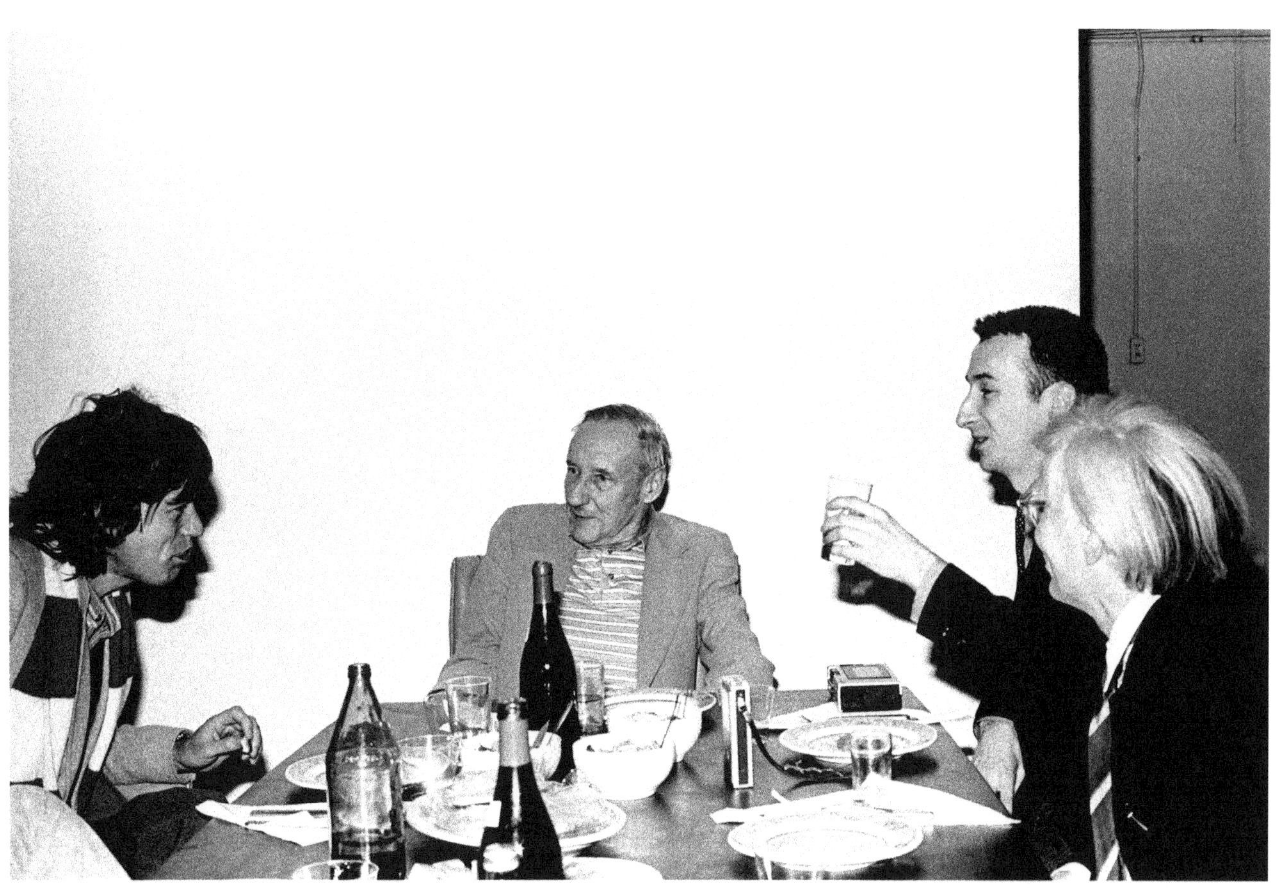

BOCKRIS: Well, I thought it would be nice to have dinner anyway, regardless of all that, right?

JAGGER: Yeah, I think that's a good idea. This is very nice pâté. I wouldn't know what it is in there.

BOCKRIS: Yeah, let's just have dinner and forget about it.

WARHOL: Yeah, Bill's so great he's just…

BOCKRIS: We had dinner the other day with Bill and Andy.

WARHOL: I'm trying to find, er… what am I trying to find him?

BOCKRIS: Young men. [changing the subject] Mick, is it true that you saw Bill a few years ago in London to talk about *Naked Lunch*?

JAGGER: Somebody was trying to put it together, but he was a bit of a shyster, wasn't he?

This raises Bill's ire toward Mick a notch or two. The "shyster," Anthony Balch, was part of the trifecta of collaborators with Burroughs and Brion Gysin on the trilogy of Burroughs films. He directed *Towers Open Fire*, *The Cut Ups*, and *Bill and Tony*, which were made in the same period—1963 to 1965—when Andy was establishing his reputation as an underground film director. Bill was extremely loyal to his friends and collaborators and was offended by Mick's suggestion that Balch was a "shyster."

BURROUGHS: You're talking about Anthony Balch. Yes, we did indeed meet at 8 Duke Street, St. James. Was it with Bianca at that time? And you decided that you didn't like Anthony. Well [he slips it to Mick], Anthony is um, in a very bad way. He's dying. But, um, yes that was the last time.

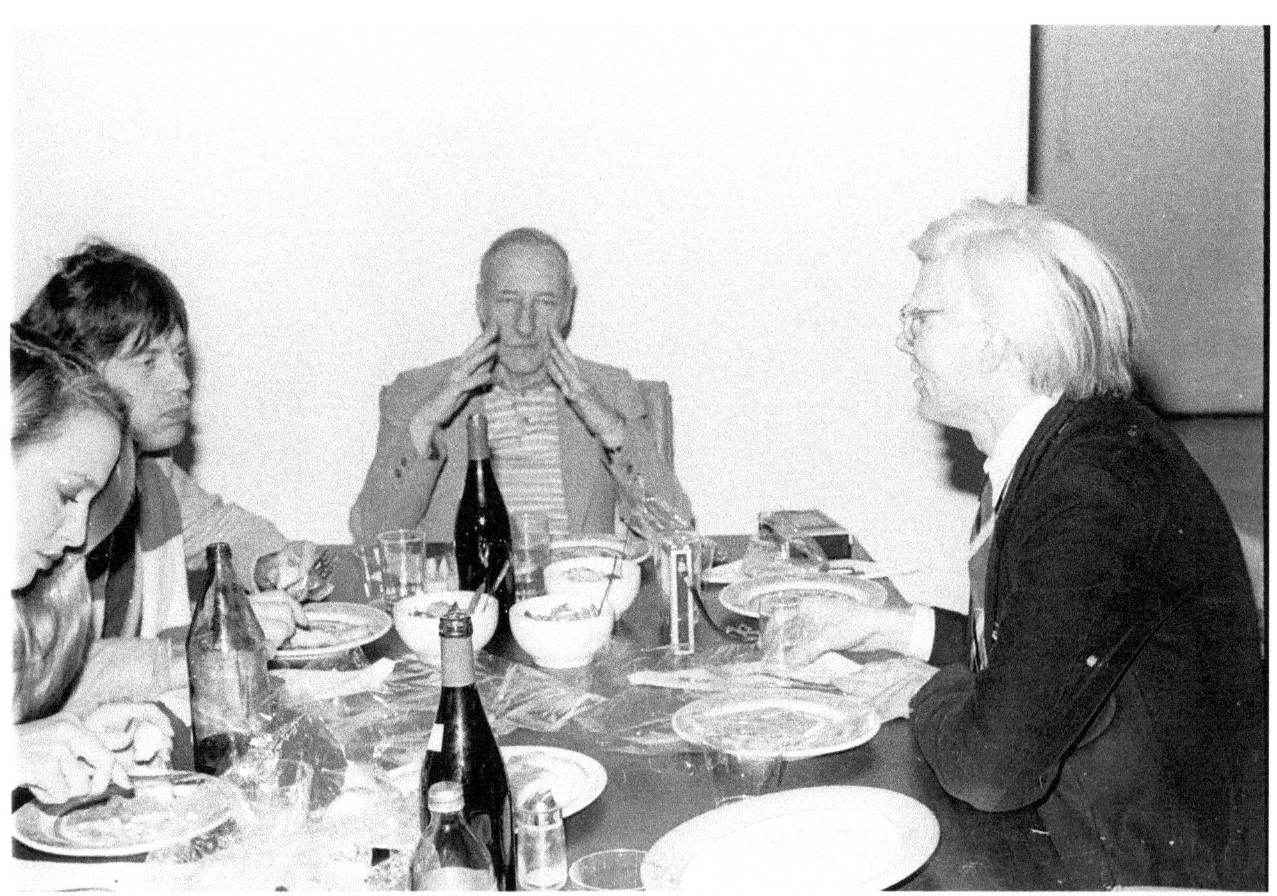

BOCKRIS: Bill just got back from London.

BURROUGHS: I stopped off to see Anthony in the hospital.

BOCKRIS: The idea was that you would play the lead in the film?

BURROUGHS: That was the idea yeah. Mick was to play the part of Lee, the central character.

BOCKRIS: It's just hard to see it as a film.

JAGGER: Right, very hard to see…

BURROUGHS: Yes, I think so. I've talked with a lot of people about it. They all seem to say the same thing—very hard to see the whole thing as a film.

Now Bill started interviewing Mick in earnest.

BURROUGHS: Mick, I am saying that the whole cultural revolution was concerned with confrontation, and wouldn't you say that this was exactly what pop music was concerned with? Real confrontation between the performer and the audience, never complete of course.

JAGGER: In *live* music, yeah.

When Mick says yes, he agrees with Bill on confrontation in rock, but Bill unfortunately does not hear him. Had he picked up on Mick's agreement, the interview might have found its ground. Consequently, Burroughs continues to interview Jagger about the cultural revolution as if he had not said yes.

BURROUGHS: I am saying that the whole cultural revolution, I'm talking about the Stones as heroes of the revolution deserving citation, you understand… Rock music is one of the most prestigious and influential forces in the cultural

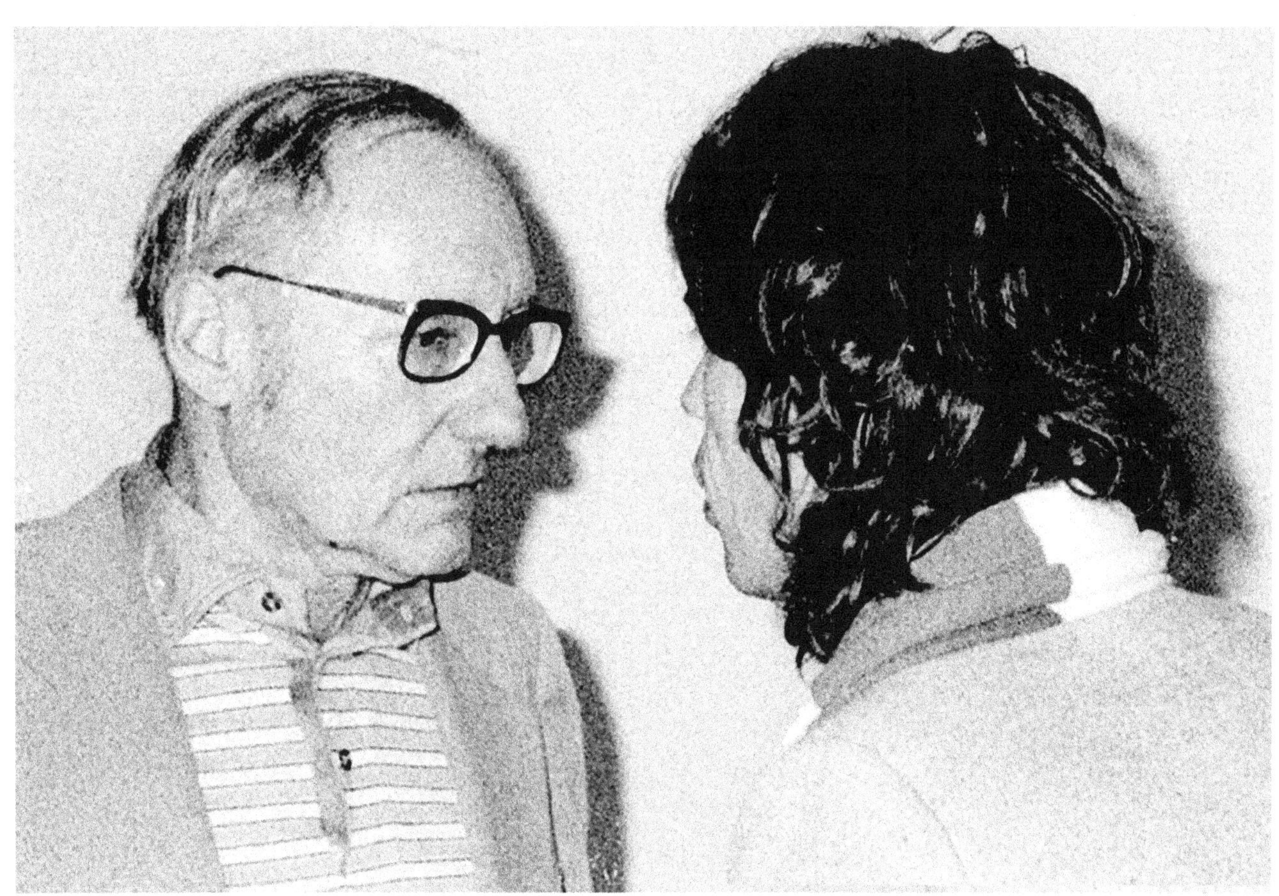

revolution because it reached millions who cannot get your songs out of their heads.

JAGGER: No, I think TV and movie images are more influential.

BURROUGHS: But I cannot get songs out of my head.

JAGGER: I can get songs out of my head but I cannot get movie images out.

BURROUGHS: Can you get rid of the music that goes round and round?

WARHOL: The music goes round and round…

BURROUGHS: The music goes round and round and it comes out here and it comes out there, and man this went on all over the world. I mean it's probably still parking somewhere in some remote island. [A terrible putdown.]

WARHOL: My favorite song was the iddy bitty bitty little what was it. No, it's the fishes the itty… do you know it?

I began to wonder if I was driving the greatest artist in the world out of his mind. Every time we tried to escape from the nightmare it pulled us back in. Now, we reach the lowest point of the interview and in fact the end of the formal interview when I questioned whether there was still a counterculture in 1980. This really sent Burroughs off into another place. It challenged everything he'd spent his life working on. "HOLY SHIT MAN!" Burroughs exploded. "What do you think we've been doing for the last forty years!?" But then Jagger and Warhol confronted Burroughs: there is no cultural revolution now. Bill's determination to make confrontation his theme turned confrontation into the curse of the night.

BURROUGHS: It would seem to me that what is happening in an evolutionary way

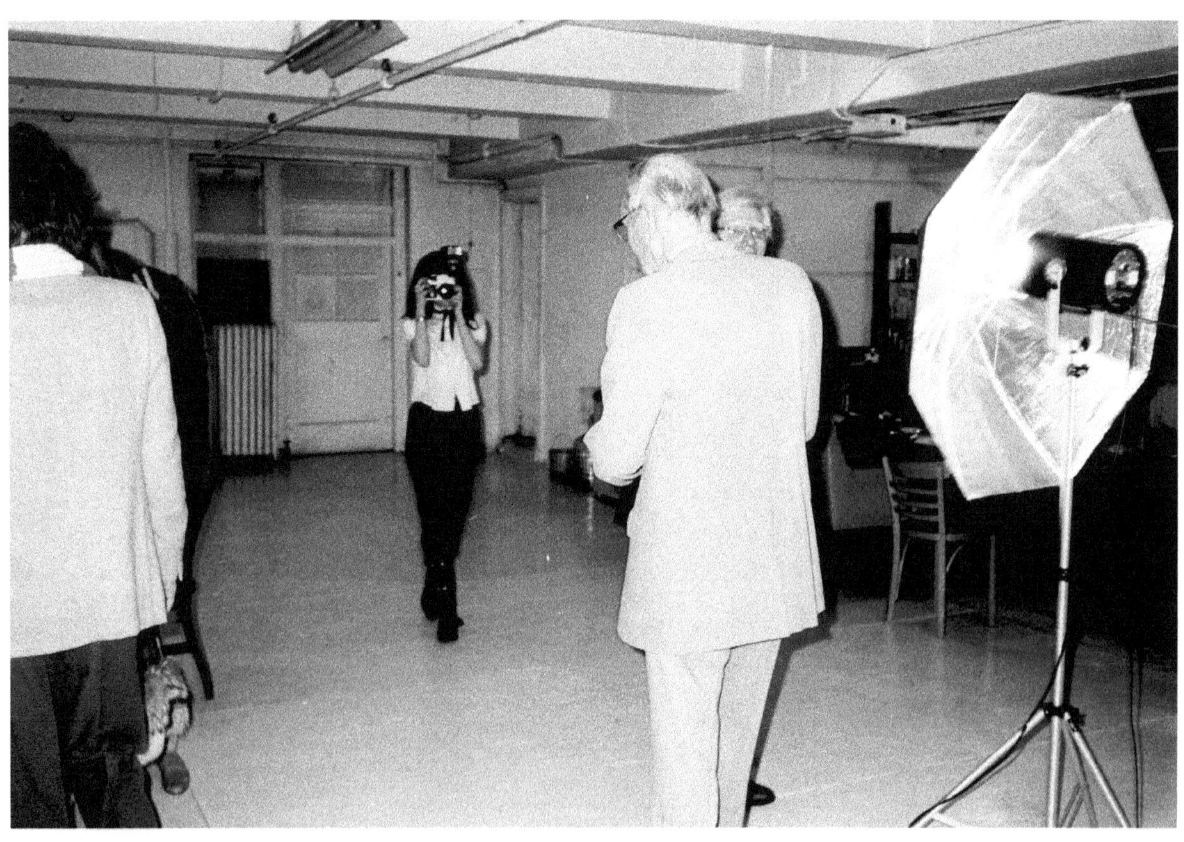

is total confrontation between all disparate groups. They got to get together one way or another. That's the way we're going to leave the planet in one piece, you see.

HALL: I think there's always cultural change.

JAGGER: There's no you know revolution now. I wouldn't think so.

HALL: It's too tiring.

I said we would soon be able to travel to other planets. Jerry said she'd like to go. Bill jumped on her line stating, "I'd love to go this second!"

RESNICK: How did you feel when Devo recorded "Satisfaction"?

JAGGER: Devo? Devo!

WARHOL: Devo keep calling me up on the phone.

When I asked Mick if he was still getting a lot of film scripts to consider, he said everything always collapsed.

BOCKRIS: Bill's big future is as an actor.

WARHOL: He wants to play you in the film, *The Mick Jagger Story*, starring William Burroughs. He's trying to study you because he's working on the part.

BOCKRIS: Who was Julian Burroughs who said he was your son?

BURROUGHS: I remember this was some sort of fraud. Yeah. Who is this guy?

WARHOL: He was a guy who was running away from the army who said he was your son named Julian Burroughs, and we starred him in a movie called *Nude Restaurant*.[1]

---

1   Also known as *The Nude Restaurant*, various versions of this 1967 film exist.

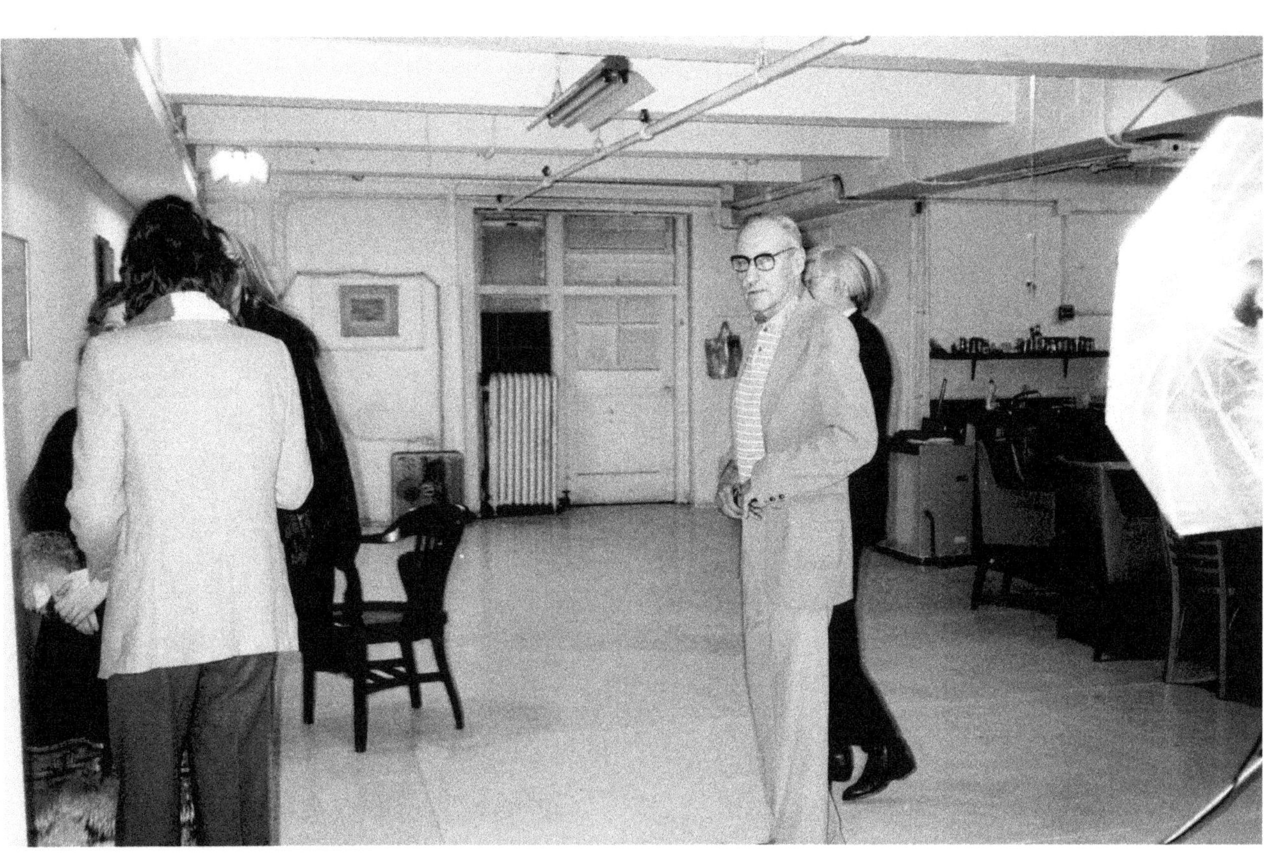

Marcia Resnick then brings up Lisa Lyons, the bodybuilder then in vogue.

RESNICK: Do you know of the female bodybuilder, Lisa Lyons?

HALL: Is she pretty?

RESNICK: Real beautiful.

BOCKRIS: Tough dyke?

RESNICK: She's beautiful.

WARHOL: Is she real skinny?

RESNICK: She's my height and weight. She's a bodybuilder.

WARHOL: Noooo…

RESNICK: I'll show you the pictures I took of her.

JAGGER: You were telling me you were really turned on.

RESNICK: Oh shut up!

Resnick had recently done a big photo session with Jagger for the cover of *High Times* magazine. Since Mick had to give Marcia permission to publish the ones he liked, they spent some time together and developed a humorous repartee.

JAGGER: You said you really liked her.

RESNICK: She's normal. She's like us. She's short and… she's great! She's normal like me. [Everyone falls about laughing.]

JAGGER: Normal like you? You think you're normal?

HALL: I'm normal.

I then asked Bill about his marriage to Ilse Klapper, whom he married in the 1930s so she could get a green card to escape from Nazi Germany. Bill explained that in New York she worked for the German playwright, Ernst Toller, as his secretary. In despair about Hitler's war, Toller would often hang himself in the bathroom during the lunch break knowing that Klapper would always come back in time to save him. But then the story got confused and the next thing we knew, Ernst Toller was dead!

Consternation ensued because Bill had left out a key part of the set up and it became harder and harder to understand it. Eventually we all understood what had happened. But not before Bill yelled ERNST TOLLER! No wonder Bill was so angry the following day. The whole thing had been a nightmare of misunderstanding from the moment Jagger opened his mouth. And it wasn't over yet.

I then remarked how Bill and Mick were dressed alike that night. As soon as we hit a funny bone, pent-up energy was released and we all started talking as if we were at a party. "Oh my God, they are!" said Jerry. "No sweater! No sweater!" yelled Andy. "What's that you're wearing?" Bill screamed. "It's a bullet proof jacket!" Andy replied. "Oh Andy! God knows you need one," said Bill suddenly right there in the middle of it.

Then I took it up a notch. "Bill shot someone," I declared. "Mick did anybody shoot you?" No. "Who did you shoot, Bill?" Jagger asked. Bill assured Mick he had not shot anybody lately. He'd been on his good behavior. The room erupted in screams of laughter. In the tapes, you can't hear anything but people laughing their heads off and talking back and forth. It was like the way things were supposed to be from the outset.

BOCKRIS: [turning to Liz] Andy got shot.

DERRINGER: Are you kidding!? You know Andy and I were on the cover of the *Daily News* together? ["A lot of people thought I shot Andy Warhol because of the picture of me and Andy on the cover of the *Daily News*" she said at the time, June 1968.]

WARHOL: No! What happened?

I thought we were home free but then talk turned to guns.

RESNICK: Oh, guns you're talking about.

BURROUGHS: Guns we're talking about here. This fucking jerk mayor that we got now wants to pass some law you know, mandatory jail sentence for possession of a gun.

WARHOL: Well, more cops were killed.

BURROUGHS: Well, so what!? You think the guys who killed a cop are gonna be deterred by an extra year in jail? Holy God, what kind of thinking is this!?

WARHOL: It's twenty years.

HALL: I thought today of walking around with one of those long things you shock a bull with.

JAGGER: Cattle prods.

WARHOL: It wasn't a cattle prod. It was a pooper scooper!

HALL: Uh uh.

WARHOL: It waaaaass…

After the meeting ended and Jagger called his driver, Marcia turned her photo lights on and took two uncomfortable portraits of Mick and Bill. Together. I took a picture of Bill saying goodbye to Mick with a hard look in his eye. This was the first and last time all three men were in the same room.

Jagger's visit had lasted for 45 minutes. In the minutes before he arrived, Andy and Bill had reached the peak of their budding friendship. Ironically, while Bill had been hammering away at rock 'n' roll confrontation, Jagger had confronted us all and taken away with him the delicate state of Bill and Andy's growing connection.

But maybe not. After Mick and his girls left, Marcia took a series of portraits of Bill and Andy together. This series of some seven dual portraits is the reward of the evening. For here Andy and Bill play out their friendship in a ballet of co-posing which climaxes when Bill puts his elbow on Andy's shoulder and Andy accepts it.

The last thing Andy said to me was, "You were terrible."

In *The Andy Warhol Diaries* for Saturday, March 1, Andy wrote: "Bill was asking Mick about the 'drug culture' and the 'revolution' and all that… I don't think he's a good writer. I mean he wrote that one good book, *Naked Lunch*, but now it's like he's living in the past."

Bill, who was upset by the way my book *With William Burroughs* made it look like he was always hanging out with famous people, said after its publication, "It isn't true that I spend my time going to parties with Andy Warhol." That was not a rejection of Andy. Bill was quite aware of his image. He did not want his fans around the world to get the impression he had joined the Jet Set.

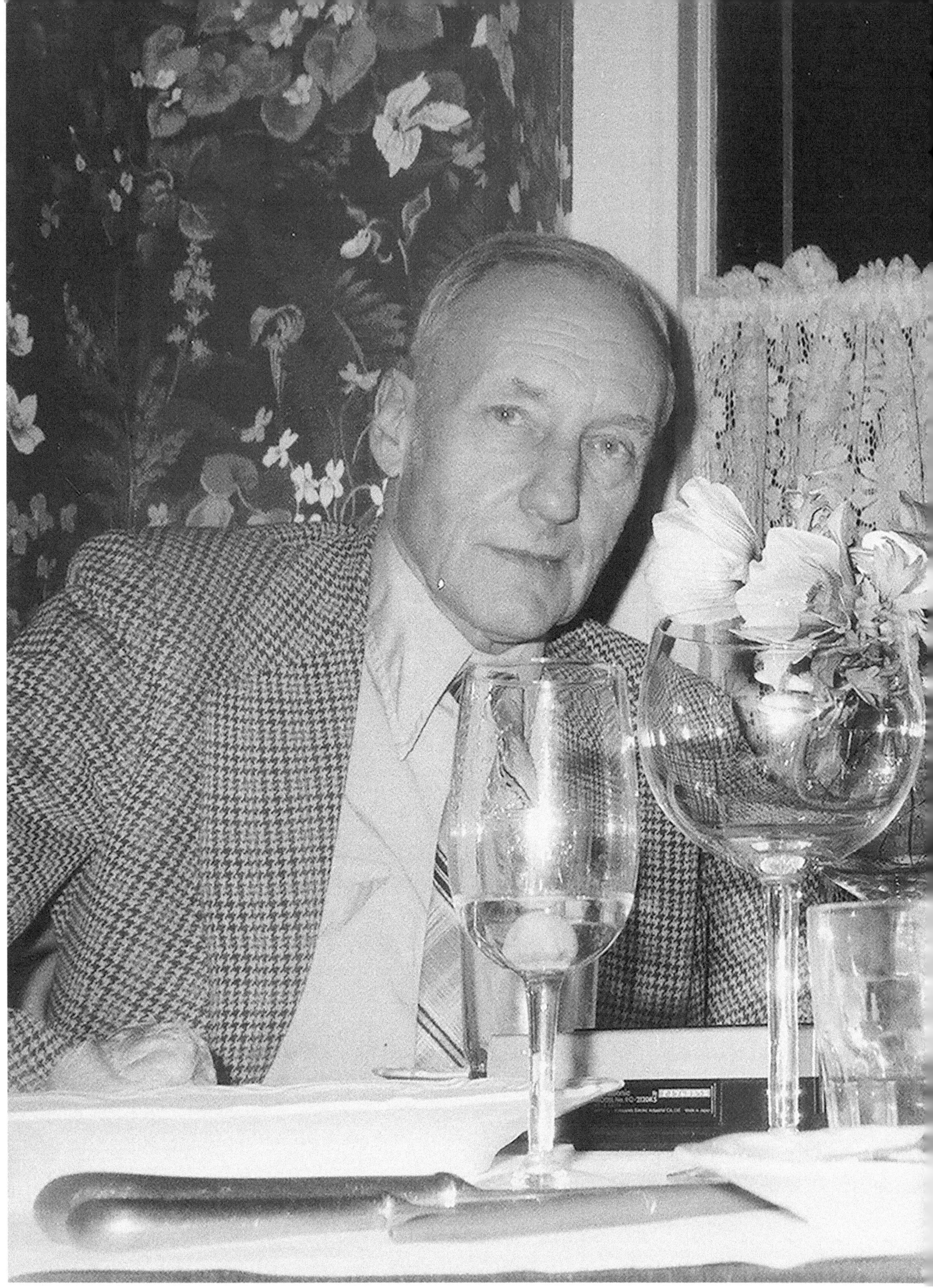

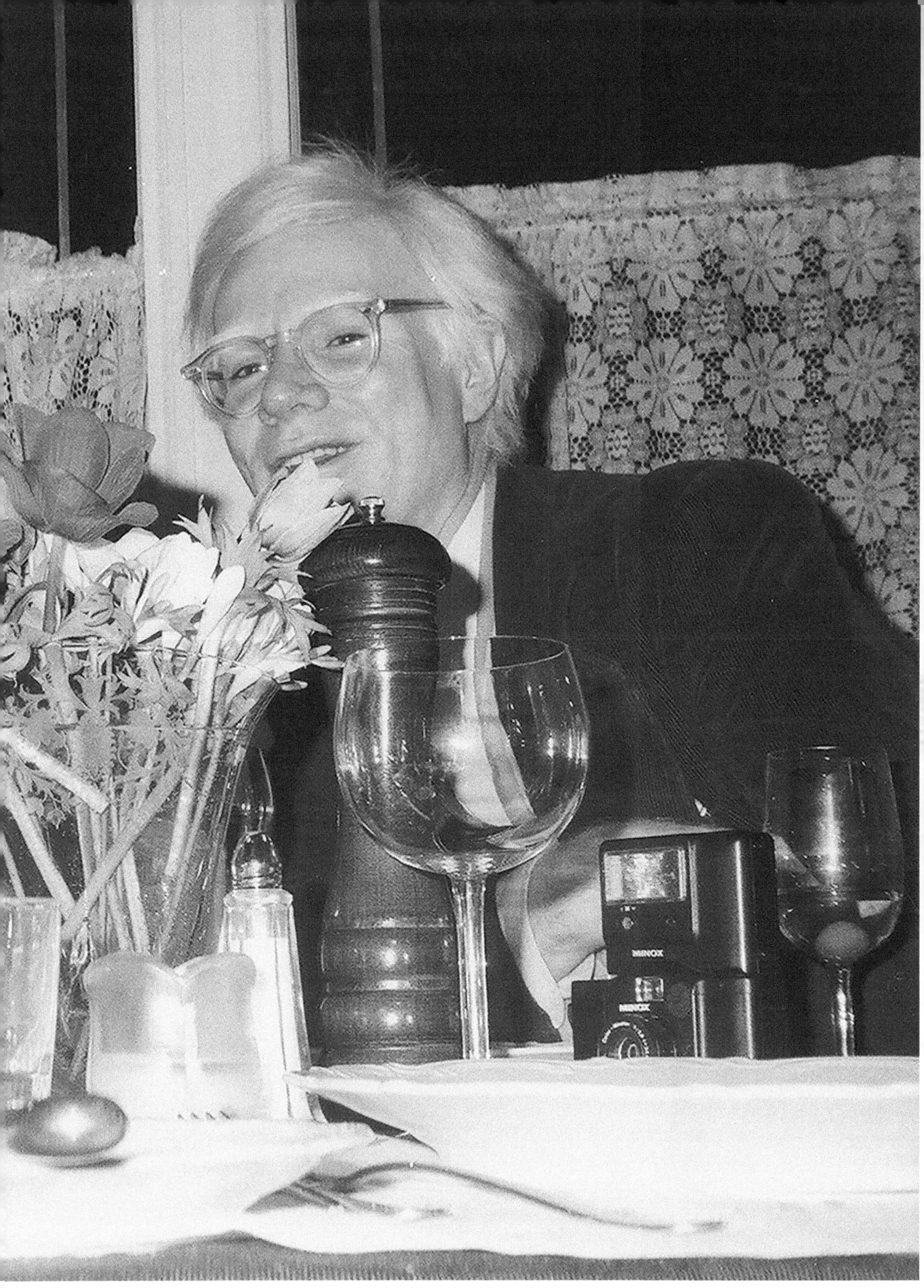

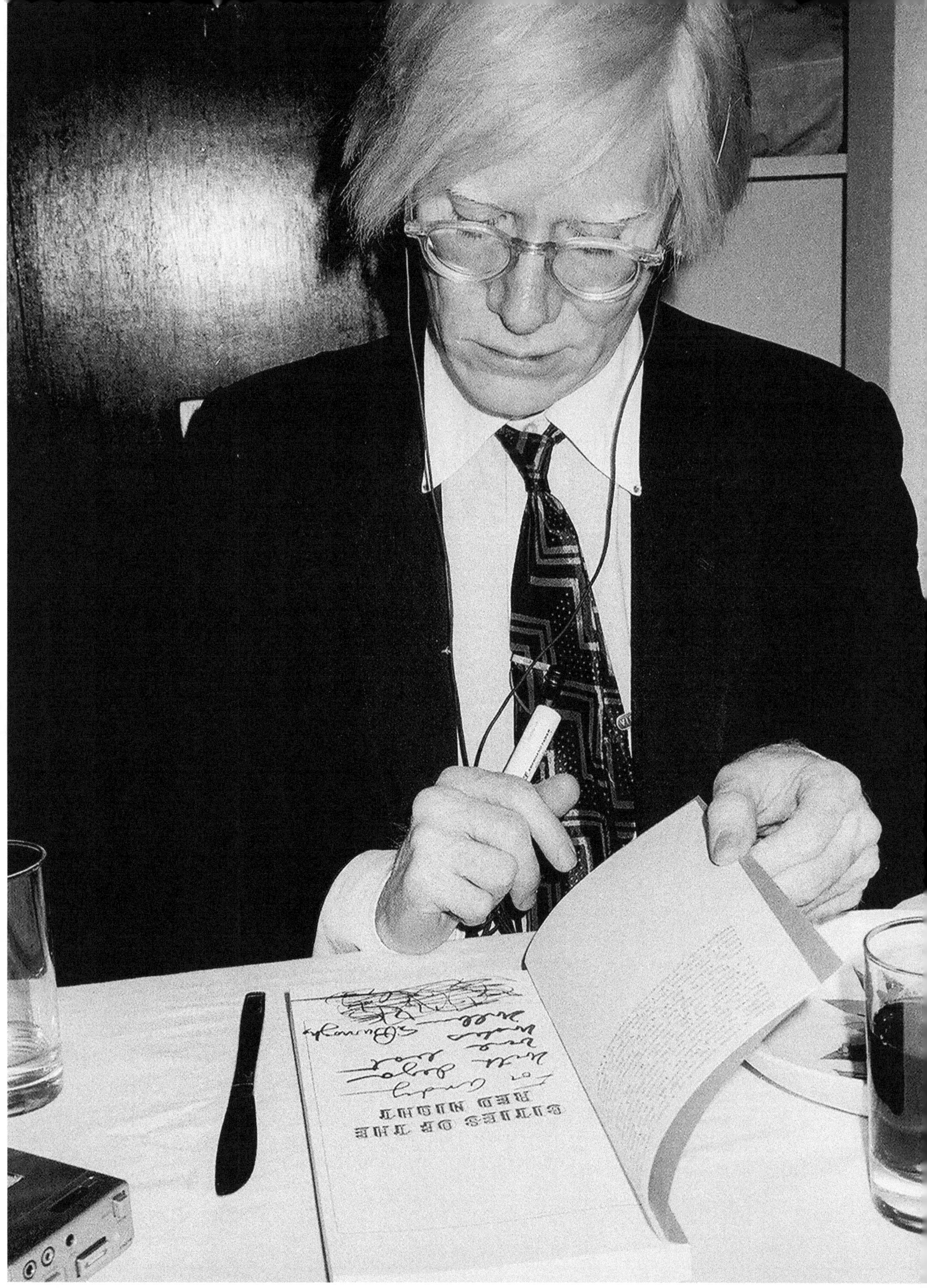

CITIES OF THE
RED NIGHT

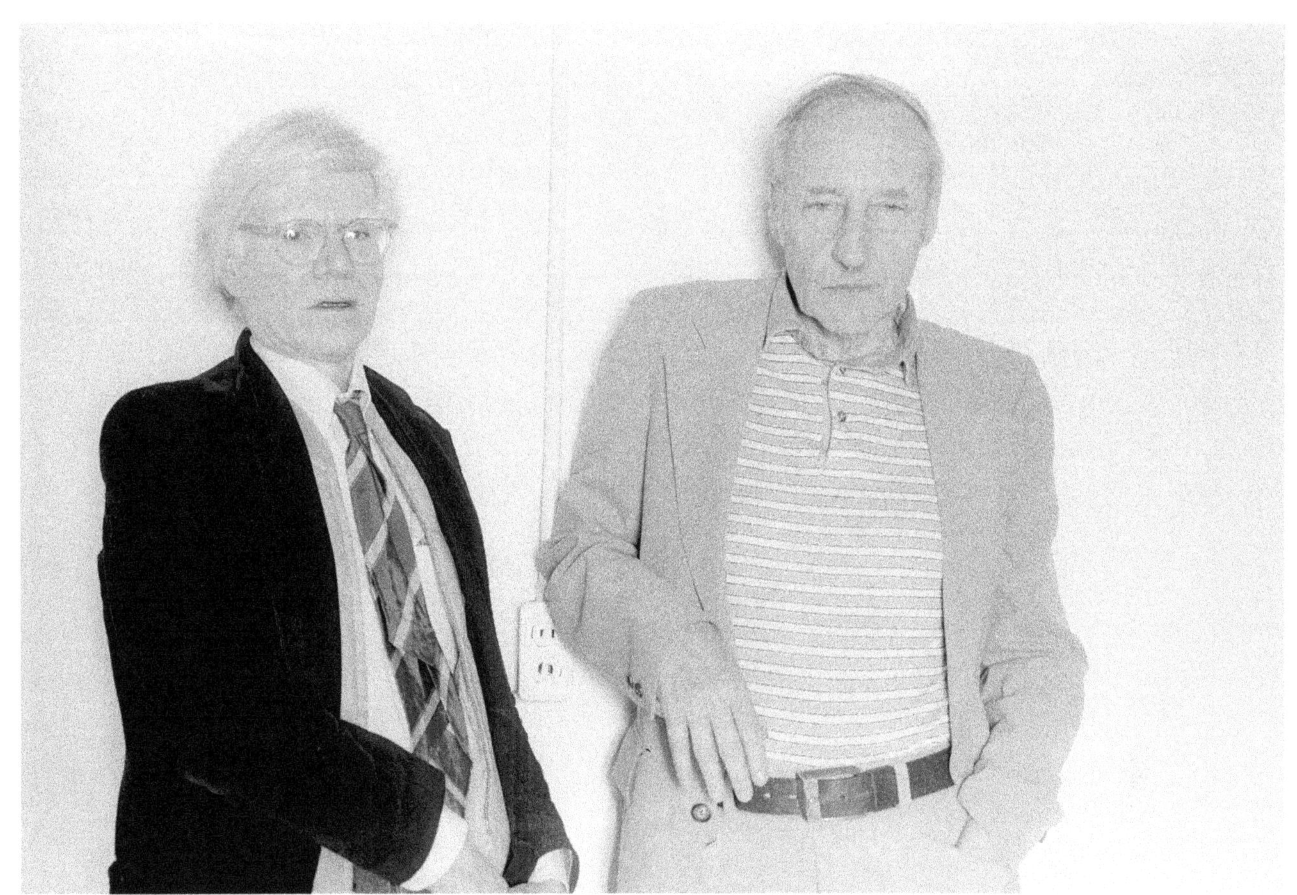

CHAPTER SIX
BURROUGHS-WARHOL DIARIES: MARCH TO OCTOBER 1980

Thursday, March 6, 1980

I took Barry Miles to the Factory at 4:00 p.m. to show him Andy Warhol's portrait of Debbie Harry. Andy was annoyed about the Jagger fiasco. "That was terrible!" he said, not amused. I tried to joke but to no avail. "What is it now?" he asked with slight exasperation. He had been giving me a hell of a lot and for what? To sit around and watch me get drunk and not be funny? I loved Andy but I couldn't express it. I froze up too much in his presence. I never relaxed with him and let myself be natural. I was never funny. I could have told him boarding school and high school stories that would have amused him to no end.

It turned out that Bill was just as fed up with me as Andy. While I was talking to Andy at the Factory, Bill was on the phone with James Grauerholz out in Lawrence, Kansas. He told James the whole evening had been a nightmare of misunderstanding and there was some question as to whether to continue working with me on my book. Other problems would soon conspire to threaten my relationship with Burroughs.

Like most people who worked with Warhol, I still ask myself "What would Andy think about this?" I think he forgave me a lot because I did produce, and in fact he was incredibly kind to me. I feel uptight just thinking about the fact that I never rose to the level that I could have. The greatest compliment he ever gave me was when he suggested we collaborate on something. "We should do something together," he said in Vincent's cubicle one afternoon. I was surprised. Write a book? "No, not a book," he laughed. Years later, I realized a weekly fifteen-minute radio show might have been really cool. But I never got back to him about it. I did not respond. I remember thinking at the time that anyone who worked with Andy lost their identity somewhere in his huge shadow. He was, after all, the greatest artist of his era and great beyond our understanding because his vision had gone so far, impacted so deeply, that he had literally changed the world. It took Lou Reed years to escape his identity as a Warhol star. But still, it was silly for me not to do it, silly and ungenerous. I should have given him anything he asked for out of politeness. It was such a privilege to work in Andy's magic universe, but nobody said working for Warhol was not complicated. A number of women who fell in love with Andy when he was starring them in films—like Edie Sedgewick and Viva—were very upset when they discovered that they simply could not get closer to him than they were. There was an emotional barrier. In the middle of so many people, Andy was essentially alone.

Sunday, March 9, 1980

David Bowie came running up the stairs to the Bunker carrying a vast arrangement of flowers in a large white vase, which he set down on the floor when he greeted William with a warm handshake and a brilliant smile. He had stipulated that there be no cameras or tape recorders; thus, there is no record of this visit save my memory and this brief exchange which I wrote down.

> **BOCKRIS:** Have you been anywhere exotic lately?
>
> **BOWIE:** Well, I mean I think New York is the most exotic place right now. Don't you, Bill?
>
> **BURROUGHS:** Yes, yes indeed. You don't have to leave New York to find the exotic. But see I think that this whole notion of only the jungle is exotic is of course ridiculous. You can find any number of exotic things in New York.

Bowie was not only charming and gracious; he was collaborative. It turned out that the purpose behind his visit was to take a Polaroid of Burroughs for a portrait he was painting. In the process of setting up a background and getting the correct light, he mentioned that the sky in the background was going to be red. This was immediately after William had completed, but not yet published, his novel *Cities of the Red Night*. Very few people knew of it. My favorite memory of Bowie's visit came at the end. As I watched from the back of a Checker cab parked across the Bowery from Burroughs' building, lit by flashing neon lights at dusk against a red night, David escorted Bill across the wide street. They looked like characters torn out of the pages of an opera, splashed down there momentarily like extraterrestrials.

Friday, July 4, 1980—Dinner with Andy, Jed Johnson, Debbie Harry, and Chris Stein at La Terrasse, the best restaurant in Harlem

I started working with Debbie Harry when writing the text for Chris Stein's book of photographs, *Making Tracks: The Rise of Blondie*. My initial plan was to tape-record a conversation over dinner between Debbie, Chris, and Andy Warhol for the book.

We met for cocktails at Blondie's West 200 58th Street penthouse. "We got it for $500," Stein reported. Its previous owner was the movie star Lillian Roth. Despite its famous tenants, the rooms were rather small. Debbie and Chris used the majority of them for storage. They spent most of their time in the bedroom running the band from their king-size bed. They were not used to entertaining at home.

The best part of their apartment was the huge terrace, which had a great view of New York. I got there before Andy arrived. We were all feeling good, but when the doorbell rang and Andy and Jed walked in the atmosphere changed. If you're not used to entertaining in your apartment and you invite Andy Warhol for cocktails before taking him to dinner, you have a lot of anxiety. Debbie was nervous and I was too.

Andy, Jed, Chris and I took our seats on the terrace. Our conversation flowed more like molasses than champagne. Then Debbie made her entrance in a white summer dress carrying a large tray of cocktails. She sat down and became the hostess with the mostest. The conversation picked up.

Everything was coming together when I was blown out of my seat by the unexpected arrival of the movie star Dennis Christopher, whose movie *Breaking Away* was a big hit the year before. His gorgeous girlfriend took a seat opposite me. I was so distracted by her seductive presence I was finding it hard to focus.

Chris put me on the spot, asking if we could take Dennis and his girl to dinner. I would have loved to have gotten to know them better, but it's hard to transcribe a tape of more than six people talking in a noisy restaurant, so I nixed it. This of course earned me Dennis' lasting hatred. And everybody put me down for being a party pooper. It was a big mistake on my part but then this book is full of my mistakes.

Debbie had made reservations for dinner at the best restaurant in Harlem, La Terrasse.

Five of us squeezed into Debbie's small silver car. Debbie drove with Andy in the passenger seat. I wedged in between Chris and Jed in the backseat. Deb suggested that we all take off our jackets, but it was impossible in the cramped backseat. By the time we reached the restaurant, the tension had melted away. Debbie is a good driver but we all made fun of her parking attempts. I took some good photographs of her getting out of the car. One of my favorite pictures shows all of them walking from the car to the restaurant in Harlem's nighttime street.

When we got to the restaurant, Debbie was annoyed because they had promised her a table by a window with a great view of the July 4th fireworks. But we got no window.

During dinner Andy and I both took pictures. Everyone but the silent Jed talked about all sorts of things like artificial insemination, Mick Jagger's new face, and how to be in a successful film. Andy said, "Magic, it's just magic, it has to be, I mean…" The conversation flowed like wine now but my tape recorder flowed like mud. This morning I discovered the tape was virtually blank because I had not realized the pause button was on. A drunken countenance may have been to blame. I had just finished a book in which I was in the habit of asking dumb questions to goose the conversation, but the conversation was already goosed. At one point Debbie told me to shut up.

Andy kept saying as loudly as he could, "I guess they just don't know who," and then he really yelled, "Blondie is!" Apparently the waiters did not recognize us until they saw *me* taking pictures and changing tapes. Only then did the chef come running out of the kitchen wearing a big white hat. He wanted to know how we had enjoyed his food. We all a loved his food but by the end of dinner Andy was also telling me to shut up.

We rode back in silence. I didn't even turn on my tape recorder. Andy Warhol's five-story Georgian mansion looked straight out of *Daniel Deronda* by George Eliot, on its tree-lined block of East 66th Street. As we approached the house, we drove through the midst of frenzied revelers all celebrating the 4th of July in the increasingly congested street. Their blurred grinning faces contrasted with the sad faces of Andy and Jed and suddenly the tree-lined block lost its glimmer and glow.

When we got back to 58th Street, we all yelled, "Let's take some drugs!" It was the same old story. Everything we do is work, including fouling our noses with potent powders and falling out behind some funky sounds. Meanwhile, Debbie thanked me for setting up the dinner. It was the first time they had ever socialized with Andy, which was sort of nuts since Debbie had been a waitress at Max's Kansas City in the 1960s and Warhol went there every night. He was also one of Chris' favorite artists, but they were shy and always very busy. I saw my job as connecting the dots and letting the dots then weave the tapestry of a relationship. Since we were all workaholics, work was the only glue that held us together.

Saturday, September 6, 1980

When "Dinner with Andy and Bill" came out in the 5th-anniversary issue of *Blueboy*, both Andy and William confided to me separately that they thought it was cool, but their handlers hated it and said it was really dumb. So I was happy.

Shortly after this, I received a call from a certain Nigel Finch,[1] who said he was directing a documentary film about the Chelsea Hotel for the BBC. He wanted to know if I could interview Burroughs. I told him that William did not do television interviews because he feels the medium is out of his control, but I would ask. Burroughs declined, adding that the only interesting things that went on in the Chelsea during his stay were events that he definitely couldn't talk about on television.

When I informed Finch of Burroughs' answer, we got drunk on martinis in the Chelsea bar, El Quixote, and at one point I told him, "The only way I might be able to get Burroughs over here is if I could arrange a dinner with him and Andy Warhol." When Finch got up off the floor where the sheer brilliance of the idea and the martinis had flung him, I mentioned the considerable costs. "We'd have to rent a suite, hire a cook, buy a dinner, and," I mumbled, sliding the check a little closer to his glass, "there is also the, uh, question of that is to say my, eeeeuuurghhmmm… fee." He blanched; however, the BBC have got it over anyone in the TV industry when it comes to recognizing and carrying out an idea. He quickly agreed to the proposal.

Before staggering out of El Quixote that night, I told myself, "Qué será será, hnnh?" I mean, Bill would probably refuse to go on television because he distrusts the medium, and Andy would refuse because he's holding out for his own satellite. In short, my chances of pulling off this operation were slim to nil, but what the hell? I'd do the best I could.

When I mentioned it to both of them in the *you-probably-don't-want-to-do-this* way, I was astonished when both men instantly agreed. However, this was the root of Andy telling me that whenever he did anything with me, he got into trouble.

---

1   English film director for the BBC, 1949-1995.

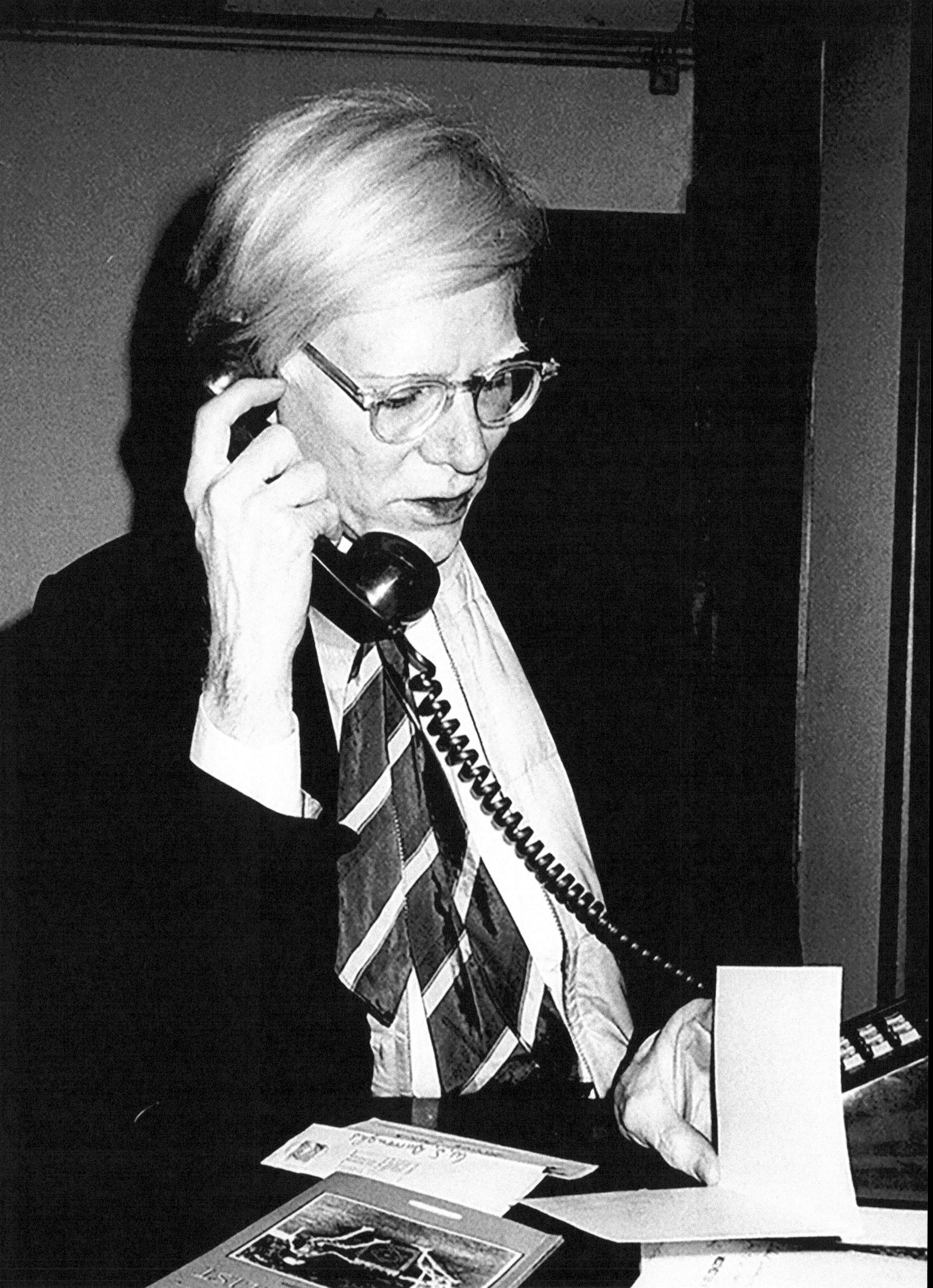

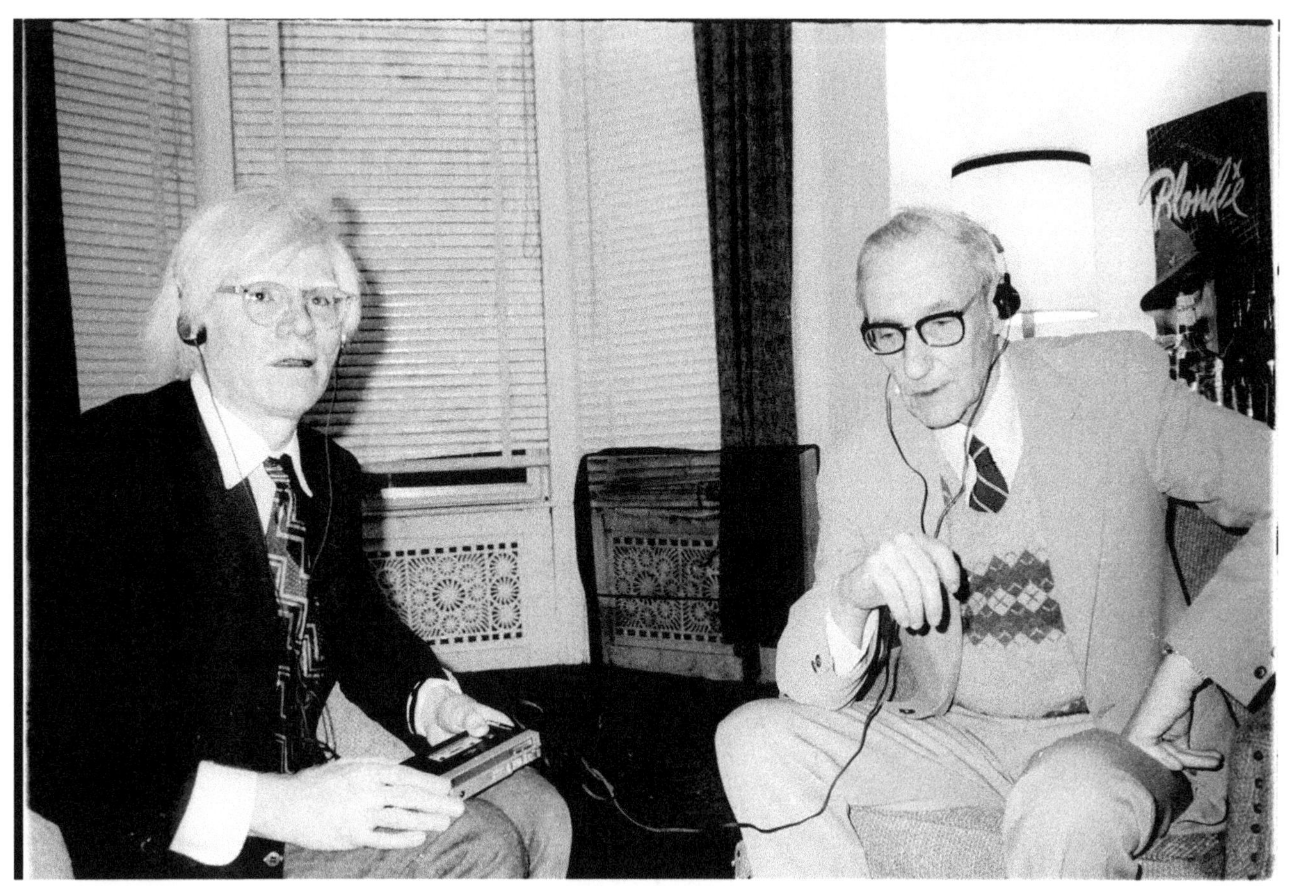

CHAPTER SEVEN
BURROUGHS AND WARHOL AT THE CHELSEA HOTEL

Madness on Christopher Street

Around 9:00 a.m. on Thursday, October 23, 1980, Miles and I were walking east on the north side of Christopher Street between 6th and 7th Avenues. We were on our way to buy the rabbit he was planning to cook for Andy and Bill at the Chelsea Hotel that night.

MILES: I knew the Arena TV crew because its director Nigel Finch and its producer Anthony Wall were old friends of mine from London. They knew I was in New York when they were making the Chelsea Hotel documentary. I told them that Victor would be the person to get Burroughs and Andy. I was asked to cook for Bill and Andy in one of the hotel's kitchen rooms. My specialty back then was rabbit with mustard sauce. We bought a good-sized rabbit, which we marinated for a couple of hours before cooking. In the BBC program, there is a brilliant close-up of a strange substance inside a large bowl with rabbit feet smeared with mustard. They focused right there and held the shot for a moment. It was pretended that Andy was going to have dinner with Bill at Victor's apartment in the Chelsea Hotel.

Interview with Miles by Bockris, New York, 2007

The Village had not quite woken up. It still had that morning sun on its red brick walls that bathes its streets and buildings in the most beautiful orange glow and makes the windows sparkle. It was an exceptionally beautiful, brisk day. As we walked along enjoying everything, I started thinking about Lou Reed, who lived in this block above where the historic Stonewall Bar had been.

I had known Lou for six years. He was a good friend. We shared a background as poets and I had even represented his book of poems, *All the Pretty People*, from 1974 to 1980. Quite recently, I had received an enraged phone call from his lawyer demanding an explanation for selling the book to an Italian publisher for $500. I vehemently denied selling Lou out for $500 and wrote said publisher a blistering complaint demanding exoneration. In fact, only the previous night I had slid an envelope under Lou's door containing a copy of the Italian publisher's angry reply exonerating me from selling them the book for $500 along with an invitation to tonight's dinner at the Chelsea.

As we were drawing level with Lou's front door, it abruptly opened. Two elegantly

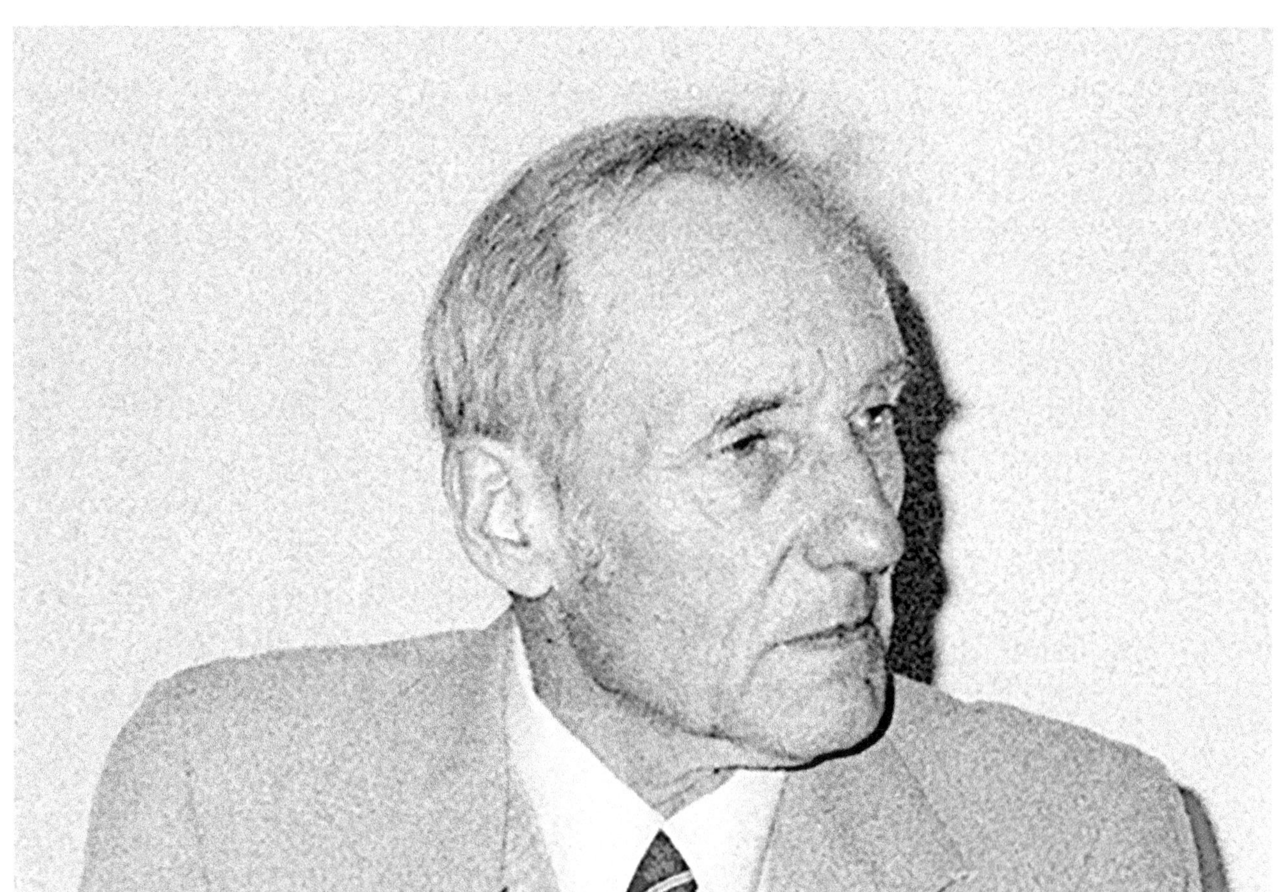

disheveled figures, clad from head to foot in black leather, emerged each clutching to their breast a dachshund: Lou's beloved Baron and the Count. Lou was with his clone who I took to be Rachel Humphreys, a beautiful drag queen who lived with Lou for several years. She was the subject of his song "Coney Island Baby."

The four of us would not have been able to navigate the narrow sidewalk in opposing directions without conversing. As we momentarily slowed, I stepped forward to embrace my friend, crying out spontaneously, "Lou! How strange to see you here now!"

Evidently, Lou had rejected both the invitation and the exoneration letter because they stepped around me gingerly as if I were a piece of dog shit. Lou's head swiveled so as to keep the twin barrels of his horrified eyes blasting contempt at me as if I were a leper. In a moment that is indelibly imprinted on my memory, I called out, "I didn't do it, Lou! I didn't do it!"

Instantly the scene broke. Lou turned toward his appendage and they marched across the street to Jackson Square Park to water their hounds next to the George Segal sculpture of two lesbians sitting on a bench that dominates the piazza. Deflated, I stumbled alongside the striding Miles, who had maintained his trademark aplomb. Whereas I remained shackled to the view that Lou Reed was some kind of human being, Miles knew better how to handle the massive emotional shift celebrity friendship creates. "You should have said, 'Cat got your tongue, Lou?'" he concluded.

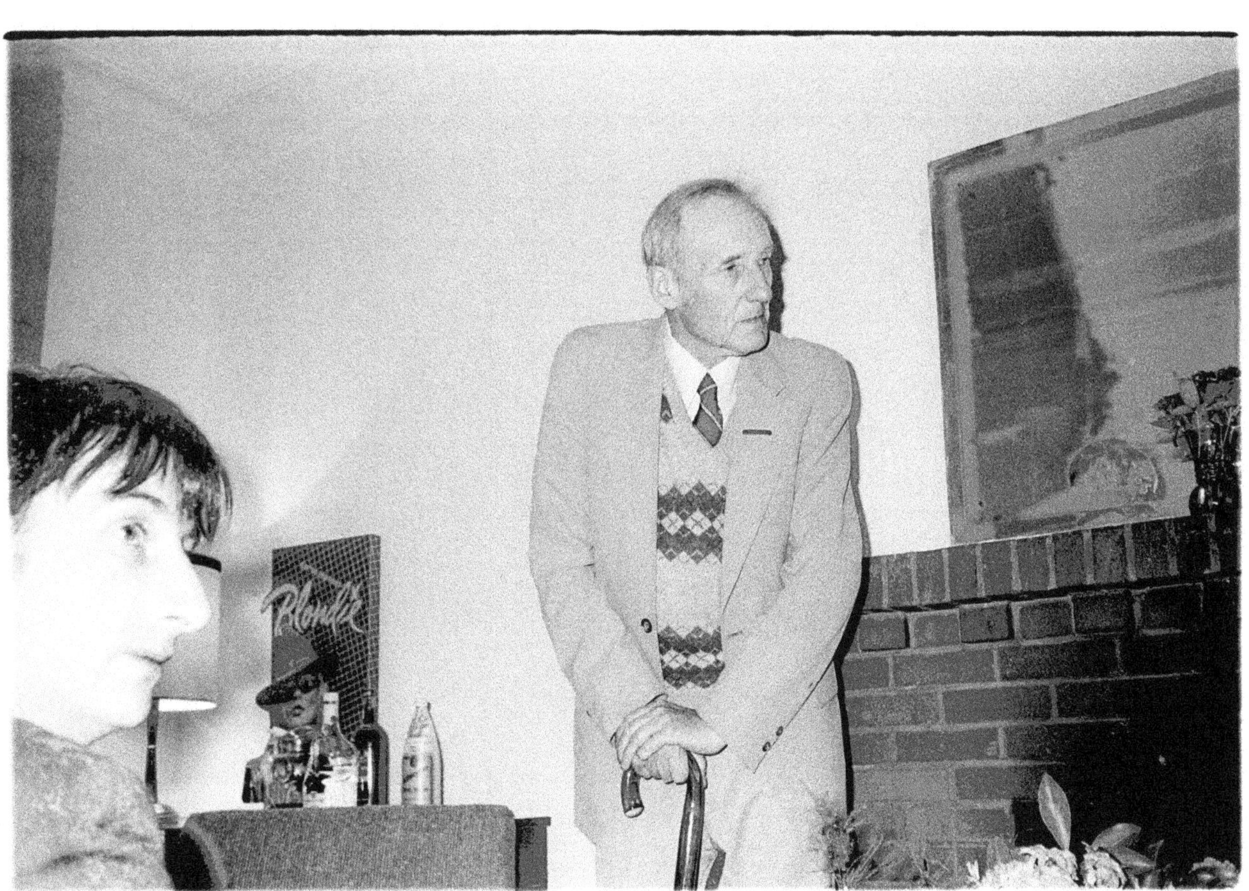

That Night

Suite 222 at the Chelsea Hotel opened onto a small dining area with a compact kitchen and beyond it a 14-by-20-foot studio apartment climaxing on a window which overlooked the back of the hotel. Bill had signed an agreement with Howard Brookner, who was filming a Burroughs documentary, to not give any filmed interviews until the documentary was finished. In order to get Brookner's permission to film the dinner, I had to agree to let his crew film it alongside the BBC. By the time both crews had set up their lights and cameras and Burroughs arrived [high on Majoun] with James Grauerholz, there were already eight people in the room. At that instant I called Andy, only to hear him hesitatingly announce he was getting "cold feet" about coming over to the Chelsea because some of his former superstars like Viva, who could be volatile at times, still lived there.

The necessity of the moment transformed me from the semi-tongue-tied-awe-struck schoolboy into the hard-charging accountant of his emotions.

"Don't worry about a thing, honey!" I cried. "I'll be right over to get you! The room is on the second floor, so we're going to walk up the stairs. We won't be trapped in the elevators with anyone! I promise you!"

"Oh, uh. Ok," he whispered. I cabbed it to the Factory. Fifteen minutes later, we piled into the dark interior of a Checker cab with two bodyguards, his painting assistant Rupert Smith who looked like Rupert Bear and an aide, Jay Shriver. Andy was upbeat and talkative. I noticed he was carrying three canes. He always overdid it. Surrounding Andy, we cut through the virtually empty lobby at warp speed and took the stairs like a football team.

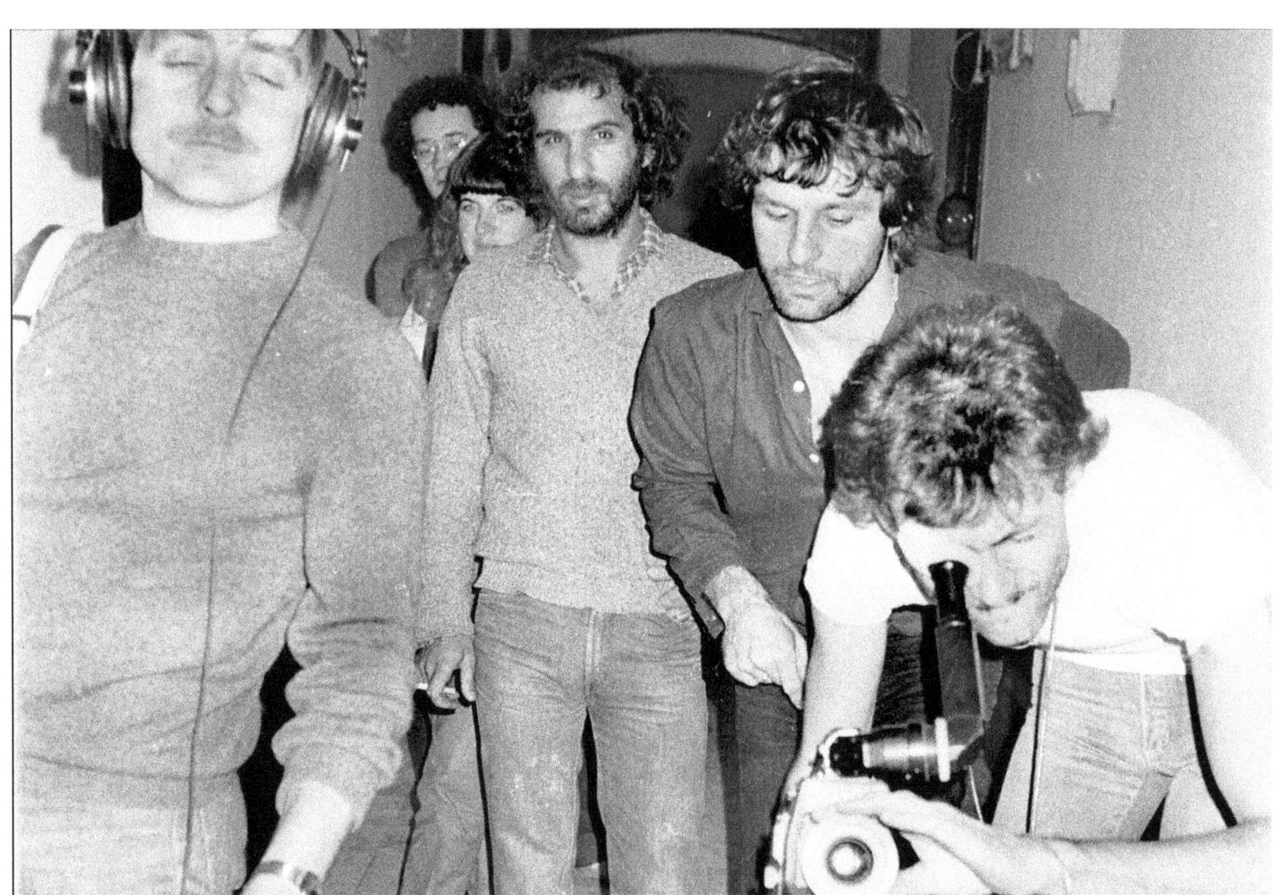

As I entered the suite with Andy Warhol, Nigel Finch slumped out of his rigid tension and mouthed a big "Congratulations!" Andy took one look at the room and whispered, "Gee, this is going to be really boring. You said it would be fun…" as he slipped his Walkman's headphones over his ears listening to an opera. The headphones would remain for the balance of the night.

Bill sat at the head of the table, Andy to his left, me to his right, respective bodyguards in the remaining seats. We were wired for sound. Two sets of hot spotlights beamed on our faces. Sound men squeezed into pretzels around our feet. It was one thing for me to sit down at a dinner table with four people with Andy in control at 65 Irving, but quite another to face the vortex of two expectant camera crews, film lights, and six hot faces—particularly when I had made no preparations. This time nobody seized control of the conversation.

Bill gave Andy a proof copy of *Cities of the Red Night*.

BOCKRIS: Ask Bill to sign it for you, quick, quick. What page do you want, the dedication page?

BURROUGHS: I'll sign anywhere, wha?

WARHOL: Would you do a drawing?

BOCKRIS: Bill hates to do drawings.

BURROUGHS: What?

WARHOL: Can you do a drawing?

BURROUGHS: Oh yes, sure. [This is interesting. Bill has *always* refused to do drawings. Even at our first dinner he made a point of it.] Well, I'll just uh…

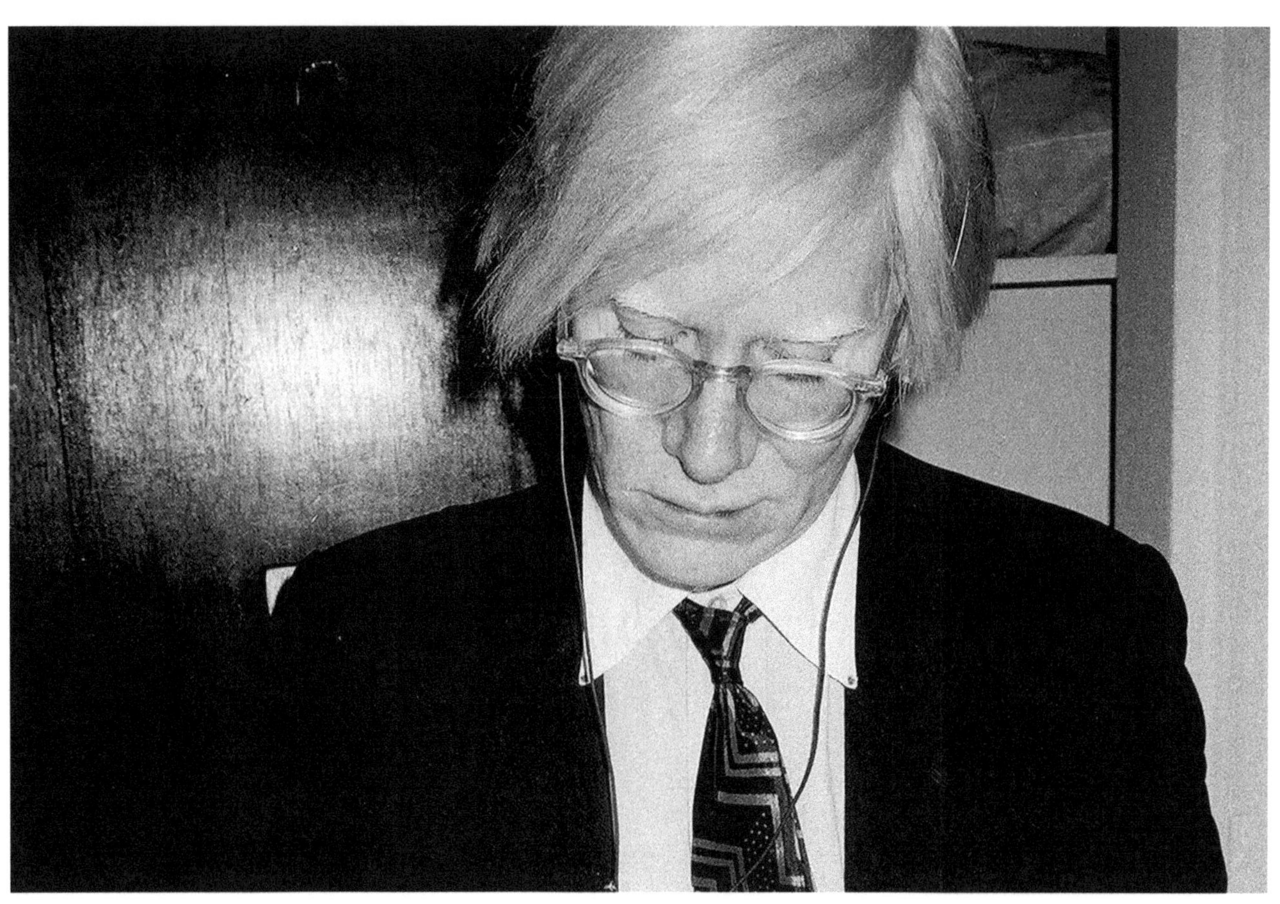

BOCKRIS: [gasping] It looks like Salvador Dali!

WARHOL: [gasping twice as much] *Ooohhh my god, uuuuhhh ohhhhh!!* More, more, on the side…

BURROUGHS: Is that…

BOCKRIS: Great.

WARHOL: Here, here, go…

BURROUGHS: Noooaaa I know everybody just wants jus… jus…

WARHOL: Gawd! This is like *aaaaawwwww!*

BURROUGHS: [businesslike] There you are.

WARHOL: *Thanks a lot!*

BOCKRIS: You're so lucky.

WARHOL: Greeeeaaat.

BURROUGHS: Uh, well there you are.

BOCKRIS: Boy that's so unique. I never saw Bill draw.

WARHOL: I think that's just… [boyish giggles]

BOCKRIS: Bill once did ten pages of drawings like that in Hollywood when he and James were out there visiting the set of *Heart Beat*.[1] At the end of the evening, he asked me if they were any good. I was snotty and said, "No!" Instantly, he threw them all in the trash can.

WARHOL: Soooo great. [He really sounds sincere and excited.] So great. Oh we're gonna, you're gonna start painting from now on, right? [See, why didn't someone set up a collaboration between Andy and Bill?]

BURROUGHS: Well, no, I'm not…

BOCKRIS: Give him a place to work at the Factory.

BURROUGHS: No, now…

____

1   1980 movie based on Carolyn Cassady's book about Neal Cassady and Jack Kerouac.

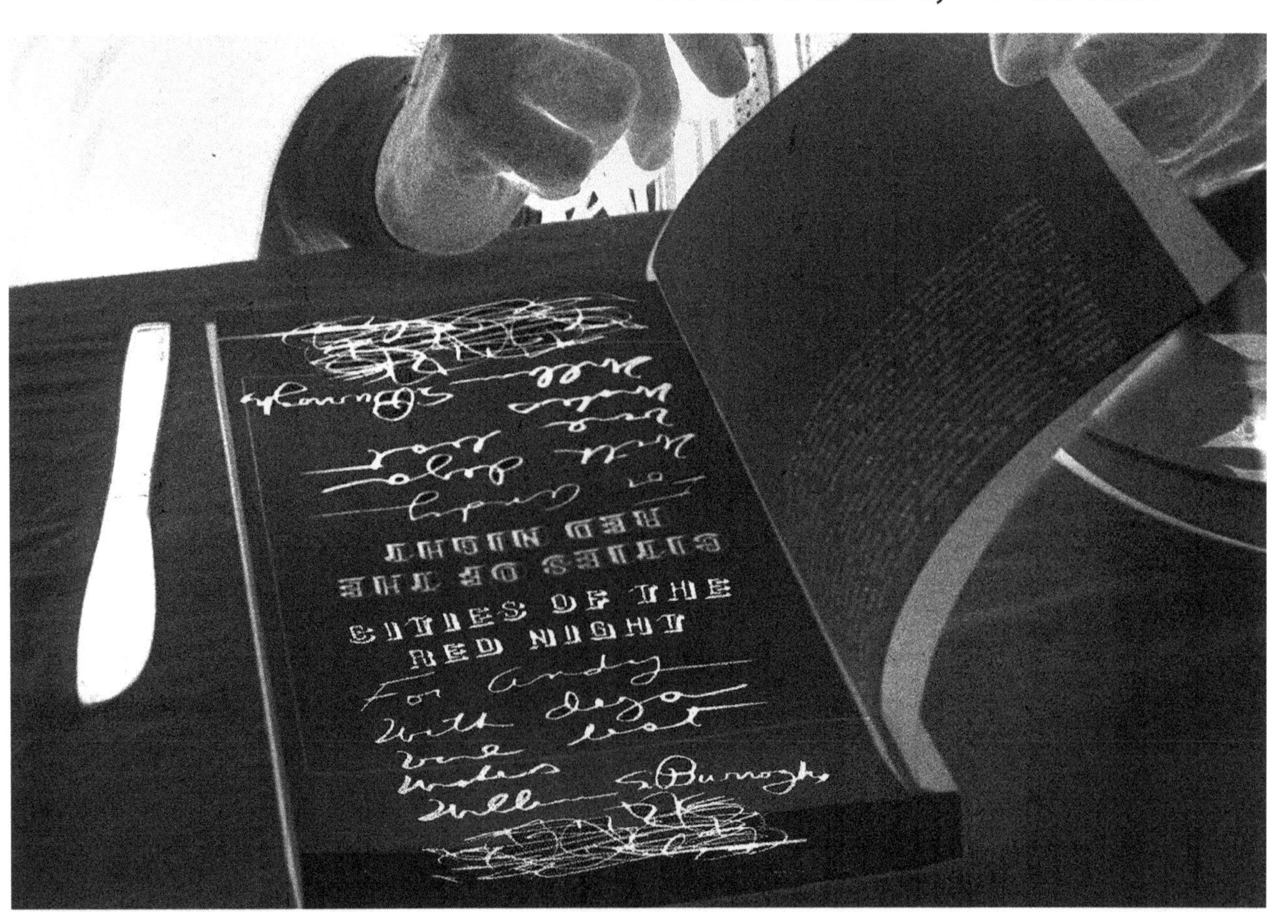

WARHOL: You've got to!

BOCKRIS: He'll give you a space, materials. All you've got to do is paint like Jamie Wyeth did at the Factory in 1977.[2]

WARHOL: I can get you… how about this tablecloth? [He sounds religiously serious.] Please do it on this tablecloth.

BURROUGHS: *No.*

WARHOL: Oh yes [strangely politely determined]. I mean it should be…

BURROUGHS: There is no…

JAMES GRAUERHOLZ: There is one drawing you can do.

BURROUGHS: …*way.*

MILES: [serving the rabbit in a mustard cream sauce] Pass these around.

BURROUGHS: What it is? It's a rabbit. Marvelous! Marvelous!

BOCKRIS: In mustard sauce.

---

2   American painter, b.1946.

When the serving dish came to me, I was so nervous, I dropped my cigarette in the cream sauce. Miles smiled.

***

Bockris: I remember dropping my cigarette in the rabbit in the mustard cream while you were serving it.

Miles: What a scandal. Why did you do that? Some kind of punk expression, no doubt…

Bockris: I wish! I was very nervous and uncomfortable. You noticed and you had a kind of Gestalt reaction.

Miles: Like, "What the hell are you doing?"

Bockris: What was the atmosphere like in the room?

Miles: In the room I felt that there was a lot, a lot of tension. Not only because there was a BBC crew filming—which

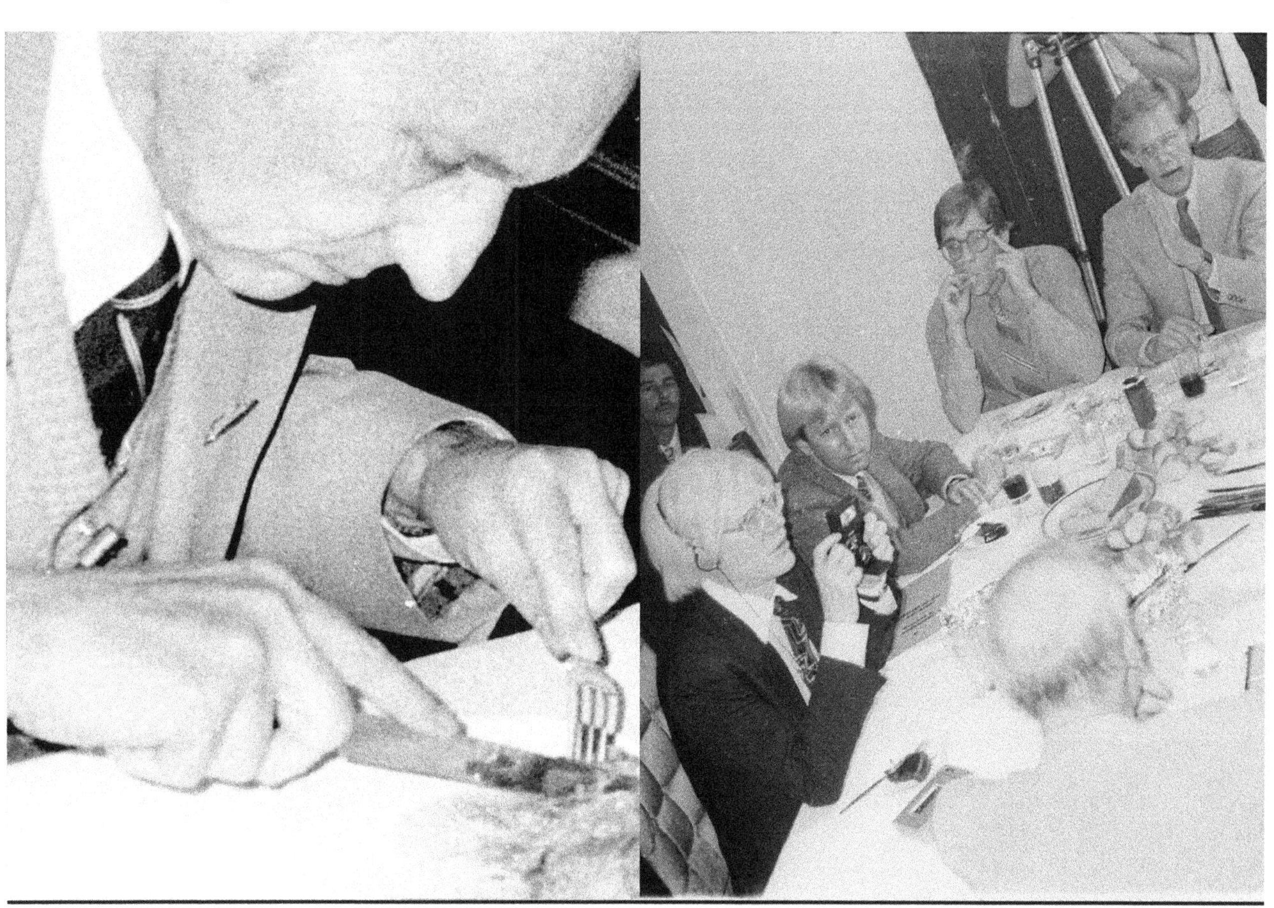

made Burroughs so extremely nervous that he would make little fishy gestures with his mouth, go very stiff, and speak in a gasping way—but furthermore, the English film crew was in turn being filmed by Howard Brookner's crew, who were making a documentary about Burroughs. So, there were two film crews with huge cameras, big sound poles, and people around with giant tape recorders. At that time the technology was like that, the recording equipment and the cameras were huge, heavy, and very cumbersome. You couldn't chat with someone like today with a webcam where the camera is barely visible. So, the cameras were a meter long and carried by a guy on his shoulder, it was like...

Bockris: It was as if a miniature spaceship with astronauts inside was slowly approaching overhead like an acid trip. People suddenly saw them and said to themselves, "Damn!"

Miles: With one person filming the other and the other filming Burroughs and Andy, any kind of spontaneity or natural chatter was practically impossible. It all seemed very forced and artificial to me.

Interview with Miles by Bockris,

New York, 2007

***

WARHOL: It's cream sauce [sounding just like another boy at the table]. You and your cream sauces. Don't you know the difference in color between mustard and cream? [Andy really lays into me for a while. I am colorblind: yellow, green, and brown all look the same.]

BOCKRIS: It's really exciting. [At this moment, small microphones looking like satellites slowly appear hovering over our heads.] You have the original book with all the mistakes in it.

WARHOL: Oh really!

BURROUGHS: There are some mistakes there. Yes, there are some there.

BOCKRIS: Where is the rabbit?

BURROUGHS: The rabbit is right here at the end of your fork.

WARHOL: It's divine.

BURROUGHS: Yes, quite toothsome.

WARHOL: This is the first time I've had hare. It's really good.

MILES: I got it at the Italian butcher. They asked if I wanted to have the head on or not, so I decided to remove the head.

BURROUGHS: I think so. It would bring up too many unfortunate associations.

BOCKRIS: Did you used to hunt rabbits, Bill?

BURROUGHS: I've shot rabbits, yes, hares, wild duck. I shoot them in the head as best I can.

BOCKRIS: But Bill, only the other day you were criticizing Hemingway for saying he liked to shoot rhinos and hares, and here you are...

BURROUGHS: Hemingway used a recoilless rifle to shoot this rhino—spew spew spew—but I don't see, I don't see any reason for killing a rhino or having a confrontation.

BOCKRIS: The great safaris are camera safaris. I went on a camera safari...

While Andy listened to opera, tuning into our conversation when called upon, Bill smiled inscrutably from within his pillow of druuuugs baby… Ironically, this turned out to be by far the most intimate, sensitive conversation I had the opportunity to tape between them.

BOCKRIS: Salvador Dali is broke.

BURROUGHS: The last time I saw him he said…

BOCKRIS: Muhammad Ali is broke.

BURROUGHS: That's much more understandable than Dali, who has been on the scene so long.

WARHOL: Well, Victor and I went to see Muhammad Ali and he had like a thousand people working for him and…

BURROUGHS: …and vice and stuff.

WARHOL: Oh, I know… I mean you could see…

BOCKRIS: But he's a survivor. He just lost this fight with Larry Holmes. It's so embarrassing, right? He didn't throw one punch. You know why? 'Cos he was so sick. He came out like a kitten, then at the end he said, "I want a rematch!"

WARHOL: We had the best time. We went to 21 and had dinner there, then you just walked right through the Warner Brothers building to Madison Square Garden and we had first row seats to see the fight. And I couldn't watch it. I was just too upset.

BOCKRIS: 'Cos you like him a lot?

WARHOL: Huh?

BOCKRIS: 'Cos you like him a lot?

WARHOL: Yeah, the whole audience loved him, and they pretended it never happened. They all went back to 21 and continued to party and pretended the

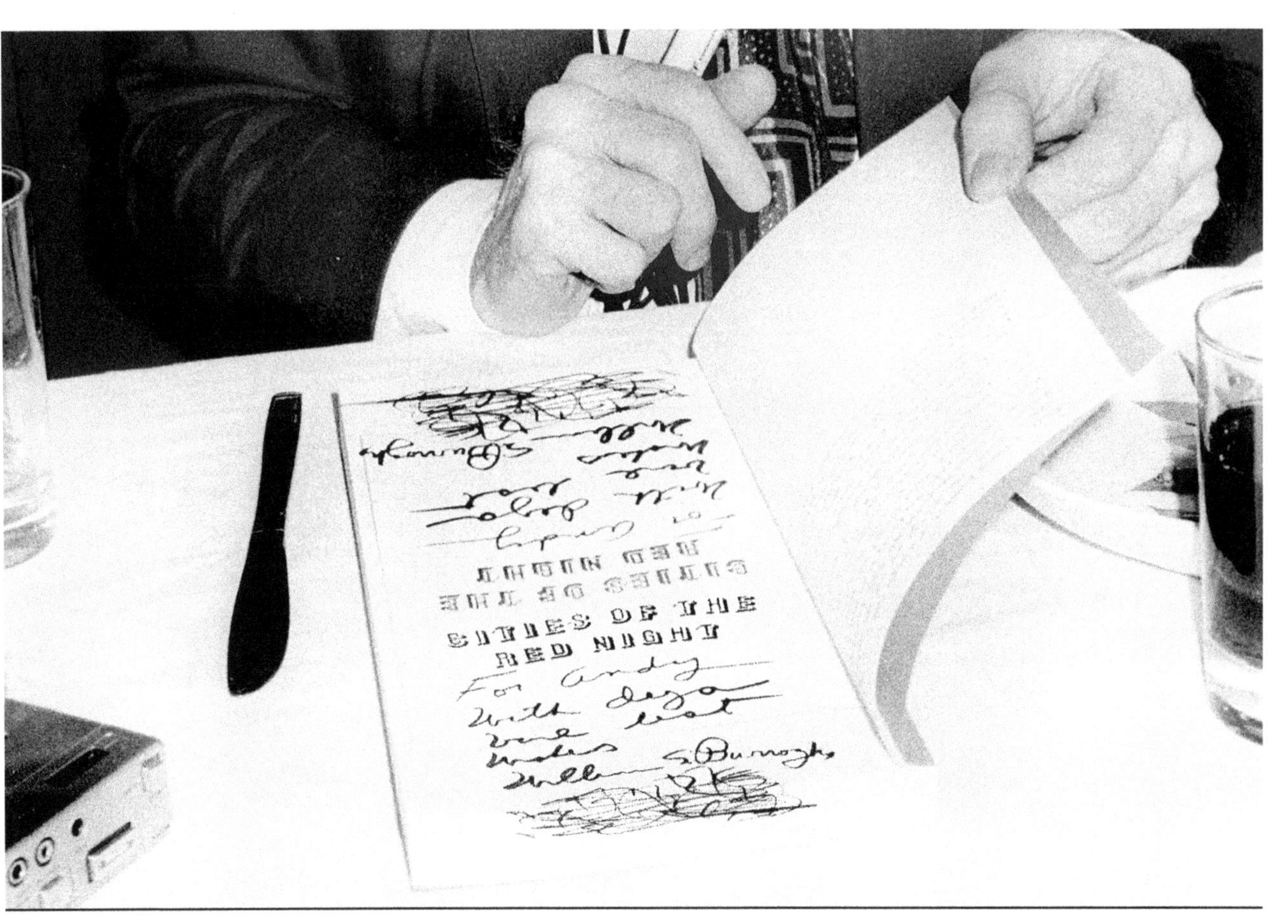

fight never happened! It was so weird. I mean no one ever mentioned that. Then I went uptown and saw a real murder, so that was more exciting.

BURROUGHS: Where was that?

WARHOL: It was at 79th Street and 3rd Avenue.

BOCKRIS: You saw people running down the street shooting each other?

WARHOL: Yeah. Well, there were these two guys trying to rob an undercover policeman, but they had other undercover policemen hiding around. So, when these three guys tried to spot him, they rushed out and shot him.

Phone rings. It is Raymond Foye calling with regrets to say that he and Henry Geldzahler, Commissioner for the Arts under Mayor Koch, would not be able to make it because they were already running late.

WARHOL: Is that Henry?

BOCKRIS: Yeah.

WARHOL: *Oh!* [becoming obstreperous] Tell him to come!

BOCKRIS: Andy says make sure you come.

BURROUGHS: A distinguished cultural functionary like Henry doesn't have time, my dear, for people like us, no no. We cannot do without him. The party will languish.

BOCKRIS: Well, why don't you come down?

WARHOL: Tell Henry to come! Tell him it's real… really fun! [sarcasm dripping]

BOCKRIS: Andy says it's so much fun here, we're having a wonderful time.

***

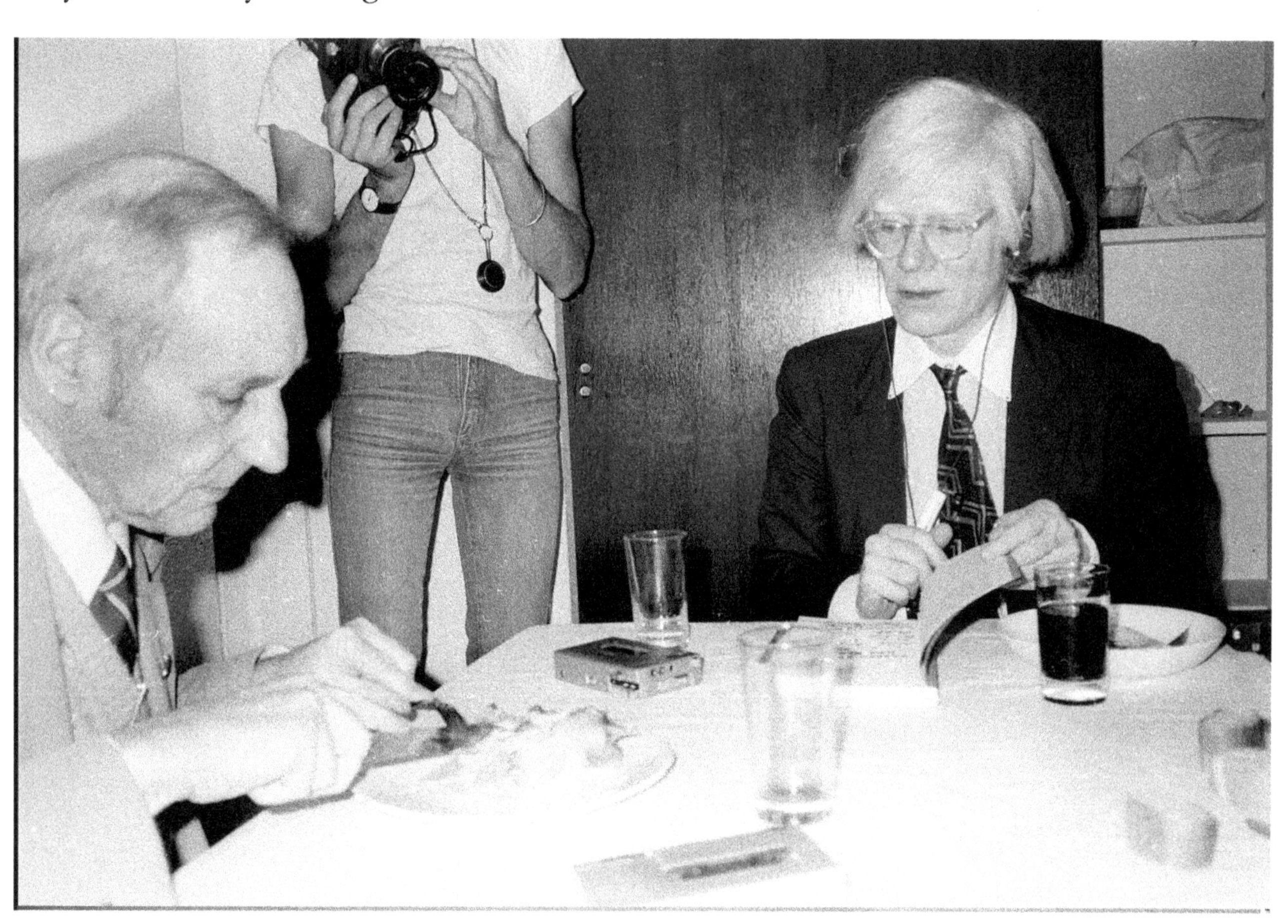

MILES: I thought Bill was being nice to Victor for doing this, because he clearly wasn't doing well, and possibly Andy neither. Even though they both spoke to each other, Victor was the third man in this triangle because they both had a relationship with him. This strange and tense result was to be expected. When Victor tried to organize social events with them, strange things happened. They knew it was going to be an awkward and strange situation if he organized it!

Interview with Miles by Bockris,
New York, 2007

***

BOCKRIS: Dylan Thomas died here after drinking 28 whiskies.

WARHOL: He was at the White Horse. He didn't die here.

BOCKRIS: Did you ever see Dylan Thomas?

WARHOL: Yeah. At the Gotham Book Mart.

BOCKRIS: Was he real fat?

WARHOL: No.

BOCKRIS: Did he look cool?

WARHOL: Yeah. He had a shirt on. [Andy is strangely serious.] He was always signing books at the Gotham Book Mart.

BOCKRIS: Did you think he was great or…?

WARHOL: No, he was great.

BOCKRIS: I'm scared of that guy in the closet! [Howard Brookner's soundman]

WARHOL: *Oh!* [Andy looks around for a minute at the cupboard where Jim Jarmusch is crouched down just behind his chair and laughs nervously.]

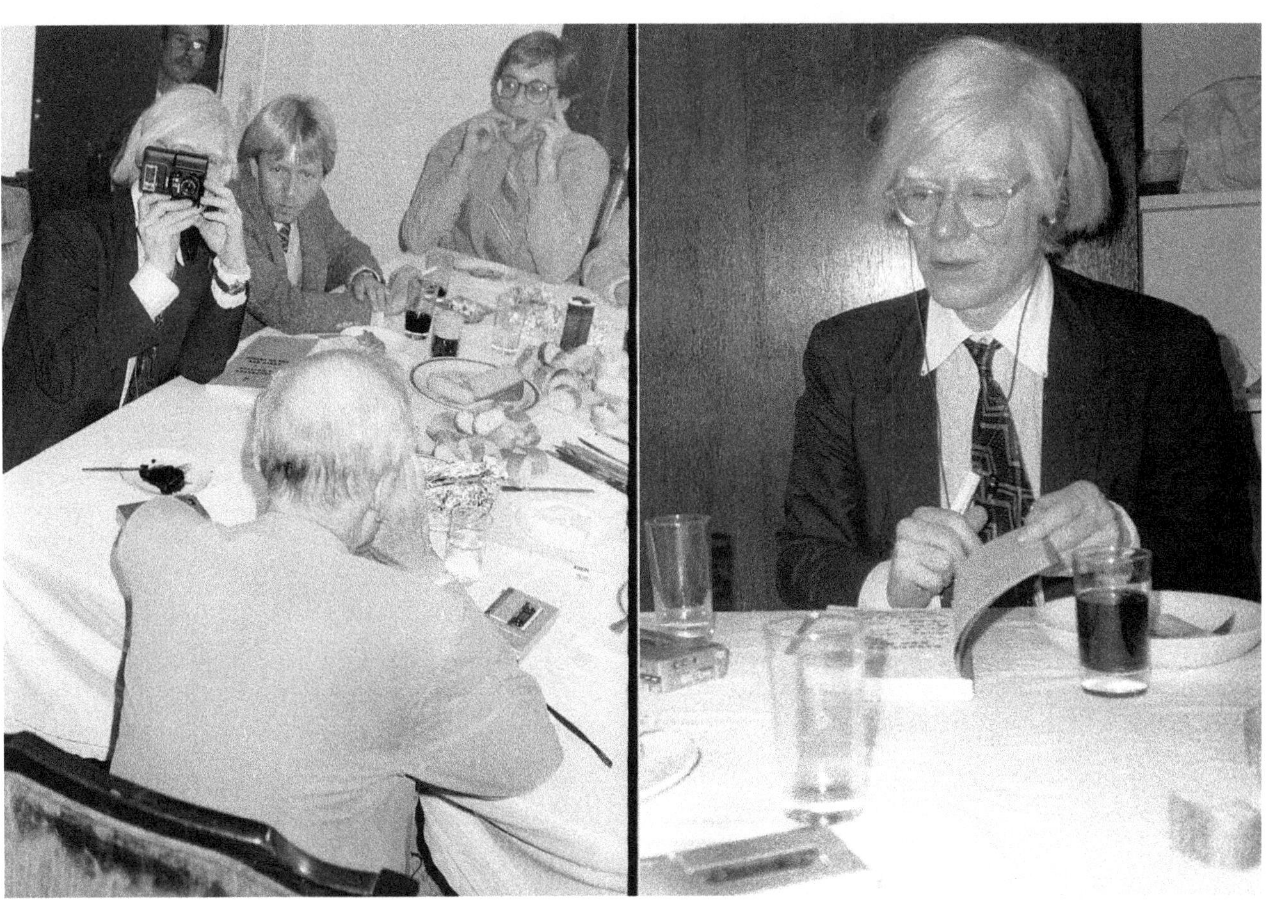

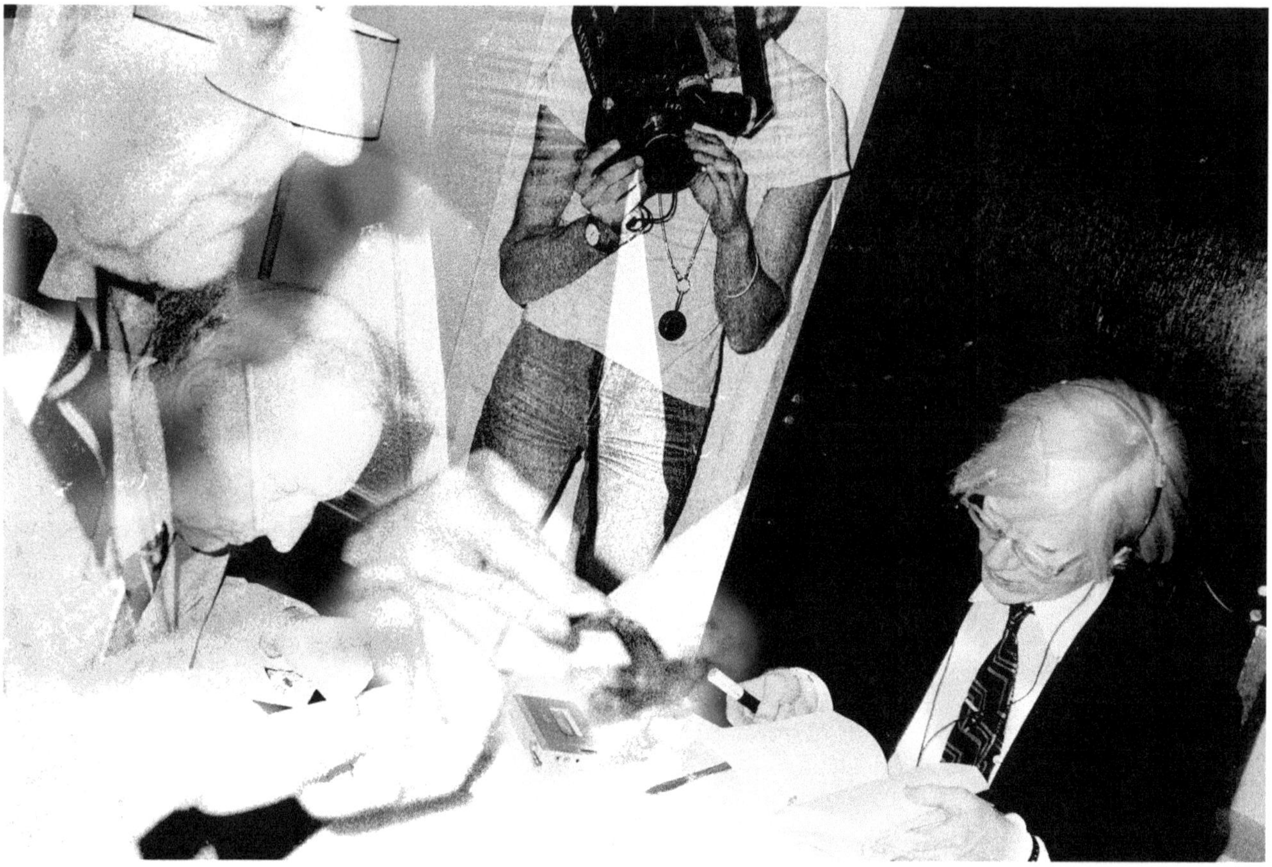

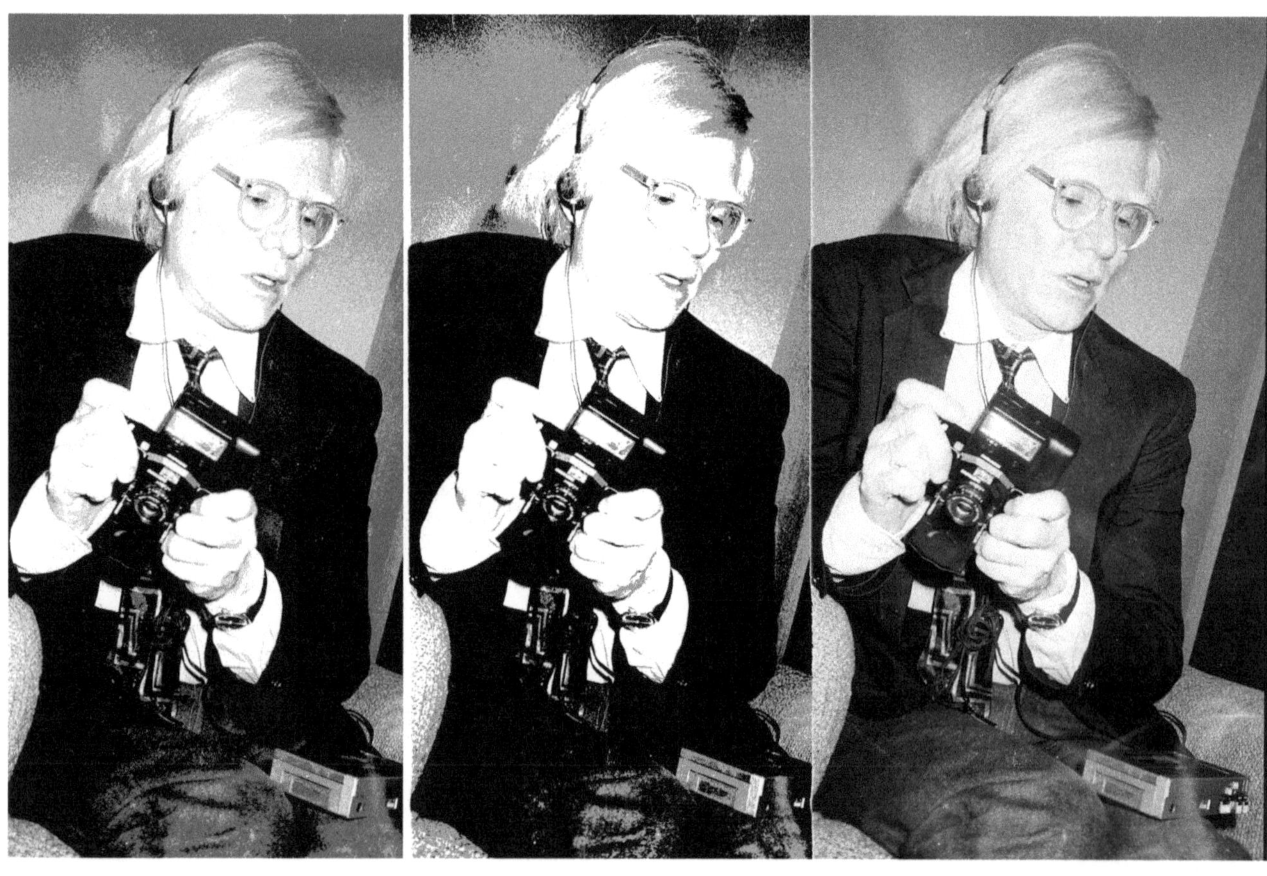

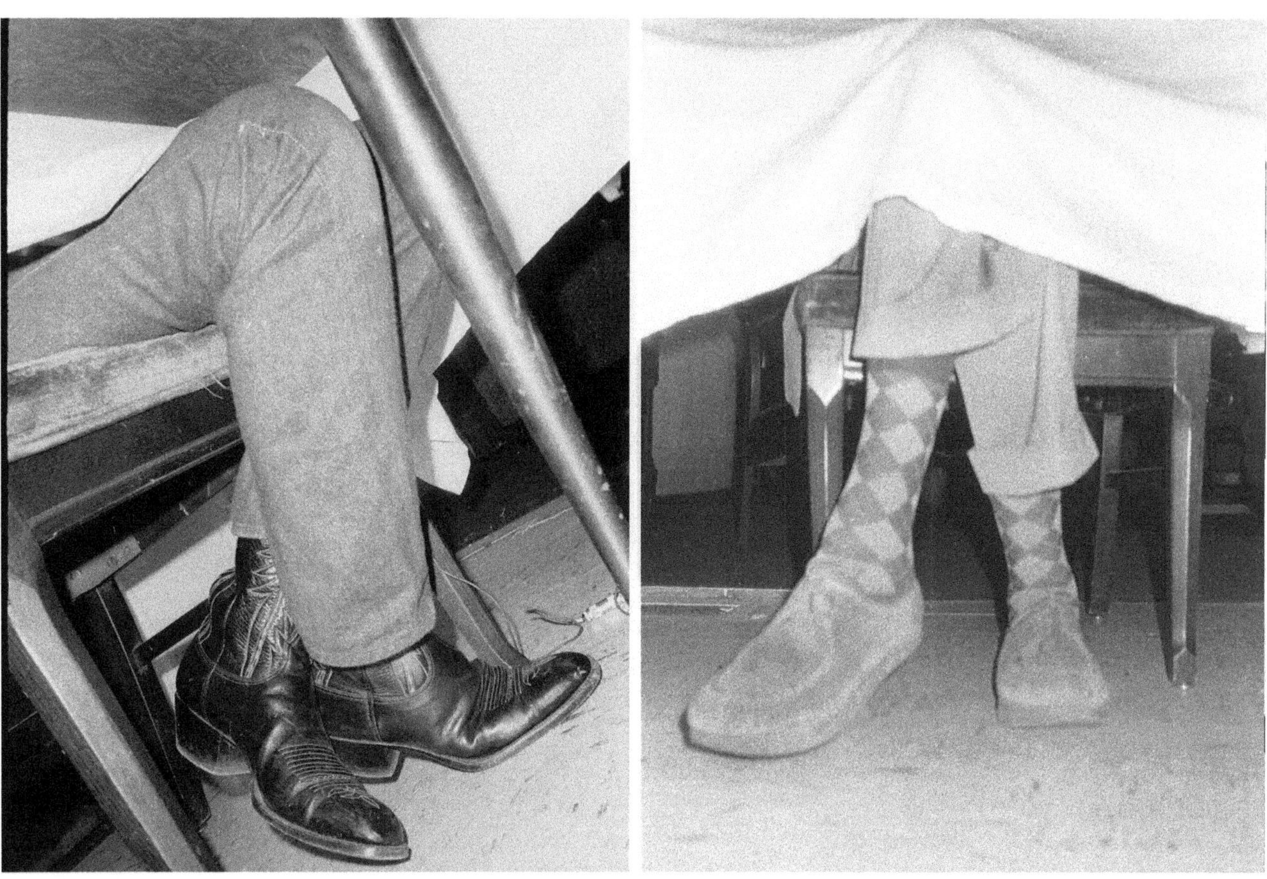

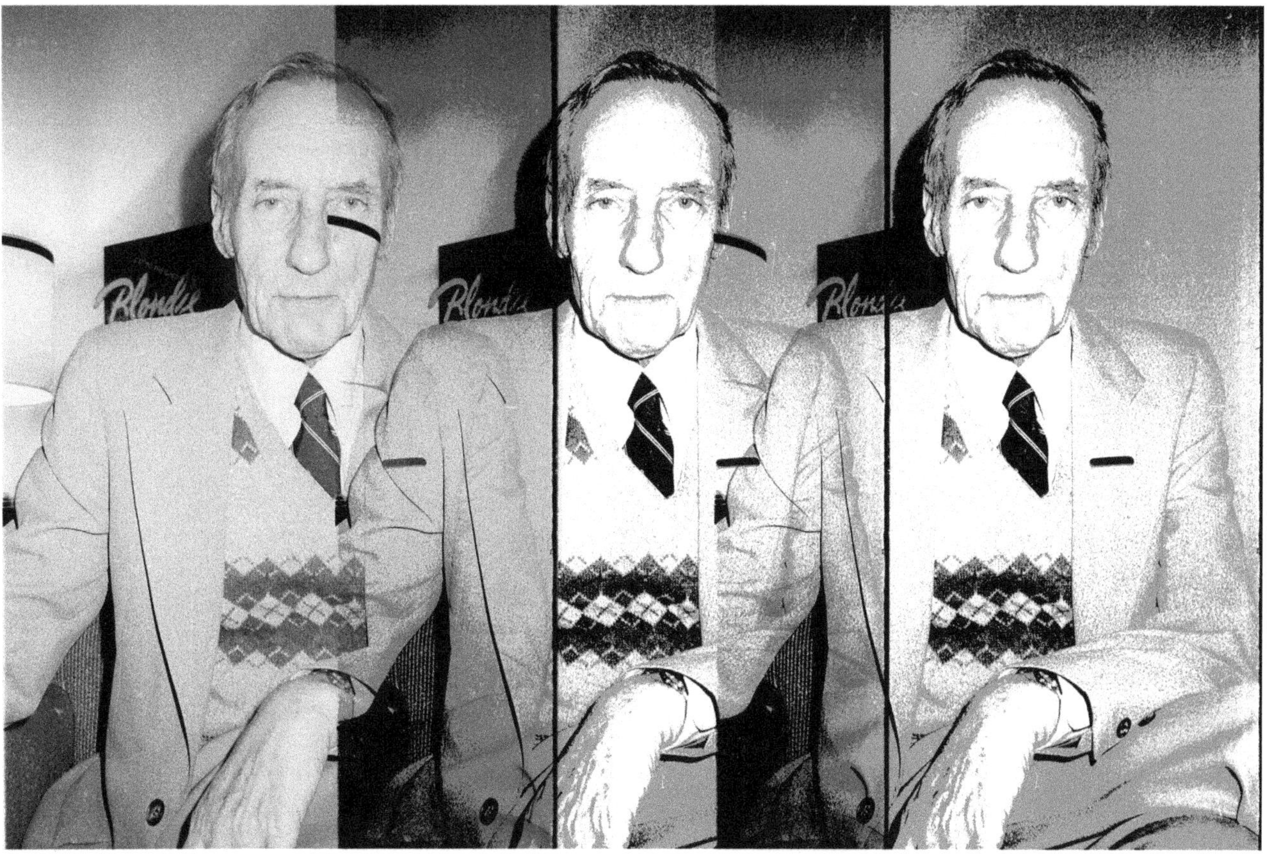

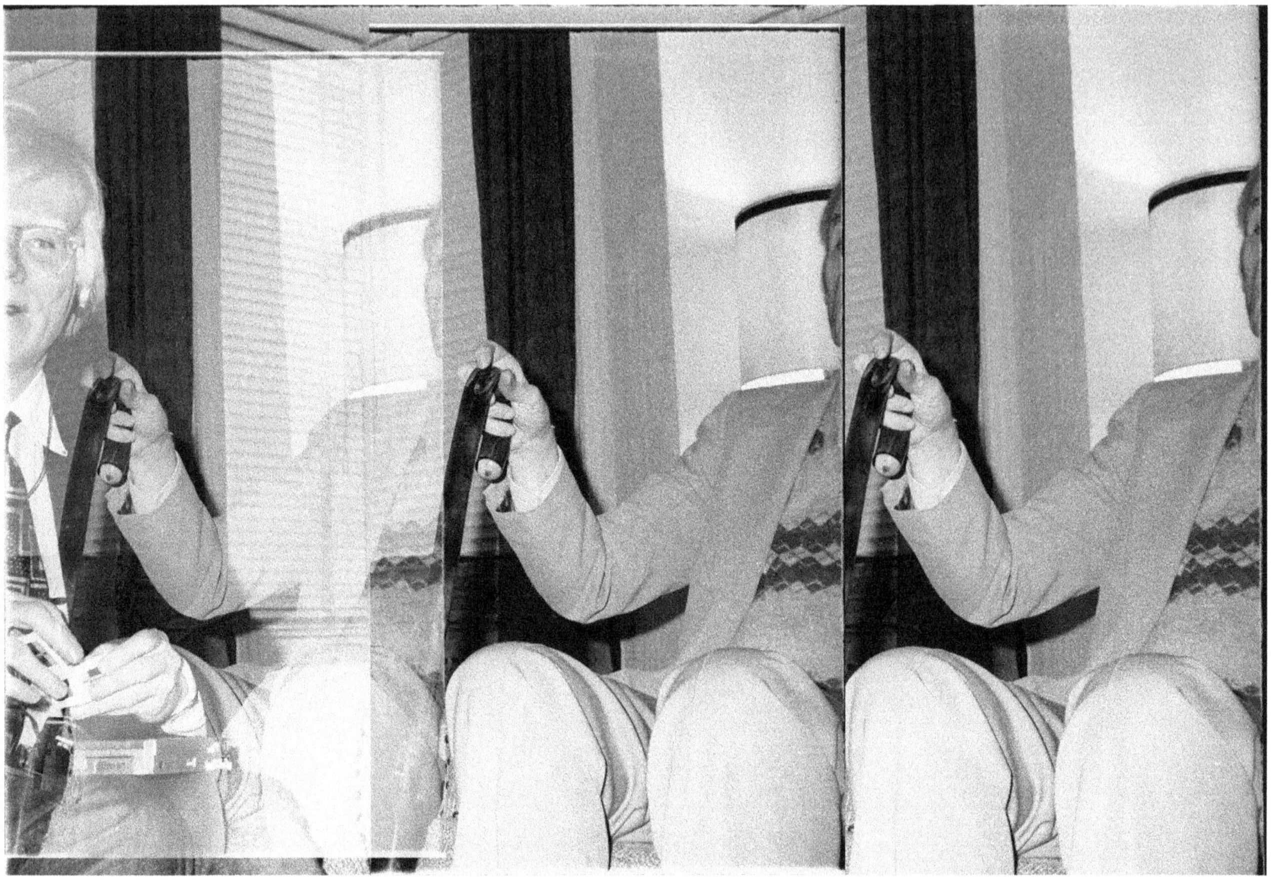

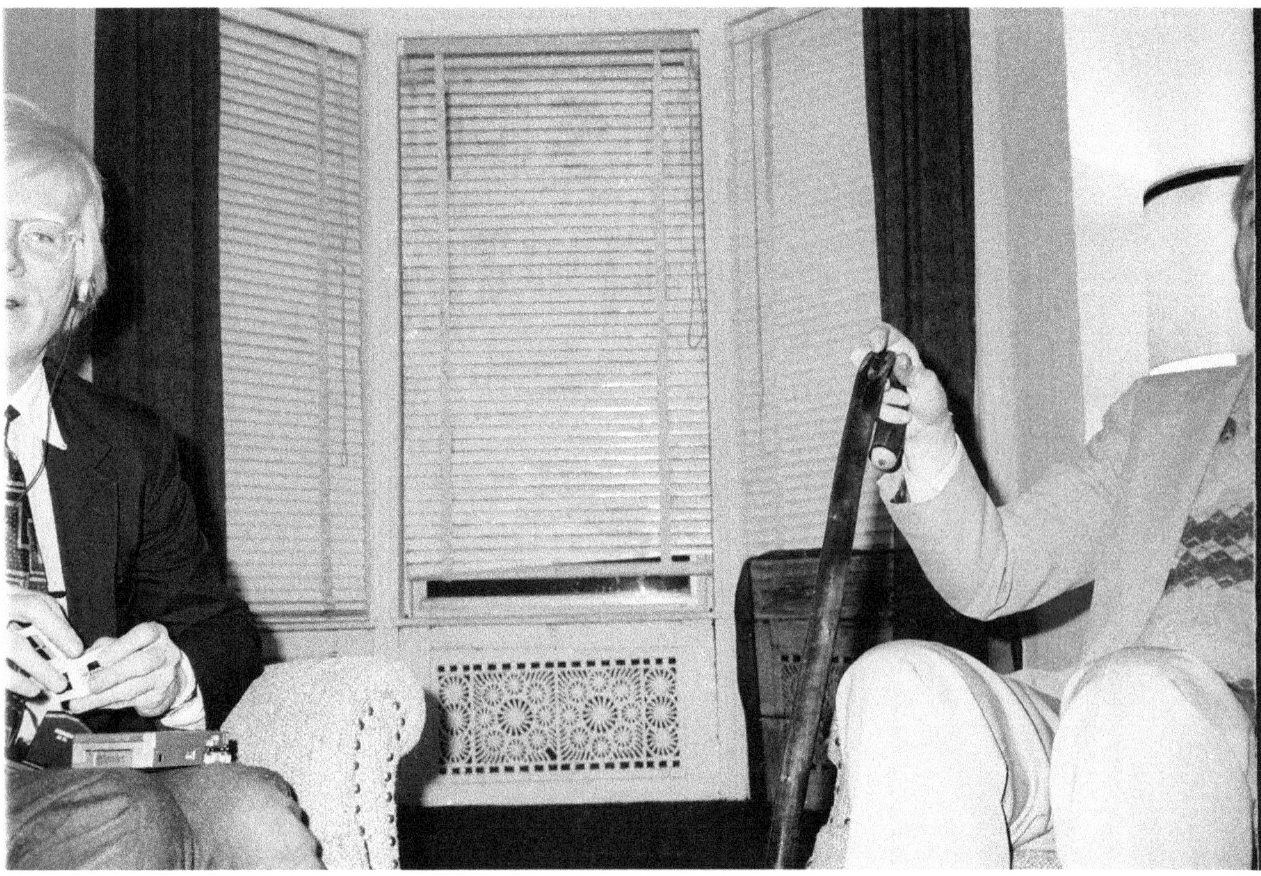

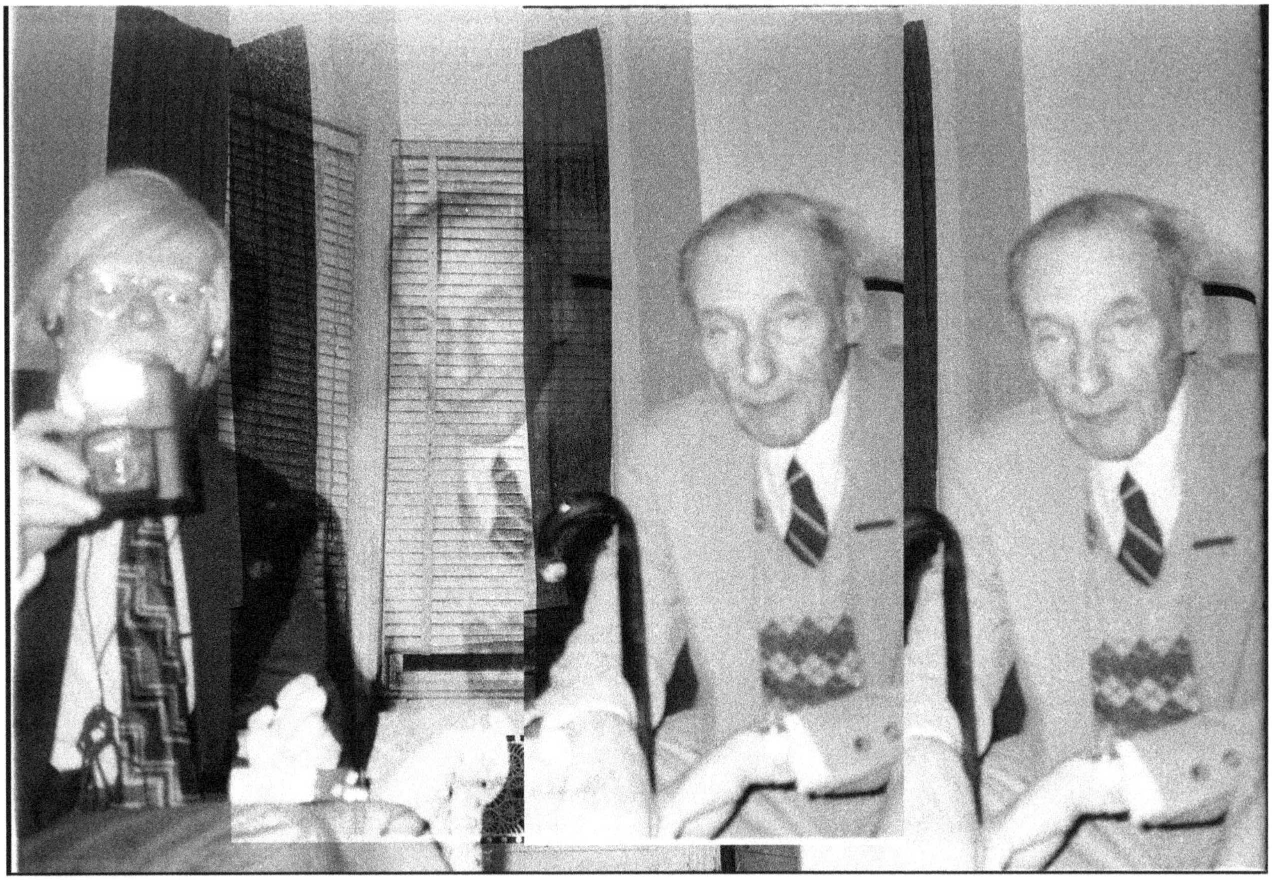

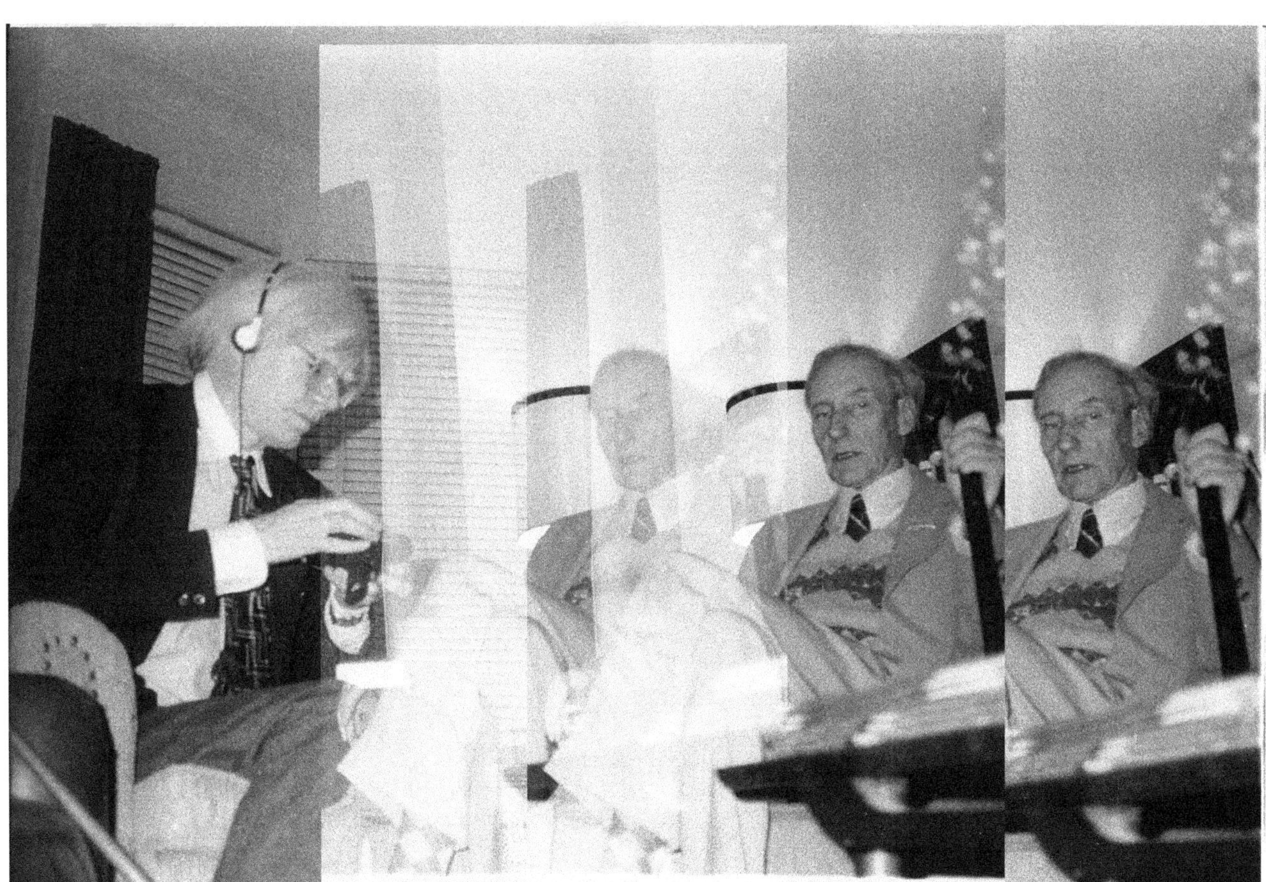

BOCKRIS: Well, you know Bill wants to move. He's planning to move to Kansas now. He's got his eyes on a house in Kansas which he's thinking about. I saw a picture and it really is beautiful: a big, old, beautiful Victorian house for $29,000.

WARHOL: You think it's a good idea?

BOCKRIS: Do I think it's a good idea?

WARHOL: Yes.

BOCKRIS: Well, it's a really beautiful neighborhood… Well, I'm just wondering out loud.

GRAUERHOLZ: Whether it is a good idea?

BOCKRIS: I think it's a good idea, very sound, because, um, it's a very good buy and the prices undoubtedly will be up there.

WARHOL: What, Kansas City? Kansas City, Missouri or Kansas City, Kansas?

GRAUERHOLZ: Lawrence, Kansas. The University of Kansas. It's sort of like an oasis.

BURROUGHS: It's quite close to the border between…

About fifteen minutes later, Andy, who was the most "alone" painter, suddenly blurted out in the voice of a very hurt little boy, "You're not going to go off to Kansas, are you? I'm going to miss you if you go off to Kansas."

BURROUGHS: Well, eeeuurummm well… I'll always be here and there.

WARHOL: Bill looks so young, God.

BOCKRIS: Bill's taste is based on some other time. He has the boarding schoolboy look and sensibility. Look at those shoes.

WARHOL: They're comfortable.

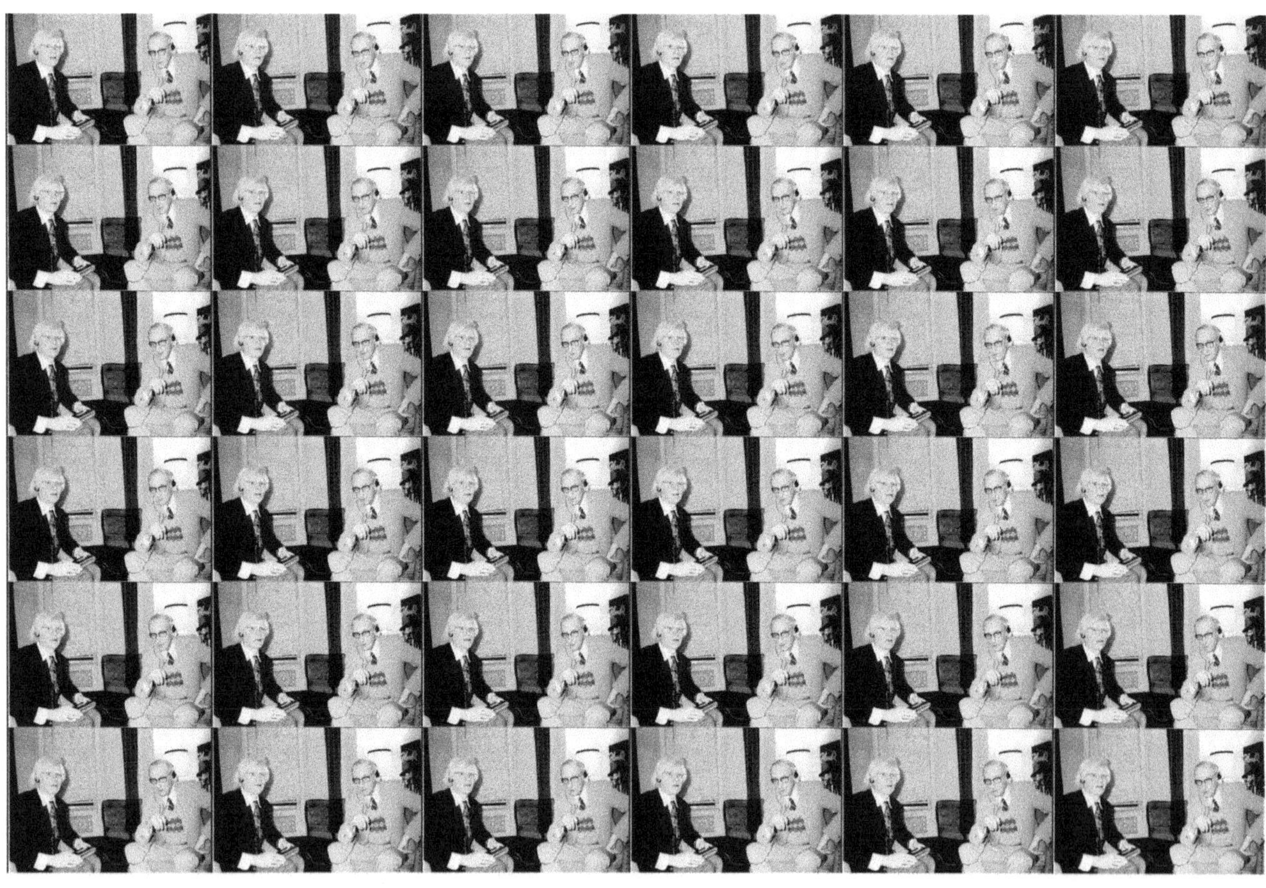

BURROUGHS: Oh, they're very comfortable. They're Earth shoes, my dear!

BOCKRIS: Did you used to wear cowboy boots, Bill?

WARHOL: He wears boxers, right? Colorful boxers. Do your boxers match? Are they lime green?

BURROUGHS: My boxers are beige.

WARHOL: *Beeeiiigge*!!! *Beige*, oh, well that's good. Look at the socks, God!

BOCKRIS: He always has those kind of socks!

WARHOL: They match the tie!

BOCKRIS: That's that whole tie-sock-handkerchief set you can buy at Klein's on Union Square.

BURROUGHS: I doubt it. I've had them for three years. They're indestructible, but I never find the like of them again.

WARHOL: Oh, really.

BURROUGHS: Then the whole breed disappeared.

WARHOL: The best. Isn't Bill the best? He's always worn a tie since I've known him.

BOCKRIS: We went on the set of *Heart Beat* in LA and had lunch with Sissy Spacek and Nick Nolte. Sissy came up to William and she said, "I'm Carolyn Cassady, Neal Cassady's wife." Then we had lunch with her and she was really exciting.

WARHOL: Oh yeah, she told me she had a walk-on in *Women in Revolt*.

BURROUGHS: Yeah, she was just like a high school teacher type, exactly.

WARHOL: [gasping] The youngest little cute girl. She looked great in the movie. She looked old. I mean, I think she's a great actress. If you ever see her, she's the littlest. I mean she's like him [Tiny

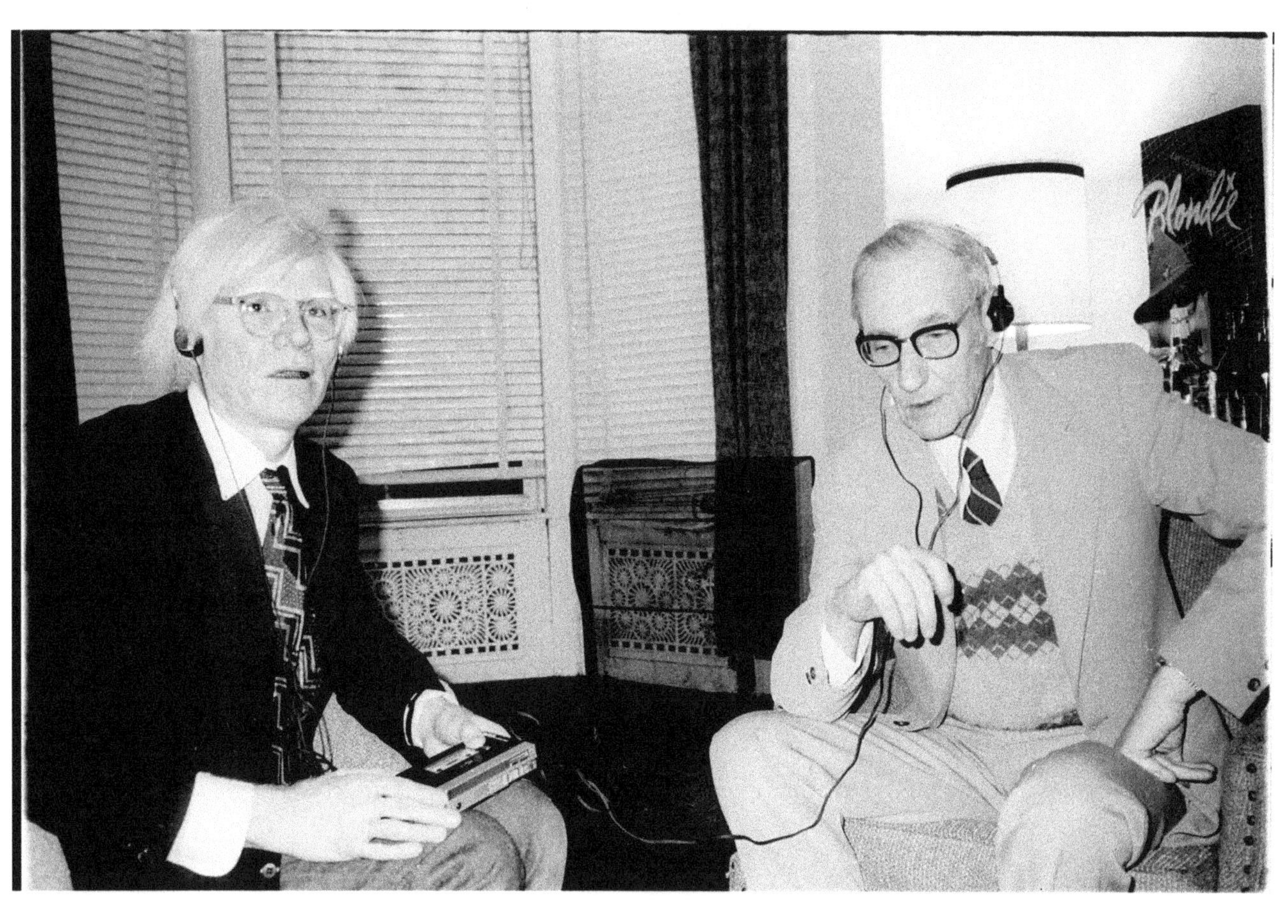

Rupert, Andy's painting assistant] with blonde hair. I didn't even know it was her.

BOCKRIS: I'm glad you liked the film because everybody hated it.

BURROUGHS: No one liked it. Everyone hated it, hated it.

WARHOL: They should have gotten Allen Ginsberg in there. I wished they used his name.

BURROUGHS: That was great, that was fantastic, the rabbit was just, yeah.

MILES: Cake or cheese next?

BURROUGHS: Cake cake cake cake cake cake.

WARHOL: Cake.

BURROUGHS: Ooohhh, that was good.

BOCKRIS: What was?

BURROUGHS: The coffee.

MILES: Victor knows how to do coffee.

GRAUERHOLZ: He's the only one in the room who doesn't!

WARHOL: There should be a kind of machine as soon as the camera starts, you start talking.

BURROUGHS: I think so.

BOCKRIS: Right. With the movie *Cocaine Cowboys,* it was really easy with that script.

WARHOL: Have you seen Tom Sullivan [the star of *Cocaine Cowboys*]?

BOCKRIS: No, but I heard he signed himself into the mental hospital for legal reasons. He felt it was safer to be in the mental hospital because the police were closing in on him. The last time I saw him, he was with his wife Winnie, but then she really did throw him out.

WARHOL: [delighting in some dirt] Nooaaaaw!

BOCKRIS: Once an old lady jumped out

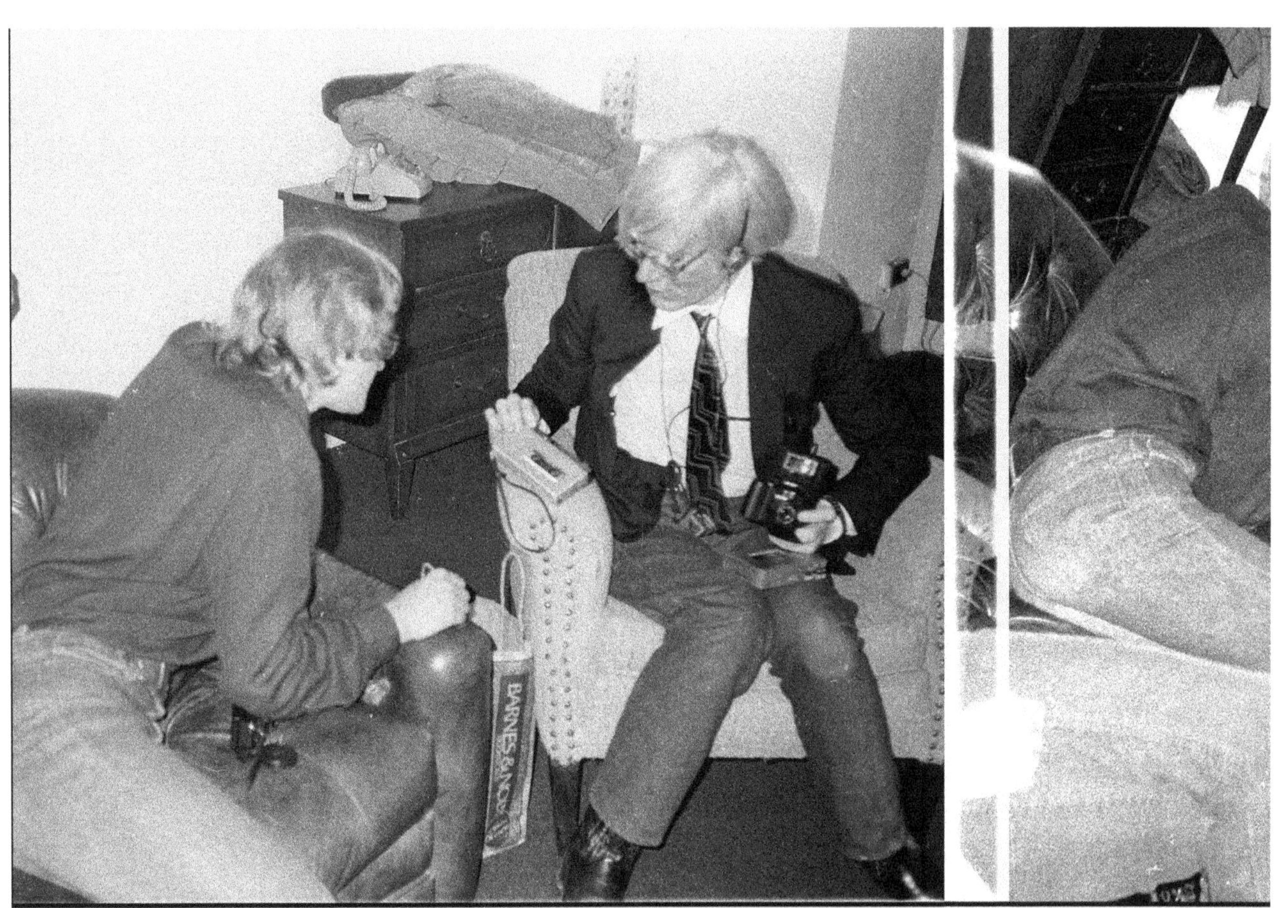

of the window and landed right next to me.

WARHOL: [excited] Really? You mean she jumped out of the window?

BOCKRIS: My best friend pulled me out of the way; otherwise, her orthopedic shoes would have hit me right on the head.

BURROUGHS: Where was she jumping from?

WARHOL: When was this?

BOCKRIS: 47th and Pine in Philadelphia. I heard the splat and then the croaking of the last breath. We were walking along…

BURROUGHS: Tell me tell me tell me.

BOCKRIS: And Johnny beside me says, "Look out Vic!" He pulls me aside and I looked up and thought somebody had thrown their laundry off the balcony by mistake, a bundle of laundry, and I looked up and suddenly *Splat!* And this horrible

kind of death rattle, eeeuuurrghhh!

WARHOL: Is anybody else coming besides Henry?

BOCKRIS: No Lou. Lou's not coming… Raymond called and said…

WARHOL: Maybe we should have asked if we could go up there?

BURROUGHS: Oh well, if you wanna go out, I'm going home.

BOCKRIS: When you made *Chelsea Girls,* did you really make it in the Chelsea Hotel?

WARHOL: Oh uuuuhhhh we made it well no we made it yeah we made it here I think in a couple of different rooms running back and forth.

BOCKRIS: Did you ever stay at the Chelsea?

WARHOL: Overnight. The best thing was when Brigid [Polk, star of *Chelsea Girls*] picked up the phone and they thought

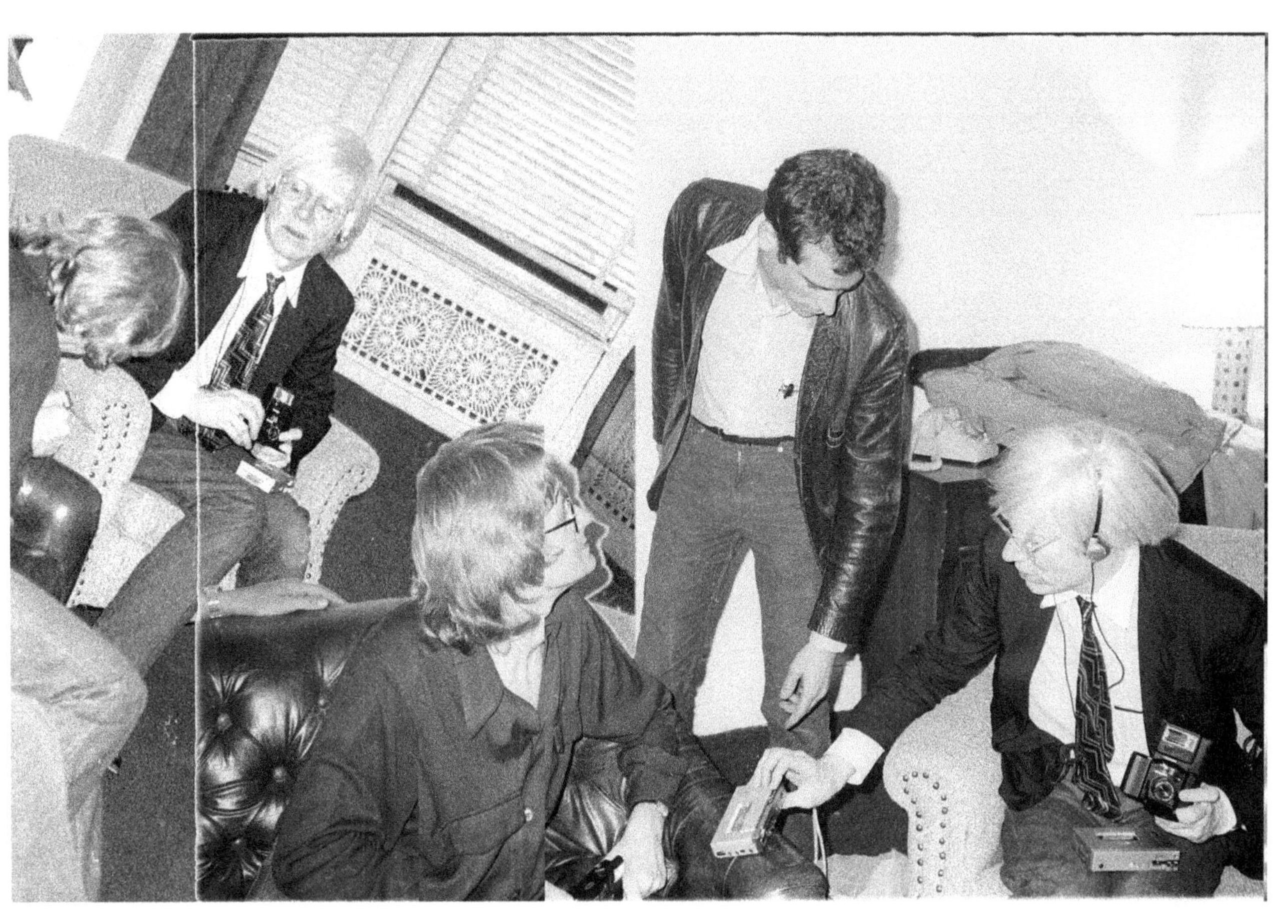

she was actually ordering up all the drugs and making a killing and stuff and they did send the police and she was really using…

BOCKRIS: You mean she had a needle in her ass?

WARHOL: No, she was making it up on the phone for anybody she'd, she'd just do it for anybody even without, she'd call up on the phone and just make it up you know "send over 80 million of these and some of that" and the police came in and they didn't find anything. I'd like to hear that story about the laundry falling out of the window.

BOCKRIS: So, I screamed out, "Oh My God, let's get out of here!" and we went and told Johnny's mother, "There's a dead lady outside…" but she had a headache and didn't believe us. The other thing was she landed on the pavement with a big splat!

BURROUGHS: Did she bounce?

BOCKRIS: No. Yes yes yes now you ask the question, she did but about two inches or something.

WARHOL: But you didn't know what it was?

BOCKRIS: Exactly. I was right next to her, right next to it like one foot away. I looked at her for about thirty seconds frozen and just ran off. She was 65. Her husband had died and she couldn't pay the bills. These were fairly expensive apartments.

WARHOL: You mean you lived in a good neighborhood?

BOCKRIS: Briefly.

WARHOL: Oh really. What are you trying to say? Aaaaaahhh it's all coming out now, family secrets.

BURROUGHS: Absolutely.

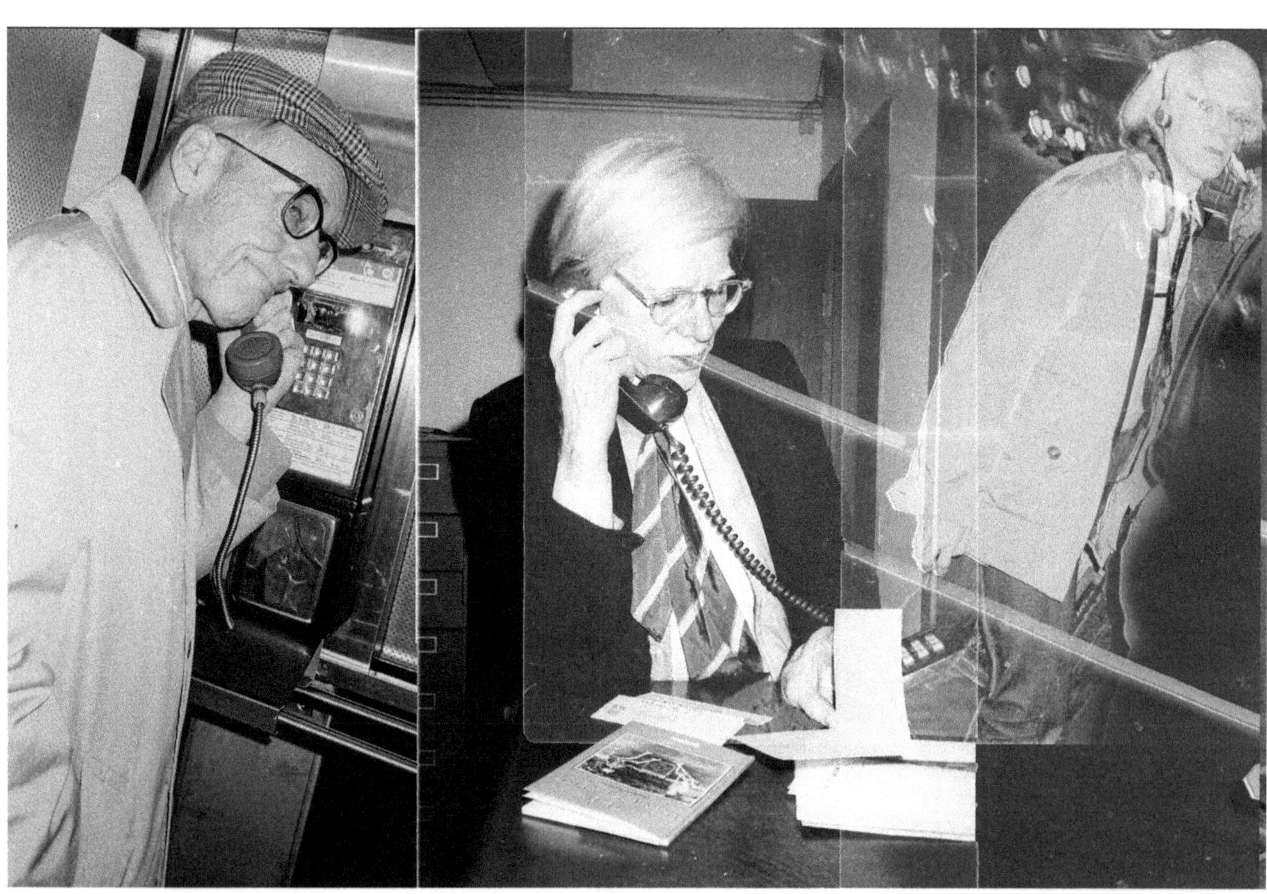

BOCKRIS: Bill doesn't hardly know me at all.

WARHOL: Oh, I know.

BOCKRIS: He doesn't even know who I am when I call sometimes.

WARHOL: Oh sure.

BOCKRIS: Did you ever see the movie Andy made with Kerouac in it?

WARHOL: God, where did you get this cake?

MILES: At the [unintelligible].

BOCKRIS: You shot it from underneath or behind? Kerouac, Ginsberg and Corso.

WARHOL: No, uh, we have it somewhere. I don't know where it is. It's part of *Couch.* Anybody who sat on the couch we photographed. From the side huh huh huh.

BURROUGHS: I mean you've got the stationary camera and what happened? Who said what happens in front of the camera is more interesting than any movement of the camera? [Andy Warhol said it.]

WARHOL: Oh.

BURROUGHS: Give me a bigger piece of cake, some sort of instrument. It doesn't have to be a fork even a knife will do.

BOCKRIS: Bill, do you think Reagan is going to win the election?

BURROUGHS: I have no idea. I just hope that Carter wins. But I don't know. You know Reagan would be very frightening, tripping out, being paranoid. *"This is the end, the end!"* everybody will say.

Walking in the Street to Get a Cab

BOCKRIS: Do you want to get a cab

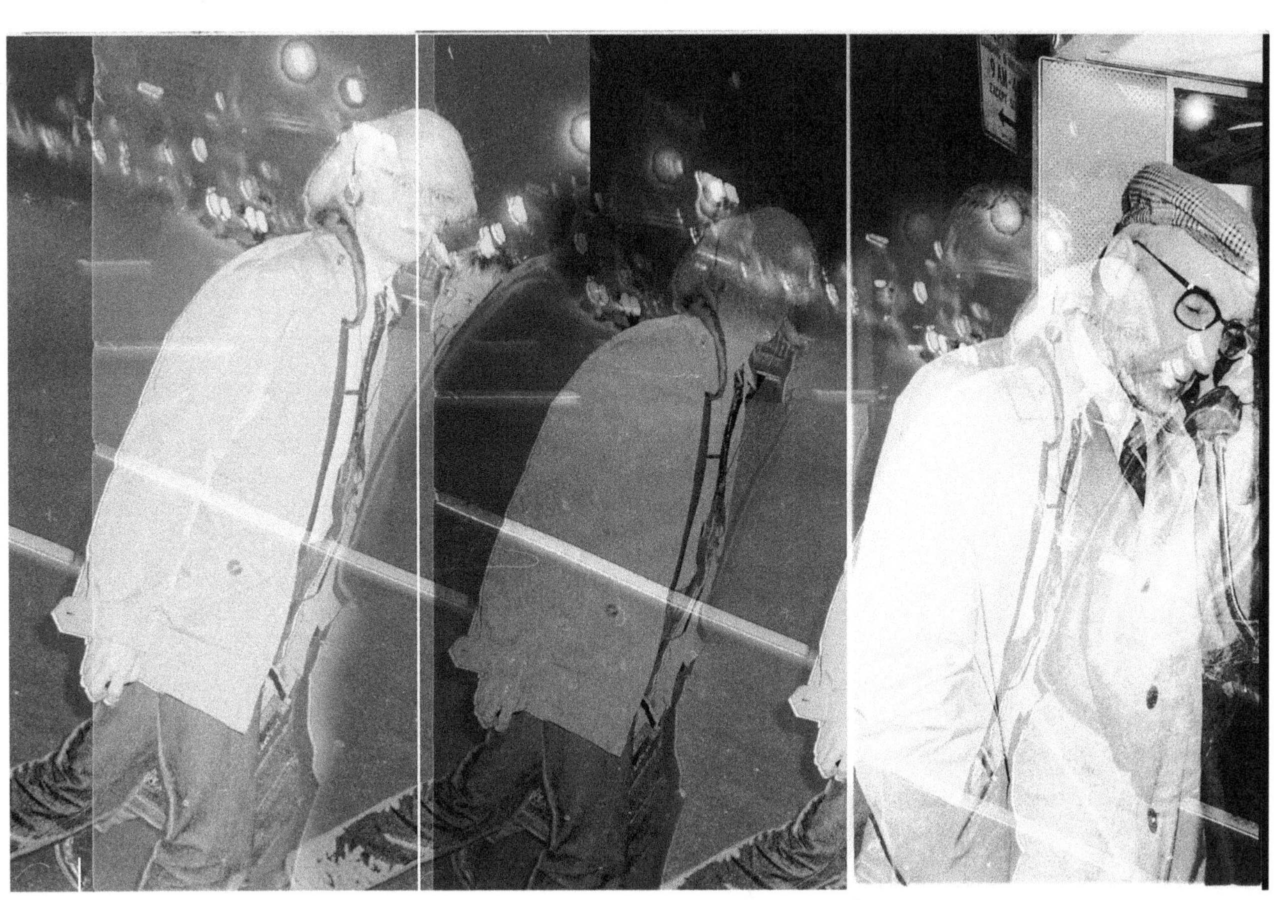

together, Andy? Do you want to take Bill home?

WARHOL: I'm not going to sign this release. I mean, they don't need a release at all.

BOCKRIS: Oh, I know it's so stupid… Bill, do you want to say goodbye to Andy before he leaves?

BURROUGHS: OK, Victor. OK.

BOCKRIS: So, you've got it, right?

William Burroughs. The Chelsea program was also attended by Nico and all kinds of people. She took out her harmonium and began to sing: *"Deutschland, Deutschland über alles"* over the images. It was a great program, really.

Bockris: I'm really hungry, I'm craving mustard and rabbit.

Miles: Eat a cookie… Look!

Bockris: I already had a cookie. I want rabbit or I will die.

Interview with Miles by Bockris,

New York, 2007

David Schmidlapp's Apartment, Lower East Side, New York, 2007

Bockris: I think these three meetings with Andy and Bill were actually very different from each other. This is a movie of the movie of the movie of Andy Warhol and William Burroughs meeting. [singing] *"Getting to know you, getting to know all about you. Getting to like you, getting to think you like me."* That's what it was. It was quite an event. People knew what we were doing. I mean, they're two lovely guys. They were the loveliest guys I've ever met (except for you, Miles). Andy Warhol and William Burroughs. So, I think there was a real mutual recognition in a way.

Miles: Burroughs is the only person to appear twice in the Chelsea Hotel documentary. The first time he is talking to Andy Warhol and the second time he is talking to Francis Bacon. It is very interesting not only that he appears twice, but that on both occasions he appears talking to the most famous painter in the United States in the world and the most famous painter in the United Kingdom in the world. It adds a different nuance to

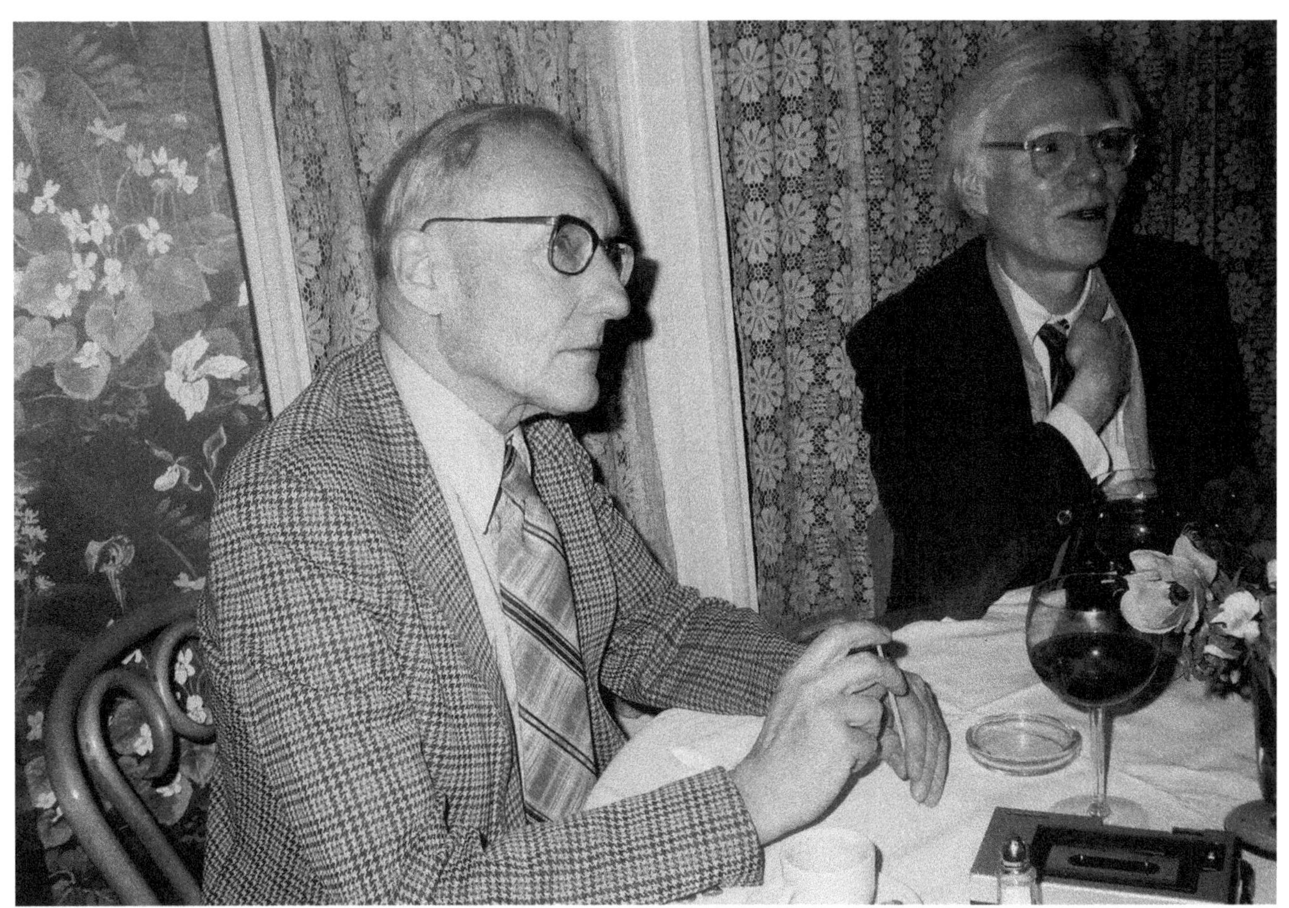

CHAPTER EIGHT
THE BURROUGHS-WARHOL
FILM FILE

by Jed Birmingham

I just finished reading a catalogue raisonné of Andy Warhol's Screen Tests. For those who do not know, Warhol shot a series of portrait films from 1964 to 1966, one of the most long-term and ambitious projects in his career as a filmmaker. Each test was about four minutes long, roughly the duration of a hundred feet of film. Warhol would place his subject in front of a camera (a 16mm Bolex to start) with instruction to face the camera until the film stopped. In many cases, Warhol would walk away from the subject as the film was shooting.

Warhol directed over 400 screen tests, and they serve as a remarkable archive of the personalities of the New York art scene and the Factory. Artists, art dealers, collectors, critics and patrons are well represented, as are the celebrities of the Factory's Studio System: Edie Sedgwick, Mario Montez, Ivy Nicholson, Baby Jane Holzer, Ultraviolet, and Taylor

Mead. Poets find a place in the pantheon, particularly poets associated with the New York School. Or should I say the Tulsa School? John Ashbery sat for a screen test representing the first-generation New Yorkers, and he labeled Ted Berrigan, Ron Padgett, Joe Brainard, and Dick Gallup "the Tulsa School." Berrigan, Padgett, and Brainard all sat for screen tests.

The Beats are represented in the form of Allen Ginsberg and Peter Orlovsky. Both poets sat on December 4, 1966. These were some of the last screen tests taken in the entire series. In an exhibit at the Corcoran Gallery dedicated to Warhol, I saw a handful of screen tests. Ginsberg's was one of them. Like many subjects, Ginsberg chooses to sit as still as possible and aggressively out-stare the camera. I also saw Ashbery's test. He, too, aggressively confronts the camera, scowling for much of the test. In interviews, Ashbery admitted to being intimidated by the process. Ginsberg and Orlovsky appeared in another Warhol film, along with Jack Kerouac and Gregory Corso, two years earlier. The film was *Couch*. It has an interesting backstory.

William Burroughs never sat for a screen test. Given the hype and excitement that surrounded Burroughs when he was in New York City in 1964/1965, this is somewhat surprising. At the time, Burroughs was an underground celebrity, a perfect subject for a screen test. Yet Burroughs and Warhol did not hit it off in the 1960s. Panna Grady, a rich heiress and a groupie of underground poets and writers, took Burroughs to meet Warhol for dinner. They went to a Chinese restaurant, where Burroughs was offended by the manners of those in Warhol's entourage and walked out.

The personalities of the two men were quite different, which must have been obvious when they met. Warhol cultivated a camp and effeminate gay persona that was the polar opposite of Burroughs' gun-toting machismo. Burroughs' letters of the 1950s are filled with his dislike for swishes, so coming face-to-face with Warhol must have aroused some level of distaste. Creatively, however, the two had much in common. Before their ill-fated dinner, Warhol arrived at Burroughs' loft with a bag of tape-recording equipment. Surely this piqued Burroughs' interest because he asked Warhol to leave the recorders at the loft.

I am fascinated by Warhol during the Factory years, and it is an interesting "what if" to me to wonder what a collaboration between Burroughs and Warhol would have been like. How would Burroughs have reacted to a screen test? If anybody could have outstared a Bolex, it would have been him. I like to think that the camera would blink, tear up, or break down under the strain of Burroughs' impassive, sullen gaze. Perhaps he would not even register on the film at all. In Mexico City, Peru, Panama, and Tangier, Burroughs stalked back alleys anonymously, melting into the shadows without leaving a trace on his surroundings. The banker's suit and the grey hat were the uniform of the 1950s Everyman. Or maybe a Nobody. Not for nothing did Burroughs' ability to blend in and disappear earn him the name "El Hombre Invisible."

Ironically, Burroughs' nondescript clothes became iconic by the 1970s. Immediately recognizable, precisely because he was invisible. The banker's clothes disguised a revolutionary: a wolf in sheep's clothing. When Burroughs returned to New York City from 1974 to 1981, Warhol was still holding court, although the Factory gave way to Studio 54. The screen tests were replaced by celebrity portraits painted for a sizable fee. Interestingly,

it was during this period—when Burroughs truly broke into mainstream consciousness—
that the two men would connect. When Burroughs lived in New York City at the Bunker,
he and Warhol met again for dinner, and the results were much more cordial than in 1965.
Victor Bockris taped several of their conversations and published them in *With Willam
Burroughs: At the Bunker*. This title was a Richard Seaver[1] book that was distributed by
Grove Press in 1981. Warhol took several Polaroids of Burroughs in preparation for a
proposed portrait, but it never came off. Burroughs never ponied up the requisite cash.
Yet the attempt was made. Even more than in 1965, Burroughs was a celebrity. Burroughs
appeared on Saturday Night Live, was the Godfather of Punk, was profiled in *People*. Such
flash and recognition captivated Warhol. The pinnacle of this type of attention would be
the Nike ad in 1994 that capitalized on Burroughs' iconic status in the realm of, not Punk,
but Cyber-Punk.

Despite the coldness of their first meeting, Burroughs and Warhol briefly bonded in
Burroughs' loft over the tape recorder. This machine proved central to the creative work
and philosophies of both artists in the 1960s. Burroughs: "I am a recording instrument."
Warhol: "I want to be a machine." Burroughs utilized the tape recorder from the late 1950s
on. In his essay "The Invisible Generation," Burroughs proclaims such technology as an
agent for revolutionary change. Warhol relied on the tape recorder for most of his literary
projects. *a, A Novel* is at its simplest a transcription of Warhol star Ondine talking about
the events of his day. Tape transcriptions made up the bulk of *Popism* and *The Philosophy of
Andy Warhol* as well. Ideally, Warhol sought to just let the tape run and present verbatim
transcriptions. There would be no stopping or re-starting of the tape, no edits, no cuts. On
the other hand, Burroughs aggressively manipulated the tape. He inched it backwards and
forwards, recording and re-recording. He cut and spliced the tape. The resulting transcripts
were heavily revised and altered. These two creative icons are on the opposite ends of the
spectrum concerning the process of editing. Yet the goal is the same: a dissolving of the
control of the artist, a striving for the impersonal.

The major difference between the films of Warhol and Burroughs is, again, the cut.
Burroughs' films are full of aural and visual cuts, and Warhol uses the cut sparingly, if at
all. Despite opposing editing techniques, the desire to displace the artist is the same. Of
course, just the reverse occurs. Reading Burroughs' cut-up texts, his personal obsessions
and style shine through. The same occurs with his films. The selection of images and
sounds betray his hand. He cannot help but impose his personal imprint. The same holds
true for Warhol. Within the seemingly very strict parameters of the screen test, extremely
individual, personal performances result. No screen test is exactly the same, even with the
same subject filmed for several different tests. If you doubt this, view the several different
tests taken of Baby Jane Holzer or Edie Sedgwick. Each test has its unique qualities. The
personalities of the sitter show through, as does that of Warhol.

Watching the films of Burroughs and Warhol from a drug perspective, I feel that their
styles could have been reversed. The drug of choice for Warhol and his art was amphetamine,
while Burroughs preferred heroin. One would expect rapid cuts of image and sound from
Warhol, and yet it was Burroughs' cut-up films that reflect the speed freak's sense and

---

1   American translator, editor and publisher, 1926-2009.

sensibility. Conversely, Warhol films like *Sleep* and *Empire* seem to capture the perspective of the junkie on the nod. Burroughs famously wrote in *Naked Lunch* that while on junk he could stare with interest at his shoe for hours. What would Burroughs have thought of a movie like *Empire?* Given his interest in editorial manipulation, Burroughs might have found it boring, preferring instead a movie like *Chelsea Girls* with its split-screen projection. Burroughs' fascination with multiple perspectives hammers home the point that the world he described is largely seen through the lens of withdrawal. The kicking junkie is besieged by sensation. Spontaneous orgasms, crawling flesh, runaway thoughts. Burroughs' art, cinematic and literary, captures and reproduces the experience of withdrawal more than the sensation of the fix. The hardcore addict fails to experience the euphoria of heroin in the same manner as a first-time user. Part of the kick is trying to recapture that initial rush. Burroughs' strong sense of nostalgia stems in part from the longing of the addict for the first fix.

As Warhol was making screen tests in the 1960s, so in a way was Burroughs (along with Brion Gysin, Anthony Balch, and Ian Sommerville). *Towers Open Fire* (1963) opens with a long static shot of Burroughs which mirrors the portraits Warhol would begin creating a year later. In *Guerrilla Conditions,* later to become the basis for *The Cut-Ups* (1966), Burroughs introduced chance and found techniques similar to Warhol's. Barry Miles writes, "*The Cut Ups* was literally that, with four reels of film being cut into twelve-inch lengths and assembled in rotation by a lab technician… No artistic judgment was made, and Balch was not even present." The similarities to the restraints imposed on the screen tests are obvious.

I am more intrigued in considering a film like *Bill and Tony* (1972) as a Burroughsian screen test. The movie consists of the image of Burroughs mouthing Balch's words, and Balch doing likewise to Burroughs' words. Balch and Burroughs experimented with merging images to form a composite person. Burroughs was very interested in such superimpositions. He states, "Anthony Balch and I did an experiment with his face projected onto mine and mine onto his. Now if your face is projected onto somebody else's in color, it looks like the other person. You can't tell the difference; it's a mask of light." He goes on: "Another experiment that Anthony and I did was to take the two faces and alternate them twenty-four frames per second, but it's such a hassle to cut those and replace them, even to put one minute of alternation of twenty-four frames per second on a screen, but it is extraordinary." Burroughs and Gysin also played with such techniques in *The Third Mind* (1977) experiments. The New Reformers photographs, produced in connection with the Colloque de Tanger in 1975, utilized such superimpositions. In 1971, Jan Herman visited Burroughs and Balch at St. Duke Street in London. At this time, the two men were making *Bill and Tony* and performing the experiments Burroughs describes above. Herman took part in these experiments and recorded a session on videotape. The results are available exclusively at RealityStudio.org.

As the video shows, Burroughs introduces montage to the screen test. Montage, collage, assemblage, like the cut-up technique, all center on the cut. In the screen tests, Warhol avoided the edit, the physical cut. The duration of the movie was dictated by the length in feet of the packaged roll of film. No takes, no director yelling cut, no splicing of the film. On the other hand, Burroughs urged a generation to cut up everything. Film, text, and audio tape were all fair game for the scissors. Warhol and Burroughs' editing techniques differed, but their goal of depersonalization (and eventual failure to achieve those goals) were the same.

Both Warhol and Burroughs were well exposed to the world of experimental film from Russian avant-garde film of the 1920s to Surrealist film of the 1930s to the New American Film of the post-WWII era. Warhol was a fixture at the Filmmakers' Co-op and a friend of numerous underground filmmakers like Jonas Mekas, Jack Smith (before their falling out), Willard Maas, and Marie Menken. These filmmakers were subjects for screen tests. Through Gysin and Balch (who distributed European soft-core films), Burroughs would have been exposed to a number of experimental films. I suspect Burroughs and Warhol were well aware of each other's films as well. *Towers Open Fire* was completed in 1963 before the underground film boom of the next year. Much of what became *The Cut-Ups* was filmed around that time. Sections of *The Cut-Ups* were filmed in the Chelsea Hotel in 1965, the year Warhol and Burroughs first met. Given his connection with Mekas and others, Warhol may have heard about Burroughs' film experiments as early as 1963. Interestingly, despite Burroughs' absence from Warhol's films, particularly the Screen Tests, they are Burroughsian in spirit (alternatively Burroughs' films are Warholian) as both men had similar obsessions and interests. Burroughs' films of the mid-1960s have images of young men in bed, of static portraits, of artwork being created in Factory-type fashion.

In fact, in 1968 a young man appeared at the Factory introducing himself as Julian Burroughs, the son of William Burroughs. The man was in fact Andrew Dungan, and his act was a con along the lines of that portrayed in *Six Degrees of Separation*. Dungan read up on Burroughs and his actual son, Billy, in the mainstream and underground media. Either Warhol was fooled or he went along with the deception. The idea of a doppelganger of this type would have appealed to Warhol. He played such tricks himself. Most famously, Edie Sedgwick dyed her hair silver and accompanied Warhol to parties and openings as a female version of Warhol. Less well-known but more on point here, Warhol sent Alan Midgette (who sat for a screen test) on a speaking tour of the United States posing as Warhol himself in October 1967 around the time of the Julian Burroughs hoax. Quite possibly, the hoax perpetrated on the Factory inspired Warhol to try it himself, although forgery and impersonation were already staples of the Factory aesthetic. In any case, Warhol cast Dungan / Julian in *Lonesome Cowboys* and *Nude Restaurant*. So indirectly Burroughs was a Warhol superstar. Burroughs may never have set foot in the Factory but his presence was felt there and bled into Warhol's films of the period. Similarly in the screen-test feel of *Bill and Tony*, Warhol proves to be a ghost in the machine in Burroughs' films.

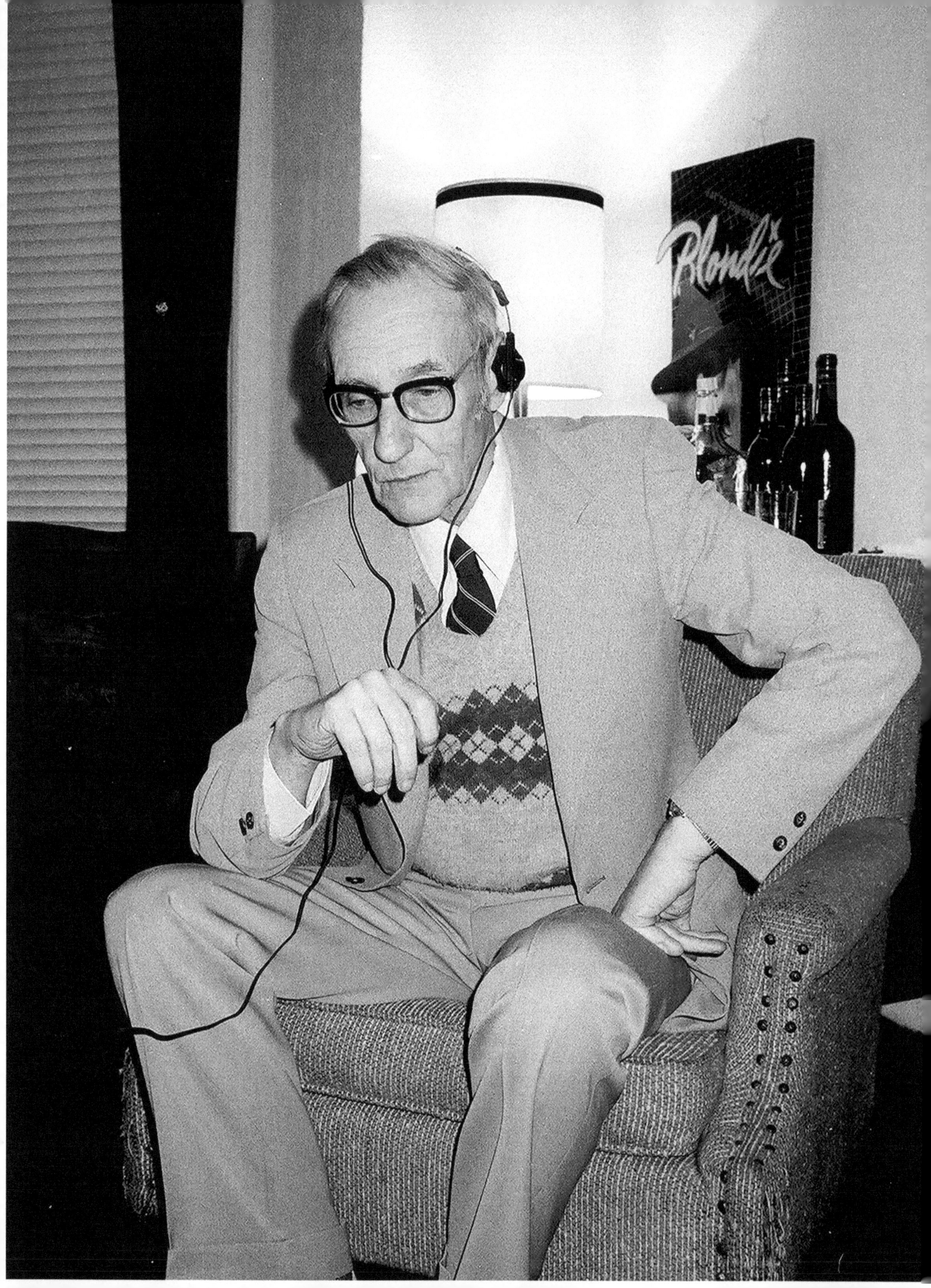
Blondie

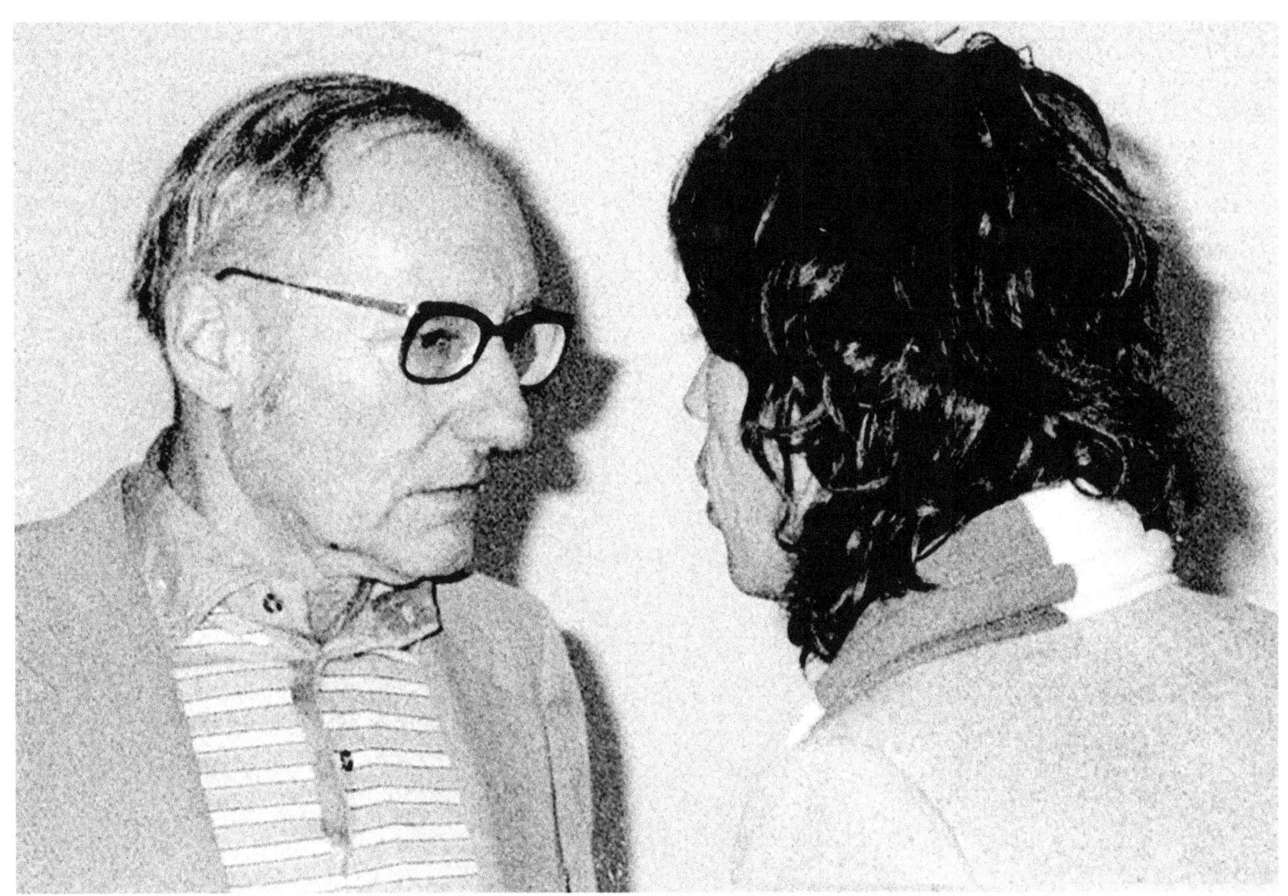

CHAPTER NINE
BURROUGHS–WARHOL: THE
AFTERMATH

Shadows creep through these conversations. Underneath each shadow another shadow trembles. They are as meaningful as cigarette smoke floating through the fake window of a movie set, and yet some fascination always pulls me back inside them. They are like conversations between ghosts. On the surface of their shared histories, Burroughs and Warhol had a staggering amount in common, but it was the hidden connections which hovered between them that give this document another resonance. They were both double agents: bold, strong, courageous men who stood up when no one else would and shattered the establishment. They were both married to their work, tortured by great romantic souls and the necessity to be ultimately alone. By the time I crawled back and forth through the arteries and conduits of their table-talk, I sensed I was stumbling along the margins of a new form. In the tradition of Charles Ludlam's deeply humane *Theatre of the Ridiculous*, I hereby name it *Interview of the Ridiculous*.

Friday, October 31, 1980

Dear Miles,

I'm thinking of putting together a manuscript called *The Burroughs-Warhol Dinners*. Rather along the lines of my early piece on Claude and Mary, *The Last Interview in Black and White*, and making a book out of it. It would be about 100 pages, I guess. There is the first dinner at a restaurant in New York as published in *Blueboy*, then dinner with Jagger at the Bunker, then dinner at the Chelsea Hotel for the BBC Chelsea Hotel documentary. I want to use about thirty photographs, approximately 75 pages of text. I originally thought that Expanded Media Editions would snap up such a book, and they probably would. Udo is always writing asking for something, but then I thought maybe better than that it could be quite a nice little number with all those different pieces and I started seeing $$$ in the air. (4:30 p.m.) I'm going to move ahead and put the manuscript and photographs together. I hope to get it done in the next couple of weeks, at which point I am going to send out a Xerox to a few places and see if I can get interest in getting it published as a book.

Love, Victor

In 2011, in the midst of finishing *The Burroughs-Warhol Dinners*, I suddenly recalled an unpublished book I'd written in 1974: *Hitler on the Moon*, which also featured William Burroughs and Andy Warhol. This fictive romp through my early seventies career as an interviewer took its lead from Andy's advice in my unpublished 1974 interview, done while he was painting his watercolors of flowers, to "Use other people's leftover answers."

The story was based on an assignment to interview Hitler on the Moon. Pulling together interviews I'd done with Warhol, Burroughs, Muhammad Ali, Allen Ginsberg and Peter Orlovsky, Lou Reed, Halston, Salvador Dali, Peter Bogdanovich, Mick Jagger, Bill Wyman, and Joe Dallesandro, I invented a world of fantastic interview subjects—from the Abominable Snowman to the Jolly Green Giant and the Loch Ness Monster. It was the last book contracted by the legendary French publisher, Maurice Girodias, a great friend, who made his name by originally publishing *Naked Lunch*, *Lolita*, and *Candy* in the 1950s.

This interview parade through Europe, Africa, the U.S., South America, and the North Pole featured a dime-store detective story about a cat burglar and a young chick related to the Virgin Mary. In reaction to a *Village Voice* piece by Alexander Cockburn that had compared a Warhol interview with Nancy Reagan to interviewing Hitler, I gave Andy the lead role as Adolf Hitler exiled to the Moon, where he is planning a comeback. Burroughs played himself as the Operator, aka Inspector Lee of the Nova Police. Allen Ginsberg played the Abominable Snowman. The dialogue in the following two scenes is exclusively taken from leftover answers from my interviews with the original subjects:

The Operator (Burroughs) launched into a spasmodic confession: "Well look, if you have any actual sexual outlet, to jack off is a betrayal of that sexual outlet. There's nothing worse than making it with someone and thinking about someone else. It's very bad and will always be detected. Look, now all I'm saying is something very simple—you're making it with someone, all your attention should be on them, you should not be thinking about someone else, or not jacking off to someone else, or not making it with someone else. I don't jack off so long as I have any alternative. Well, of course I jack off if I don't have an alternative. Now, for example, there was a whole year or two in Alexandria where I had plenty of boys. I never jacked off. Why in the hell should I jack off? No. Nononononono. This is all wrong. If you have actual sexual outlets, why in the hell should you jack off? [Everyone arguing] But if I have any sexual outlets, I will never jack off. I'll tell you exactly what I think about it. I think that if you think that, you might as well just jack off all the time. You never make it with anyone. This is the basic fear, my dear, this is fear. Fear which is of death, which is regret."

Hitler on the Moon, Chapter Six

Hitler (Warhol) continued: "The point is, it would be easier to live in a totalitarian society. You're told what to do, and things like that, so it's just much easier. Nobody wants to work anymore. But, you know, just working is more fun; it's like that magic person who comes along. Stay young and work. Take domestic positions. I think those are the most glamorous positions, you meet the most interesting people. You can just watch. Success isn't anything. Some people think it is. I don't know. I mean, some people think it's… I don't know. I just work all the time mostly, but not as much as I did before. I don't work hard at all; read newspapers, watch television. I play two sets at one time, there are so many good things on T.V. What you should do," Hitler was saying, "is just use somebody's leftover answers."

Hitler on the Moon, Chapter Eleven

From: *Memory Chips, The Bunker Diaries* by Stewart Meyer
Sunday, November 23rd, 1980

Found Bill working on a manuscript with Bockris, Victor's *With William Burroughs: A Report from The Bunker* book, which they're doing final copy on. I've seen enough to know this is going to be an important book to people who know Bill's work and a way of interesting the uninitiated. People have an image of Bill as a chilly piece of work, a living Dr. Benway. And Bill doesn't discourage this persona, I think it is a protective cloak. But it should be penetrated at least partially because what you've got behind those chilly blue white panther eyes is a very loving and sweet ol' fuck who cares more than he should about his species and always responds to sincerity. Indeed, the old Doc's taught me as much about friendship as about writing.

Victor's book is culled from conversations which he transcribed, so of course there are errors. Hard to hear tapes sometimes. They're pouring (sic) over these pages and it's a pleasure to watch. Bockris did an early interview with Bill I read in a European art magazine, and has maintained a steady contact with him. During the Nova Convention Victor acted as an aide, and was very helpful. I sat quietly, not wanting to spatter the focus, but it was fun to watch. After a while they took a break and I rolled a fat bone of Thai.

Sunday, Late August 1981

It was a hot Sunday afternoon and I was sulking over *Negative Girl*, a piece of writing I could not pin when I spotted Warhol's in-house photographer, Christopher Makos, sitting at a traffic light in his brilliant aquamarine blue Italian sports car. The handsome, tanned Chris with his shiny gold hair and Germanic features was the last person I wanted to see at that moment. In fact, I was unshaven and sloppy, and in no condition to see anyone. Hugging the wall, I was zipping around the nearest corner, shoulders hunched against intrusion when I was hooked by a stentorian bellow, "*I really liked your book!*" that was so commanding I couldn't help but spin around and stare. I could not see who was in the backseat yelling, but trotted over to the car and found myself squinting down at a grinning, wigless Warhol, a white handkerchief knotted at the four corners of his head, perched in the tiny backseat with the legs of his last love, the athletic Jon Gould, athwart his lap. "I really liked *With William Burroughs*," he enthused. "I read it twice. I read it. Then I read it backwards. It was so fabulous. How did you do that? Did you do it all by yourself? I mean God! It was so great. It was the best!" After a difficult silence in which he asked what I was doing and I mumbled, "trying to write," the light changed and the car, with all of its occupants laughing their heads off, roared away.

Monday, December 8, 1986

At the end of the very worst year of my struggle to pin down my Warhol biography, I gave a dinner party for William Burroughs, Allen Ginsberg, Debbie Harry and Chris Stein, Richard Hell, Jean Michel Basquiat, James Grauerholz, and the owner of the Mudd Club, Steve Mass. Burroughs, Chris, and Debbie had come directly from the Factory where they had been filmed for Andy's TV show, *Andy Warhol's Fifteen Minutes*. William had left a gift for Andy—one of the shotgun paintings he had painted that year following Brion Gysin's death. When Bill began to worry that the previously shot artist might get the wrong impression, Chris called Vincent Fremont who assured him that Andy took these things in his stride.

Andy Warhol Died on February 22, 1987

I had known Andy for seven years at the time of his death, and it came as a surprise to me to learn that he was a devout catholic—a surprise that, when considered, is not a surprise but somehow appropriate. He was a very private person who was able to maintain reserve without any trace of chilliness or hauteur.

William Burroughs

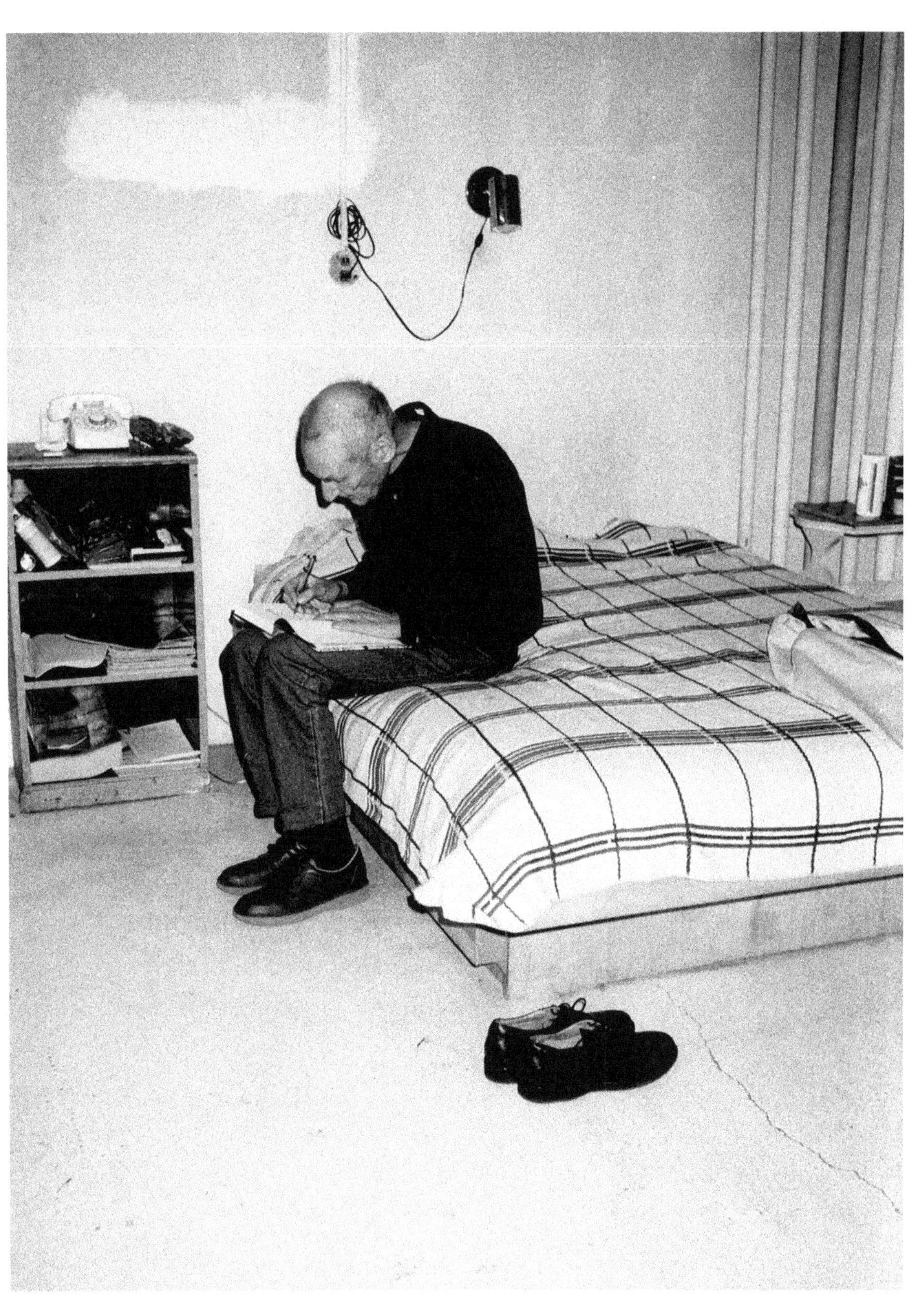

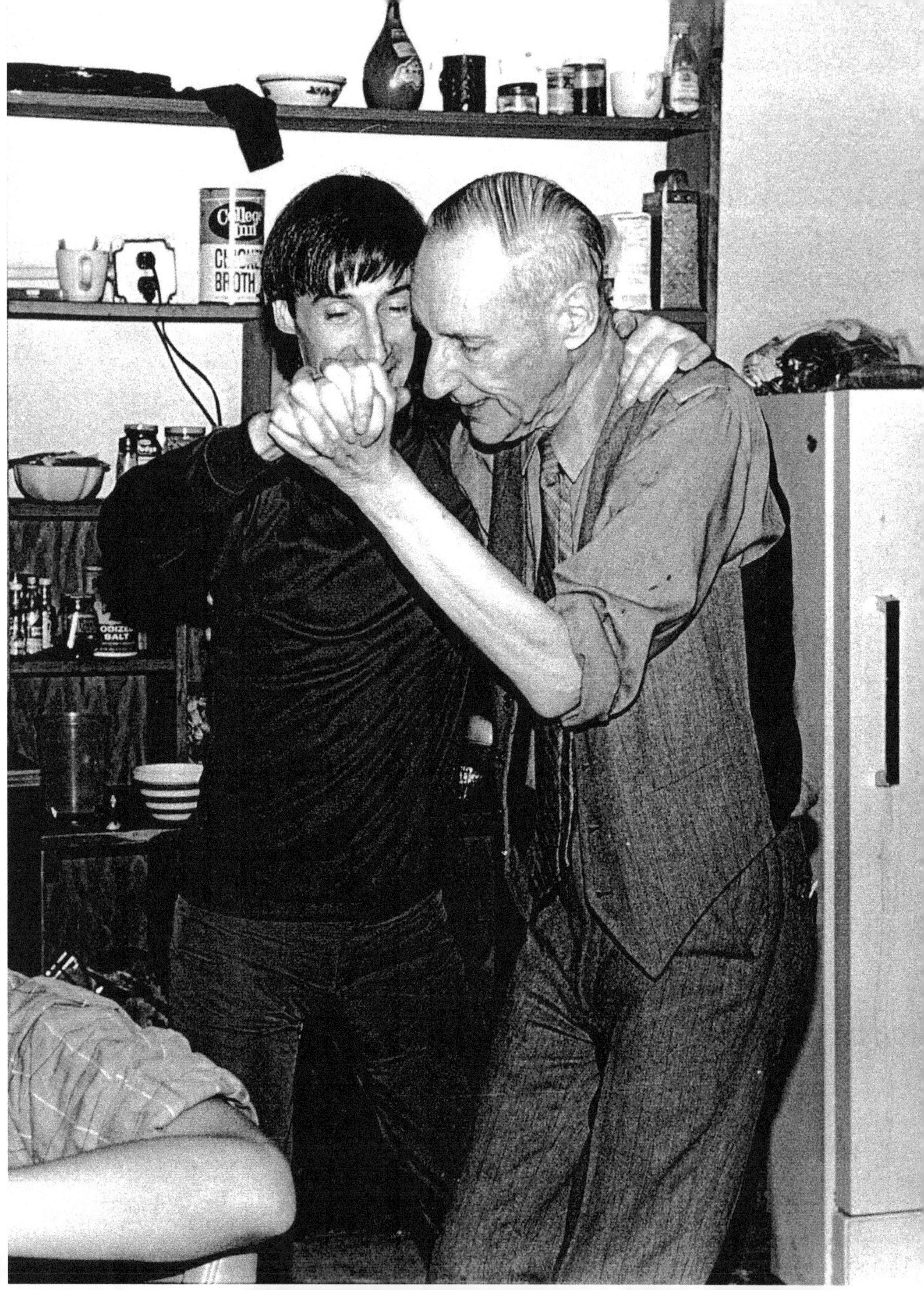

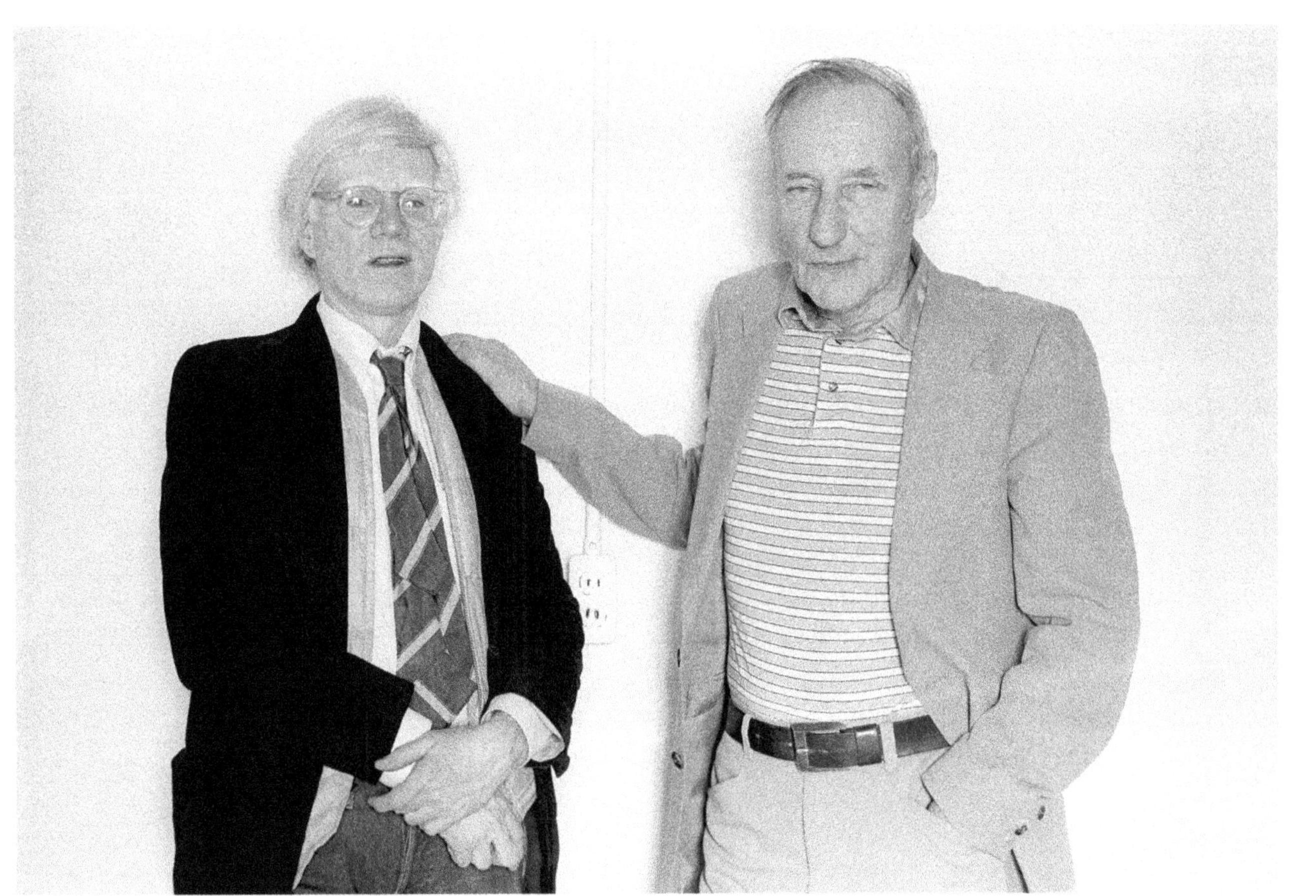

CHAPTER TEN
WILLIAM BURROUGHS AND ANDY WARHOL: THE BIOGRAPHY OF COMPARISON

"Like Warhol, Burroughs was an outsider who perceived the death drive that lay beneath his country's materialistic propaganda."

- Jon Savage

In the future, no one will write biographies of one person; all biographies will be about two people. There will be *The Biography of Comparison* in which one life reflects upon the other, and *The Biography of Collaboration* in which two people join forces to create a third mind.

William Burroughs and Andy Warhol's lives seem to be woven into the fabric of the counterculture. Both these unofficial legislators of their times were born in spooky moments of the 20th century: Burroughs on the eve of World War I in 1914; Warhol in poverty on the eve of the Great Depression in 1928. William attended the Los Alamos

Ranch School for boys in New Mexico, which was later the base for the creation of the atomic bomb. Andy's seventeenth birthday on August 6, 1945 was the same day the U.S. Air Force dropped the atomic bomb on the people of Hiroshima, Japan. He would paint the mushroom cloud explosion in his *Death and Disaster* series.

Both artists grew up knowing they were gay when being homosexual was illegal. They suffered tremendously. Both were branded as freaks in their teens and made to feel ugly. Privately, Andy and Bill were passionate romantics, whose emotions would have overwhelmed them had they been allowed to flourish. Instead, each man married his work and dressed for the office in costumes that best expressed their engagement—Andy like Elvis in the dance sequence from *Jailhouse Rock*; Bill like a patrician banker in a suit and tie. Both became the definition of cool in the 1960s. Both became in my view militant homosexuals and, starting in the mid-'70s, icons of Gay Liberation.

Bill often spoke of buying an old motel and turning it into a finishing school for young men called the Final Academy. He would live in the big house at the center of the compound, and each of the cabins would be occupied by one or two pupils, just like the boys in his novel *The Wild Boys*. There were to be lessons in fishing, shooting, reading, and having sex with each other in perfect harmony.

Andy's version of Bill's scenario was to preside over a male brothel. There would be a large room the size of the silver Factory. Andy would sit at the top end of the room behind a large desk, empty except for a cash register. As he surveyed his dormitory, to the left and right of him, single beds lined the walls at intervals, a young man lay on each bed. Customers came in and paid Andy a sum of money to rent a young man depending on the amount of time they wanted. In his ultimate scenario, Andy would quietly glory in keeping an eye on serial scenes of rampant sex on every bed. After living, Andy once wrote, the hardest work is having sex.

Why are the fantasies so similar?

Regardless of that check out this quote from Oliver Harris' book, *William Burroughs and The Secret of Fascination*:

> What then does it mean for Graham Caveney to claim that there is "nothing hidden in Burroughs' image, no secret to be decoded" or for Timothy Murphy to say that since "he hides nothing, he has no secrets which can be revealed?" Taking up the myth of transparency that El Hombre Invisible has himself promoted, they approach Burroughs as another Andy Warhol, the great American icon of blank ambiguity. "Warhol," writes Steven Shaviro, "is mysterious and charismatic not because he is so good at keeping his inner life secret, but because he has no secrets to keep." Does this direct challenge to hermeneutics, to the deciphering of any deep meaning, apply to Burroughs, let alone fit Warhol? Or might we say of Burroughs what Hal Foster says of

Warhol, that "the fascination is that one is never certain about this subject 'behind': is anybody home, inside the automaton?" Foster's open question preserves a vital ambiguity and allows him to read Warhol's image as both deep and shallow, both referential and simulacral. The alternative is a situation that combines a certain philosophical integrity with a radical short circuit of any grounding whatsoever. When an interviewer asked, "How do you see the relationship between your public image—there's a William S. Burroughs archetype—your body of work, and yourself, the actual man?" To his total consternation, Burroughs replied: "There is no actual man."

Their public careers in America took off in November 1962. Warhol's groundbreaking one-man New York show of paintings opened at the Stable Gallery in New York on the 7th. Grove Press published Burroughs' *Naked Lunch* on the 26th. Both works polarized their fields. Both men went on to confront their mediums by developing machinelike techniques, which appeared to remove the artist's emotions from their work. Burroughs' cut-up technique drove the majority of his peers and critics around the bend. Warhol's silkscreen technique confused and annoyed his detractors, who chased him until he died. Whereas painters like de Kooning might spend a year on one canvas, Andy Warhol took less than five minutes to produce a painting.

Burroughs' entrance onto the world stage took place at the Edinburgh Writer's Conference in August 1962, where he was quoted saying, "I am not an entertainer." In the 1960s, his carefully constructed image and rare public appearances never let his audience relax or get to know him. Comments like "Love is a con put down by the female sex" mirrored the attitude of his alter ego, Inspector Lee of the Nova police. With his banker's drag, pale enigmatic blue-lipped face, and his uncomfortable aristocratic distance, William Burroughs faded into the boardroom portraits of his faceless ancestors. He was a sheep-killing dog. He did not want to be recognized.

In this composition of negatives, he was a scary motherfucker, just like his partner in time Andy Warhol. The pop artist's hoodlum entourage, his drop dead sound bites—"I don't believe in love; I want to be a machine"—and films like *Blowjob* made *Time* magazine call him "Puke's Bad Boy" and "The blond guru of a nightmare world." He had crossed over with the errand boys and the gooks, chewing gum, drinking Coca-Cola, and calling out Jackson Pollock.

Signature voices became their shields. Andy combined Marilyn Monroe's and Jackie O's gliding whispers with a soupcon of Marlon Brando's monosyllabic mumbles to create an instantly recognizable, hypnotic voice. Bill cut the crisp vowels of F.D.R. on the radio into the pellucid tone of Kate Hepburn to create an electronic voice that reflected its times.

In each case, I was entering the world of a monarch operating out of his own headquarters, surrounded by his own followers, who had been one of the biggest stars of the counterculture in the 1960s. The faces of William Burroughs and Andy Warhol flash repeatedly from the media kaleidoscopes of the 1960s like frightening masks of a cultural apocalypse. If the counterculture had its Mount Rushmore, Andy's Slavic slab of stone face would have stared out at America next to Burroughs' last American dream face, next to Bob Dylan and Lenny Bruce. They were the Guard!

Between them, Burroughs and Warhol took on the most powerful of all American syndicates and cartels—the FBI, *Time-Life*, the CIA, and the Ghost of Eisenhower's military-industrial complex. There could be no quarter and no prisoners.

Both men mastered the interview and the photo session, recognizing them as forms they could control, and using them effectively to establish their images. In 1969, Warhol began *Interview* magazine. In 1970, Burroughs put out a book of interviews with himself conducted by the French writer, Daniel Odier, called *The Job*.

As spiritual leaders of their tribes, William Burroughs and Andy Warhol were the two most subversive artists in the United States. Warhol was under FBI surveillance. Burroughs was under Narcotics Police surveillance.

Both thrived on negative publicity. "We are constantly under attack!" was the motto of the Factory. "We must hold The Bunker at all costs," became Burroughs' signature statement.

Andy Warhol was famous for being shot and almost killed by a woman. William was famous for shooting and killing his wife.

Both made an enormous impact in the sixties but managed to live beyond that decade to do equally well in the seventies and even better in the eighties.

Both were vilified by the establishment press but went on to become bellwethers of their times.

Both lived at the center of an entourage of disciples.

Both were trendsetters and fashion plates.

Both lived their lives as movies which they wrote, starred in and directed.

Both were addicted to their work and never took vacations. Their work was their life.

Both were satirists who used America and its people as their primary source and subject.

Do you realize that the woman who shot Andy Warhol referenced William Burroughs Cut-Ups in the title of her SCUM Manifesto, *The Society for Cutting Up Men*?

The extraordinary number of similarities and parallels between them made William Burroughs and Andy Warhol seem like partners in crime. There were people who wanted to kill both of them.

Their images went through parallel public declines in the confusion that ended the 1960s and cast a fog over the early 1970s. After Warhol had been shot and almost killed in an assassination attempt in New York on June 3, 1968, some of his followers said he was but a ghost of the man he had been. When Burroughs returned to New York in 1974, he was teaching a class in creative writing at the City College of New York and did not think he could write fiction anymore. Both men had momentarily lost their hold on the times which they had foreseen and, in great part, brought into being by creating new populations of Burroughs and Warhol people.

In Washington, something was happening that would go a great distance towards changing this. After President Richard Nixon's 1972 landslide election, the Watergate scandal forced him to resign in 1974. This transformation of the wheel of fortune brought Burroughs back to America and back to the limelight, finally recognized as a prophet in his own land. Meanwhile, in the words of Norman Mailer, Warhol replaced Nixon in the culture, becoming "America's Regent."

The biggest thing they shared in common was working from the center of an entourage which doubled as a collective. It's one thing to have an entourage devoted to an artist in the field of entertainment; it's another altogether for each member to work in some specific capacity towards the success of the artist's work. Warhol's Factory was well known as a modern Bauhaus. When I knew Burroughs, he also worked from a space with a name where his followers regularly gathered and worked. Burroughs' Bunker operated on the same principles of love and tension as Andy Warhol's Factory. However, the manner in which each man inspired his disciples reveals a core difference between Burroughs and Warhol.

Andy had a global organization with layers of workers devoted to him for his blessing. He was an original in being able to put people to work for his benefit in a way that benefited them even more. [My case is a good one to examine.]

Bill had a far less mechanical organization or sense of how to use people. If you were in his inner circle, you benefited enormously from the generosity of his soul, his openness to emotion and sensitivity to pain. He possessed few of Andy's defenses, but then he needed less.

Andy was the most attacked artist in America. He was a true *Grimm's Fairy Tale* character made up of the themes of his times. An Everyman. A genius and a clown. He knew how to harness the power of fame with a cartoon image. Bill had no such abilities or thoughts. His was a far more individual, hands-on, less manipulative scene. He certainly did not encourage people to fight for his attention.

As lifelong teachers Andy and Bill were equals. And as Godfathers of Punk and Professors of the University of Manhattan they were equals. Burroughs influenced as many fields as Warhol without the incredible cultural machinery that led Andy to have a social secretary, a business manager, a Girl of the Year, and bodyguards. This pauper prince and made-for-media culture hero was truly all the things he pretended to be.

Bill was not a game player. He wrote for the salvation of his soul and for the salvation of many souls. If you treated him as I did, he was capable of giving you collaborative love.

By the beginning of the 1980s, both men were more widely known international figures than ever.

William Burroughs was the greatest writer in the world. Andy Warhol was the greatest painter in the world.

Andy Warhol was also a writer. I believe that in the future, Andy Warhol will be recognized as the author of at least three classic books: *a, A Novel, The Philosophy of Andy Warhol,* and *The Andy Warhol Diaries.* In everything he did, he was involved with conceptual works, with signs and labels and codes. With life and death. He was a black magician from a background of violence and death, madness, fire and rage, all of which he pulled together in himself to become the strongest artist in the world. To be with Warhol was to rock through the zeitgeist, people shooting from all sides. Everything Andy did was great. Andy is for the ages.

William Burroughs was also a painter. Between 1986 [after Brion Gysin, who taught Bill how to draw, died] until his own death in 1997, he produced over 100 paintings and had shows throughout the U.S. and Europe. Burroughs first exhibited talent as an artist when he designed the cover of one of his Olympia Press books, *Naked Lunch.* His eye for framing and composition can also be seen in his 1950s photographs. In 1986, William became the painter Andy had encouraged him to be in 1980. Everything Bill did was great. Bill is for the ages.

I first interviewed Andy Warhol in the second Factory at 33 Union Square West in the fall of 1973. He was in the jet set, traveling back and forth between New York and Rome, filming *Dracula* and *Frankenstein.* The Mao paintings were just making their way into the world. I interviewed him for a British underground magazine, Emma Tenant's *Bananas,* about his "Return to Painting!" The following day, I returned to take some photographs of Andy taking Polaroids for the commissioned portrait of an industrialist's wife. At one point, he took a phone call and could be heard saying, "Oh… er… through the head! Oh, only through the ear? Gee… he must be very sick… oh… oh really? Well, I'll come up and see him sometime."

"What happened?" his subject asked him.

"Oh, a friend of mine got shot at Serendipity. Do you ever go there?"

Her eyes shot out of her head for a split second, then she said, "I used to, but I never will again!"

"Oh, no, no, this was at night," Andy said, looking a tad concerned lest he might affect the reputation of that place. The small talk trickled on.

In a quiet moment before I left, we were standing next to one of the four pristine transparent glass-top desks which furnished forth the new Factory's organizational principles. We were staring at a 1960s portrait of Andy's face on the cover of the *Saturday Review.*

"I look different now, Victor," he whispered.

There was something endearingly intimate on the borders of that frozen moment. Years later, he told me it was at that time he had fallen in love with me. Of course, that was just a phrase. Andy fell in love with thousands of people for five minutes, but there was something lonely and lost inside me then to which he responded. Later, as Lou Reed would point out, I became a monster.

I first interviewed Bill in the fall of 1974. He was sixty and had only just returned to the U.S. after twenty-five years of self-imposed exile and settled in downtown Manhattan. At that time, he seemed to be a little burned-out by too much work and too many isolated years in London writing those wonderful books: *The Last Words of Dutch Schultz*, *The Wild Boys*, *Port of Saints*, and *Exterminator!* Nobody recognized him on the streets. Some of his American fans even thought he was dead.

After twenty-five years of avoiding narcotics agents, Burroughs was apparently so uncertain of his reception in the U.S., I heard he thought my partner and I, who were dressed in matching Brooks Brothers suits, were from the CIA. Hence his puzzling refusal, in an otherwise monosyllabic interview, to admit the existence of the Russian novelist Alexander Solzhenitsyn. In fact, the first interview was so bland that there was nothing in it I could publish.

Two weeks later, we tried again over dinner at my apartment. This time it went extremely well. Afterwards, as we were walking down the street to get him a cab, William put his arm around my shoulder in an avuncular fashion and said, "It's all up to you now, Victor." I was twenty-five and had little if any sense of what I possessed that could have resulted in such remarks. I have never had such an intimate connection with any of my other subjects after doing an interview.

Shortly after Burroughs arrived in New York, Allen Ginsberg introduced him to a young man from Kansas. James Grauerholz would be Burroughs' amanuensis for the final twenty-three years of his journey on earth. Twenty-three happened to be Bill's favorite number. Around the time I met William, he told James he did not think he could continue to write fiction. The first effective thing James did was set up some local readings. As soon as Burroughs started to give public readings of his work in New York, a brush fire was lit. Apart from the album *Call Me Burroughs*, recorded in Paris in 1959, his voice had rarely been heard. And Bill was a great performer of his writing, with perfect comic timing and a delivery as good as the famous Victorian novelist, Charles Dickens, who did several reading tours of the United States.

My first significant solo piece—the Rosetta Stone you might say of my twelve-volume mythology for the counterculture—was a profile of Burroughs, "Information about the Operation." I wanted to do something special but struggled to find a form. Finally, four weeks into the work, I walked up and down my apartment determined to succeed or fail that night. A couple of hours later, out it came fully formed: the layout of a multi-layered profile in twenty-three different scenes. It was published in Ian Hamilton's London-based *New Review*, April 1976. Appropriately enough, I published a parallel profile of Warhol.

Again, the same thing happened. I couldn't find the form. I stayed up all night. It finally came out around 6:00 a.m. fully formed. It was published in New York's *National Screw*, July 1977. It included the line, "Who does Andy Warhol remind you of most? Muhammad Ali." I was introducing *The Biography of Comparison* by underlining this curious fact. These were unique experiences. It wasn't just that I turned out two strong individual pieces. In both cases, they laid the groundwork for the book I would write about each man.

Burroughs and Warhol were, among other things, spiritual and exemplary leaders of the Gay Liberation Movement. In my opinion, they did more to bring homosexuality via art into the mainstream than any other artist except Allen Ginsberg, who deserves equal citation for parallel achievements. In fact, before I brought them together, one might say that Allen was the crossover figure between the Burroughs and Warhol camps. Allen was Bill Burroughs' closest friend and colleague from the 1940s until Allen's death in the 1990s. He also made a point of being the bridge between the Beats and Warhol in the 1960s. He appeared in Warhol's film, *Fifty Most Beautiful Men*, and with Jack Kerouac and Gregory Corso in Warhol's mid-sixties epic, *Couch*. Ginsberg also defended Warhol against verbal onslaughts by Corso and others. In turn, Andy attended Allen's poetry readings in New York and London and often spoke highly of him in interviews. In April 1966, Ginsberg even appeared onstage with the Velvet Underground during their victorious month-long run at the Dom on St. Marks Place, the central artery of the Lower East Side.

One of the reasons that I had hesitated about arranging a dinner for Andy and Bill was because Burroughs was particularly sensitive to the tastes in paintings of his closest collaborator, Brion Gysin, who introduced Burroughs to the cut-up method. One of Gysin's greatest paintings hung on the wall above Burroughs' desk at the Bunker. Gysin was a space-age artist himself, but unfortunately, Brion was strictly anti-Warhol, so the loyal Bill had never really looked at Andy's work. As it turned out, the paintings would perfectly reflect the books and vice-versa. Thus, Andy Warhol's paintings would have been perfect covers for William Burroughs' books.

In a hitherto unrecognized development, it turns out that no two comparable counterculture figures had as much in common as William Burroughs and Andy Warhol. They were both great visionaries of America's post-war cultural revolution that changed the way many of us saw life and lived it. And we are still beginning to really digest the full value of their contributions.

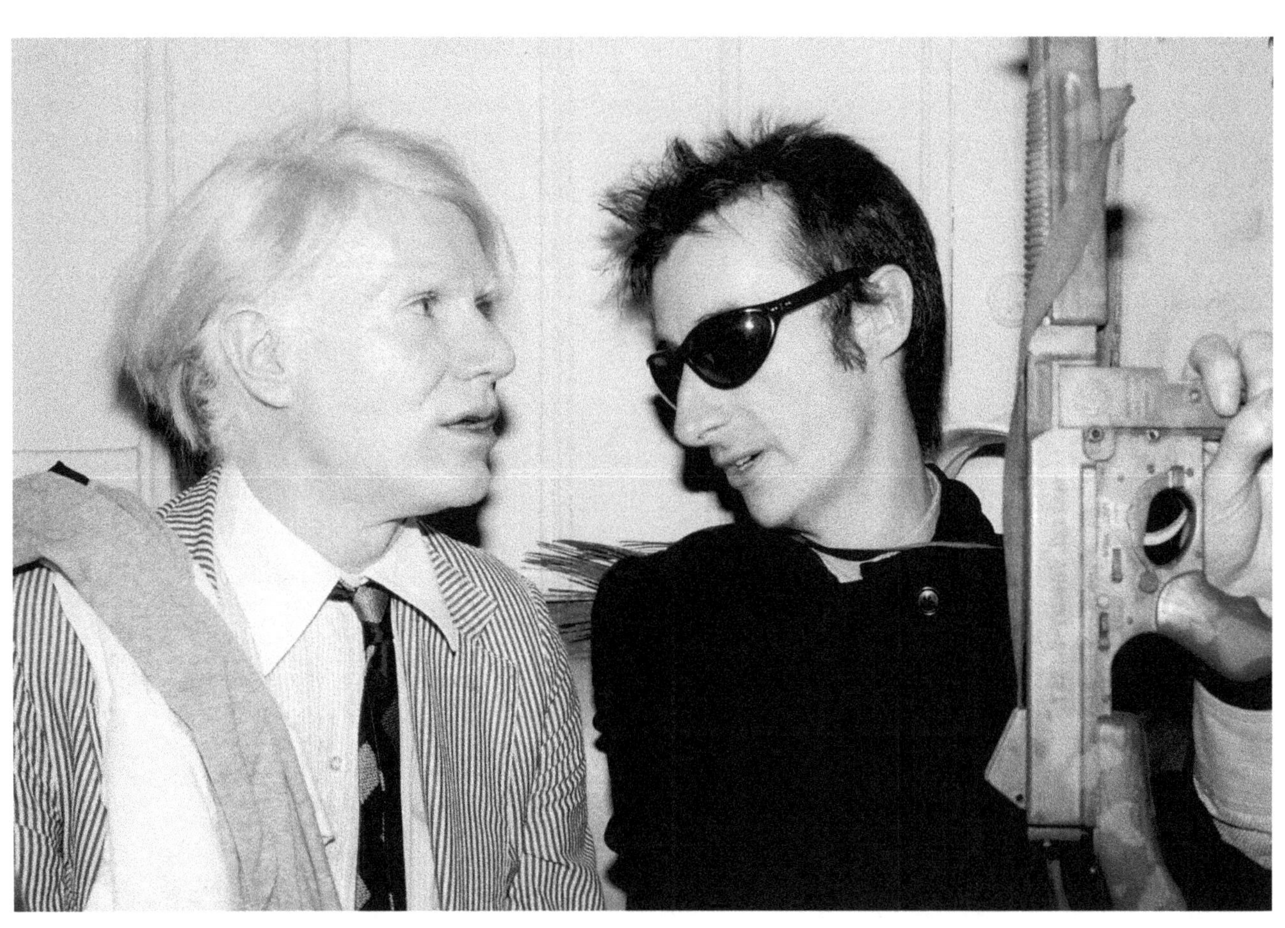

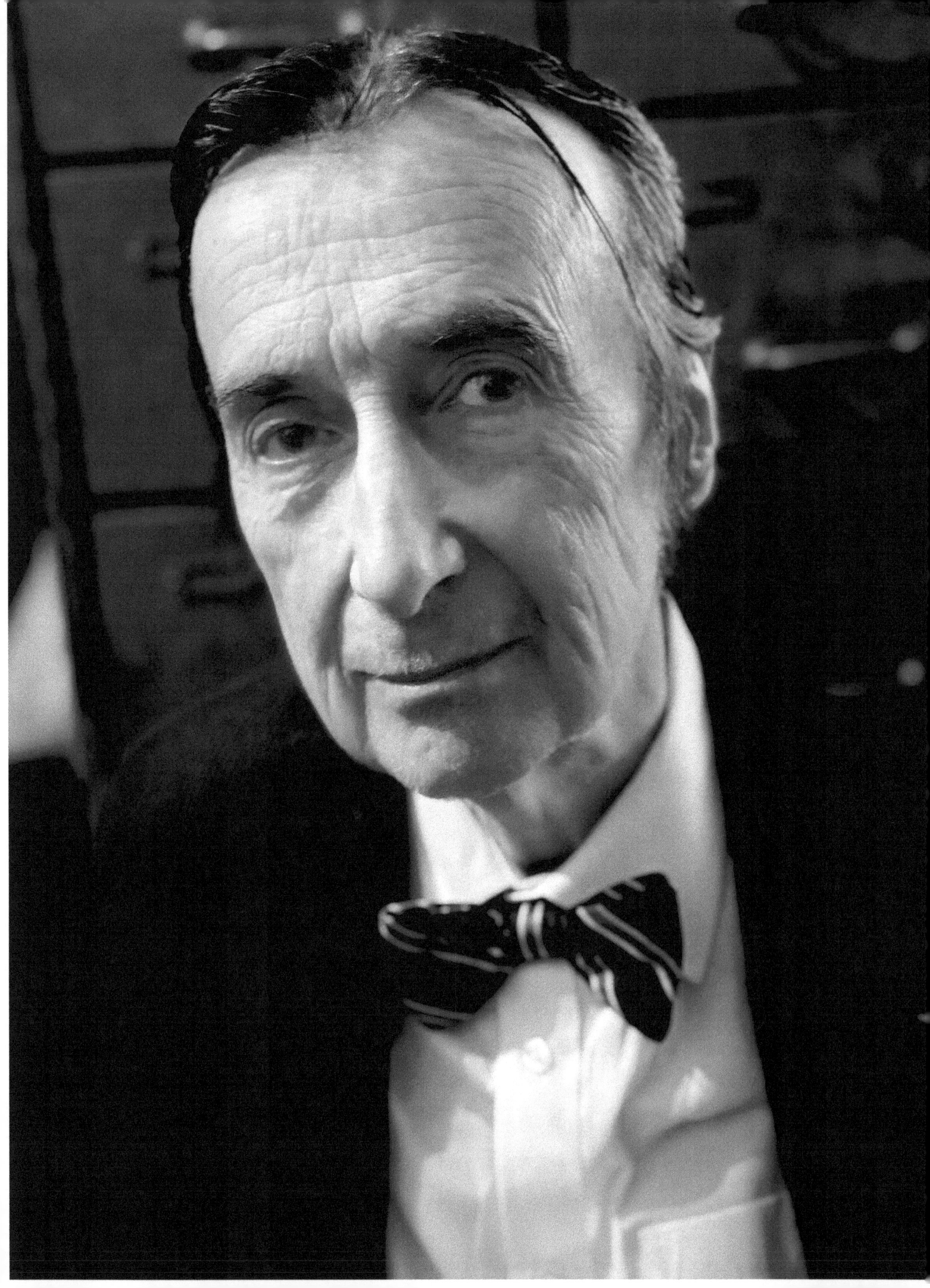

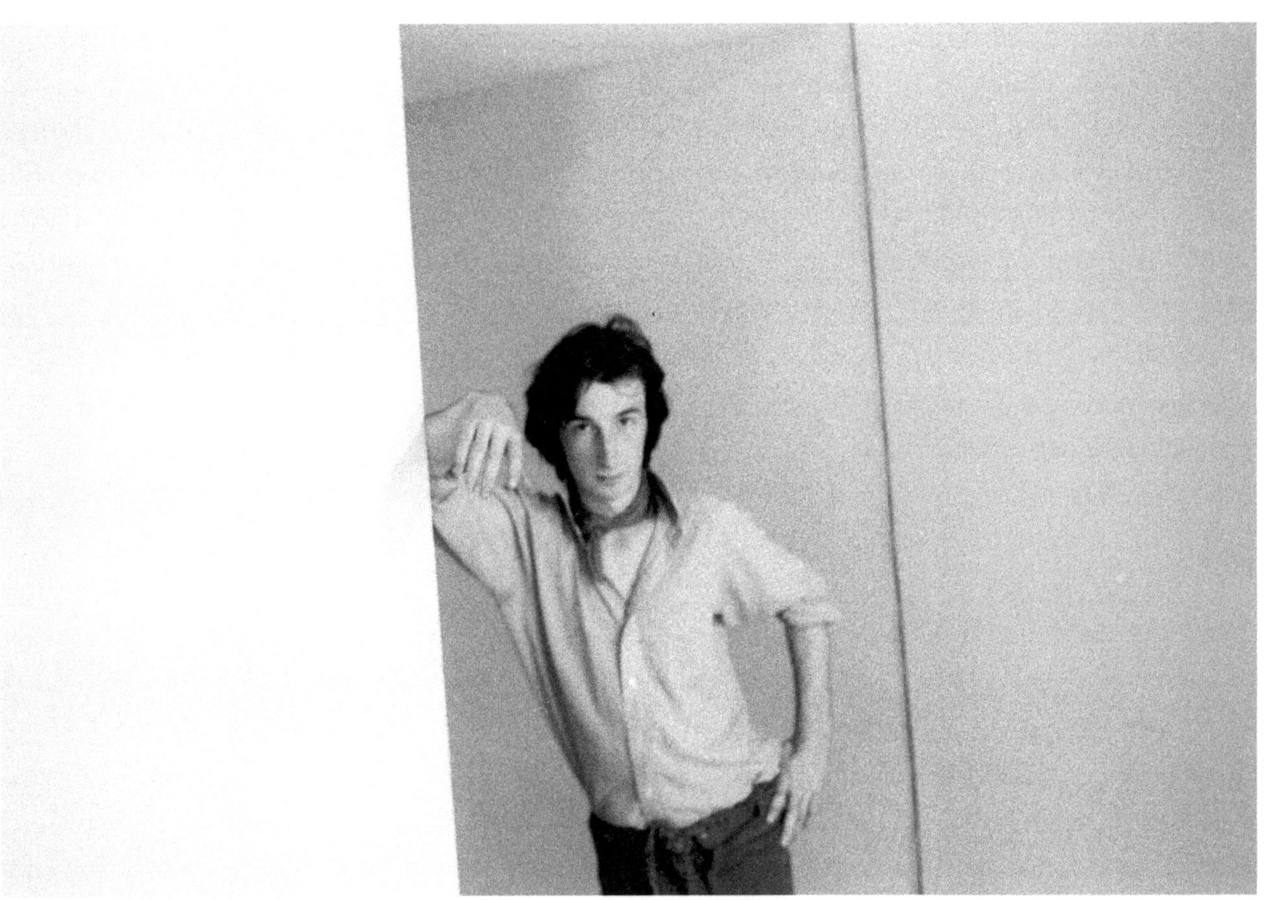

The Tables Turned:
An (Extended) Interview with Victor Bockris

By Leon Horton

Poet, publisher, photographer, writer, and all-round bon viveur, Victor Bockris is regarded as the foremost chronicler of the New York counterculture scene of the 1970s and '80s. He has written biographies on Patti Smith, Lou Reed, Andy Warhol, Keith Richards, and Muhammad Ali—as well as *Uptight: The Velvet Underground Story*, *Making Tracks: The Rise of Blondie*, and *With William Burroughs: A Report from the Bunker*. Andy Warhol said of him: "Victor Bockris has more energy than any person I know… He's always tape-recording and taking pictures. I can't keep up with him."

Victor Bockris is an interviewer's dream. Of course he is, just look at his career—he's a master at the form. When I first approached Victor in the summer of 2020 to ask for an interview, I had little expectation he would even reply, let alone agree to talk to me. Why would a writer of his calibre, a man who counted Burroughs and Warhol among his friends, even deign to open my email? I needn't have worried. Not only was he delighted to be approached, but—as I would soon discover—his ability to hold court, to consider each of my (occasionally dumb) questions with a care and attention normally reserved for newborn babies, to answer in streams of colourful recollection, expansive, and somehow erudite, made the whole experience easy for me.

New York in the late seventies/early eighties has taken on a semi-mythical quality. Warhol at the Factory, Burroughs at the Bunker… and Victor was there, in the thick of it, all the while recording: disastrous dinner parties with Mick Jagger and Lou Reed; falling out with Patti Smith; spilling red wine all over Burroughs just before a reading at the Nova Convention; hanging out with David Bowie, Susan Sontag, and Christopher Isherwood… Victor's life and work reads like a Who's Who of late 20th century counterculture—notes from the underground—and plays out against an epic backdrop, which, while not always as glamorous as it might sound, never ceases to be fascinating.

I was delighted when the original interview appeared in *Beatdom #21*. It ran to, I think, just short of 12,000 words, and featured many of Victor's personal photographs. It also had the distinction of being my first interview to make it into print rather than online, which never ceases to be a joy. When the letterbox clacks and you tear open the packaging and flick through the fresh pages and smell the print—and then, there it is, your name, your by-line, right there in a book. Best drug I know.

This, though, was the problem. When the drug wore off, I wanted more. By necessity, I was always trying to bring the questions back to William Burroughs (which was right for *Beatdom*) and I felt there was so much more we should have talked about. Happily, Victor agreed and we continued onwards, delving deeper into his life and work. For this extended interview, Andy Warhol is brought more to the fore, given equal footing with Bill, and we take time to discuss interviewing Salvador Dali, writing a book about Blondie with Debbie Harry and Chris Stein, taking a taxi to the airport with Robert Mapplethorpe, and, of course, the very book you are currently holding.

For this edition, I was delighted to ask more questions about the craft of writing and Victor's own methods (what do you expect when two writers start chatting?), to be given the opportunity to broaden the scope of the overall interview, and to remove one or two questions which frankly didn't work or didn't go anywhere. Do we really need to know who Victor would kill if he was given total impunity? No, we don't, because he circumvented that now dead question with the skill of a Zen master. In the end, it is better to sit back, let Victor talk, and see where he takes you on this rollercoaster…

No one is innocent, but some of the guilty got out alive.

Victor has led the most extraordinary life with some of the most important artists and writers and musicians of his day. When we completed this interview, in July 2022, he was kind enough to say this was "the best interview I have ever done. And I've done a great many." That kind of accolade I will take smiling to my grave. I hope you agree with him.

Leon Horton (September 2022)

* * *

HORTON: Victor, with a wealth of interviews, photography, and biographies under your belt, you could easily put your feet up and rest them on your laurels. Yet here you are, in your early seventies, riding your bike in the Florida sun, giving talks and interviews and currently writing your memoirs. Are you slowing down any, or is life as frenetic as ever?

BOCKRIS: Writing is a way of life. Thanks to the international audience I have developed over the past fifty years, and the internet, I have a higher profile than ever. My daily life has changed little from what it has always been. I get up, clean up, take a bike ride to get the *New York Times…* and after reading it, I get to work. Right now, I'm working on a three-part BBC documentary about Andy Warhol and a documentary about Keith Richards' first wife Anita Pallenberg, and Nick Dimino is making a documentary about me. I answer interview questions. The interview is my favourite form, I think of it as a literary form comparable to a short story.

The larger work shadowing all of this is my memoir. Never talk about what you are writing. A growing book inside me is like a jealous lover. If I went out at night while I was writing the Warhol book, the book would not emerge so easily on the following morning. It would prove a little harder to find. If I stayed in, the book was eager to get together. Never forget, your book can kill you.

HORTON: How do you work? Do you write on a computer or by hand?

BOCKRIS: I have always written by hand then typed it on the computer; largely because my mind moves fast and I can write by hand faster than I can type. At the moment I am changing this because it takes twice as long if you have to type it up. I've always thought of writing a book as an athletic task.

HORTON: Why do you write?

BOCKRIS: I am addicted to writing. I don't feel whole unless I write. I write because I believe I have something to share with my readers. The intercourse between writer and reader is really special.

HORTON: Looking back at your life and work—living, breathing and documenting the New York countercultural scene from the 1970s onwards—from poetry to art to music to literature, Warhol to Burroughs to Blondie and beyond—you have created a body of work that stands as testament to a place and period that has come to hold immense cultural significance. Do you feel the weight of that on your shoulders?

BOCKRIS: It is not a weight. It is a joy to have a mission to care for that body of work and add to it. Beat-Punk is the subject I am always writing about. This place and period have certainly come to hold immense significance, but I don't think anyone has quite captured it yet.

VICTOR BOCKRIS: These combination book ideas are strong. Nobody is doing that. That's my new forte.

BURROUGHS AND WARHOL AT

THE CHELSEA HOTEL (1980)

HORTON: Your latest book, *The Burroughs-Warhol Connection*, brings together the twin towers of Andy Warhol and William Burroughs, both masters of their own scenes, in a series of transcribed conversations. Reading it, I felt—God, I hope this doesn't offend you—but I felt like I was up in the viewing gallery watching brain surgery on these two greats, with you as the surgeon rummaging around in their cracked-open craniums…

BOCKRIS: When I recorded the first dinner between Andy and Bill for *With William Burroughs*, it felt like the ultimate achievement. All the dinner parties I recorded for that book were unique in their own way, but the conversation between Bill and Andy surprised both of them. When.it was originally published in the 15th anniversary of *Blue Boy* September 1980, they were both happy about it, but their handlers were annoyed because I'd caught both men talking in a way they did not talk in public. The fact that there were three dinners with A and B in 1980 was coincidental. When I set up the dinner with Jagger at the bunker, Bill insisted we invite Andy. The BBC commissioned the Chelsea Hotel dinner for their Chelsea Hotel documentary. As early as December 1980, I wrote Miles I was planning to do a book of conversations and photographs— but I did not find the right form until David Schmidlapp and I created the Burroughs-Warhol Photo Tapestries in 2003. I am thrilled that it is finally coming out in the English language. Yes, I guess I was rummaging around in not just their cracked-open craniums, but in the many sides of their faces, and the growing regard they had for each other.

HORTON: I think Burroughs fans will see *The Burroughs-Warhol Connection* as a sequel to your 1981 book *With William Burroughs: A Report from the Bunker*—which it is in part— but in terms of structure it bears some similarity to *Uptight: The Velvet Underground Story*. Experimenting with form has been a major part of your *œuvre*, hasn't it?

BOCKRIS: Every book I've written has a form dictated by its subject. It took me some time to see this though. I used the table talk form to write the Burroughs book because Bill was most talkative and sharp over cocktails and dinner. I took five years to complete *Warhol: The Biography* largely because I could not find the right form. I finally realized I had to write it in conversational prose mirroring Andy's way of writing his books. You are correct that I saw *The Burroughs-Warhol Connection* in the form of *Uptight*, half text half pictures.

HORTON: Throughout your career you have been variously described as "The Poet Laureate of the New York Underground," "Always exciting and energetic" (by your close friend and fellow writer Barry Miles), and "a 150-pound bundle of sometimes irritating energy." That last one was Ted Morgan in his biography *Literary Outlaw: The Life and Times of William S. Burroughs*—we'll get to Morgan later—but how would you describe yourself?

BOCKRIS: Thin. Gaunt. Fragile. Strong legs. Well-dressed. Sharp. Energetic. A good conversationalist, who particularly likes talking with girls. Has many faults. Keeps trying to learn how to live.

HORTON: You were born in Sussex, England, in 1949, but your family moved to Pennsylvania when you were just four-years old. You are an American citizen in every sense and yet, to me, you retain a distinct "Englishness." I'm aware you were sent back to England (to Rugby Public School) as a boy, but was your childhood schizophrenic?

BOCKRIS: Not sure if schizophrenic, certainly split. Apart from one heroic period, when I was eight and led a gang of eight guys and eight girls at Lea School in West Philadelphia, I was pretty much a wimp by the time I returned to England age ten. Few games. No sense of self. But when I moved back to England in the fall of 1959, I started making progress. I became Head Boy at my prep school Great Ballard, starred as Shylock in the school play, edited the school magazine, played cricket in the first eleven etc. At Rugby, I won a Distinction for Writing during my first term. By the time I was fifteen, I was progressing on all fronts at Rugby: academic, sports, social. A British boarding school education is much better than any other kind of school because when classes are over, you don't go home alone, you engage in games and conversations and trips and adventures with your best friends. You're being educated all the time. I was also the singer in our band.

Just as I was about to sail into being sixteen at Rugby, my father yanked me out without warning. By March of 1965, I was going to Central High, Philadelphia's primary all boys high school. The extreme culture shock I experienced in the cross-over brought my role down from the leader of the band to second-in-command. I was no longer the Lone Ranger, I became Tonto.

See, my life was based in cricket and soccer and English styles of conversation and comportment, but compared to my new American friends I was naïve in terms of girls and the wild life beyond school in cars and at parties. I could have played the field at our sister school Girl's High, but I didn't know how to handle the intercourse. I was, at first, too badly cut up by the abortion my father had performed on my education, just to hurt my mother.

HORTON: Why did your father want to hurt your mother?

BOCKRIS: That was in Another Land.

HORTON: Do you remember when you first realised you wanted to be a writer? Who were you influenced by?

BOCKRIS: I first wanted to be a writer when I was four. I copied out the first paragraph from *The Adventures of Robin Hood* and showed it to my great aunt. She was enormously impressed, but she soon caught on. I started writing poetry in 1965 after I fell in love with a flawed thirteen-year old beauty from Girl's High who was way ahead of me in sophistication and imagination outside the box.

"If you raped me," she cried out over the phone in a clutched voice of brushfire excitement one steamy afternoon. I knew I could not satisfy that kind of lust, as much as I admire her to this day. I was one of those prim boys who said very seriously, "Of course I wouldn't have sexual intercourse with her, father. She's thirteen, for Christ sake." Meanwhile, I was attracted to her all the time. It was wonderful and horrible. I still dream of her. I started writing long Ginsberg-Dylan style lyrics about her.

Who was I influenced by? My best friend at Rugby, Andrew Russell, told me to write as plainly and clearly as I could "because people already had a hard time reading."

I have been influenced by everybody I have ever known: certainly Dylan Thomas, Ginsberg, Kerouac, Burroughs, Simenon, Sartre, Camus, Genet, Ungaretti, Creeley, Lenny Bruce, Bob Dylan, Andrew Wylie, Bobbie Bristol, Tom and Connie Pickard… Among biographers: Boswell; among pop biographers: Albert Goldman and Barry Miles.

HORTON: Barry Miles has written extensively about the Beat Generation, of course. Did the Beats play a part in your formative years?

BOCKRIS: The great trade-off I made when I moved from Rugby to Central High was that I replaced my best friends and collaborators at Rugby with the three American artists I encountered in Philadelphia during the summer and fall of 1965: Bob Dylan, Allen Ginsberg, and Andy Warhol. This was when I also started reading books by Burroughs, Ginsberg, and Kerouac, along with books about the Beats. I am still reading them. Kerouac's *Visions of Cody* and Warhol's *a, A Novel* are two seminal and related books in the Beat canon. And the first inspired the second. The Beats, the Dylan-Warhol-Stones Schools, and the Punks are three generations of artists who emerge out of each other to coalesce in the mid to late '70s.

HORTON: In 1971, you graduated with a BA in Literature from the University of Pennsylvania—where you contributed material to the *Pennsylvania Review*, much of it your own poetry—and along with Andrew Wylie and Aram Saroyan, founded Telegraph Books, again publishing poetry. Is poetry still a big part of your life?

BOCKRIS: My underground poetry press Telegraph Books and Jeff Goldberg's magazine *Contact*, which picked up where T.B. left off, were celebrated in that great mid '90s celebration of Small Presses of the Lower East Side, at the New York Library on 42nd and Fifth Avenue. T.B. published the cutting-edge voices of the early '70s. The poetry scene in New York and London was a strong base of the counterculture when it was most vulnerable. I'm proud of my two books *In America* (Telegraph Books, 1972, US) and *The Victor Bockris Special* (*Joe Dimagio Magazine*, 1972, UK). Since then, I never stopped writing poetry. I wrote this poem last week:

SOMEBODY ELSE'S PENIS

Somebody else's penis in her mouth

Somebody else whose cock is much bigger than mine

Making her come five times

I used to die of jealousy now I pay her $50.00

To describe each event in as much

Detail as possible. After all he's dead

While I'm still aroused just watching her at seventy

Dance in front of her CD player in a grey pleated mini skirt

And knee socks just as when she first told me to fuck her and

Rape her - "just rape me and fuck me," she said - aged twenty-four

Even then I was incapable of communicating efficiently with my cock

And had to decline

Now I love her more than ever. Now I want her all the time

Between seventy and seventy-nine.

HORTON: Is poetry purging?

BOCKRIS: That's a good question. Poetry as a record of events or insights like in "America / all we / do is work" is a turn on, a reliving of sexual thrills or a cool take on the current situation. I don't find it purging. Sometimes it can take you deep into yourself, it can trap you, it can cut you, amuse you or confuse you. I've never felt purged of all the things I've done, but now I think about it maybe I should try to purge myself. "Sorry ma, sorry pa....who knew you were unaware....of meee!"

HORTON: How did Telegraph Books come about?

BOCKRIS: When I graduated from the University of Pennsylvania, two brothers, Ralph and Jerry Weiman, who ran a reprint house, the Folcroft Press, which I worked for part time, gave me as a graduation gift my own underground poetry press for one year, all expenses paid. We could publish one book per month. Meanwhile, during my final year at Penn, I had become friendly with a Harvard grad one year older than me named Andrew Wylie. We actually drove across the country during that summer of 1971 making plans for my press all the way. By September, when I returned from a vacation in London, Wylie had moved to New York and opened the Telegraph Books shop on Jones Street in the West Village. I remained in Philadelphia where the press was. During our first editorial meeting at the Telegraph Books shop, Wylie suggested we publish Aram Saroyan, who was at the time the most famous young poet in America. After some heated discussion, I agreed. Andrew called Aram in Cambridge, Massachusetts, and several hours later, he joined us. Before the meeting ended, he had accepted my invitation to join the editorial board. Thus, it was that I went from being totally unknown in the poetry world that year to becoming by the fall of 1972 a celebrated poet in Philadelphia, largely on the back of Telegraph Books. Working with Wylie and Saroyan provided me with my first great triangular collaboration. Saroyan and Wylie equally influenced my first book, *In America.* Few people knew that 1972 was the first year since 1960 when the counterculture was wide open to new voices and new faces.

HORTON: In 1971, you saw Patti Smith perform at St Mark's Church Poetry Project in New York. You subsequently published her first book of poems, *Seventh Heaven*, through Telegraph Books. Did you realize then what an important international artist she would become?

BOCKRIS: We gave a great Telegraph Books reading in London with her in January 1972. She was dynamite. It helped launch Patti in England. We also did photo sessions with most of our authors. "Patti Smith dominated the sitting with a pro-dynamism that was as unmistakable as it was charming," Aram Saroyan wrote in his memoir about Telegraph Books, *Friends in the World.* "There she was, braless in an oversized Harley tee-shirt and black pants, perhaps a hundred pounds in all. She was clearly already a star: it was just a question of getting the message out to the world."

> **VICTOR BOCKRIS:** Would you consider yourself to be the greatest poet in New York City?
>
> **PATTI SMITH:** Um, the greatest poet in New York City? Um. Shit, I can't think of what to say. I don't think I'm a great poet at all. I don't even think I'm a good poet. I just think I write neat stuff.
>
> PATTI SMITH'S FIRST INTERVIEW (1972)

HORTON: In your interview with Patti, you asked her "If I was to offer you a reading tour with three other poets, who would you choose as the three other poets?" She chose Jim Carroll, Bernadette Mayer, and Muhammad Ali. Who would you choose and why?

BOCKRIS: Tom Pickard, John Weiners, and Andy Warhol's Robot. I did a bunch of readings up north in England with Pickard in 1972. We had a lot of fun. I gave a reading with Weiners in Philadelphia. The sensitivity and pain of his voice touched my heart. A theatre producer built a Warhol robot in the mid 1980s. It was going to read

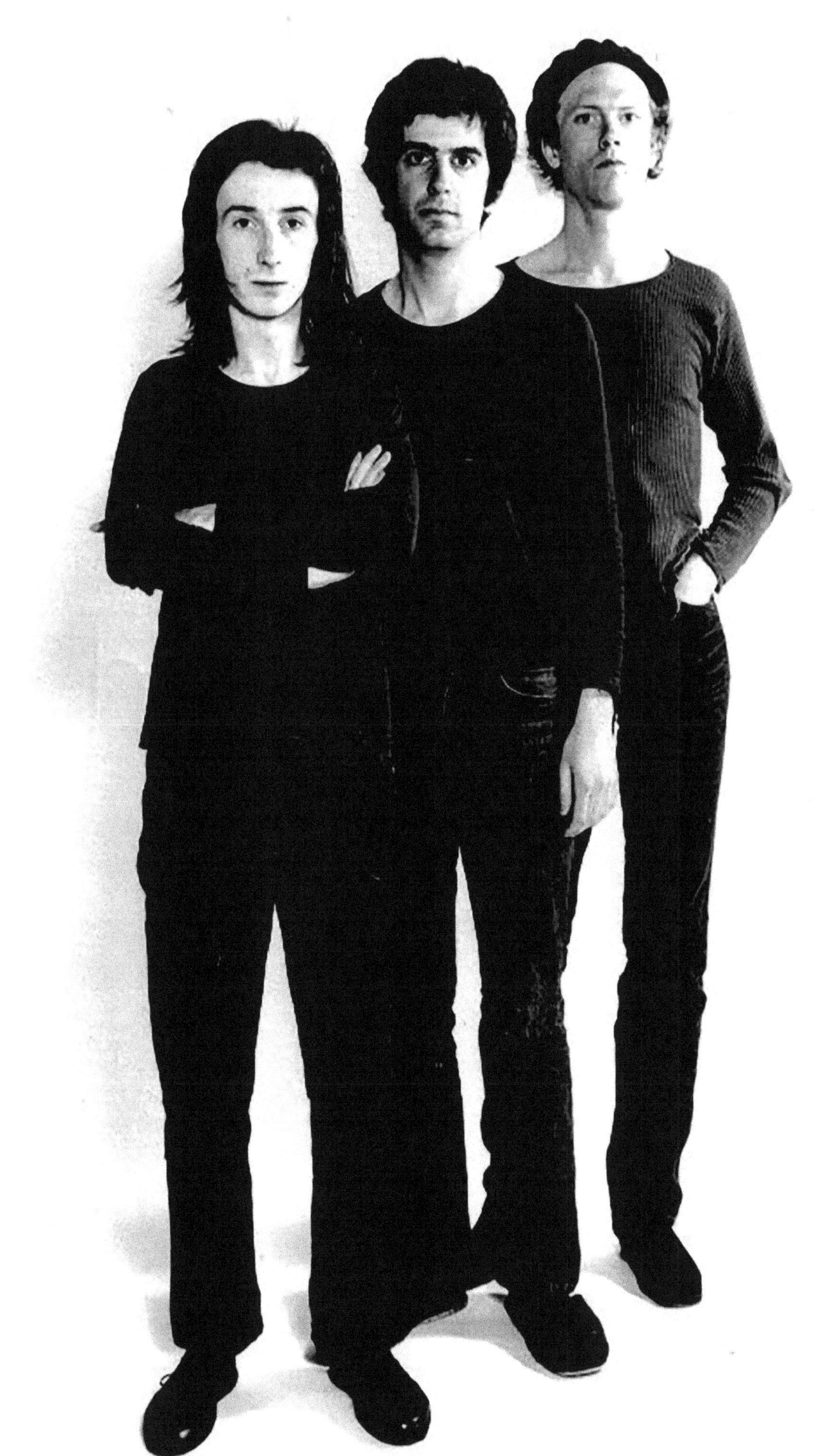

from Andy's *The Philosophy of Andy Warhol: From A to B and Back Again* in a Broadway show, which never happened. I always wanted to see Andy succeed as a writer.

HORTON: Forming the Bockris-Wylie writing team with Andrew Wylie, you more or less moved permanently to New York in 1973. Was that a suck-it-and-see decision, or were you chasing something specific?

BOCKRIS: By the time I moved to New York with my new girlfriend, Bobbie Bristol, Wylie and I had already put together a book of fifteen interviews with poets, *The Life of Poetry*, with an introduction by Eric Mottram (never published). And we had definitively switched from writing poetry to doing interviews, which I saw as the poetry of the human voice. By the time Bobbie and I took the train from Philadelphia to New York on September 12, 1973, Wylie was living in a grand sixth floor apartment overlooking Gramercy Park. Bobbie and I moved into a beautiful one bedroom, large living room with a fireplace and high ceiling at 110 East 17th Street around the corner from Max's, three blocks east of the Factory. And four blocks from Wylie's place.

In fact, I came to New York to launch Bockris-Wylie's plan to interview the one hundred most intelligent people in the world. We had come up in the world and were perfectly placed to launch our invasion of the city. A year later, we were interviewing Salvador Dali, Muhammad Ali, Andy Warhol, Mick Jagger, William Burroughs, Roman Polanski, and Lou Reed among many others.

HORTON: Wait…What? You interviewed Dali?

BOCKRIS: Yes, we interviewed Salvador Dali at one of the Sunday night open house parties he gave in his Mortuary Parlour off the St Regis Hotel's King Cole Bar. It was a magnificent scene. Dali, who had just come across the Atlantic on the Queen Elizabeth, sat at the top of the room and held court that night with La Principessa and the King— titles he made up and bestowed upon them in his own magic universe. He talked in a combination of Spanish, French, and English, which we understood precisely. Back story: previous Sunday we'd come with tape recorder and been dismissed by Dali in two minutes. This Sunday, Andrew had a ninety-minute Sony tape running in the inside pocket of his double-breasted jacket. The problem was the tapes only lasted for forty-five minutes a side. The way Salvador was going we were going to have to make two tape switches. Right before Andrew had to fake a run to the john in mid brilliant Dali rap, Andy Warhol came in and sat down right behind us with his entourage. "Going to change your tape?" he all but yelled as Wyle tried to slip away. Andy would try to stir up a storm in a teardrop. Dali loved being interviewed with a little pizzazz. We got him going on sex, politics, murder, the lot. He was hilarious. We captured him as I had never seen Dali captured before. Dali had been living like this since the 1920s. He was a surrealist through and through, he lived a surreal life with a surreal wife and he had a very good time. For Salvador Dali, life was a parade. He was also in the present not the past. He liked Andy a lot. They had known each other for years.

HORTON: Do those tapes still exist? I don't like to think what they'd be worth to a biographer…

BOCKRIS: It took us two long afternoons to transcribe our tapes because they were often hard to hear. In those days, we worked so constantly and so fast, we often taped over tapes. I grab my head in horror when I think of what we did not collect. I remember Goddard saying he destroyed all his records of making a film and we thought it was the right pop approach. Meanwhile, the interview was published in all its glory in Charley and Pam Plymell's *Coldspring Journal*.

HORTON: Interviewing the 100 most intelligent people is seriously ambitious. Did you hit your target? Who made number one?

BOCKRIS: Ali, Warhol, and Burroughs were all number one. Particularly because I would go on to write books about all three of them. In fact, the books grew out of the interviews. I think we interviewed about forty people. Once, we interviewed Max Von Sydow in LA and Francois Truffaut in New York the following day—in French. At the time, I looked and dressed exactly like Jean-Pierre Léaud, who starred in most of Truffaut's biggest hits in the 1970s. We had so much fun doing these interviews, in part because we were being published in Playboy's *Oui, Penthouse, Viva, People*, and Andy Warhol's *Interview*. Unfortunately, no one we knew read any of those magazines except *Interview*.

HORTON: You were present in 1974—again at St Mark's Church—the night Patti Smith announced on stage that William Burroughs had returned to New York. It's a moment that has gone down in countercultural history, across numerous accounts and biographies, but was it really that significant? I mean, he'd spent several months in New York only nine years previously, this was hardly the return of the prodigal son…

BOCKRIS: William Burroughs return to New York in 1974 was a deep event for the Underground. First, because it came in the same year President Nixon was forced to resign. Nixon had overseen the vicious attack on the political counterculture, which had almost succeeded in squashing it. Burroughs return to New York to stand as our new leader in the return of the counterculture was of immense significance. In fact, this period of significance starts right here. At the same time Burroughs returned, the original punk bands started playing CBGBs, Andy Warhol had his great Mao show in Paris and moved to the new Factory at 860 Broadway. Bob Dylan released *Blood on the Tracks*; Lou Reed, *Rock n Roll Animal*. Muhammad Ali won back his heavyweight championship crown after beating George Foreman in Africa. The party was just beginning in downtown New York. Allen Ginsberg won the National Book Award for *The Fall of America*. The rest of the seventies would be led by these heroes of the artistic counterculture. The seventies took what the sixties had spawned and brought it into the mainstream.

HORTON: What sort of reception did the crowd give Patti's announcement?

BOCKRIS: A cheer went up. Burroughs was a much-loved figure at St Marks. The other thing is on his previous attempt to return to live in New York in 1965, Burroughs had been set up for a narcotics bust. It never happened because Herbert Huncke, the guy who was supposed to set him up, warned him instead.

In 1974, it was safe for Bill to return. The time was right in so many ways. During the seven years he lived on the Lower East of New York, William Burroughs became the King of the Underground and the Godfather of Punk. The climax of his rise came at the Nova Convention in December 1978.

HORTON: You later fell out with Patti—or should I say, she fell out with you. Was that because of your biography? You were pretty scathing in parts. You certainly took her High Priestess of Punk image down a peg or two. Shortly after publishing *Seventh Heaven*, you said, "the sweet, playful girl, who had been so excited by our acceptance of her book, had changed to a wrathful harpy overflowing with anger." You're not exactly pulling your punches.

BOCKRIS: First, there was a falling out with Patti because, unbeknownst to me, one of my partners at Telegraph Books told her we would pay royalties. There were no royalties, no contract. We just did our best to help the poet along. *Seventh Heaven* was good for Patti's reputation. She was a big hit at the reading I set up in London.

The interview I did with her in '72 is one of her best. I was only interested in celebrating Patti. But when she started to make it, she made a big thing of attacking people. T'was too starved an argument for my sword. As for the Smith biography, it is my worst book. I should never have written it. I was sick, burned out, and under insane pressures. I deeply regret writing such a shit book. She deserves a great biography.

> **VICTOR BOCKRIS:** Would you give up writing tomorrow if you could continue performing in some other way?
>
> **PATTI SMITH:** No, I can't give it up, I have no choice.
>
> **VICTOR BOCKRIS:** Is that really true?
>
> PATTI SMITH'S FIRST INTERVIEW (1972)

HORTON: You must have found yourself in the same room as Patti since then. Are things more cordial these days?

BOCKRIS: The last time I saw Patti was at the New Year's Day reading at St Marks Church Poetry Project in 1995. She was sitting in the front row when I came on stage and announced that I would be reading from the US edition of the Patti Smith biography (which is superior to the UK edition). Patti got up and went backstage and I proceeded to read one of the best sections of the book to much applause. The thing is, man, I have absolutely nothing against Patti. I really don't know where this idea we are enemies came from. I would never spend the time it takes to write a biography about somebody I did not admire. The thin book was 100% my fault. I wish I had written the great book I could have written. The best thing that can happen to a rock star is a great biography. I know my books on Keith and Lou were good for them. Why do you think Keith wrote his life story?

HORTON: In 1974, you interviewed Burroughs for the first time for *High Times*. What can you tell us about that?

BOCKRIS: No. I interviewed Burroughs for the first time in 1974, but not for *High Times*. That was in 1978. In fact, Bockris-Wylie interviewed Burroughs twice in 1974. The first time we went over to his apartment at 77 Franklin Street, Wylie and I were dressed in Brooks Brothers suits and bowties, and carried matching briefcases. He was accompanied by his new assistant James Grauerholz. We were huge fans of Burroughs' books and glowing with the intensity of admiration. However, we got nothing out of him and finally stopped trying. When we phoned around, it turned out he thought we were CIA. ("Yeah I'm a CIA agent, baby, what's wrong with that?") In retrospect, it was understandable because we were dressed like CIA agents, and he was still paranoid back then.

Anne Waldman, poet and head of the St Marks Poetry Project, assured him we were alright, and a second interview was set up at my apartment—over drinks, joints, and dinner. Once again, Bill came with James. "He's the best there is," Bill told us, "I can use him in my biz." Grauerholz would help guide Burroughs career over the next twenty-three years and was beside him when he died in 1997.

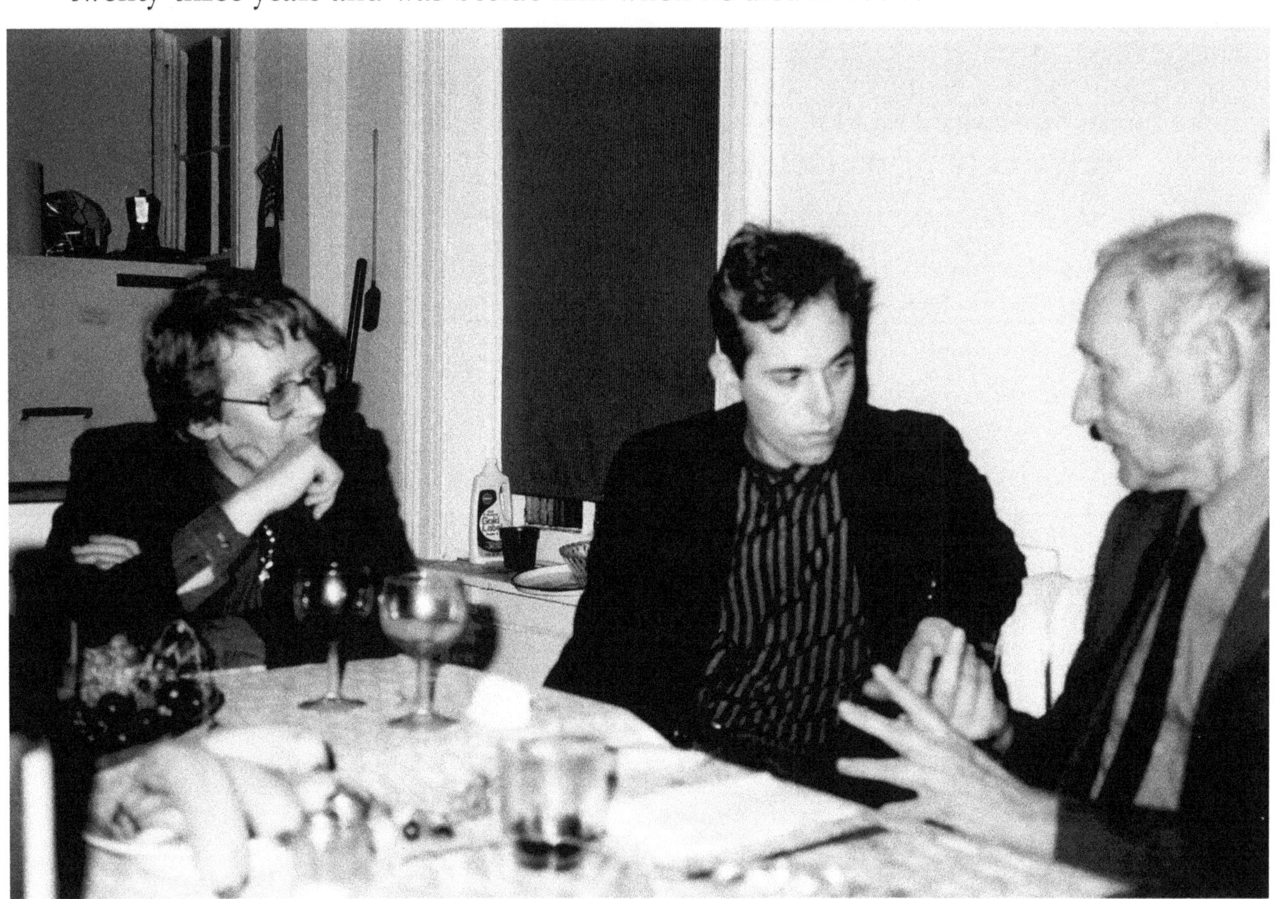

This was one of Bockris-Wylie's star interviews. We asked Burroughs every question everybody wanted to ask him, and he answered in detail with great verve and humour. As I walked him to a cab that night, he put his arm around my shoulder and said, "It's all up to you now Victor!"

Two days later, we dropped the interview off for his approval. Several days after that we got a call from a very different sounding Burroughs, asking us to come over at five. When we got there, we met a grim-faced Bill and James. They thought we had tricked Bill into talking about sex by telling our own sex stories. Burroughs refused to OK the interview. I think James had a lot to do with this because Bill said he was upset we didn't put our personal sex stories into the interview. Anybody who had been interviewed as much as Burroughs had to know no magazine is ever going to run the stories of the interviewer, unless they themselves are a famous person. Anytime a young guy would get Burroughs' attention, James would try to get rid of them. In this way, he did a great deal of damage to, for example, Malcolm McNeil and others.

Wylie and I ended up walking back home in a torrential rainstorm and were soaked to the skin in our Brooks Brother suits and soggy bowties. When we got to my place, Andrew flipped out, called James, and yelled at him. We were now *persona non grata* at Franklin Street.

We could have published the interview, but out of respect for a man we admired as much as anybody we desisted.

HORTON: Has that interview ever been published?

BOCKRIS: Part of it is published in this interview:

> **BOCKRIS–WYLIE:** Are you jealous?
>
> **WILLIAM BURROUGHS:** I can be, yes. I regard it as a flaw in myself. Jealousy is awful. It's the most disgusting thing. But I will tell you how you deal with this. You do absolutely nothing.
>
> DINNER WITH BOCKRIS–WYLIE AND
JAMES GRAUERHOLZ (1974).

HORTON: In 1975, you split with Andrew Wylie, began writing on your own and later joined Warhol's *Interview* magazine and Tom Forcade's *High Times*. In "Andy Warhol the Writer" (published in *NYC Babylon*, 1998), you relate how Warhol told you the best way to interview someone was "with no questions and no preconceptions—with as empty a mind as possible." It's a remarkably fresh approach, but the idea terrifies me; it goes against everything I've been taught. Did you really work in that way?

BOCKRIS: Yes. I interviewed Keith Richards and everyone else for an hour and a half with no preconceived questions. The idea is to turn the interview into a cocktail party conversation or thereabouts, to informalize it. Andy was going for voice portraits in his interviews. If you could capture the way your subject talked, you could bring the reader into the room. That was always my aim: to capture not so much what my subjects had to say but the way they said it.

One reason this time was of immense significance was there was a feeling by the late '70s of all being in this together. Keith, for example, took my Burroughs book *With William Burroughs: A Report from the Bunker* down to his house in Jamaica, where he and Anita kept hiding it from each other so they could get to read it.

We were all part of this huge time. For me, one way to look at it is to assemble a list of all the works each person put out over those five years and look at what was made in that period.

HORTON: In his 1979 book *Exposures*, Warhol described you as "a brilliant young writer who only writes about three people: William Burroughs, Muhammad Ali, and me." Is that a backhanded compliment or just Andy's sense of humour? He *was* familiar with your other work?

BOCKRIS: It was a forehanded compliment. I always related to Warhol as one writer to another. I am a serious fan of his writing. I really got turned onto it by his March 1973 cover story in *Rolling Stone* about Truman Capote's memories of the Stones' spectacular 1972 US tour. This is a tremendous piece of conversational prose.

When I read *a, A Novel*, I was convinced it was a classic. Bockris-Wylie put Andy on the list to get our weekly columns and interviews in Philadelphia's underground paper *The Drummer*.

Plus, we sent him other things. When I compared him to Muhammad Ali in a profile in *National Screw*, he wrote about it in *Exposures*. I actually wrote the first draft of that book.

HORTON: I recently watched the three-part BBC documentary *Andy Warhol's America*, in which, erudite and expansive as ever, you feature a great deal. How did you find the experience?

BOCKRIS: First of all, I love working with the BBC. Secondly, the director Francis Whately was particularly good to me on camera and off. It was a good experience. I always love talking about Andy. As for watching the series—which was not telling the story of Andy's life but relating it to the America he lived in over the years from 1928-1987—I thought the first two films were really well done, but that the third fell down on sticking to the myth that by the late seventies and eighties he was just painting for the money. Nothing could be further from the truth. As time goes on and the "experts" become people who never met Andy Warhol and have little idea what he was about, we drift into unearned critical opinions that will lead us ultimately into fiction. But I still think Francis Whately did a herculean job. *Andy Warhol's America* is for the Ages.

> **INTERVIEWER:** Do you see yourself as a creator, or more as a
> magnet who attracts other talents?
>
> **ANDY WARHOL:** More like a pencil sharpener.
>
> UPTIGHT: THE VELVET UNDERGOUND STORY (1983)

HORTON: Much has been written about Warhol's often vampiric, hoarding nature—in his business and personal relationships as well as in his art. In your critically acclaimed *Warhol: the Biography* (1989)—one of the most insightful portraits of both the man and the artist—you go to great pains to pin down, illustrate, and explain this part of Warhol's persona, without ever losing sight of the fact that this was merely one shade of his shadowy character. What was your personal relationship with him like?

BOCKRIS: Andy was a teacher and the Factory was like a school. I used to go there at the same time as Catherine Guinness and we used to see it as a boarding school, which I think is most accurate. Most people lasted for a year or two and were moved on. I started working freelance for Andy in 1977 and finished in 1983. I contributed regularly to *Interview* magazine. In the *Interview Box Set* (2002), I had more interviews reprinted than anybody except Andy. I was employed to come up with ideas for films or TV shows and was the front man at a meeting with *Saturday Night Live* to do a Warhol show. He helped me with the Burroughs and *Uptight* books. In fact, Andy did more for me career-wise than any other person except Andrew Wylie. On the other hand, I was never able to be myself the way I could be with Burroughs. The fact I was not gay limited the extent to which I could have become much closer to him than I was. We had fun together. The greatest compliment he gave me was on the day he said, "We should do something (a work of art) together." He was the most fascinating man I ever met. He suffered a great deal. He was electrifying to be around. The Factory was like a court.

HORTON: I get the impression *Interview* magazine was chaotic at the best of times. Is chaos fuel for creativity?

BOCKRIS: *Interview* was not chaotic. It was brilliantly run by Andy, Fred Hughes, and Bob Colacello during its greatest period, 1974-1982. If there was chaos, it was fun chaos. Bob Colacello wore so many hats working for Andy, I think he became increasingly overworked, but there's no doubt Bob did a great job with *Interview* magazine

HORTON: What do you think was your best work for the magazine?

BOCKRIS: The conversations I mentored and recorded between first Christopher Isherwood and William Burroughs, and then Susan Sontag and Richard Hell. Both pieces are in my book *NYC Babylon: Beat Punks* and in the *Interview Box Set.*

> **VICTOR BOCKRIS:** Isn't it possible for a man and woman to have
> a relationship…

SUSAN SONTAG: I should hope so.

VICTOR BOCKRIS: …where they don't have to live together or get married, but where they can see each other naturally or something?

SUSAN SONTAG: I like the way you say "naturally". Yes, sure it is.

RICHARD HELL: That's the only way to live.

SUSAN SONTAG MEETS RICHARD HELL (1978)

HORTON: In *NYC Babylon* you say that Christopher Isherwood has been your favourite writer since you were 15 years old. What was it like to meet your favourite writer?

BOCKRIS: Christopher Isherwood was my favourite writer from fifteen to twenty-two. My all-time favourite writer is Jack Kerouac. *Visions of Cody* is a mind-blowing book. Meeting Isherwood was a thrill. From the moment I picked him and Don Bachardy up at the Algonquin Hotel, until the moment I put them into a cab to return there five hours later, was like being in a movie. Christopher Isherwood is Christopher Isherwood, a character of legend but right there in front of me. Every word he said was part of another book.

In fact, he ended up writing about me in his 1978 diaries. The first meeting was in late 1976. Then in October 1978, I gave a party for Burroughs at the Tropicana Motel in LA, to which Chris and Don came. A few days later, I accompanied William to his house so Don could draw his portrait. I sat in the kitchen with Christopher, who was wearing his boarding school cap, drinking sherry, and talking about ghosts. I cherish the moment, but in his diaries he complained that Bill always travelled with an entourage.

HORTON: Warhol and *Interview* magazine clearly played a hugely important part in your life and development as a writer, and yet, unlike your biography of Patti Smith, you kept yourself absent from the narrative of *Warhol: The Biography*. Why did you do that?

BOCKRIS: I don't think it's appropriate for the biographer to appear in his subject's book because it upsets the balance. You can include yourself by writing, "According to one reporter," etc, etc. Also, despite the many things I did with Andy—and my place in that period—I don't think anything I did played a significant role in the large life I was writing for him.

HORTON: My favourite moments in *Warhol: The Biography* are when you talk about his relationship with the remarkable artist Jean Michel-Basquiat. I'm obsessed with Basquiat at the moment, I keep dreaming we are married and living in a New York loft apartment. Do you think, if he were alive today, I'd be in with a chance? Sorry, no, that isn't my question. What I'd like to know is how much you were privy to their friendship…

BOCKRIS: I knew Jean before he met Andy and he was wonderful: warm, sweet, and appreciative. He liked me because he wanted to be a writer. I used to see Andy and Jean

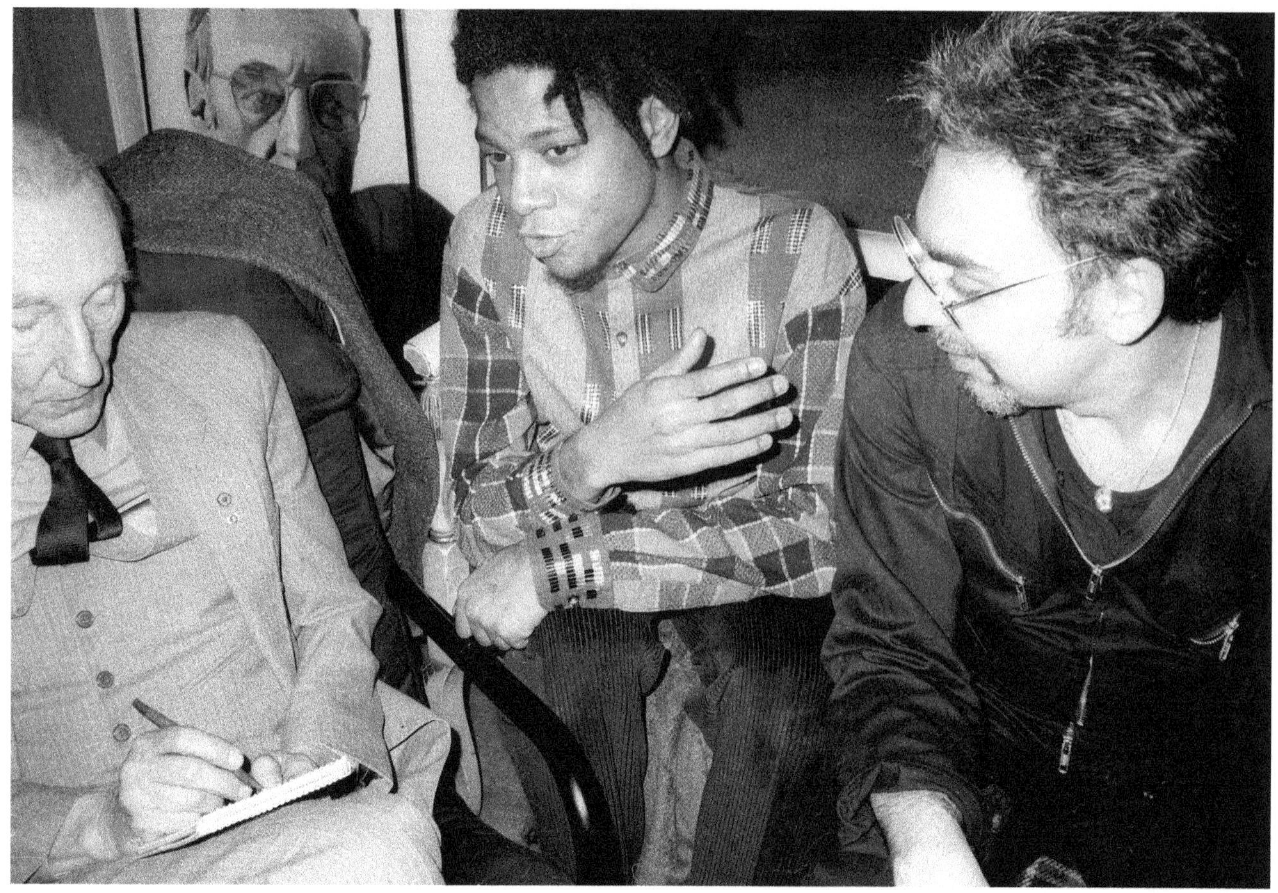

sweep into Area like the glamorous stars they were. The relationship was good for both of them, but Andy taught Jean to be more aloof and Jean started giving people the thousand-mile stare. The problem he had was the same as anybody who came under Andy's sway and tried to act like him. Nobody could pull off Andy's aristocratic stand except Andy, who was a true peasant Prince. Andy tried hard to help Jean to stop taking heroin and learn how to manage his money, but like so many of the Warhol Superstars, Jean was so deeply wounded by his father before he met Andy, there was nothing Andy could do to stop him killing himself. It was exhilarating to watch them together, but it was so sad in the end. I think Andy's sudden shocking death in 1987 in part triggered Jean's death in 1988. Being a shooting star is such a thrill; but in the final moments, feeling tired, sad, sick, and in the face of death, is horrible and filthy.

HORTON: Is it difficult to suppress your own prejudices and presumptions when writing biography?

BOCKRIS: I approach the biography as an opportunity to celebrate the achievements of my subject. I had a lot of prejudices and presumptions about Andy Warhol, Keith Richards, and Lou Reed. I thought they were all great artists whose contributions to our lives as I saw them at the time were always enlightening and uplifting. I knew all three men to varying degrees and I knew them all to be profoundly good people; people who had helped to shape the styles and attitudes as well as the basis of life in the counterculture. One of the hardest things to communicate about this time is the extent to which we all lived almost completely inside this counterculture. All our judgements and ways of being grew out of the work of these artists and others of their ilk. I felt that if I could bring them alive people who were frightened by them would be better able to appreciate and take part in their work. So yes, the books are drenched in prejudices and presumptions. They are also accurate books. Accurate biographies. Those are the books I stand on whenever anybody measures me. Those plus *With William Burroughs* and *Uptight*.

HORTON: Reading *Warhol: The Biography* in tandem with *Uptight: The Velvet Underground Story*, a clear picture of Warhol's working relationship with Lou Reed emerges. At times, they were brothers-in-arms, albeit with ever-shifting loyalties, on other occasions like a disenfranchised father and truculent son. Did they see each other as kindred spirits?

BOCKRIS: According to Lou, Andy told him, "You are doing the same thing with music I am doing with paint." If you think about what that implies it's a high compliment. Remember at the time they met and worked together (December 1965 - June 1966) Andy Warhol was the most famous artist in the world and a powerful culture hero in America. Lou was a complete unknown. The fact of Andy's support of Lou's work and the band made Lou much more pliable in Warhol's hands than at other times. Has there ever been a producer in music history who plucked an actress out of Fellini's *8 ½* and placed her in front of the lead singer of a band as hard as the Velvet Underground? That these two men could work on those levels says a hell of a lot for the art of collaboration. Both Warhol and Reed were profoundly collaborative artists.

> **ANDY WARHOL:** The whole time the album was being made, nobody seemed happy with it, especial Nico. "I want to sound like Bawwwhhhb Deee-lahhhn," she wailed, so upset because she didn't. The Velvets didn't want to turn into a back-up band for a chanteuse, but ironically Lou wrote the greatest songs for her to sing…
>
> UPTIGHT: THE VELVET UNDERGEROUND STORY (1983)

HORTON: Warhol's influence on the formative years of the Velvet Underground is well known, but aside from the multi-media travelling circus that was the Exploding Plastic Inevitable and foisting Nico on the band, Andy afforded them complete artistic control, something all but unheard of in the music business. So why did Reed grow to resent him?

BOCKRIS: It came down to business. The R&R business is hard, artists surrounded by creeps. Fact was Andy and Paul Morrisey were not good R&R managers. They did not get down in the dirt with the record company executives and fight for their band. After the album was recorded, it took nine months for it to come out. Lou was thrilled that the *Velvet Underground and Nico* album existed, but he got a little bummed out when it brought him little recognition. First, the album was advertised as a Warhol happening. The only name on the cover was Andy Warhol, and in a highly unusual development "Produced by Andy Warhol" was part of the title. Meanwhile, all the press went to Nico, who was perceived as the singer in the band since she sang both songs on the album's first single. A lot of people say Warhol had nothing to do with producing the album. On the other hand, if Warhol had not brought Nico into the band and gotten Lou to write several songs for her to sing on their album, we would not have the album we have. No doubt the VU had their music together when they met Andy, but it was Andy who brought in Nico. Moreover, as a first-time recording band, the VU would never have been able to record the album as they did without Warhol's insistence to Tom Wilson (producer at Verve, the record company) that it be recorded the way they heard it. Surely, Andy Warhol helped to get that music down on vinyl through thick and thin in the months just before he made his second greatest work of 1966, *Chelsea Girls*. Lou Reed grew to resent Andy because he could never sustain a relationship with anybody more powerful than him. Andy and Nico were just so much cooler than Lou was. They called him Lou Lou at the Factory. He was astonished by them—by the whole thing. He never stopped talking about Warhol for the rest of his life. The problem was that once Lou betrayed Andy on the managerial contract, and insisted the money go to the band instead of Warvel (the management company run by Paul Morrissey and Andy Warhol) Andy never included Lou in anything he did again. Andy was, after John Cale, the greatest collaborator Lou ever had, but Lou was sensitive to the betrayal by the father. Andy never betrayed Lou.

HORTON: *Uptight: The Velvet Underground Story* is an extraordinary piece of work—part oral biography, part rock history. How did you hit upon the form for the book?

BOCKRIS: The book was originally Barry Miles' idea. He was running Omnibus Press in London in those days (1982). He came up with the idea that I should collaborate with Gerard Malanga (who played a significant role in the band's performances as the whip dancer) on a book about the Velvet Underground. We talked about it over the summer of 1982 as I was doing book tours of England on *Making Tracks: The Rise of Blondie* and *With William Burroughs: A Report from the Bunker*. We decided because they were an art band the book should look like an art catalogue. I flew back to New York in September and got to work with Gerard. He really lit the book on fire when he found Nat Finkelstein's great trove of Velvet Underground pictures at the Black Star Photo Agency and started talking on the phone with Paul Morrissey and Billy Name, who had both played central roles in the VU's Factory Adventure. Morrissey managed the band with Warhol. Billy was Lou's Zen buddy and the Factory photographer who best captured the atmosphere of that dynamo. As Gerard built the photo archive and got me on the phone with Sterling and Maureen I began to weave together a text that took something in part from the WB book and other interview pieces I'd done. I love the humour that runs through *Uptight*. It mirrors its subjects: authored by Bockris—

Malanga, edited by Miles, who chose its designer, Neville Brody. Everything, from the various typefaces Miles insisted on to the balance between pictures and text made by Brody, helped to make it a rocket ship of a book. In fact, published in 1983 it was Omnibus Press's flagship book through the 1990s.

HORTON: How much did Malanga contribute to the finished book?

BOCKRIS: The book was a fifty-fifty collaboration between Gerard and myself from conception to delivery. Gerard was the glue that held the disparate pieces of the book together. His deep inside knowledge and personal connections in that Factory world of the 1960s took us to the studios of many photographers. He also contributed his diaries from which we quoted. As I said above, Miles's vision and Brody's ability to weave the photos and texts were all an integral part of the book's unique form. It was first published in London. I remember getting the first copy in the mail in New York. I cut a caper around my apartment screaming like a thirteen-year-old-girl.

HORTON: By 1978 your friendship with Burroughs had developed to the point where, with the advent of the Nova Convention [a three-day series of seminars and performances in Burroughs' honour] and with James Grauerholz questioning his own ambitions, you became—for the duration of the convention, at least—in the words of Barry Miles, "Bill's personal assistant." Did that foment jealousy among his other close friends? I'm thinking of John Giorno in particular. I imagine him coveting such a role.

BOCKRIS: John Giorno would never have wanted my role. He was one of the stars of the show, plus he ran the Nova Con in tandem with James. The reason I was given the role as Bill's personal assistant during the evening sessions was because I had introduced Bill and James to Tom Forcade [owner and editor of *High Times* Magazine] out in LA that October, and Forcade put up the initial seed money for the Nova Convention. Meanwhile, Bill, James, and I had a ball out in Los Angeles: visiting movie sets, hanging out with Paul Getty Jr., getting high, and laughing. This was when I went from being a journalist to a friend. Then, back in New York in mid-November, Tom Forcade shot and killed himself. I was shattered. James told me he had not seen Bill as upset as he was on hearing of Tom's death. I think they saw giving me the assignment as a way of helping me move on from Tom, with whom I had been very close. It worked out well for all of us.

HORTON: The Nova Convention is considered a convergence that cemented Burroughs' influence on music and established his reputation as "the godfather of punk"—a moniker he firmly disputed—with performances from Patti Smith, Frank Zappa, John Cage, and Laurie Anderson. What are your abiding memories of those three days?

BOCKRIS: Jumping down from a shelf in Bill's dressing room just before he went on stage and spilling my glass of red wine all over his trousers ("All over my trousers, man!"); making eye contact with him backstage right before he went on to do a great reading; telling him there was a bomb scare at the after-show party at Mickey Ruskin's.

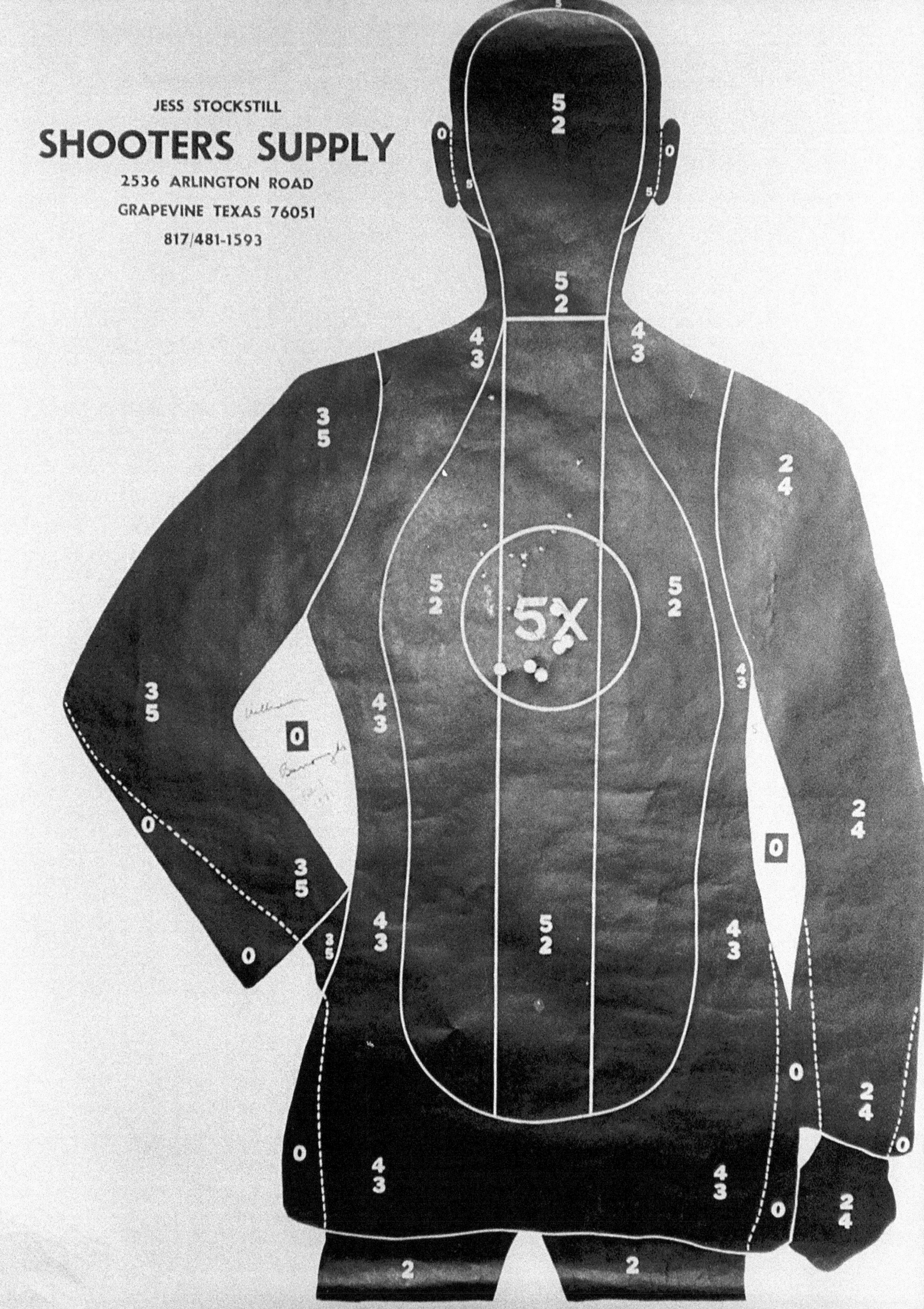

JESS STOCKSTILL
SHOOTERS SUPPLY
2536 ARLINGTON ROAD
GRAPEVINE TEXAS 76051
817/481-1593
5X

"THERE AINT NO BOMB MAN and we're not going anywhere," he said. He was enjoying every moment of this once in a lifetime celebration of his life and work.

HORTON: From around 1974 to 1981 you organized the series of dinner parties that would ultimately be published as *With William Burroughs: A Report from the Bunker*. Andy Warhol, Susan Sontag, Lou Reed, Tennessee Williams, Debbie Harry, Allen Ginsberg, Mick Jagger, Christopher Isherwood, Joe Strummer… The guest list goes on and on—it's one hell of a roll-call—but how did you first hit on the idea for such an unusual book?

BOCKRIS: One night after interviewing Bill over two afternoons in Boulder, Colorado, for *High Times* in August 1978, I was having dinner with him and some amigos. At one point, when he saw me obviously astonished at the level of play in the ongoing conversation, he said, "The best stuff is always off tape." At that moment, I swore I would only interview Bill over drinks and dinner. Andy had been doing this for years. Thus, all the conversations in *With William Burroughs* were conducted over drinks and dinner.

The book was first published in Italy as *Con Burroughs* in December 1979. It was only after recording a dinner conversation between Bill and Andy Warhol that in February 1980 I realized I could cut all the dinner transcripts up and reorganize them by subject. That's what really turned that book into, as Gerard Malanga wrote me, "A work of art." One of the best creative experiences of my life.

HORTON: The book is much more than a series of remarkable dinners, of course, but one that really stands out for me—one described in detail in *The Burroughs-Warhol Connection*—is the disastrous meeting with Mick Jagger. It is certainly clear that Jagger not only didn't want to be there, but also that he didn't seem to know *why* he was there. He comes across as positively paranoid in fact. With Warhol, Jerry Hall, music journalist Liz Derringer, and New York photographer Marcia Resnick all in attendance, the strained conversation and palpable discomfort practically leaps off the page…

BOCKRIS: This "nightmare of misunderstanding," as Bill called it, was based on the fact that Keith Richards wanted to meet with Bill. Considering his recent brush with incarceration regarding the Toronto heroin bust, the Stones' team wanted to block a meeting between Keith and Burroughs. The fact was that Keith proved impossible to pin down to a date and the deadline for my book was approaching. Liz Derringer was a good friend, so she stepped in to make a date with Mick.

I should have known that trouble was brewing when neither Bill nor I had enough money to buy a good dinner for our guests. The trouble really began when Bill could not remember why we were there. In the end, I think I captured a more interesting and revealing conversation than I might have had things proceeded positively. And Marcia Resnick took thirty-six photographs of the event. That dinner is best read in the context of *The Burroughs-Warhol Connection*.

VICTOR BOCKRIS: So, Mick, did you ever shoot anyone, or did anyone ever try to shoot you?

MICK JAGGER: No.

VICTOR BOCKRIS: Bill shot someone, and Andy got shot, let's see…

MICK JAGGER: Who did you shoot, Bill?

WILLIAM BURROUGHS: It's a long story. It's a bad story. But I haven't shot anyone right lately. I assure you of that, Mick. I been on my good behaviour.

THE CAPTAIN'S COCKTAIL PARTY (1980)

HORTON: Ted Morgan in *Literary Outlaw* says Jagger stayed for fifteen minutes. Did it feel longer?

BOCKRIS: Ted Morgan did not like me because I was young and had more intimate access to Bill than he did. This was something he could not understand. Jagger stayed for forty-five minutes.

HORTON: What was Morgan's problem? He spent little time at the Bunker, I believe, while writing his biography, and yet he seems to hold you responsible for everything he didn't like about what went on there.

BOCKRIS: Biography is a hellish art form because the biographer has to find a different form for each of his books, and Morgan never got his Burroughs form right. Look at it from his perspective: he was a prizewinning biographer who had tackled some of the greatest subjects of his times like Roosevelt and Churchill.

I had offered to write Bill's biography, but I think Bill and James Grauerholz wanted the more experienced and higher profile Morgan. Morgan had known Burroughs since 1972. Yet he was uncomfortable with homosexuality and did not understand Bill's relationship to heroin at all.

Furthermore, biographies demand from three to five years to research and write. This was also an authorized biography. As time went on—and cracks started to appear in the book's carapace—Bill interposed James between himself and Ted. James was a great amanuensis, but he had a fatal flaw. He liked to maintain control by interfering in affairs he did not fully understand. In the final stages of the book, Ted, James, and Bill were not talking. And I believe Morgan associated me with this cabal.

In fact, I had nothing against Morgan and nothing to do with his problems. He just saw me as an opportunist. He was blinded by his own frustrations. My problems with Morgan only came after the book's publication, when he turned against Bill and started telling a lot of lies about him in public talks. Ted Morgan's mind, as it were, had been blown by writing the biography of Burroughs. In retrospect, I sympathize deeply with his problems.

HORTON: Let's talk about the Bunker for a moment. A disused YMCA locker room, a large concrete space with no windows, no natural light and a bathroom with a row of urinals and cubicles—it sounds such an oppressive environment to live and work in. I mean, I feel depressed if I leave the curtains drawn for a day. Burroughs lived there from 1974 to 1981. How did it suit his temperament? Did it impact on his mental wellbeing?

BOCKRIS: On the contrary, the Bunker was a place of light and adventure, which emanated largely from the force of Bill's drive to write *Cities of the Red Night*. When the doctor was in, his typewriter thundered through the afternoons. Like Warhol, Burroughs personality was the opposite of his image as a cold distant oracle. He loved having drinks and dinner with his inner circle, loved telling and listening to stories. His face lit up when he was making contact.

I've described the Factory as a boarding school. I would say the same about the Bunker. After dinner activities included target practice with air pistols and blowguns. It was an old boys' literary salon, to which I brought a certain flash perspective. I strongly suggest you publish a section of Stewart Meyer's *Bunker Diaries* in *Beatdom*. This is the best unpublished book on W.S.B.

Furthermore, 222 Bowery was a landmark building. Rothko had had a studio in the swimming pool. John Chamberlain, of the Car Crash sculptures, used to live on the top floor. It was an artist's sanctuary. The Bunker fit Bill like a warm glove. In March 1980, I witnessed this conversation in the Bunker, which puts it in context of New York City in those days:

> **VICTOR BOCKRIS:** Have you been anywhere exotic lately?
>
> **DAVID BOWIE:** Well, I mean, I think New York is the most exotic place right now. Don't you, Bill?
>
> **WILLIAM BURROUGHS:** Yes, yes indeed. You don't have to leave New York to find the exotic. But, see, I think that this whole notion of only the jungle is exotic is of course ridiculous…. You can find any number of exotic things in New York…
>
> THE BUNKER MARCH (1980)

HORTON: Such a hermetic habitat coincided with Burroughs suffering writer's block and using heroin once again. Is there a correlation there, or am I reading too much into it?

BOCKRIS: Bill's writer's block was not unrelated to his son's slowly dying or to his ongoing financial hardships. So far as I know, between 1974 and 1977 Bill did not use heroin. I was with him in 1978 in LA when he started using again. Most people misunderstand Bill's relationship to heroin. The fact is, to start with Bill took small amounts of opium,

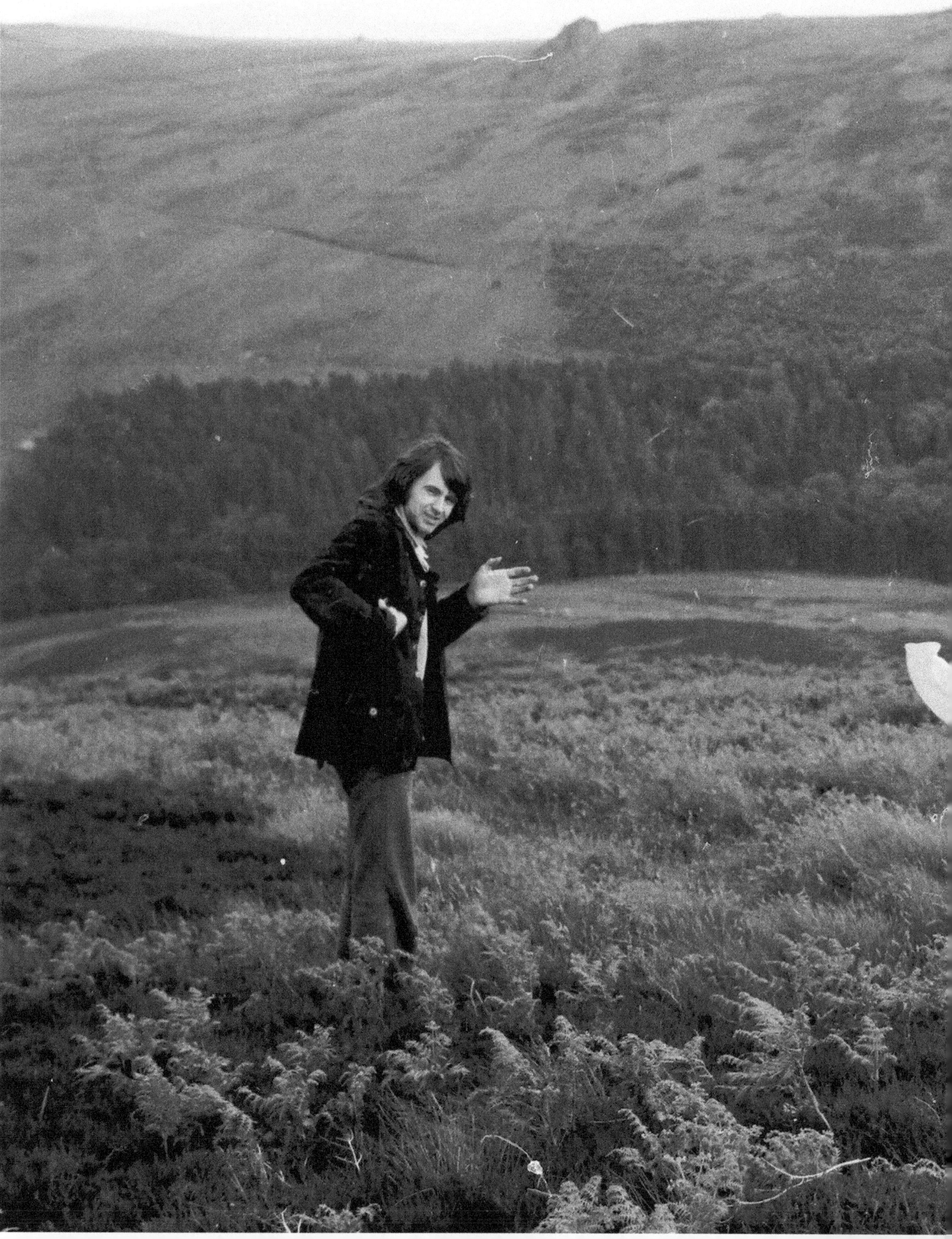

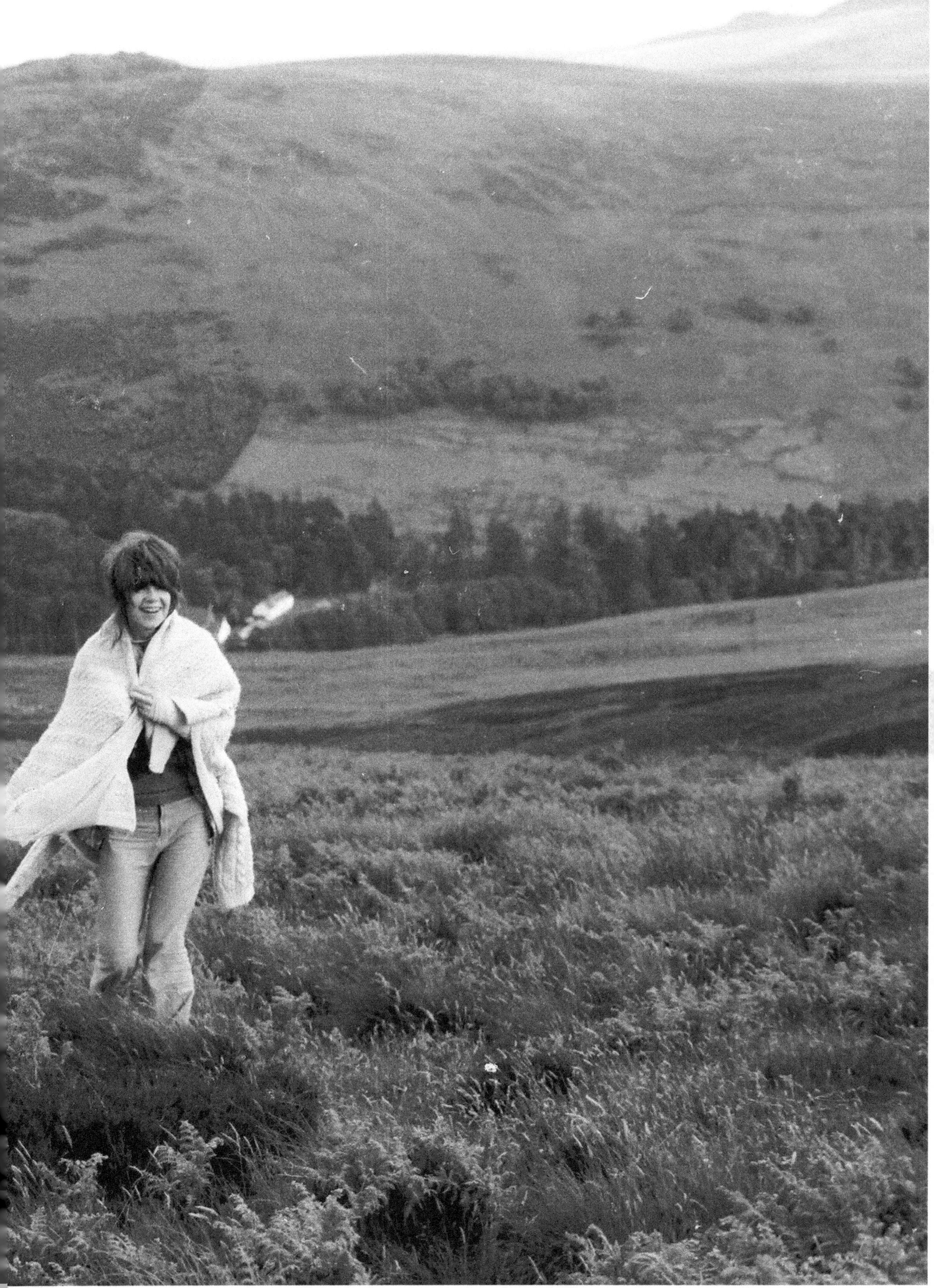

which gave him the space to write well, without interruption by constantly intruding problems. From thereon, he became addicted to heroin again and made good progress on *Cities of the Red Night*. People need to be better informed. Used in moderation, heroin can be extremely useful in one's work. The problem comes with long-term addiction when the drug can take away everything from your ability to work to your soul. I would never recommend anybody use heroin; it is the most seductive and destructive drug. Bill got off it in 1981. He was a very strong man.

HORTON: How did life at the Bunker compare to life at Warhol's Factory?

BOCKRIS: This is a good question. Life at the Factory (in 1980, the year I introduced Andy and Bill) and the Bunker was similar in that it evolved around the superstar at its centre, each populated by men devoted to furthering their respective master's career. Both Bill and Andy had multiple productions going on.

Of Burroughs inner circle, John Giorno was putting out albums of Bill reading his works; Howard Brookner was making a documentary about Burroughs; I was writing a book about him; Stewart Meyer was driving him and keeping a diary. All these products had a positive effect in building up his audience. Meanwhile, Bill was producing his monthly *Crawdaddy* column "Time of the Assassins" and writing his big novel *Cities of the Red Night*.

Of Warhol's inner circle, Bob Colacello was putting out Andy Warhol's *Interview* magazine, Vincent Freemont was developing Andy's TV show, Ronnie Cutrone was Andy's painting assistant, and Fred Hughes was the business manager who turned the Factory into Andy Warhol Enterprises. Both places hosted meetings with other artists. Both relied on their exotic company and the voice of their leader to create a creative and intoxicating atmosphere.

HORTON: According to Barry Miles in his biography *Call Me Burroughs*, Burroughs had mixed feelings about *With William Burroughs*. Miles quotes from a 1981 interview in *Talk Talk*, saying: "There are some good photographs in it, but I could have lived without it." Barry is elsewhere very complimentary, saying Burroughs "enjoyed the razzmatazz that Victor brought to his life" but his seeming ambivalence towards your hard work must have stung a little bit.

BOCKRIS: Yes. I'm sorry Miles did not quote instead a remarkably positive review of the book by the writer Seymour Krim in the *Chicago Tribune*, but I understand why he used that quote. In fact, one night I was sitting next to Bill at the Bunker when I stumbled on the quote and humorously passed it to him. He responded by writing a dedication to me in a recent art catalogue, which said essentially that it was the product of shifting loyalties. In other words, Grauerholz, Brookner, etc., were trying to persuade Bill that I was taking advantage of him. I think I made around $2,500.00 from the book, a little more from foreign sales. Part of the problem was, just when I got going on the book, James left Bill to move to Kansas with Burroughs' archives. He kept running his business from there. Thus, James did not appear in the table talk. He should have, and would have had he been there.

Let me add that Miles has written more intelligently about me than any other single writer. He has also been my closest friend since 1978. The conversations we have had over the years have played a large role in shaping my thoughts and my writing. The friendship also has its own pedigree. In 1973, Allen Ginsberg introduced us, saying we had a lot in common and would like each other. Thank you, Allen! Meeting Miles changed my life. I miss seeing him as much as I used to.

HORTON: Miles mentions that some members of Bill's circle felt threatened by your presence and attempted to turn him against you. Without risking a lawsuit, is there anything you'd like to say about that? It sounds like people were claiming some sort of ownership over the man, which is frankly ridiculous, as though they were vying for control of him…

BOCKRIS: When people become part of an entourage, there are always struggles between its members for closeness to the star. Miles witnessed, with humour, the attempts of the gay men around Bill to close me out because I was not gay or was not an addict. Grauerholz (not an addict) and Brookner both resented the close conversations I had with Bill around this time. They refused to understand how much Bill enjoyed my conversation and, for the most part, talking with people I bought to him. Everything I did was done out of sincere love for my subject.

HORTON: Personally, of the many interviews, books, and biographies I've read about Burroughs, I think *With William Burroughs* stands shoulder to shoulder with Miles' *Call Me Burroughs* and Burroughs' *The Job* as the three most insightful portraits of both man and writer. Were you pleased with it? Did you achieve what you set out to achieve?

BOCKRIS: Thank you. Yes, I was immensely pleased with the results. *With William Burroughs* was my first solo book, apart from my two books of poems. I started working on the book in January 1979; I did not discover its perfect form until February of 1980, one month before the deadline. It was always going to be based on Burroughs' table talk, but it was not until I recorded the Burroughs-Warhol dinner that I decided to cut up all the dinner transcripts and reorganize them by subject. I found the perfect form for *With William Burroughs*. Andy was one of the biggest fans of the book.

HORTON: There is a wonderful account of a 1979 dinner with Lou Reed at the Bunker, which you relate in *Lou Reed: The Biography* (1994). Reed was late, somewhat inebriated, and rather than apologize for his tardiness, you wrote that he "proceeded to take apart each of Burroughs' cocktail guests with deft one-liners that perfectly pinned their weakest points." Who was present, and what exactly did Reed say to them?

BOCKRIS: When I approached the Bunker with Lou and his entourage, almost one hour late, I had no idea Bill had a number of guests. Present at the table were Bill's driver and connection Stewart Meyer, Bill's close friend and upstairs neighbour John Giorno (star of Warhol's first movie *Sleep*), and Ted Morgan, accompanied by an attractive young woman. Lou went around the table asking peoples' names then commenting on them. Now, you have to understand that Morgan was a French aristocrat called Sanche Charles Armand Gabriel de Gramont, who changed his name when he moved to America. So when he answered "Ted Morgan," Lou responded incredulously: "Ted?" Lou not only hit a raw nerve, he made Morgan look like a fool in front of his girlfriend. There was a sudden freeze in the atmosphere, but Lou rescued himself by hurrying on to Bill, asking him if he had cut off his toe to avoid the draft, or slept with his publisher in order to get his book published.

HORTON: Neither of which was true, of course. What was Burroughs' initial reaction to all of this?

BOCKRIS: Bill immediately picked up on Lou's satiric references, and responded playfully to each barb. The meeting ended on a friendly note when Bill did something I had never seen him do before. He walked Lou, his wife Sylvia, and his guitar player down to the street and shook hands with him next to Lou's limousine.

> **LOU REED:** See, I know you wrote a lot of other books, but I think *Junkie* is the most important because of the way it says something that hadn't been said straightforwardly…. Is this boring you?
>
> **WILLIAM BURROUGHS:** Wha?
>
> DINNER WITH LOU REED (1979)

HORTON: *Lou Reed: The Biography* is a genuinely loving portrait of an extraordinary artist who gave his life to music, an industry known for eating its young. It's clear you adored the guy, despite his failings, but how did your relationship change over the years you knew him?

BOCKRIS: *Lou Reed: The Biography* was the name of the British edition. The British paperback replaced the hardback text with the text of the U.S. book, *Transformer: The Lou Reed Story*. I presume you read the British paperback.

HORTON: Um… no, I read the hardback.

BOCKRIS: If you ever get a chance to pick up the paperback you'll find a much more completed book with better construction and infrastructure throughout. I was lucky in meeting Lou in 1974, when I interviewed him about *Rock n Roll Animal*. Lou also thrived on good conversation. We connected so well that day he invited me to have dinner with him that night. I couldn't go, but when we did meet for drinks a few days later, Lou was the sweetest most charming man I'd ever met. From '74 to '76, I saw him when he was in town, or talked with him on the phone. He always gave me good advice on how to survive in the New York Underground.

HORTON: I read somewhere that Reed had previously been very complimentary about *Uptight: The Velvet Underground Story*, but how did he feel about your new biography?

BOCKRIS: This is a complex issue. In the months following the book's US publication, three different rock writers from the US, Australia, and France on three different occasions told me the same story. Each one said they approached Lou asking if he would grant them an interview. On all three occasions, he asked, "Have you read my biography?" When they all responded "No", he replied, "Go away and read that book then come back and we'll do an interview." On the other hand, Lou's wife Laurie Anderson, for whom I have the upmost respect, has treated me since Lou's death as if I am an enemy.

This brings up a vital subject: Why do rock stars, whose careers would have been shadows of what they became without the intelligent interviews, reviews, and books published about them, treat rock writers like deadly enemies? This is a mystery that deserves to be investigated. I have always written out of love for my subjects. And I believe my biographies have been popular among their fans. They are parades of their achievements and advertisements for their albums.

HORTON: After his death in 2013, you updated the biography (re-titled *Transformer: The Complete Lou Reed Story*), something you have done with several of your other books. Is it the biographer's lot in life to be forever rewriting their work? Where does it end?

BOCKRIS: I've updated *Uptight: The Velvet Underground Story* and *Keith Richards The Biography* three times successfully. I think my update of *Transformer* was not as successful. However, I did discover how much Laurie's and Lou's albums during their partnership were like epistolary novels. They both sang back and forth to each other, responding song by song to what the other had said. I think this is kind of unique. Nothing ever ends.

HORTON: James Grauerholz took a certain amount of flak from some quarters when he convinced Burroughs to give up the Bunker and move to Lawrence, Kansas, in 1981. Do you think it was the right thing to do? What was the feeling among his New York friends?

BOCKRIS: James got a lot of flak, but it was a brilliant move – as the years flickered by and we approached the era of AIDS, Bill's life was increasingly in danger from shared needles. Furthermore, if you look at the patterns of Bill's life, he always moved after six or seven years—from Tangier to Paris to London to New York to Lawrence, his final address.

There was a lot of bad feeling from people who were going to miss the man who had become the centre of their lives. On the other hand, few people noticed how hard Grauerholz was on Burroughs during his first year in Lawrence living alone on the outskirts of the city, often leaving him alone for several days at a time. No wonder Bill called Learnard Avenue, where he finally bought a house, Learn-Hard Avenue.

However, the bottom line was that Grauerholz gave Burroughs twenty-three years of a highly productive life from 1974 until Bill's death in 1997. Sixteen of those years were based in Kansas, where Burroughs really flourished and was surrounded by a devoted crew of assistants. Moving to Lawrence was the right thing to do in spades. What he missed in conversation he gained in product.

HORTON: Was there life at the Bunker after Burroughs left?

BOCKRIS: Not sure what you mean. Was there life at the Bunker? John Giorno oversaw the Bunker during Bill's absence, but Burroughs continued to use the place on regular visits to New York.

Personally, I lost my place at the Bunker, the Factory, and at Debbie Harry and Chris Stein's Upper East Side mansion all at the same time. Bill left town, Blondie broke up, and Andy would not let me come to the Factory during the time I was writing his biography. Living in New York always provided me with new routes once others had closed.

HORTON: Speaking of Harry and Stein, in 1982 you collaborated on *Making Tracks: The Rise of Blondie*. What can you tell us about that?

BOCKRIS: I was about two thirds of the way through the Burroughs book when I signed the contract to work on *Making Tracks* with Chris and Debbie. This was a wonderful project and they were inspiring to work with. Of all the people I met in New York during the 70s and 80s, they were the most inspiring and the most fun to work with. And the book worked out very well. The only problem, and it was a big problem, was that I took an absurd amount of time to write the text. It really breaks my heart when I think back on what would have happened had the book come out at the same time as *Autoamerican* [Blondie's fifth studio album] when it should have, or could have. We had a wonderful editor in Fred Jordan, one of the Grove Press heroes who played such a large role in bringing so many major European writers into print in the US. Yet I hardly saw him except for a couple of good lunches. Despite my ongoing affection for Debbie and Chris and good memories of working with her on the text and Chris on the photos and layout of the book, I cannot forgive myself for falling down so badly on the job. I regret that I was not able for contractual reasons to work on Chris' other books of photographs. I feel like I let him down. We are still friends.

HORTON: Are the stories about the animosity between Debbie Harry and Patti Smith true?

BOCKRIS: No. This was a minor matter and for a short time. It's been blown out of all proportion.

> **BOCKRIS:** Why can't you just tell the story that Patti Smith came up
> to you and told you to get out of rock 'n' roll?
> **HARRY:** 'Cause it's tacky.

STEIN: Yeah, just leave it out.

HARRY: Just say around this time people came up to me and told me to get out of rock 'n' roll. Patti wasn't the only one. I was pretty horrible. I deserved to be told to get out of rock 'n' roll. I was pathetic. Horrible and pathetic. I was very shy and stiff.

AN INTERVIEW WITH DEBBIE HARRY (1996)

HORTON: You lived in New York through the AIDS epidemic—that must have been a horrifying experience…

BOCKRIS: It was horrifying to the max. I lost a number of good friends to AIDS. It was also terrifying because it was never clear in those days whether it would cross over into the hetero community. I had some narrow escapes with girls who shared needles. AIDS also had a terrible effect on the counterculture's lifestyles. Everybody stopped picking everybody up, which meant a lot of people were dropped hard and broke.

HORTON: The extraordinary, controversial photographer Robert Mapplethorpe succumbed to AIDS, of course. You interviewed him in 1977, in the back of a taxi on his way to the airport. This was before he became famous. Did he sense what was coming?

BOCKRIS: Robert was a lovely guy. He was also very ambitious and lived, breathed and dreamed photography. He had an important backer in the collector Sam Wagstaff. Essentially, he succeeded as greatly as Patti Smith and Sam Shephard did—because he explored dark worlds with intrepid daring and brought back the pictures.

Did he see it coming? Absolutely. He was always going to be successful. The extent to which his work collided with his times and to some extent killed him only emphasises how much he was at the centre of the zeitgeist in those heady late 1980s, when the counterculture was reeling from the effect of AIDS. I once asked him, "What's your favourite part of your body?" and was impressed when he answered, "My cock." I shall always remember him and his work as courageous, beautiful and tough.

MAPPLETHORPE: I think photography is a perfect medium for this era. It's so quick. The idea of belabouring a painting, working for a month at one image is just not conducive to this period of time.

ROBERT MAPPLETHORPE TAKES OFF (1977)

HORTON: When I look at his work—the beauty of his composition—I realise that the line between perception and reception, between what we delineate as either art or pornography, is as thin as a politician's promises. "Look at the pictures," homophobic Senator Jesse Helms exhorted when he tried to have Robert's sex photographs banned.

What is it about sex, or the depiction of sex rather, that makes some people so apoplectic?

BOCKRIS: In Mapplethorpe's case, the photos fed on the age-old fear that the black man has a bigger penis than the white man. Bottom line: sex is a private act people do not talk about. Anytime you bring sex out into the open in whatever form, it challenges peoples' sense of privacy. Since World War II, sex has marched into prominent view on so many stages. It's still controversial. Bill Burroughs once opined that most peoples' sex lives were so disappointing, they cringed at other people expressing their joy in making love. This may be the case. Sex is certainly hard to write. In a way, it is a sad subject.

HORTON: I recently learned that you edited Burroughs' 1985 collection of essays *The Adding Machine*. There are some extraordinary pieces in there: "The Name is Burroughs," "Sexual Conditioning," "Remembering Jack Kerouac"—routines and reflections on writing, the cut-ups, space exploration, mind control, and how to become invisible. You must have had a great deal of material at your disposal. How did you make your choices?

BOCKRIS: This is an intriguing question. The fact is we had very little material to choose from, because Burroughs secretary-cum-manager James Grauerholz never sent us the essays he had in the Burroughs archives in Lawrence, Kansas. I did track down a number of these fugitive pieces. I don't want to hurt James, but at the same time I was striving to put together *The Collected Essays* that would have established Bill as a major essayist, James was putting together another book of essays, *The Burroughs File*, for City

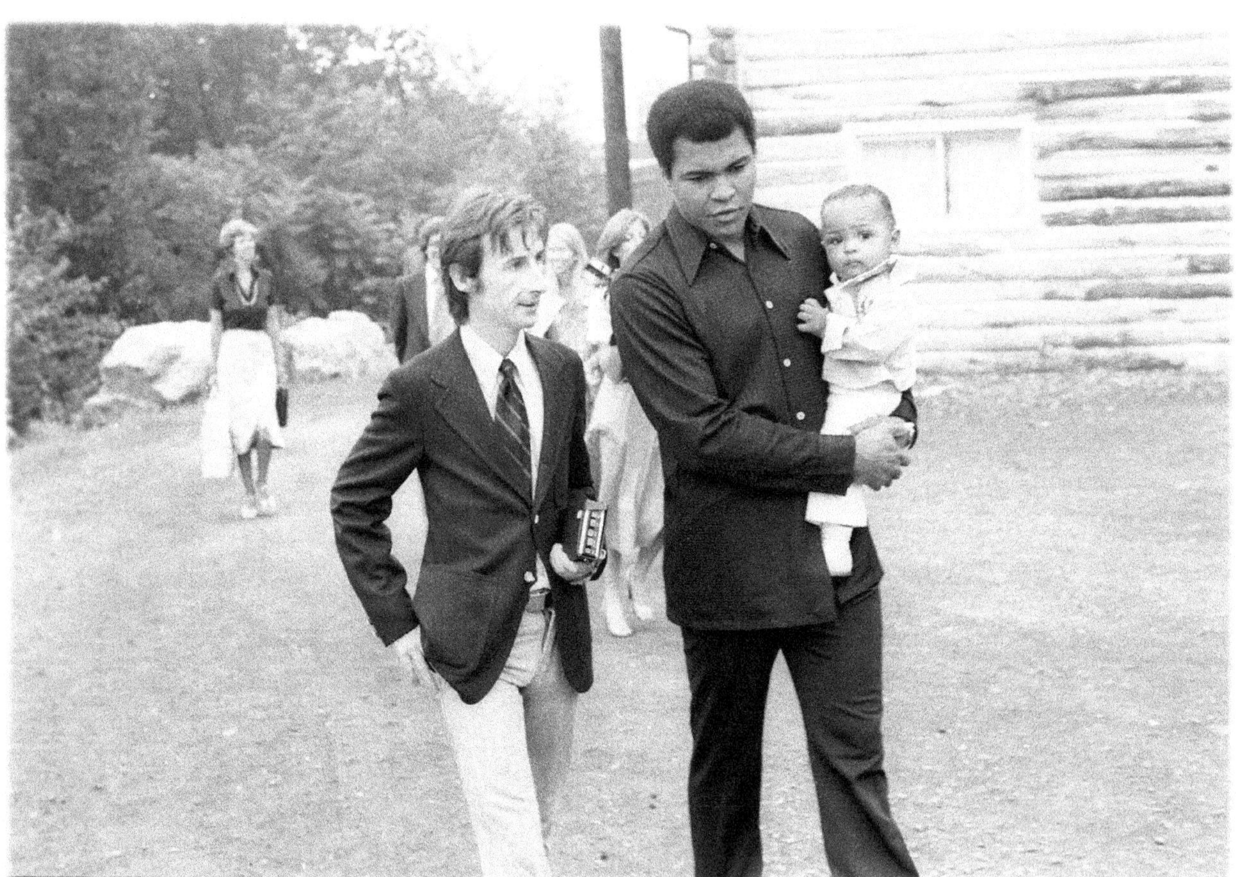

Lights. An opportunity to do *The Collected Essays* was missed. Years later in 2014, James wrote a bizarre introduction to a new edition of *The Adding Machine*. He stated that my attempt to edit the book had fizzled. He claimed he put the book together, but finally gave up on any attempt to describe how it had been sequenced, because of course he had not sequenced it. In fact, James appears to hate the book. He never did a minute's work on the entire volume, apart from hiring Stewart Meyer to type the manuscript I gave him onto a computer. Bill and I put together *The Adding Machine* in the Bunker, between 1980-1981, as we were both publishing our new books: *Cities of the Red Night* and *With William Burroughs.*

HORTON: Much of your writing was published at the fag-end of the 1980s into the '90s, when in quick succession you produced *Warhol: The Biography* (1989), *Keith Richards: The Biography* (1992), *Lou Reed: The Biography* (1994), *Patti Smith* (1998), *Muhammad Ali in Fighter's Heaven* (1998), *NYC Babylon: Beat Punks* (1998), *What's Welsh for Zen?* (1999)… Of all your books, mentioned here or not, which do you feel are the most successful in revealing something new about their subject?

BOCKRIS: *Warhol: The Biography* took me five years to research and write. It remains, thirty years after its publication, the only real biography of this extremely complex artist. The book puts Andy Warhol's work in context of his childhood in Pittsburgh, and brings the man alive as a passionate romantic, quite opposite to his public image. It also reveals him as the super intelligent, well-read, and in the words of Mailer "the most perceptive man in America." It is full of illuminating stories by his teachers and school friends, peers, critics, lovers, enemies, and family members.

Keith Richards: The Biography invented a new form for rock biography. Even Keith, who claimed he had not read it, told the *Chicago Tribune* that I was a good writer and that he heard I had done it in a new way. Anita told me she and Keith hid my Burroughs book from each other during a vacation at Point of View in Jamaica because they both enjoyed reading it so much.

Muhammad Ali said he had never read a book in his life, yet he went out of his way to publicise my book *Muhammad Ali in Fighter's Heaven*. He put together a book of his favourite photographs, *Muhammad Ali in Perspective*, including one of himself and his wife Lonnie reading my book with satisfied expressions. In 2009, Lonnie wrote me a card saying she was reading the book to Muhammad before he went to sleep at night. I believe he liked the book because it recorded the last period of his life that was under his control, before it was taken out of his hands and controlled by his profoundly immoral manager. The book is a celebration of Ali's voice. By the time that manager, Herbert Muhammad, had done with him, Ali had lost his beautiful voice forever. That was not a coincidence.

With William Burroughs: A Report from the Bunker revealed the kind, generous, funny side of Bill. I wanted to call it *Dinner with William Burroughs*, but the old-fashioned editor thought that was not appropriate. The point is anybody reading the book can pull up a chair and listen in to Bill's table talk. The book has been published in seven countries. Still in print here.

HORTON: Do you ever read reviews of your books?

BOCKRIS: Certainly. I have learned a lot about my writing by reading reviews of my books starting with Kenneth Bluford's review of *In America* in the Philadelphia underground weekly *The Drummer* in October 1972. I've been very lucky to receive good reviews for all of my books—although I cannot kid myself, they were also reviews of their subjects.

HORTON: What's the worst thing you've ever read about yourself?

BOCKRIS: "Victor Bockris is a terrible person. Everybody knows it." (At least they do now!)

> **VICTOR BOCKRIS:** Do you think alcohol addiction is as hard to kick as drug addiction?
>
> **KEITH RICHARDS:** Yes, I think so. All these things are very individual. One drug will have a different effect on one person than on someone else. I can booze for weeks and months and get lushed every night, and then, because I have a change of environment or whatever, I can stop and just not miss it
>
> AN INTERVIEW WITH KEITH RICHARDS (1977)

HORTON: I was blown away by the scope of *Keith Richards: The Biography*. It truly is a unique book. As with *Uptight*, you utilize elements of oral biography that lend themselves to a much more intimate and immediate experience for the reader—puts them in the room as it were. It's a technique I thoroughly intend to steal somewhere down the line, but did you envisage that form from the very beginning, or was it more of an organic process?

BOCKRIS: Biography is one of the most challenging literary forms because, for all you might learn about its structures and methods, each biography must find the form its subject requires. I don't think you can go into a biographical project knowing its form. Discovering it has to be an organic process. I made two decisions when I began the book: I would let Keith tell the story as much as possible, understanding that whereas he might not always be accurate in his accounts, he is giving us his emotional truth and that was more valid to me than straight facts. I would interview as many of the main women in his life as I could because women knew Keith best. The book is basically a parade of his achievements.

HORTON: In *The Burroughs-Warhol Connection* you talk in some detail about both artists' respective—"dual" is the word you use—influences on music: Warhol with Lou Reed and the Velvets, Burroughs with the likes of Patti Smith and David Bowie. However, the band you most closely relate to both men is the Rolling Stones. Why is that?

BOCKRIS: Since the Velvets, Warhol influenced hordes of musicians and bands. Burroughs influence on rock deserves a book of its own. Apart from introducing into our vocabulary the phrase Heavy Metal, his books supplied the names for a number of bands from Steely Dan to the Insect Trust. I am surprised both Andy and Bill have not been voted into the Rock n Roll Hall of Fame. The reason the Rolling Stones are the most prominent band in this case is because the first time they visited the States in 1964, the Stones met Andy Warhol. A friendship between Jagger and Warhol led to Andy's cover design for *Sticky Fingers* (1971) and *Love You Live* (1977), as well as the Jagger portraits Warhol did in 1975. When Andy died, Mick Jagger made one of the most astute comments about him.

The Stones' affiliation with William Burroughs emerged in the Nick Roeg film *Performance* starring Jagger and Anita Pallenberg. There are numerous quotes from Bill's writings in the film. Also, Jagger met with Burroughs in 1972 to discuss making a film of *Naked Lunch*. Both Keith and Anita often referenced him. The Joujouka album, *Brian Jones Presents the Pipes of Pan at Joujouka*, was William's favourite record for many years when I knew him. The Rolling Stones were influenced by countless other artists. Andy Warhol and William Burroughs were two of them.

HORTON: The 1990s saw a revival of interest in the counterculture, with the release of movies such as David Cronenberg's *Naked Lunch* and Oliver Stone's *The Doors*; numerous books including *Naked Lunch* and Kerouac's *On the Road* finding a new audience; and Patti Smith's return to music after 17 years of self-imposed exile… It's a strange question to ask a biographer, but do you think there are inherent dangers in looking to the past?

BOCKRIS: On the contrary, the past is a goldmine. Chroniclers of such significant periods as the triumphant Beat-Warhol-Punk collaboration that brought us out of the '70s into the '80s are indispensable. Otherwise, such vital historical movements would be lost under the rubble of time—and we would have no idea of how we got from there to here. History – *Her*story – is mighty relevant today.

> **VICTOR BOCKRIS:** I'm confused by the nineties. Historically, the last five years of any decade are supposed to be a fantastic time. But nothing's happening!
>
> **DEBBIE HARRY:** There's so much information, Victor. People are too aware of history, too informed. There's going to be a new perception, a new idea of what people are.
>
> AN INTERVIEW WITH DEBBIE HARRY (1996)

HORTON: You interviewed Burroughs again in 1990 for a piece titled "Calling Dr Burroughs." That interview has subsequently taken on legendary status—not least, if you don't mind my saying because you sound like you're having a full-on nervous breakdown. At one point, with Burroughs taking on the role of pacifying doctor, you exclaim that you are "suffering from a strong sense of invasion." Strident doesn't even begin to describe your state-of-mind in that interview. What the fuck was going on?

BOCKRIS: I reached the zenith of my career when the Warhol book was published in 1989. For the first time in my career I had the money to be mobile and all doors were open to me, but at this juncture I made the biggest mistake of my life. Instead of investing the money I was making in the Underground—from which my work had sprung—I chose to join forces with my new girlfriend and help her buy a house in Republican Connecticut to live in with her six-year-old daughter.

By the time I joined Bill and James a year later, I was reeling under the realization of what a dreadful mistake I had made. It was when I was trying to sleep in the Eldridge Hotel in Lawrence—between days interviewing Bill—I started twisting in the wind of my own disaster. I also had a broken wrist and a worried penis. And I was beginning to depend on substances other than of my own making to remind me who I was. I was falling apart, man. The good Doctor tried to put me back together.

HORTON: A worried penis? I've had lover's balls before now, but what the hell is a worried penis?

BOCKRIS: A worried penis is a penis which has strayed from one's wife to interact with one's mistress, leaving it vulnerable to transmitting a sexual wound. A worried penis constantly reminds its master of said infraction by regularly sending out a disturbing pulsing sensation. Imagine spending a sleepless night with a penis which will not stop pulsating.

> **WILLIAM BURROUGHS:** *(dignified)* I have never been a journalist.
>
> **VICTOR BOCKRIS:** Well, come on, you're always talking about the press, the press, the fucking press…
>
> **WILLIAM BURROUGHS:** You're crazy, man!
>
> **VICTOR BOCKRIS:** Of course I'm crazy!
>
> **JAMES GRAUERHOLZ:** You're lashing out, Victor.
>
> CALLING DR BURROUGHS (1990)

HORTON: At the top of the interview, you asked Burroughs "Were you ever in your life what you would describe as a frightened person?" to which he responded: "ARE YOU MAD? Like most people I live in a continual state of panic." I'd like to ask you the same question: Have you ever been a frightened person? What crawls up the back of

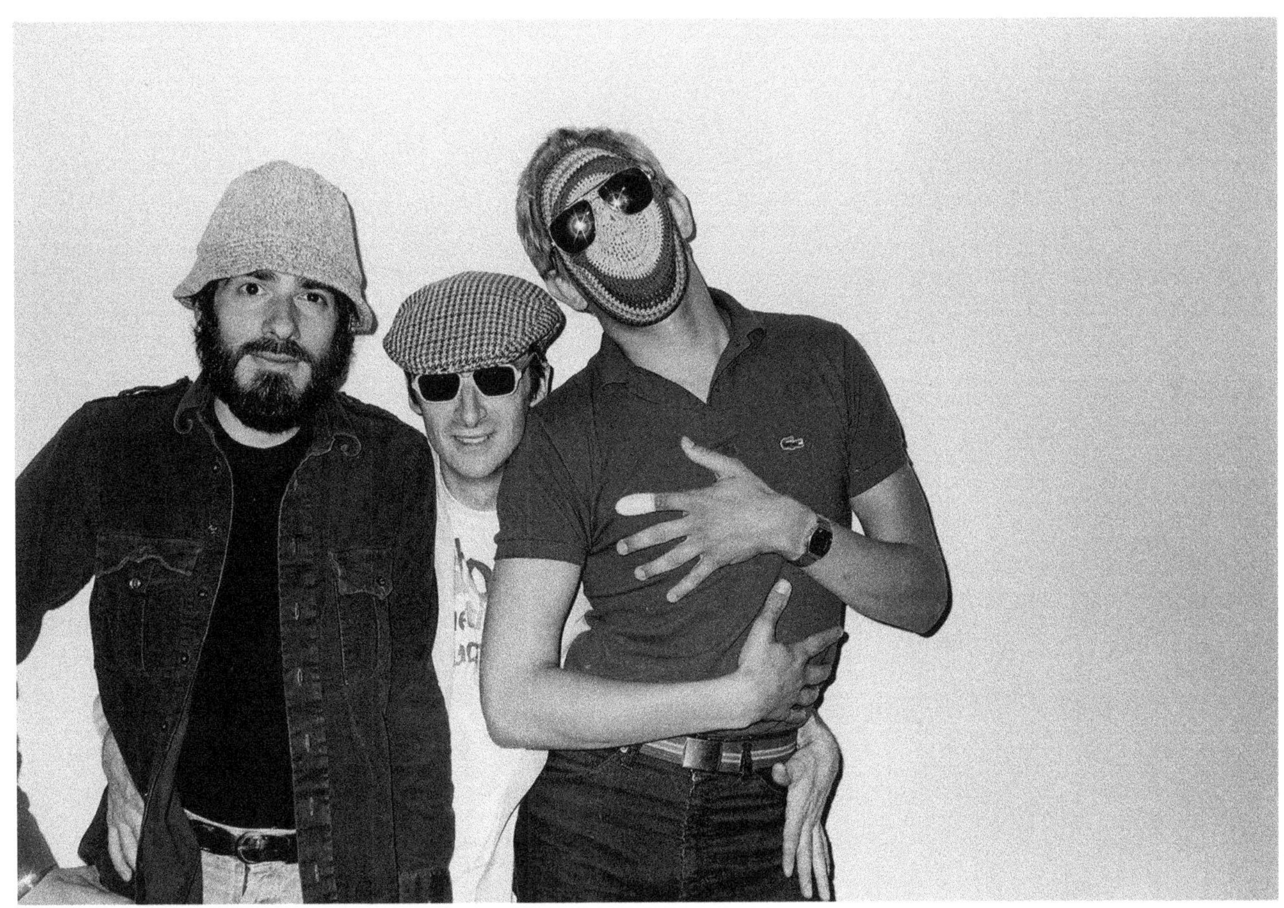

your throat in your nightmares?

BOCKRIS: Ha ha! I used to be plagued by certain fears from my childhood: an old lady jumped out of a sixth-floor back porch and would have landed on top of me if my best friend Johnny had not yelled, "Look out Vic!" I was terrified of being roasted alive on a spit and eaten by six-foot tall cockroaches standing on their hind legs. More recently, I am plagued by waking in the middle of the night in a cold sweat remembering the shocking moment I thought George C. Scott's car ran over Marlon Richards outside Keith and Anita's country house Frog Hollow in South Salem, New York. When bad things I did in my past leer up at me in broken dreams, I quiver in the sheets and curse the fact that I have never learned how to live.

HORTON: We've talked a great deal about your relationship with Burroughs, but what about others associated with the Beat Generation? I know you met Ginsberg on several occasions—he was a guest at many of the dinners you organised—but did you know any of the others?

BOCKRIS: Oh, yes. I had the honour to meet and hang out with Carl Solomon to whom "Howl" is dedicated; Herbert Huncke, who invented the term "Beat." He bent over backwards in the street one day, his arms flung out at his sides, exclaiming, "What a beautiful day man!" I was good friends with Terry Southern, loved Susan Sontag, had dinner with Gary Snyder; hung with Bob Creeley, Ted Berrigan, Anne Waldman, Robert Duncan, Michael McClure, Claude Pélieu, the actor Rip Torn, Mary Beach,

Charles Plymell, and big time Norman Mailer. I knew Corso, briefly, near the end of his life—beautiful cat.

> **VICTOR BOCKRIS:** Are there any mysteries?
>
> **GREGORY CORSO:** Generally, no. Personally, one.
>
> **VICTOR BOCKRIS:** What's the one?
>
> **GREGORY CORSO:** I don't know who I am.
>
> INTERVIEW WITH GREGORY CORSO (1973)

HORTON: Did you get on well with Ginsberg?

BOCKRIS: Allen Ginsberg was good to me on many occasions in New York and London. One afternoon, I visited him an hour before he was embarking on a tour of Yugoslavia with Peter Orlovsky and his guitar player Stephen Taylor. That night, I told Bill how good Allen had made me feel. "Yes, Allen has that effect on people," Bill responded agreeably. He loved Allen. It was hard not to love Allen, but I think Allen had a hard time loving himself, even in his sixties.

He thought my book on Bill was too chic, which it probably was, but I don't think Allen or Bill really saw it for what it was. In 1973, Allen introduced me to my best friend [Barry] Miles, which changed my life. Like I said, Allen always made me feel good.

HORTON: It concerns me, with the rise of so-called "cancel culture," that many of the artists and writers we've been talking about might find their work and reputations in the firing line. Am I right to be worried? Are we facing a new censorship, or is it just a passing phase?

BOCKRIS: All phases pass, but some leave more wounds behind than others do. I was recently talking to my sister Anna on the phone, bemoaning the state of affairs in the so-called United States. She pointed out that every generation, as it gets older, cannot understand the actions of its youth. At the moment, however, we are watching the collapse of the American Empire and the devastation of this country in a very real way. Frightening Fascism is on our doorstep. You might say the gates have been breached. Fascism is here. Meanwhile, when you look at the history of the arts in America, the great names remain. Andy Warhol is bigger than ever. In fact, the majority of my subjects are still discussed and celebrated. Censorship has come and gone, our greatest artists from the 1950s to the present remain. We still reference Oscar Wilde. Ali remains. The Stones continue rolling.

HORTON: Warhol passed away in 1987, Burroughs in 1997, Reed in 2013… When was the last time you saw each of them?

BOCKRIS: My friend Stellan Holm photographed me late one night standing next to Warhol at Area in 1986, the year before Andy died. This was when I was not allowed to go to the Factory because I was writing his biography. Typical of Andy's kindness. Besides, by then friends were telling me he was saying he hoped I would make a lot of money out of the book.

By the time Bill died, despite still corresponding with him, I was deep in a bad hole and had not seen him for two years.

I last saw Lou Reed in 1979. After we saw him at the Bunker, I went backstage at the Bottom Line to see Lou in his dressing room. Lou had never been as affectionate as he was that night.

However, a year later his book of poems *All the Pretty People* was published in Italy. He had asked me to find a publisher for the book. In the introduction, the editor Anna Abate claimed the publisher had paid me $500 for the manuscript. Although I got the Italian publisher to write a letter denying any such payment, which I sent to Lou, he never forgave me. Of course, Lou was well known for being extraordinarily nice, then extraordinarily nasty. I think he thrived on it. He was delusional.

I did almost bump into him coming out of his Christopher Street nest one beautiful morning in October 1980, but he refused to speak. Miles, who was striding on next to me, commented, "You should have said, 'Cat got your tongue, Lou?'"

HORTON: Did you go to Burroughs' funeral?

BOCKRIS: I went with Bill to his son William Burroughs Jnr's Buddhist funeral in New York, but no, sadly, by the time of Bill's death I was too sick and broke to make it. A lasting regret.

HORTON: Sick and broke? What happened?

BOCKRIS: I had made that terrible mistake of getting involved with and living with a woman and her young daughter. This upset my focus on the work. I should have married the books; instead, I split my affections. At the same time, somebody I had completely trusted betrayed me in a way that made it difficult to keep going financially. Bottom line, I did not take care of myself. I worked for too long without a proper break and I abandoned my calling without even knowing it. Meanwhile, I had been using mucho drugs and alcohol to keep going between these two worlds. I became a mess, a horrible stinking mess! A group called Virgin of the Birds recorded a song called "Victor Bockris," written by lead vocalist Jon Rooney. He accurately pins 1998 as a turning point in my career.

HORTON: I've seen the video on YouTube. It is a wonderfully melancholic tune. Are you melancholic by nature?

BOCKRIS: My career took something of a nosedive in 1998 with the publication of my only bad book *Patti Smith: A Biography*. I carried on through 2001 with *Rebel Heart* (with Bebe Buell), but just as it began really taking off after many great reviews 9/11 stopped everything. I am not by nature melancholic, although I like the word. I am a celebrator of oft-misunderstood cultural icons, who has taken great joy in his life and career.

That's not to say I have not been through some very dark periods in my life.

HORTON: If there is one widely accepted but inaccurate perception of Burroughs the man, inadvertently or even deliberately created by yourself or others, one that you would like to take this opportunity to correct, what would that be?

BOCKRIS: That he lived at the centre of the Beat-Punk scene I was trying to create around him in *With William Burroughs*. Not that I regret it. The book still stands, hard, tall, and erect. The fact is Bill rarely went out; he did not hang with famous people. In the evenings, he mostly enjoyed the company of his inner circle—drinks, dinner, conversation, target practice. I invited Norman Mailer to one of those dinners. Mailer declined on the grounds he found Burroughs hard to talk with. He could be, but not at the Bunker surrounded by his inner circle who all loved him. He was loquacious, very funny, and very warm.

HORTON: Same question for Andy Warhol. Is there anything you would like to set straight there?

BOCKRIS: Andy Warhol was a paradox. He was a bolt of lightning, a font of joy in creation, a Lord of the Universe. He was also a tragic figure because despite all the success all the wealth and the thousands of people he befriended over time, Andy possessed an almost Russian sense of sadness that came from the sufferings of a childhood in Depression Pittsburgh: the death of his father when he was thirteen, the near death of his mother a year later. In the end, he was immensely lonely. When you exist on the highest plane of existence, there are very few people up there with you. So many of them had died. The other thing I'd like to set straight is that Andy was a truly magic person. Undoubtedly, the single most fascinating person I ever met.

HORTON: This is pretty much a rhetorical question—a pretty stupid one, I know, but I have to ask: was he a changed person after he was shot by Valerie Solanas in '68?

BOCKRIS: According to people who knew him before he was shot, yes. The underground film star Taylor Meade said he was like a ghost of the person he had been. Lou Reed said his presence alone was more powerful before he was shot. As somebody who knew Andy, from 1973 to 1983, then spent five years interviewing people from every corner of his life for my book, I can add this: it took him a long time to recover from the shooting. By 1975, he had regained a lot of the energy, drive, and focus that made him so unique. Then I had that experience of feeling the intensity of his strength as I walked along with him.

One of the negative effects of the shooting was that it distanced him from some of the crazy but creative young women he had surrounded himself with in the sixties. His openness to everyone who flocked to him at the Silver Factory inspired him to make for example *Chelsea Girls*. This side of him emerged again when he threw himself in with the young artists of the 1980s: Basquiat, Haring, etc. He started dressing in black leather again and appeared to have rediscovered a more youthful self. However, Andy

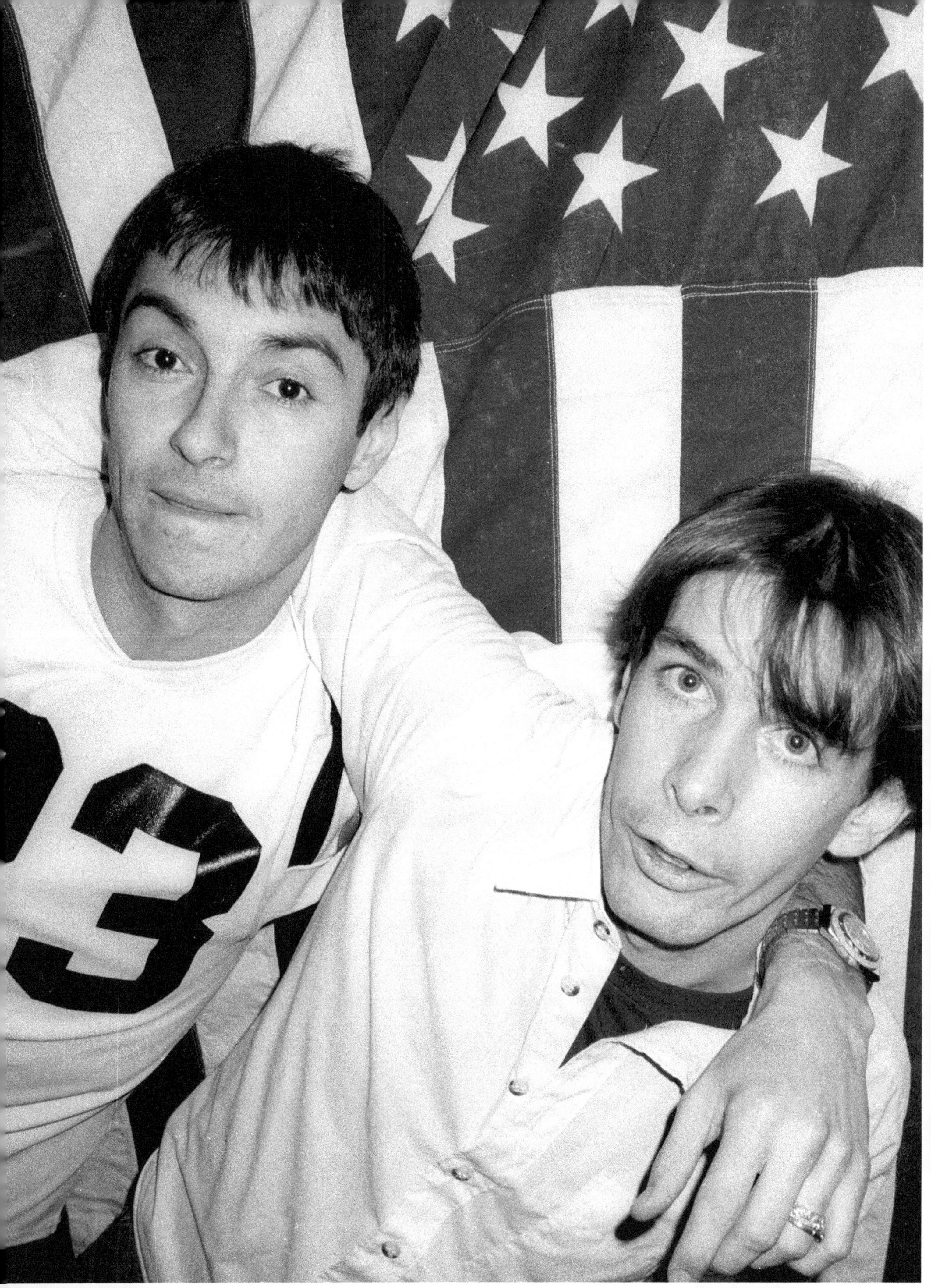

was badly damaged by the shooting. He lost his spleen. His body never fully recovered. So yes, Andy was changed by the shooting, but he was not a different person.

HORTON: Did it affect his art?

BOCKRIS: I resent people who try to say he never did such strong work as he painted in the 1960s. He retired from painting to make films in 1965. He returned to painting with his Mao portraits shown in Paris in 1974. Those paintings were as good as anything he did in the sixties. He did so much work in the seventies and eighties. I don't think that work has been properly adjudicated. In terms of comparing it to his sixties oeuvre, I think the *Shadows* (1979) and *The Last Supper* (1987) and many other works from the *Hammer and Sickle* series (1976) to the last *Self Portraits* (1986) are all as good a anything he did during his first Pop period between 1962 and 1964.

HORTON: What is your favourite Warhol art?

BOCKRIS: In 1966, my family moved into a new house and my father bought a number of paintings to decorate it. If I had been able to buy some Warhol paintings that year, what would I have bought? I think the *Marilyn Diptych* (from the first Stable Gallery show in 1962) is probably his greatest single work. I have a lot of affection for the long yellow *Last Supper* painting, which I saw as another Death and Disaster painting. If I had to choose one work, I guess it would be *White Disaster*—the *Death and Disaster* painting, based on a police photograph, of a beautiful young woman who jumped from a building and landed on top of a car; looking like a model at a photo shoot.

> **VICTOR BOCKRIS:** I have to, sort of, take Burroughs and Warhol as parallel figures. Two people who, in the late 50s and 60s, stood up for what they believed in. Made no pretence about it. Were totally out front about it. At that time, that was absolutely outrageous.
> WILLIAM BURROUGHS: A MAN WITHIN (2010)

HORTON: In Yony Leyser's documentary *William Burroughs: A Man Within*, you said, "It's because of Burroughs and Warhol and what followed in their wake that the whole gay liberation movement sprang up." As a gay man, I have difficulty in furnishing Burroughs with such an accolade. To me, he was far too transgressive an outsider figure, even for gay culture…

BOCKRIS: Each to his own vision. Of course, I go too far, but I was influenced in my late teens and early 20s by interviews with and photographs of a gay Burroughs. They all seemed to point to the life of a man I greatly admired who was gay. Also, I travelled around Los Angeles with Bill and James in 1977 and recall introducing Bill to Governor Jerry Brown. Brown understood Burroughs was out there to support Proposition Six in support of gay rights; after that, Bill and entourage haired over to the Pleasure Chest to check out the sex toys. Don't forget, Bill and I invented "The Order of the Grey

Gentlemen"—a collection of predominately gay men who would patrol the subway looking for muggers. Anybody who did not see the enormous impact Andy had on getting homosexuality accepted knows little about him. When Andy came to New York in 1949, he refused to hide his gay identity. I think of him as a militant homosexual. Half the people at the Silver Factory were gay long before being gay became acceptable in New York. He was the most famous gay man of his times.

I loved the gay men I saw pass from obscurity in 1973 to celebrated status in 1974 in New York. In the 1970s, more than half of my closest friends were gay. And that came through hanging out with the Burroughs and Warhol gangs. It's like, I would have been gay had I not been so crazily turned on by all those stimulating punk girls, man. Don't forget them in my saga. The great photographer Marcia Resnick looms large.

HORTON: Yes, let's talk about Resnick for a moment. You've been friends since 1977, and much of her work as a photographer runs along parallel lines with your writing. It seems only logical, therefore, that you would collaborate on the 2015 book *Punks, Poets & Provocateurs, NYC Bad Boys 1977–1982*. How did that project come about?

BOCKRIS: Working with Marcia Resnick on her magnificent book of portraits, *Punks, Poets & Provocateurs*, was a wonderful example of long-term collaboration, particularly because Resnick is—and is not—a collaborative artist. Her photo sessions are classic examples of collaboration. She controls the sessions by dressing provocatively and dancing toward her subjects in a fantasy seduction. She always captures her subject at a moment of climax, often while sitting on their lap or leaning over them in close proximity. However, as soon as the session is over she wants to be left alone to go into the dark room and develop her pictures. After that, she held a firm grip on her work. She knew that she was unique and she always did it her way. She was a control freak.

Yet we had known each other so well that she was able to turn my input to her advantage. During the time Resnick took the portraits, I introduced her to Andy Warhol and William Burroughs. One of the best things about our book is that once she had sated herself on punk rockers, Marcia photographed Burroughs as much as she photographed Johnny Thunders. *Punks, Poets & Provocateurs* is the first book to put together artists from the Beat Generation of the 1950s, the Warhol Generation of the 1960s, and the Punk Generation of the 1970s. This recognition of the Beat-Punk-Generation had long been a subject I wanted to write about. Thus, working with Marcia on the book was not only the best collaboration I ever had with her, it also inspired me to focus my memoir on this subject. Collaboration on Collaboration.

HORTON: Photography, of course, looms large in many of your books. In *The Burroughs-Warhol Connection* alone there are over 100 photographs by Resnick, David Schmidlapp, and yourself. How important has photography been to your career?

BOCKRIS: Photography became important to my career in the fall of 1977. As I began to circulate between the Warhol Factory, the Burroughs Bunker, and CBGBs, I discovered that many of the people I started to visit were photographers. They would always show me their contact sheets of black and white photographs. These contact sheets were like diaries of what was going on in my three worlds. Christopher Makos, Marcia Resnick, and Gerard Malanga influenced me, as did Bobby Miller, Bobby Grossman, Erica and Elizabeth Lenard, and so many others. Andy Warhol was always taking photographs, so I bought the camera he was using then: a Konica autofocus flash camera. I have perhaps a thousand black and white pictures I like. I'm just about to open a website to make them available for publications and fine prints. Photographs have always been an integral part of my books and my writing and my life.

HORTON: What do you think of the New York art-lit-music scene today? How has it changed?

BOCKRIS: You may be asking the wrong person. Every time I visit New York, I find myself running around with Marcia—going to opening parties and shows by the same people I knew back then. I love the new music, films, and literature I hear about or see, but I don't know the current scene.

Tell you what: we are in for a huge deep look into our culture after this pissed culture we've been slathered with these last few years. One reason I am galloping to completion of my explosive memoir.

HORTON: Is it harder these days to make it as a writer?

BOCKRIS: No. Writers can always make it. People always want to read about what's happening. James Michener told me that, and he knew what he was talking about.

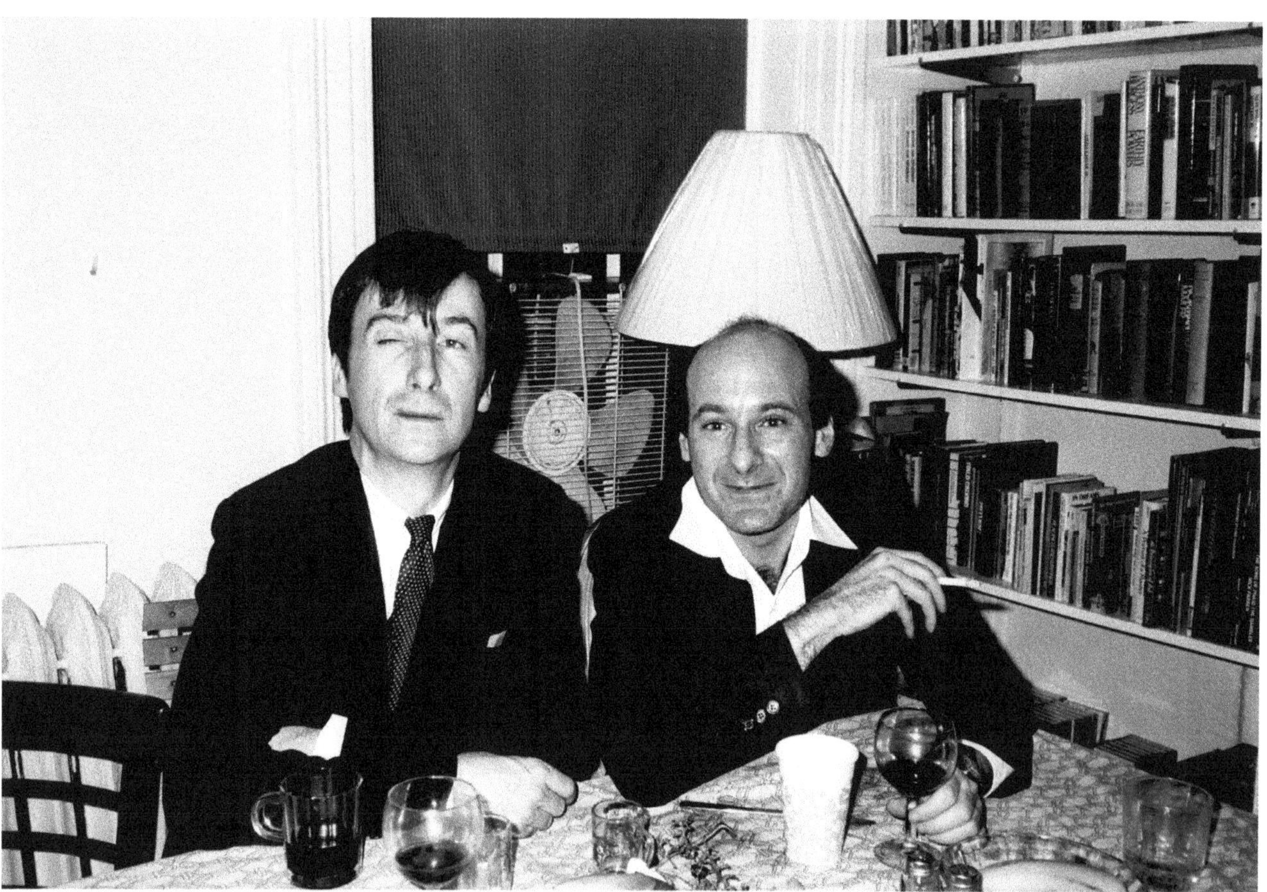

HORTON: As you move forward in life, do you find your interests—your concerns and beliefs—shifting at all?

BOCKRIS: ARRRRRGGGHH… uh, no. That's the problem. I'm still in love with the same girl I fell in love with in 1977. I'm still writing about all those people I wrote about in the '80s and '90s. I still dress the same way I dressed in the 1970s. If this was a movie would they call it *The Throwback*? No. It is necessary to travel. My mind is travelling all the time!

It's only recently that I've come to realize how little I've changed over the past fifty years. At a certain point around the late 1980s as I finished the Warhol book, I started to like myself. I liked who I'd become. I even liked the way I looked. 1989 was the first year I started to make money. I was forty. I had all sorts of plans: to go to yoga camp, to meditate, to clean out my system. I knew I had a long career in front of me and I wanted to be clear, healthy, and strong. But as soon as I met the perfect woman and fell in love, all that went out the window. I appropriated all those funds to rescue her from a damning marriage, etc. Had I really known myself I would not have made this dire mistake. People who abandon all for success are often successful, but their success often cannot be sustained because at some point they will step into quicksand without seeing it.

> **VICTOR BOCKRIS:** The most difficult thing in a writer's career is to keep on writing. The odds are very much against a writer being able to write to his satisfaction throughout his life. He has to keep traveling intuitively. He has to get off boats and planes to keep looking for new scenes he will need to write twenty years later. He may have to involve himself in other people's dreams.
>
> INTRODUCTION/WITH WILLIAM BURROUGHS (1982)

HORTON: Do you still get pleasure from writing? What I mean is, rather, do you still draw pleasure from the process of writing?

BOCKRIS: I think the practice of any craft is pleasurable so long as you stay on your spot. However, if you lose your spot, lose your footing and, for example, over-write or piss in your own bed, it can become harder to enjoy the process. Writing depends on strength of character. I will never let go of writing as the base of my life. I actually don't do very much where I am currently living when I am not writing. I have been writing my memoir for a long time. Will I ever unlock its combination? And if I don't, if I die by mishap or laziness, who would ever know the pages that already exist? Saying this urges me to act fast before I lose it. You can write yourself out of a book inadvertently. There's a two-way street between pleasure and writing. It's not just about how you feel in relation to the writing—it's about how the writing feels about you. This may be truer in writing books because there's a certain point in writing a book when you realize the book has developed its own legs. It begins to stand up on its own. If one was writing every day then suddenly stopped writing and took a trip, that writing would not be immediately available when one got back. Foreplay is needed, seduction even. I guess one of the better things about the writing process is the joyful experience of working in collaboration with your living book, giving and getting that love.

HORTON: Do you want to write until you can't anymore?

BOCKRIS: Yes, I want to write until I die. I want to die writing like Burroughs, who wrote one of his most profound sentences right before he left for the hospital for the last time. "Love? What is it? Most natural painkiller what there is." But I don't want writing to kill me. I mean, there are times when I imagine a time when I don't have to make money. Would I still write? I'd like to write long letters to all my friends. I wrote this lyric during the 2020 Pandemic:

> Before I die I want to be young
>
> Before I die I want to be golden
>
> Before I die I want to tell
>
> All my friends how much I love them,
>
> But I'm speechless
>
> And I'm speechless

HORTON: What will it say on your gravestone?

BOCKRIS: "He Wrote it as It Wrote him."

HORTON: You recently told me that you see your major works as trilogies—the Warhol/Richards/Reed biographies and the Burroughs/Blondie/Velvet Underground portraits. Where do you think this new book, *The Burroughs-Warhol Connection*, fits into that?

BOCKRIS: The trilogies you mention came out of the natural progress I was making through my times. The books I published between 2012 and 2022, *The Burroughs-Warhol Affair* (same book different title) in France, Spain, and Japan, and Marcia Resnick's book of portraits with my text, *Punks, Poets & Provocateurs*, looks back at the great days between 1977 and 1983. When I put together my Collected Works in X Volumes, *The Burroughs-Warhol Connection* will come in between *With William Burroughs* and *Uptight: The Velvet Underground Story*. By the time I complete my memoir and two other books, I will be able to discover new trilogies within older ones.

HORTON: What works are in the pipeline?

BOCKRIS: After I finish my memoir, I plan to write a book about Andy Warhol, the

Writer. Makes me think how most of my life I've only thought of my life in terms of writing books. I've been in a long time period of isolation that crept up on me after my father's death in 2013.

More recently, I elected to go deeper into it on my own. I have many good friends I could be in touch with, but I've bought into the romantic notion that I won't shave until I finish my memoir! I hardly feel capable of talking until I finish it: my testament, my answer to myself, my explication of where I went wrong… I'd like to say the future holds A, B & C for me.

HORTON: In October 2022, you attended the unveiling of a plaque commemorating the former home of Burroughs and Allen Ginsberg at 206 East 7th Street, where they lived in the early 1950s. How did that feel?

BOCKRIS: It felt weird and wonderful. During their time on East 7th in the fall of 1953, Allen and Bill worked on *The Yage Letters*. Kerouac was coming by at the weekends and one day he gave them the manuscript of *The Subterraneans*. This led Bill and Allen to ask how he wrote the book and Jack responded by writing "The Essentials of Spontaneous Prose."

It was a heady time among these literary explorers. Bill would go to Tangier to write *Naked Lunch*. Allen would go to San Francisco to write "Howl." I was aware of all this as I mingled with some thirty people on the sidewalk. That flat was like a launching pad. I wanted to jump up and tell everybody about all the work produced there. It was both poignant and thrilling because one could not help thinking about the future.

I took away from that event the need to write about the highpoint of American Civilisation as I saw it in New York in the 1970s and early '80s, the last time America had a strong culture of its own.

About the Interviewer

Leon Horton is a countercultural writer, interviewer and editor. Published by *Beatdom*, *International Times*, and *Beat Scene*, his numerous essays and interviews include "Hunter S. Thompson: Fear and Loathing in Utero"; "The Beaten Generation: Burroughs, Ginsberg, Thompson… and the Battle of Chicago"; "Charles Bukowski: Only Tough Guys Shit Themselves in Public"; "Where Marble Stood and Fell: Gregory Corso in Greece"; "Gerald Nicosia: In Praise of Jack Kerouac in the Bleak Inhuman Loneliness"; and "Painting Typewriters: An Interview with Bill Morgan." He recently edited a book about Gregory Corso called *Ten Times a Poet*.

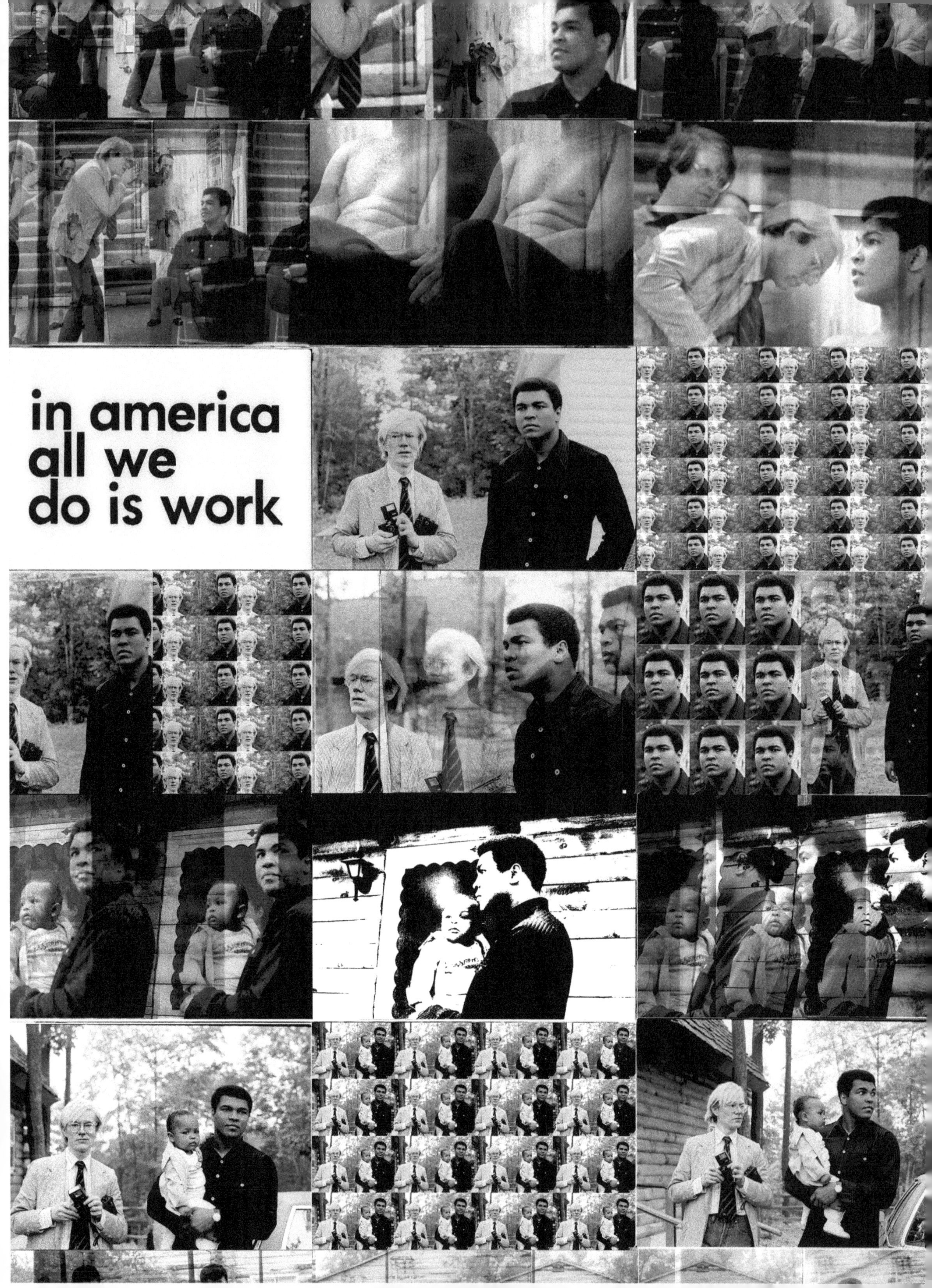

in america
all we
do is work

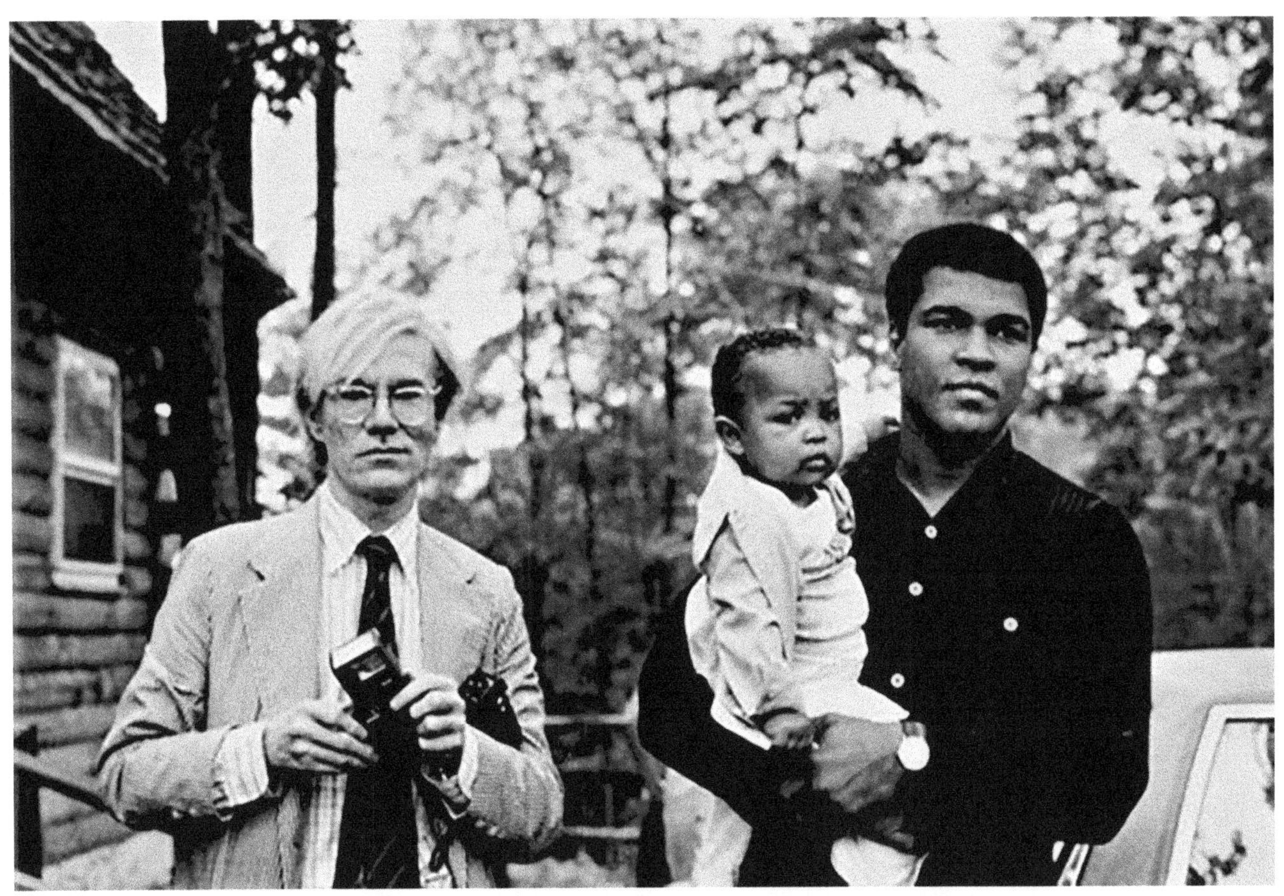

THE PHOTOGRAPHS

I do believe in teachers, though I would say, if you meet your teacher blocking your path to enlightenment, cut him down. That's the old Buddhist terminology. If you meet Buddha on the path to enlightenment, cut him down. But any action against the hero or the star system, which is taken out of resentment or anxiety or jealousy, will only lead to more resentment, anxiety, and jealousy, and so can't be of any usefulness. To cut the teacher or the hero or the media star down in a spirit of resentment is a mistake and will lead perhaps to the only permanent hell that does exist. It's called the Vajra hell, the unbreakable Vajra hell, which is refusal of intelligence, refusal of awareness.

Interview by Bockris with Allen Ginsberg

National Screw June 1977

The Burroughs-Warhol Connection is half text and half photographs. Without the visions of David Schmidlapp, Marcia Resnick, Bobby Grossman, Jenny Moradfar Meyer, and Robert de Marrais, the book would not exist. In addition, it was my collaboration with David on the Bockris-Schmidlapp Tapestries that gave me the idea for this book.

THE BURROUGHS-WARHOL PHOTO TAPESTRIES

The three Burroughs-Warhol Photo tapestries in this chapter are the genesis of *The Burroughs-Warhol Connection*. Between 2001 and 2005, David and I formed a team, Bockris-Schmidlapp. We were a complimentary mix. David is a soulful man. Working with him is a pleasure because he is right there with you, but he also knows when to say yes and no. We had a marvelous time working on our first effort, *The Ali-Warhol Photo Tapestry*. When Andreas Brown, proprietor of the Gotham Book Mart, looked at the piece, he said it reminded him of a Warhol *Death and Disaster* painting. We also showed it to the director of the Warhol Museum. He had been intrigued enough to suggest we add some words to it. We adopted that idea on the first *Burroughs-Warhol Photo Tapestry*.

We began by looking through all the photographs of Andy and Bill that I had taken in 1980. We divided them up by the three dinners. In each case, David and I would attempt to make a design with the original pictures. Once we had a basic design, we would then photoshop the images and created the pieces using repetition, multi-images and juxtaposed positions. All three pieces were designed and built by Bockris and fellow photographer David Schmidlapp under the name Bockris-Schmidlapp in 2005. Each 60"x 32" piece consists of 24 black and white images. We intended to show them in public spaces such as libraries, reception rooms, corridors, subway installations, etc.

BURROUGHS-WARHOL PHOTO TAPESTRY #1

On February 1980, Andy Warhol, William Burroughs, Andre Leon Talley, and Victor Bockris met for dinner at a restaurant called 65 Irving. Bockris took twenty-four photographs of the event. This tapestry is unique because it is the only one in which we included words from the dinner transcript along the bottom of each grid.

BURROUGHS-WARHOL PHOTO TAPESTRY #2

On March 1, 1980, Victor Bockris, Andy Warhol, Marcia Resnick, Mick Jagger, Jerry Hall, and Liz Derringer came to dinner at William Burroughs' Bunker at the landmark building 222 Bowery. Marcia Resnick and Victor Bockris photographed the event. This tapestry is unique because Marcia Resnick took 20 of its 24 pictures.

BURROUGHS-WARHOL PHOTO TAPESTRY #3

On October 23, 1980, Victor Bockris, William Burroughs, James Grauerholz, Andy Warhol, Rupert Smith, and Jay Shriver met for dinner in Room 222 at the Chelsea Hotel. Victor Bockris photographed the event. This tapestry is unique because it was filmed by Alan Yentob, Nigel Finch, Anthony Wall of the BBC, and Howard Brookner, who was under contract to film a documentary about Burroughs. All four filmmakers and our chef Barry Miles appear in the tapestry.

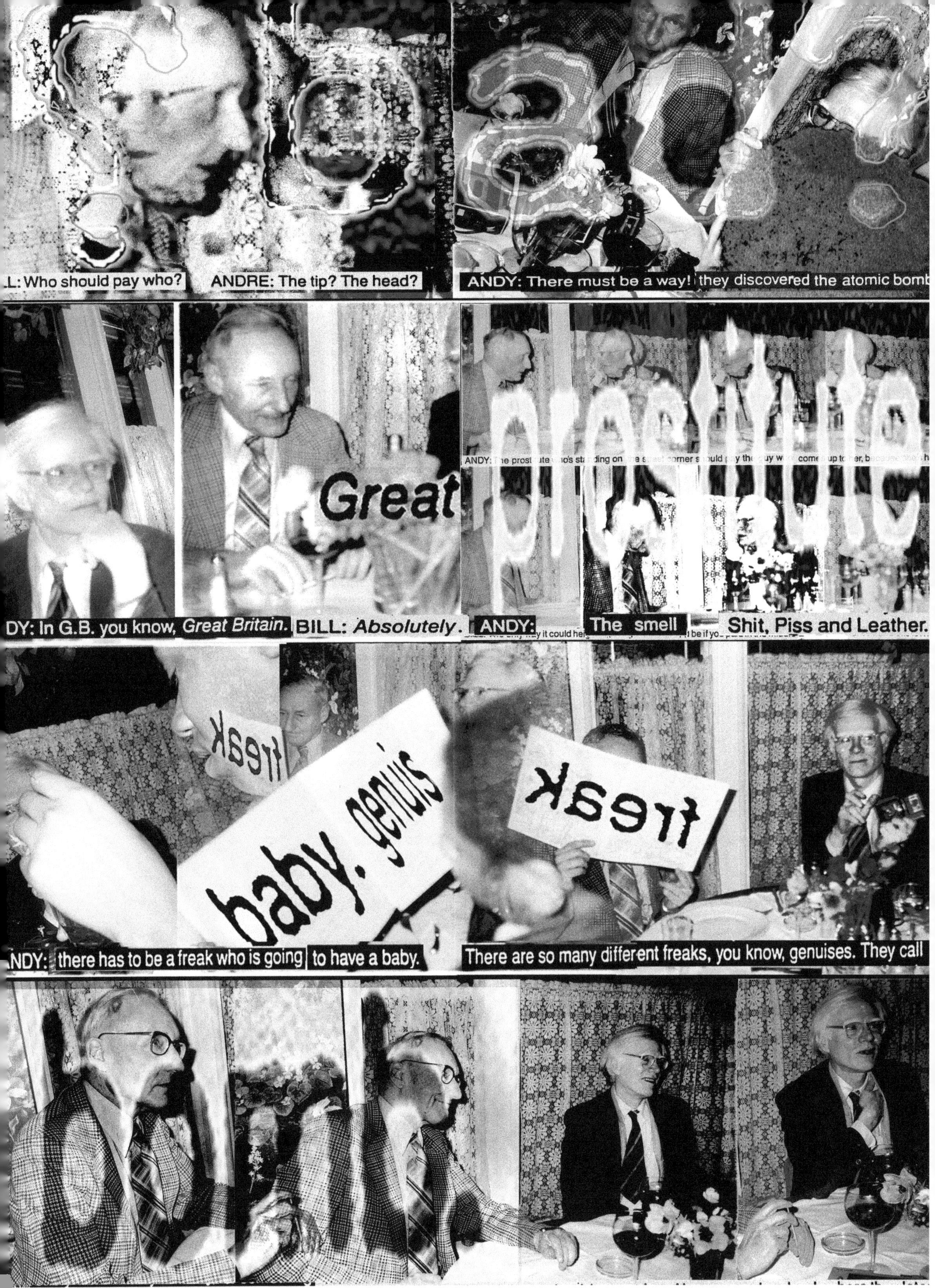
L: Who should pay who?
ANDRE: The tip? The head?
ANDY: There must be a way! they discovered the atomic bomb
Great
ANDY: The prostitute who's standing on the street corner should pay the guy who comes up to her, because wh
DY: In G.B. you know, Great Britain.
BILL: Absolutely.
ANDY:
The smell
Shit, Piss and Leather.
freak
baby. genius
freak
NDY: there has to be a freak who is going
to have a baby.
There are so many different freaks, you know, genuises. They call

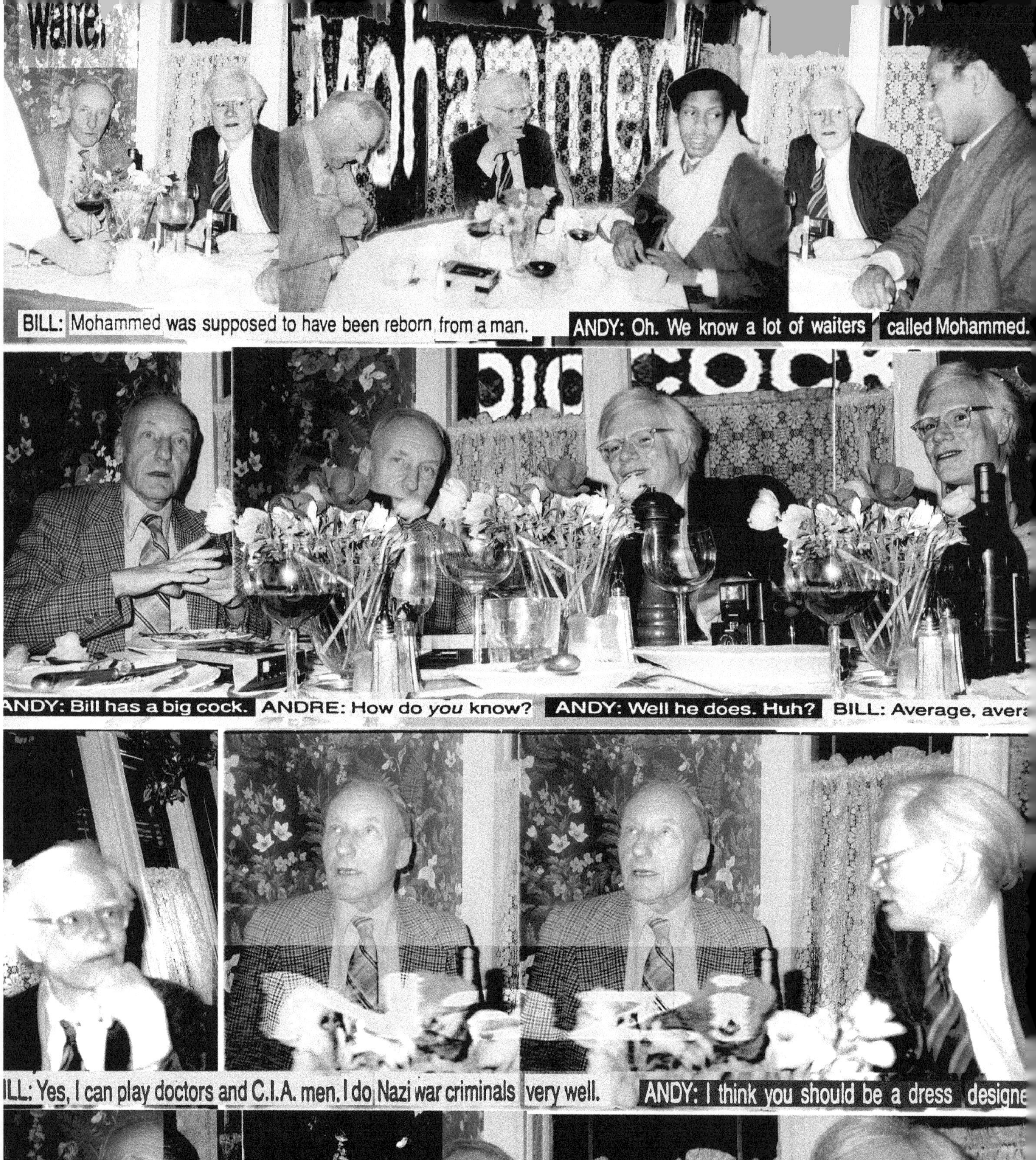

BILL: Mohammed was supposed to have been reborn, from a man.
ANDY: Oh. We know a lot of waiters called Mohammed.
ANDY: Bill has a big cock. ANDRE: How do you know? ANDY: Well he does. Huh? BILL: Average, avera
ILL: Yes, I can play doctors and C.I.A. men. I do Nazi war criminals very well. ANDY: I think you should be a dress designe

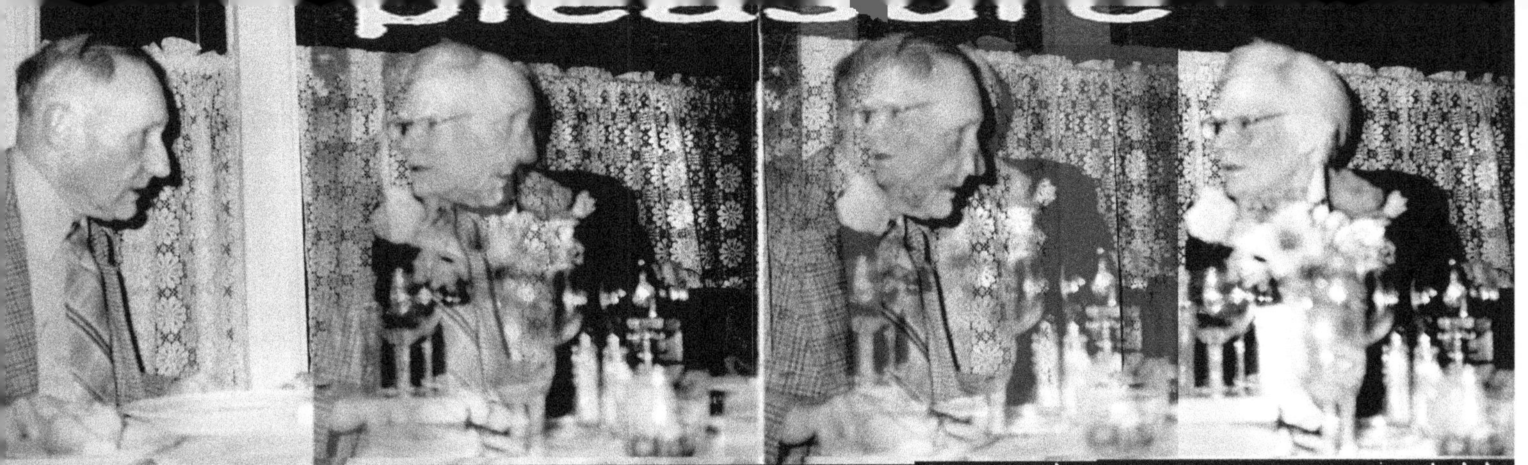

ANDY:The prostitute who's standing on the street corner should pay the guy who comes up to her, because she's ho

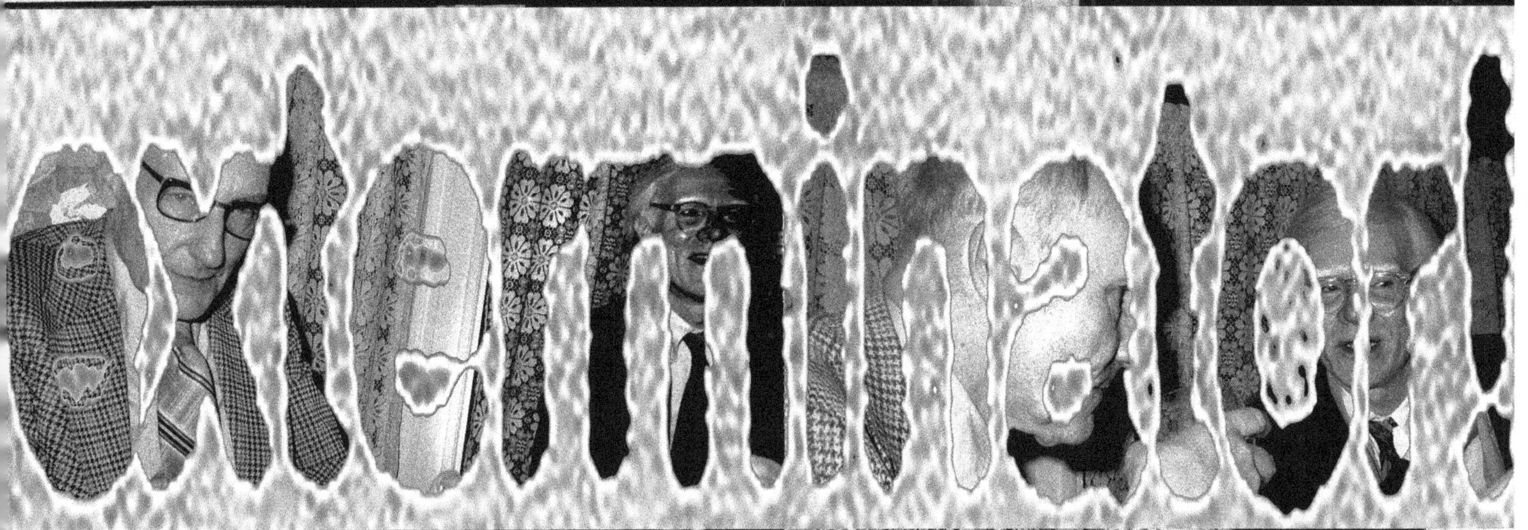

: It was the best job I ever had. ANDY: But I used to come home and I used to be so glad to find a little roach there to talk

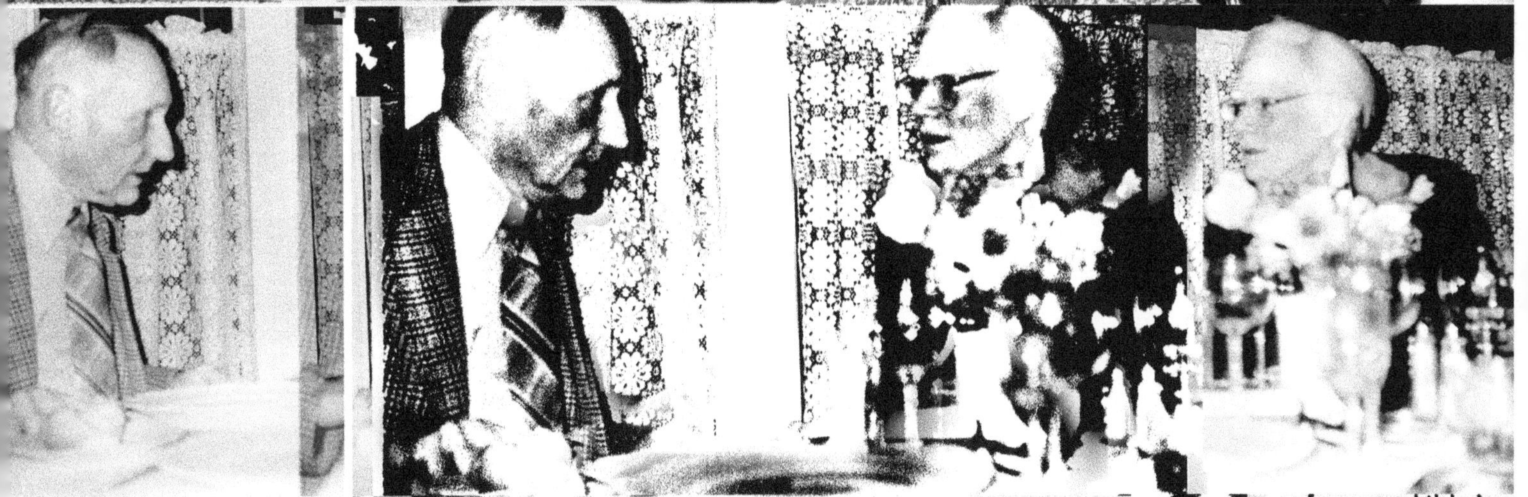

L: The only way it could heighten the   pleasure would be if you paid   in the middle   of sex and this is . .

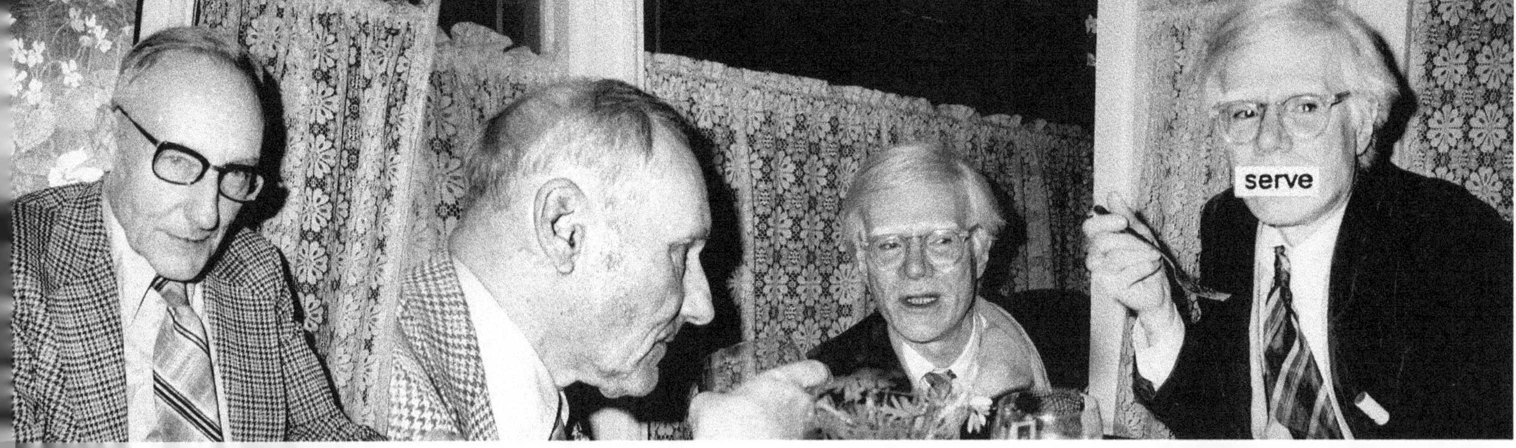

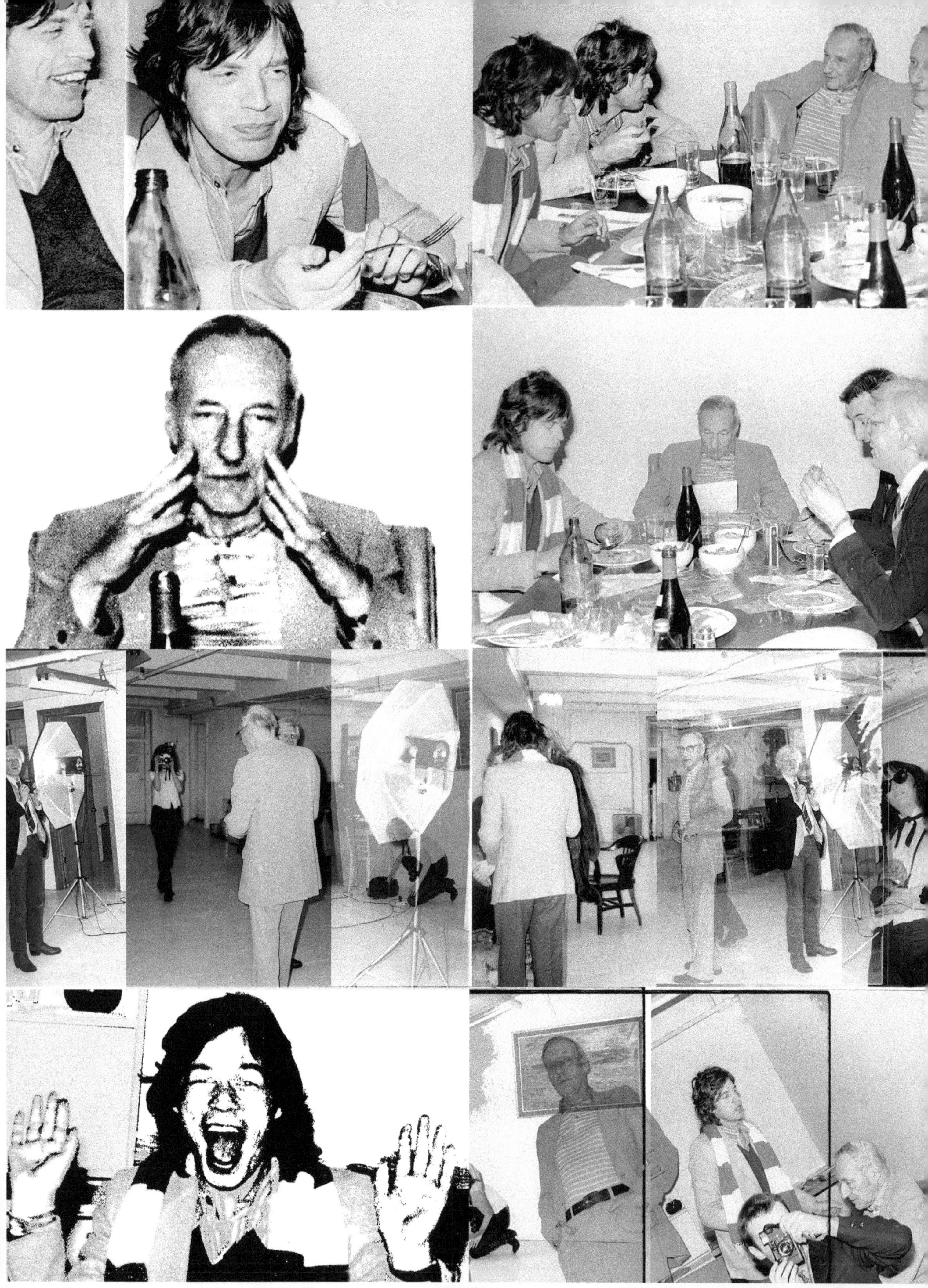

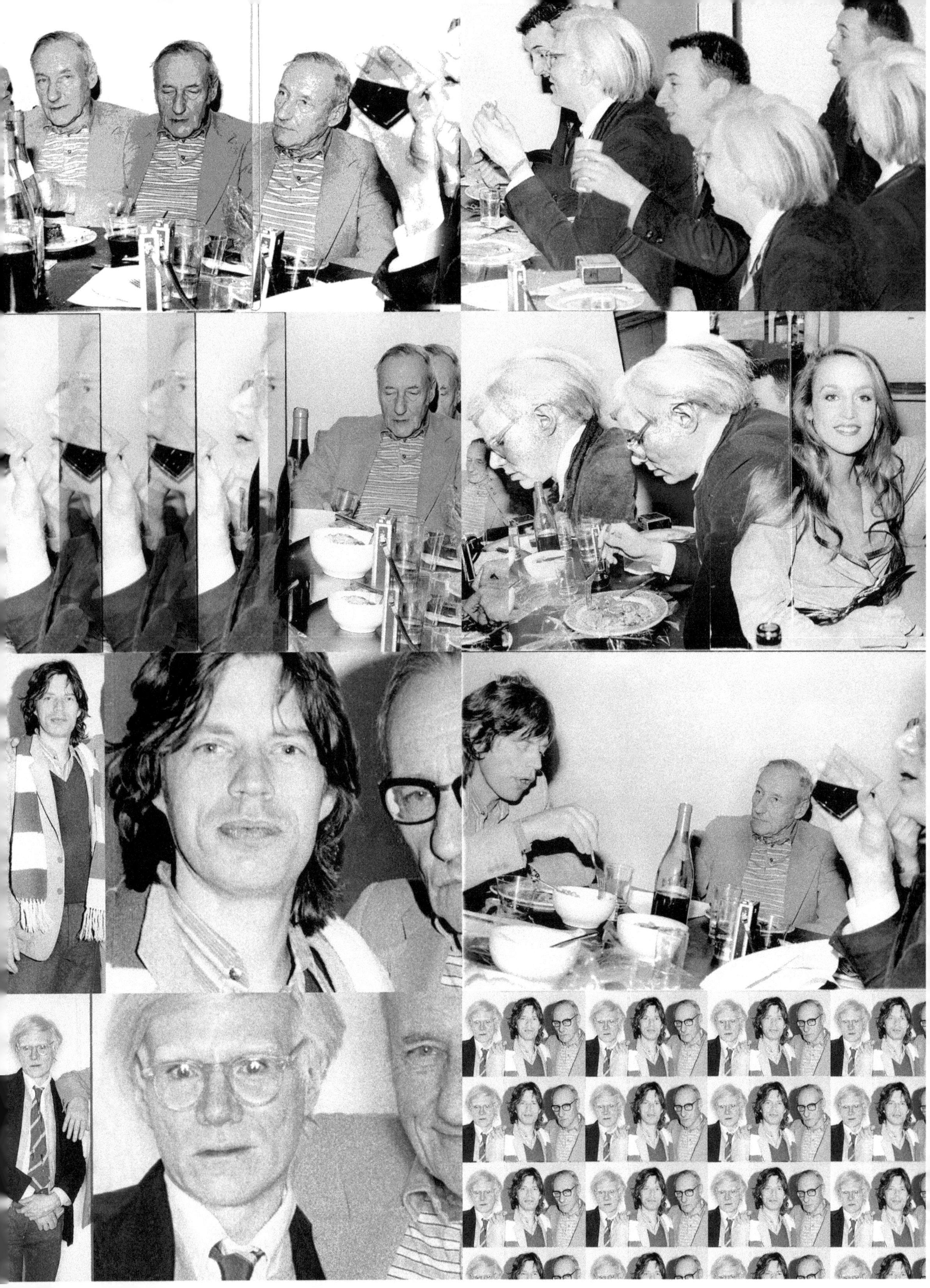

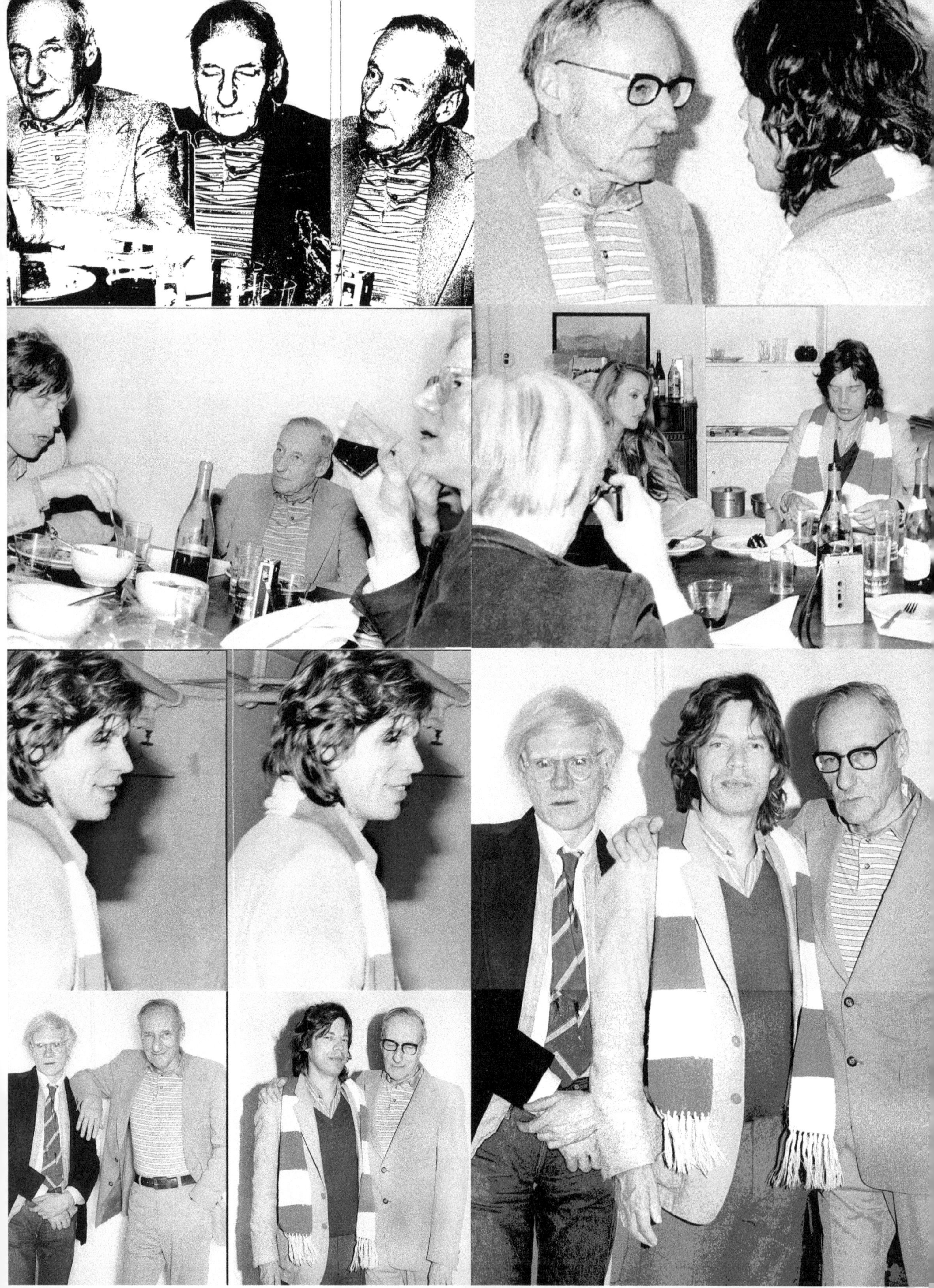

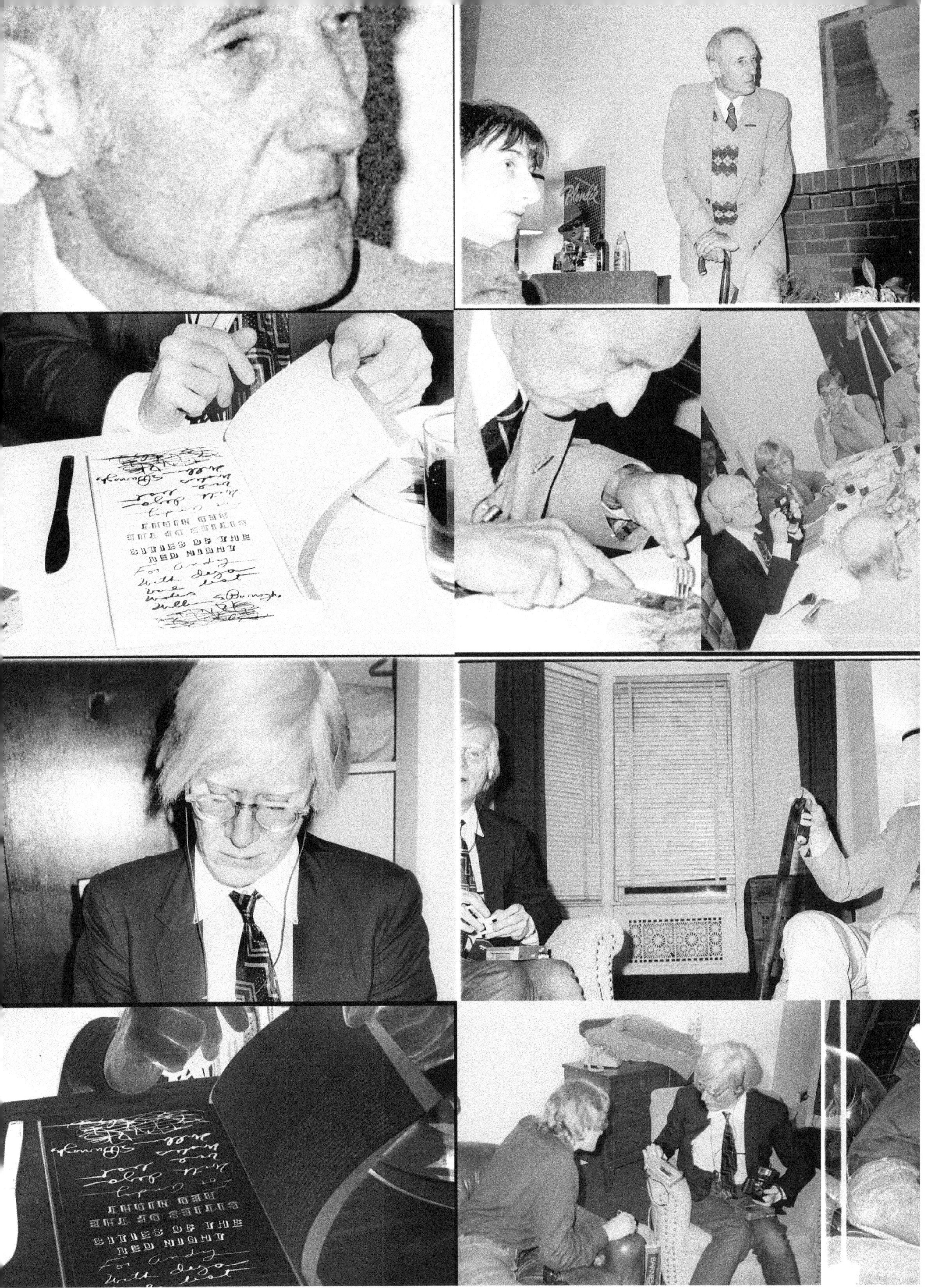

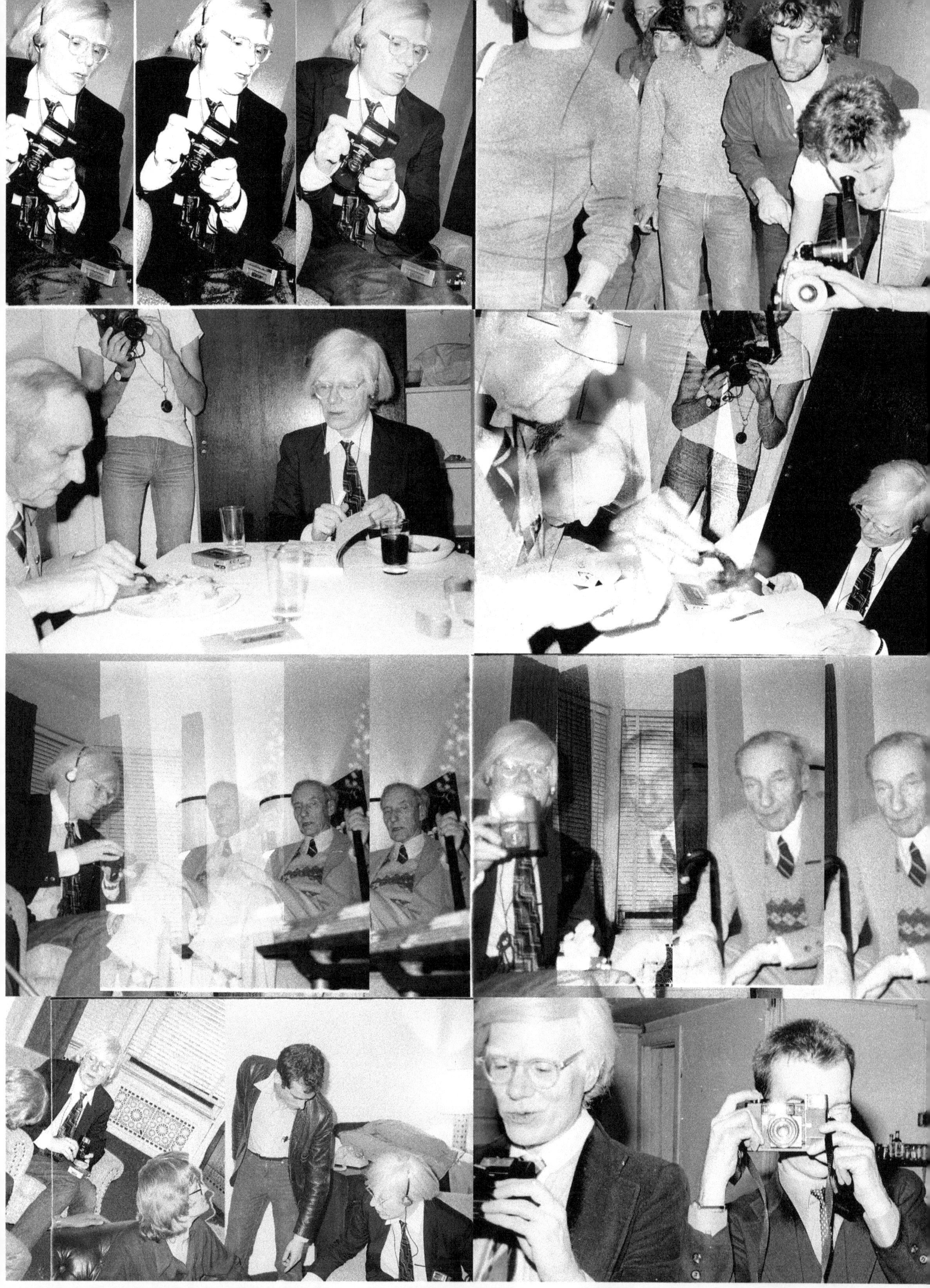

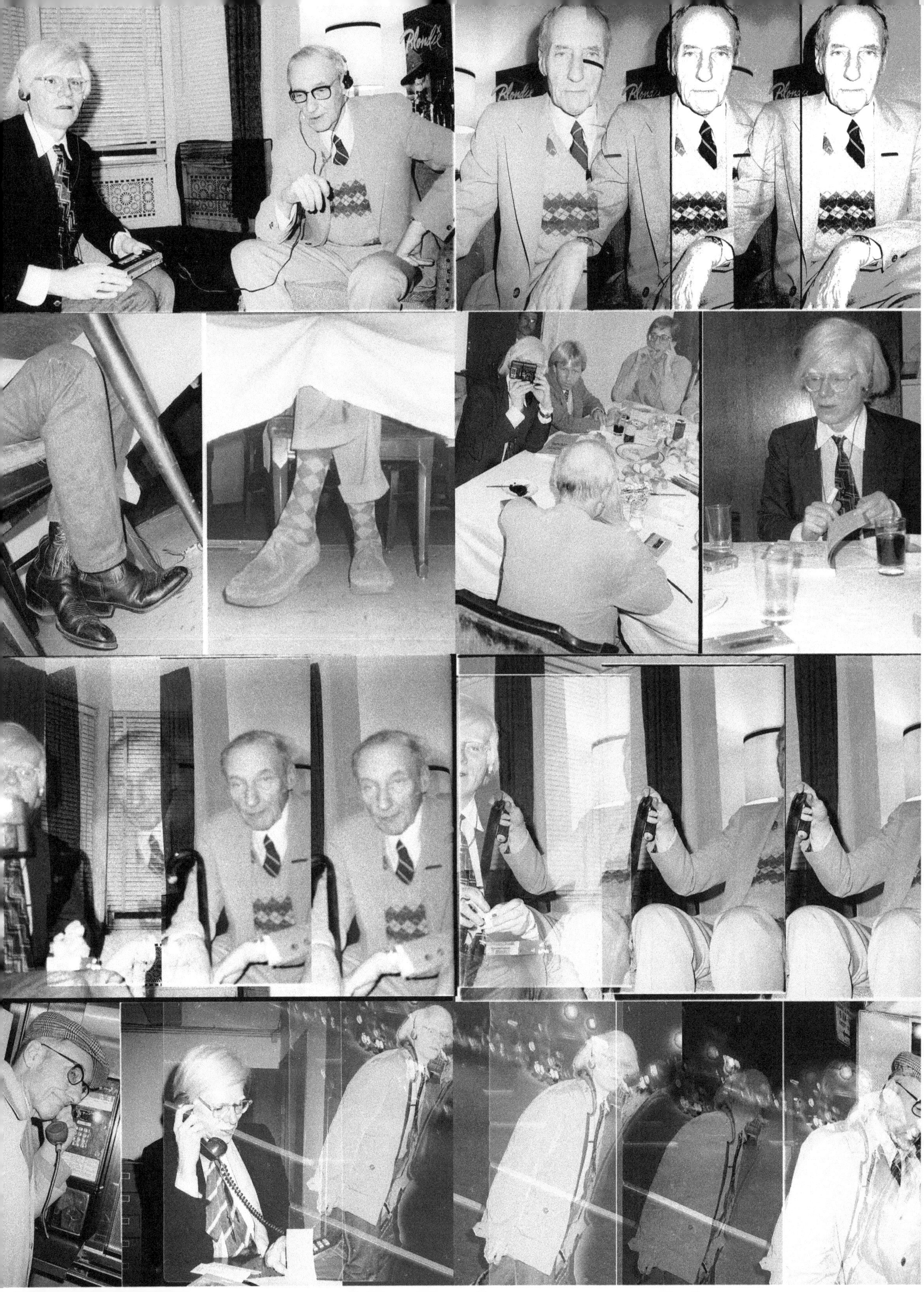

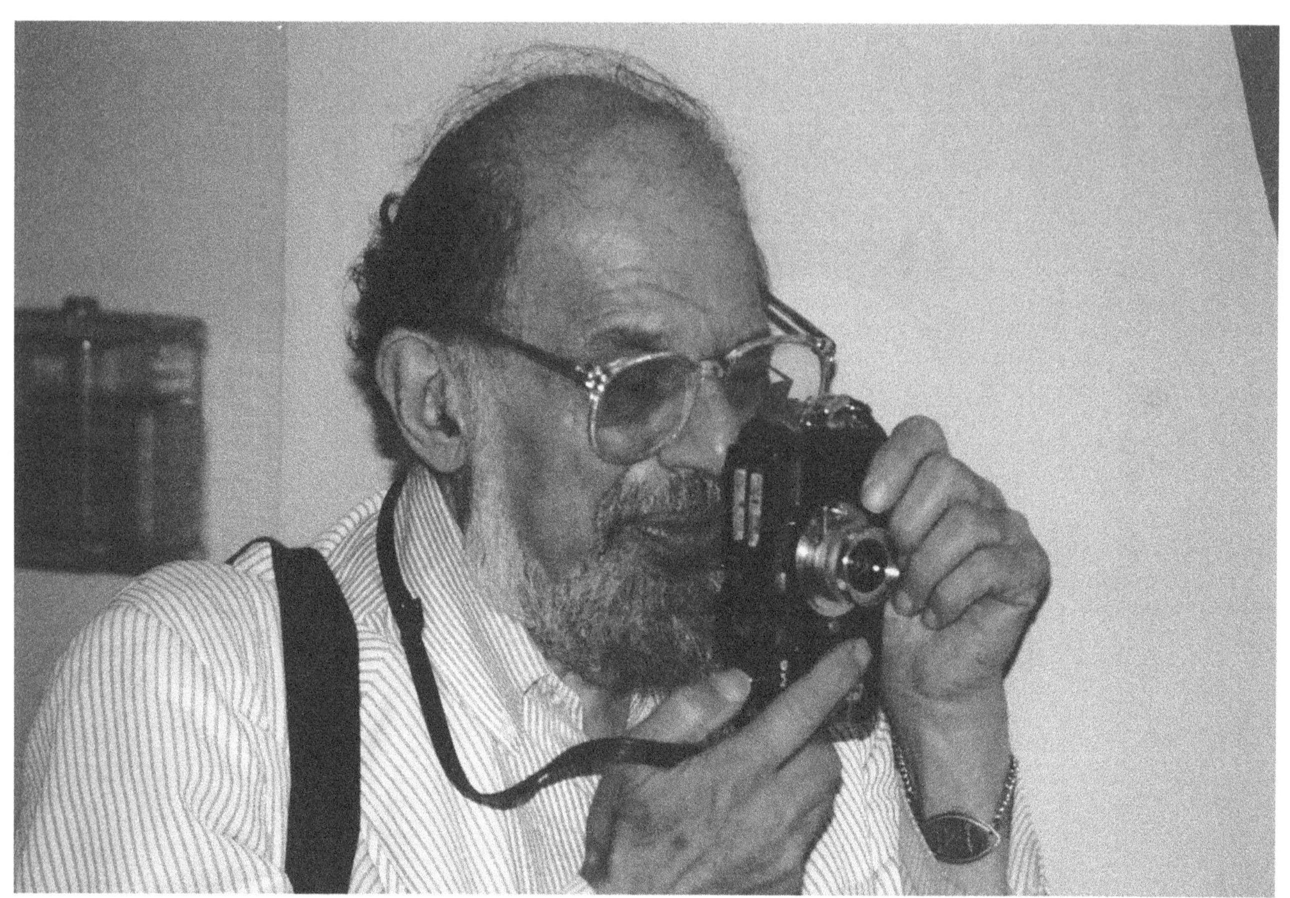

ON THE PHOTOGRAPHERS

MARCIA RESNICK

by Victor Bockris

Marcia Resnick was a smart girl and a bit of a smart aleck. I think she'd been an art teacher. She was curious. She was looking for something through her lens. She found it. She wanted to photograph bad boys and bad girls and she did and seemed to discover in the process, she was a member in the club. Every door opened, from Burroughs' Bunker to the Contortions' dressing room. Sharp eye, sharp ear, sharp dress, sharp tongue, Marcia cut the scene like it was butter. And when she got to the center, she liked it and decided to stay.

Glenn O'Brien, Writer 2005

Born in Brooklyn, New York, photographer and educator Marcia Resnick first exhibited her art at the Brooklyn Children's Museum when she was five years old. She is an alumnus of the Cooper Union and did her graduate work at California Institute of the Arts. Her photographs are exhibited internationally and are in major museum collections, including the Museum of Modern Art, NYC; Metropolitan Museum of Art, NYC; National Portrait Gallery, Washington DC; George Eastman House, Rochester; Museum of Fine Arts, Houston; New York Public Library; Jewish Museum, NYC; Rijksmuseum, Amsterdam; and Getty Museum, Los Angeles. Her work has also been published in numerous books and periodicals that include the *Paris Review* and *Rolling Stone*. In 1975, she also self-published three artist's books: *See*, *Landscapes*, and *Tahitian Eve*. Her autobiographical book of photographs about female adolescence, *Re-visions*, was published by Coach House Press, Toronto, 1978. Her book of portraits, *Punks, Poets & Provocateurs*, was published by Insight Editions, San Rafael CA, 2015.

She was part Patti Smith, part Mary Hartman, and part Diane Keaton. She was a scintillating conversationalist, always laughing, always on the edge of tears. She took a picture with all of herself, as one laughs with one's whole being. Her own coy style echoes the primordial boldness of punk and new wave music. Each portrait session featured Resnick's rare knack for capturing her subjects at that precise instant that defines them. "As soon as a subject enters the lens of my camera, he is coming into a relationship and having a conversation with me and becoming part of what I want to say about the world."

Resnick had a relationship with both of our leading men, who were among her heroes of the 1960s. In fact, when we started going through her portraits to decide how to organize them in *Punks, Poets & Provocateurs,* I was surprised to discover, after Johnny Thunders, she had taken more pictures of William Burroughs than anyone else in the book. I remember her 1978 photo session with him. I threw a party to welcome him to Los Angeles in my suite at the Tropicana Motor Motel on Sunset Boulevard. It was beginning to get dark when Resnick took Bill and James down to the pool. Some of her best portraits of William were taken that night. At the Nova Convention that December, Bill welcomed her into his dressing room where they clowned around taking photographs. The climax of her Burroughs portfolio came in 1981 during a long session at her studio at 530 Canal Street. Her best Burroughs portraits were published widely in magazines, in documentary films, in books, and on book covers. The images of Burroughs in this book are among her best portraits.

Although she did not take such a volume of pictures of Andy, he seemed to feel the same kind of affection for her as Bill. After the Mick Jagger dinner, Andy took Marcia aside to discuss the dangers of photographing Kenneth Anger. In one of Marcia's sessions with Andy, he let her photograph him as an odalisque lying on the couch at the Factory. When Andy died, her picture of him at the Mudd Club graced the cover of the *Village Voice*, a monument to her vision of the great artist.

Marcia's series of pictures of Andy and Bill capture the emotion that was already there before they walked to the wall. Andy rarely liked to be touched and Bill maintained an aristocratic distance but Marcia captured the connection between them. Two things rise from the surface of these portraits. Both men work together posing away in every frame in a ballet that climaxes when Bill lays his arm casually on Andy's shoulder and Andy accepts it. Resnick's series of Burroughs-Warhol portraits capture the rare spirit of collaboration.

Resnick reached the peak of her journey as her pictures graced the walls of her retrospective, *As It Is or Could Be*, at the Eastman Kodak Museum in Rochester in 2023, the reward of the true artist who stays the course against all odds.

DAVID SCHMIDLAPP

By David Schmidlapp

Photography has been my applied and extended medium for the past five decades. It has been the binding thread for all my artistic endeavors, which have included photomontages and layouts, slide and light shows, projections and installations, experimental filmmaking and cinematography, publishing and performance.

In the late '70s, I was a regular contributor with my "photo-pages" in the trendy style section of a downtown art weekly, *The Soho Weekly News*, where I produced, photographed, wrote, and designed my own photo-stories. By 1980, I had developed a craft of dazzling slide and light shows, lighting up the clubs and art spaces in downtown NYC. For the next three decades, I created light shows, installations, and "photo performances" in countless international venues, diverse as the National Film Theatre, London (1983); the Kitchen, NYC (1986); Universal Nightclub, Barcelona (1992); the Harvard School of Design (2000); and the Museum of Modern Art (2018). MoMA also recently acquired 30 of my ephemera from my "downtown" shows from 1979 to 1984.

In the early '80s, I created what has been claimed to be the first publication that focused on contemporary "urban" youth culture. The *IGTimes* was definitely the first publication of the inner-city art and culture that derived from the painting on subway cars by New York City's youth. I published and edited this "zine" for a decade. I also organized the *Aerosol Armada*, a multi-media slide / lecture / throwdown, painting executions in countless international venues ranging from prestigious universities like Yale and museums like the Rock and Roll Hall of Fame to Youth Centers from Italy to Hawaii. Complete sets of *IGTimes* are now collected in several notable libraries (e.g., Stanford University and Fales Library at New York University). The entire archive consisting of thousands of pre-digital artifacts (e.g., correspondences, zines, trades, news clippings, photos, writings, and layouts is housed in the Hip Hop Collections at Cornell University Library).

In the mid-'90s, I went back to filmmaking and made an award-winning experimental film, *Big Time Operator* (45min), with my aging father, a professional actor who was recovering from a brain injury. MoMA also recently acquired my 1981 film, *Not Quite Love*.

Collaboration has been a strong element in my work. I have worked extensively with musician and painter Walter Steding, who provided much of the music in my films and "projection performances." The legendary inner-city artist and hip-hop pioneer, Phase2, was instrumental in the development of the *IGTimes*, orchestrating many of our projects into the millennium. In the mid-'90s, I had a close association with visual artist and filmmaker Steve Staso, working on many of his film projects as a cinematographer and a collaborative mind.

In the early 2000s, I formed an artistic partnership with the biographer Victor Bockris, in which I re-worked his extensive archive of photos and audiotapes of our '60s icons: Andy Warhol, William Burroughs, and Muhammed Ali. Together we created the concept of the "Photo Tapestry," a retelling of events between these legendary men in a photo montage.

BOBBY GROSSMAN

by Glenn O'Brien

I don't remember exactly when I met Bobby. He was just there. I guess I met him when he was working with Richard Bernstein, the artist best known for doing all the wonderful covers of *Interview* that most people thought were done by Warhol. Richard was a painter, but much of his work was in illustration and he was, along with Jean-Paul Goude, one of the first to explore the collision between painting and photography. Richard's studio was the old ballroom of the Chelsea Hotel and Bobby was staying there at the ground zero of bohemia, up on the ninth floor. Although he was really mild-mannered, Bobby had a way with people. He was easy to be around and he was always around. He stuck to us like lint.

Bobby was a very talented illustrator—he had gone to art school at RISD with the Talking Heads—but he liked to take pictures and pretty soon he developed a talent for being in the right place at the right time. Or the wrong place at the right time. It seemed like Bobby always had his black leather jacket, his Wayfarer shades and his camera and wherever you went, he was there. Despite the black leather and shades, there was something cute about Bobby that made you want to hug him. He was sort of a teddy bear. Maybe it was his t-shirts, which were manga before anybody ever heard of manga. And then there was the Woodstock t-shirt that Bobby wore when I cast him as a nodding out junkie on a bombed-out block in *Downtown 81*. I wish the t-shirt was more prominent in the shot. That was the idea—you start out looking for peace and love and you end up in the garbage.

Bobby took so many pictures we sometimes wondered if he had film in his camera. He was at the Factory, CBGBs, the Mudd Club, Max's, Studio 54, or the club of the moment, and he knew everybody. He was sort of the punk Ron Galella, except that everyone liked him. What's not to like about Bobby? He is so nice and smart and uncommonly polite. He was never on assignment. I don't think Bobby really thought about what he was going to do with the pictures, but I do think he knew that they were important. That he was documenting history. In a way, he was a combat photographer, except instead of bombs and bullets, it was drugs and alcohol, and instead of the Vietcong, it was bouncers.

He became the official photographer of my cable show, *TV Party,* early on. Like everybody else, he worked on the show, he showed up, and kept showing up, and became a part of the *TV Party* gang. Bobby was the perfect photographer for a TV show because he didn't get in the way of the cameras. Well, not that often. And even though he would sometimes spill a drink, he was very agile with his camera. If you look at the contact sheets, all the pictures are good.

One of the reasons they are so good, aside from Bobby's great eye, is that he was not some interloping intruder but was friends with his subjects. This is the insider backstage real deal. Bobby knew he was shooting history even when people might have thought he was just killing time. His work is a fantastic time capsule opening onto a wild and strange world where everything seemed possible.

JENNY MORADFAR MEYER

By Stewart Meyer

Jenny was born in Tehran, Iran, attended early school years in NYC, and returned to Tehran as a teenager. Then she returned to the USA to enroll at the School of Visual Arts to study film and photography. In the early 1980s, Jenny was a frequent dinner guest at William S. Burroughs' Bunker. She was often the only woman in attendance but always felt welcome and at ease. She refers to Mr. Burroughs as a "kind and gentle man who loved cats and was respectful of all animals."

Early exposure to the Persian language provided a window for Sanskrit studies in India and at Columbia University in New York. Her interests broadened to include a yoga practice and an exploration of Yoga philosophy, culminating in her becoming a certified yoga instructor. Jenny's knowledge of Sanskrit and Yoga philosophy contributed to a well-rounded teaching style that added richness to her subjects.

"DOCTOR" ROBERT DE MARRAIS

by Victor Bockris

"Doctor" de Marrais contributed his comic interpretation of the mythic nature of the Burroughs-Jagger-Warhol dialogue at the heart of the *Burroughs-Warhol Connection*. He was a Gonzo Mathematician. A catalyst into the mysticism of mathematics and the esoteric. He lived in New York and Boston. He was a fine fellow, a creative man with a good heart. We are grateful to him for his insights. Unfortunately, the Doctor is out. He died many years ago. But now he lives on in this book.

VICTOR BOCKRIS (the Photographer)

by Victor Bockris

In the early sixties Bockris lived in London with his mother and his sister, Anna. When he was twelve, he filled in a survey called "Why I Like to Drink Milk." He wrote back, "I like to drink milk because I am small, and it makes me grow." The next week, he received a Brownie camera in the mail. In the next couple of years, he took a lot of photographs of his closest relatives. When he saw *A Hard Day's Night*, he bought a 35 mm camera and took photos of his friends at one of the top boarding schools in England, Rugby, pretending they were the Beatles. He continued to take photographs of his contemporaries in the

US, UK, and Russia. When he started working with Andrew Wylie at Bockris' company, Telegraph Books, they documented their activities in black and white pictures. Bockris' photographs of Muhammad Ali were featured in Philadelphia's underground paper, *The Drummer*, and their book *Ali: Fighter Poet Prophet* (Freeway Press: New York, 1974). He later composed *Punk Poets*, a collection of photographs of the Telegraph Books scene in America and England.

In 1977, Andy Warhol took him to visit Muhammad Ali as his photographer. Six of Victor's portraits of Muhammad Ali and Andy Warhol were published in Bockris' first book of photographs, *Nothing Happens* (Nadada: New York, 1978). Bockris began to focus on unexpected combinations of artists like Burroughs and Lou Reed; Debbie Harry and Andy Warhol; Marianne Faithful and Anita Pallenberg; and Jean-Michel Basquiat, Chris Stein, and Burroughs. In 1980, Bockris took the photographs of Burroughs and Warhol that were later shown in the Burroughs-Warhol Photo Tapestries by Bockris-Schmidlapp. In 1981, his photographs appeared in *With William Burroughs: A Report from The Bunker* (Seaver Books: New York, 1981). In 1982, he toured England for the publication of *With William Burroughs* and had his first one-man show of his Burroughs photographs at the B2 Gallery in London. In the winter of 1984, *Radar* magazine out of Basel, Switzerland, published a Victor Bockris issue, *The Bockris File*. It contained a collection of his writing and photography. His photographs also appeared in many magazines, as well as his books *Warhol: The Biography* Frederick (Muller: London, 1989), *Beat Punks* (DaCapo: New York, 1998), and *Muhammad Ali in Fighter's Heaven* (Hutchinson: London, 1998).

Victor Bockris took over two hundred photographs of William Burroughs, some of which were featured in his second book of photographs *Burroughs Reloaded* (Pam Books: Paris, 2017).

As much as Victor loved taking pictures, he loved the photographers with whom he discoursed like Robert Mapplethorpe, Chris Makos, Gerard Malanga, especially Marcia Resnick, Bobby Grossman, Bob Gruen, Bobby Miller, and many others including Erica and Elizabeth Lennard.

Photo Credits

Cover photo. William Burroughs and Andy Warhol, 1980 by Marcia Resnick.

10. Allen Ginsberg (the receiver) sitting, William Burroughs (the master) standing. The Bunker 1984 by Victor Bockris.

12. William Burroughs, Head Boy, at the Chelsea Hotel Dinner, October 1980 by Victor Bockris.

13. Andy Warhol – William Burroughs, Portrait Series 1980 by Marcia Resnick.

23. William Burroughs Victor Bockris Portrait for With William Burroughs 1981 by Marcia Resnick.

25. Andy Warhol – William Burroughs Series 1980 by Marcia Resnick.

26-27. Andy Warhol pins William Burroughs, Portrait Session the Factory, February 1980 by Bobby Grossman.

28. Andy Warhol Portrait Session 33 Union Square Factory, 1973 by Victor Bockris.

29. Bill, Bianca and Andy, The Factory, February 1980 by Bobby Grossman.

30. Damita Richter with The Rolling Stones second EP Five by Five, 1979 by Bobby Grossman.

33. Bill leans back, Andy watches, The Factory 1980 by Bobby Grossman.

34. Victor Bockris, William Burroughs and Andy Warhol, The Factory 1980 by Bobby Grossman.

35. End of photo session, Warhol and Burroughs, The Factory 1980 by Bobby Grossman.

36. Bill says Goodbye to Andy, who invites us to dinner. Bobby Grossman.

37. Bill looks into the next chapter, Andy Warhol partially obscured by Andre Leon Talley, 65 Irving Place New York 1980 by Victor Bockris.

38-39 Andy Warhol's Polaroids of William Burroughs at The Factory February 1980 by Bobby Grossman.

40. Portrait of Andy Warhol with Earphones at The Chelsea Hotel October 1980 by Victor Bockris.

41. Andy Warhol – William Burroughs Series by Marcia Resnick.

42. First Dinner Tapestry Bockris-Schmidlapp.

43. First Dinner Tapestry Bockris-Schmidlapp.

44. First Dinner Tapestry Bockris-Schmidlapp.

45. First Dinner Tapestry Bockris-Schmidlapp.

46. First Dinner Tapestry Bockris-Schmidlapp.

47. First Dinner Tapestry Bockris-Schmidlapp.

48. First Dinner Tapestry Bockris-Schmidlapp.

50. First Dinner Tapestry Bockris-Schmidlapp.

51. First Dinner Tapestry Bockris-Schmidlapp.

52-53. Cartoon by Doctor de Marrais

54-55. Double page spread Mick Jagger talks to William Burroughs, The Bunker March 1, 1980 by Marcia Resnick.

56. Jagger and Burroughs by Marcia Resnick.

57. Burroughs-Jagger-Warhol Multiple by Marcia Resnick and Bockris-Schmidlapp. 1980.

63. Jagger and Burroughs by Marcia Rersnick

64-65 Bill Burroughs, Mick Jagger, Andy Warhol Double Page spread by Marcia Resnick.

66. William Burroughs by Marcia Resnick.

67. Marcia Resnick by Victor Bockris.

68. Andy Warhol by Victor Bockris.

69. Group shot at table by Marcia Resnick.

70. Andy Warhol, Jerry Hall and Mick Jagger by Marcia Resnick.

71. Bill Burroughs by Marcia Resnick.

72. Mick Jagger and Bill Burroughs by Marcia Resnick.

73. Mick Jagger, Bill, Burroughs Victor Bockris and Andy Warhol by Marcia Resnick.

74. Jerry Hall, Mick Jagger, Bill Burroughs and Andy Warhol by Marcia Resnick.

75. William Burroughs and Andy Warhol by Victor Bockris

76. Leaving 1 by Victor Bockris.

77. Leaving 2 by Victor Bockris.

80-81 Bill Burroughs and Andy Warhol at their First Dinner by Victor Bockris.

82. Andy Warhol at the Chelsea Hotel October 1980 by Victor Bockris.

83. Andy Warhol – William Burroughs Series by Marcia Resnick.

88. Andy Warhol on the phone in the Bunker by Victor Bockris.

89. Andy Warhol and William Burroughs plug in at the Chelsea Hotel by Victor Bockris.

ACKNOWLEDGEMENTS

From the 1970s to the present, I have had the privilege of working for some of the best underground and/or counterculture magazines in the United States and Europe. From Philadelphia's underground weekly, *The Drummer*, where Andrew Wylie and I published a poetry column, "The Electric Generation," under the pen name Bockris-Wylie, to *Contact* and *Traveller's Digest* through *Interview* and *High Times*, including *New York Rocker*, *The Soho Weekly News*, *Night Magazine*, and *Night/Italia*, *Index Magazine*, *Blackbook*, *Another Man* (UK), *National Screw*, and *Gadfly* too, I've worked with some of the best editors I've ever known. Andy Warhol's manager Fred Hughes once told me how much he liked my profile, "Andy Warhol in Three Pieces," but wished it had been published in a more prestigious magazine than *National Screw*. I understood what he meant, but I liked being published in periodicals that did not ask me to rewrite the piece their way. These editors appreciated the input of creative writers. But it was more than that. Writing for the counterculture was like being part of a large international family. I shared the visions of these editors. They supported my writing and my lifestyle and I supported them.

The Burroughs-Warhol Connection is based on the collaboration of many spirits, including the readers. Thanks to everybody in the cast and crew. We owe a debt of gratitude to Jed Birmingham for allowing us to include his perceptive comparison of the films of William Burroughs and Andy Warhol in Chapter Eight. Thanks to my colleague and friend Glenn O'Brien for his essay on Bobby Grossman and quote on Marcia Resnick. They were originally published in Bobby Grossman's new book of photographs, *Low Fidelity*. Thanks to the artist Marcia Resnick for her luminous photographs of Mick Jagger, William Burroughs, and Andy Warhol. Thanks to my closest friend over many decades Miles for cooking such a good dinner for the BBC's Chelsea Hotel film and for his astute comments herein. Thanks to Stewart Meyer for his piece on Jennifer Moradfar Meyer and wisdom on William Burroughs. Thanks to Robert de Marrais for his interpretation of the Bunker dinner inside the front and and back covers. And with a very special thanks to my collaborator on Photo-Tapestries, David Schmidlapp, for everything he did in working with me over many years to make this book, and its earlier editions in French, Spanish and Japanese, possible.

In this book, I have quoted from various sources, including some of the following:

Title page. William Burroughs at the Jack Kerouac: King of the Beats Conference at the Jack Kerouac School of Disembodied Poetics in the Naropa Institute in Boulder Colorado, 1982.

Title page. Andy Warhol says it all at the top of his game in this rare television interview done in Boston during his single most creative year, 1966.

Preface. I love that the third quote is Allen Ginsberg explaining why Andy Warhol and William Burroughs are so cool. "Ginsberg on Heroes" by Victor Bockris, *National Screw* June 1977.

18. Robert Palmer on the Nova Convention, *The New York Times* December 4 1978.

55-56. This quote from page 55 of William's novel *Naked Lunch* published in 1959 is a vision of punk rock written fifteen years before the Ramones first played CBGBs.

57. And in the next quote eighteen years, later we have Bill telling Raymond Foye (under the pen name Ray Rumor) about his support of the Sex Pistols. *Search & Destroy*, San Francisco, where punk was strong, 1977.

58. In this quote Bill waxes lyrical about Mick Jagger in the 1960s. "Burroughs on Famous People" by Victor Bockris, *National Screw* 1977. There was a good deal of good feeling between Burroughs and the Rolling Stones.

59. In this parallel quote Andy presents his own account of Mick Jagger. *Exposures*, page 59, by Andy Warhol and Bob Colacello, Andy Warhol Books/Grosset & Dunlap, New York 1979.

60. Keith Richards wondered why William Burroughs encouraged him to take the apomorphine heroin reduction cure. Interview by Victor Bockris, *High Times* 1978.

87, 94, and 108. Miles becomes the droll commentator of the Chelsea Hotel Dinner, giving it a whole other color. From an interview by Victor Bockris New York 2007.

109–113. Jed Birmingham's essay "Burroughs-Warhol Film File" is from his website *Reality Studio* 2009.

117. The first two quotes are from the unpublished novel *Hitler on the Moon* by Bockris-Wylie, New York 1974. Burroughs and Warhol play strong roles in the novel. The words they are speaking come from interviews we had done with each man.

117. The Memory Chips quote is from Stewart Meyer's unpublished *Burroughs Diaries*. Meyer's snapshot of Bill and I working on the galleys of *With William Burroughs: A Report from the Bunker* captures the warm collaborative atmosphere in Mr. Burroughs' Laboratory at that time.

119. William Burroughs' statement on Andy Warhol's death was released in 1987.

121. Jon Savage's quote is from his article, "Cut Ups Go Pop: William S. Burroughs and a Mashed-up Future" in *Cut Ups, Cut Ins Cut Outs: The Art of William Burroughs*, Kunsthalle wien 2012. I love Jon Savage's contribution to this book. His perceptive sentence sits on its page life a bolt of paint. It is against the grain of this book, that's why it's so perfect. And so true.

122-123. The quote is from *William Burroughs and The Secret of Fascination* by Oliver Harris. This is my favorite quote in the book.

142. "The Poetry of Performance: An Interview with Patti Smith" by Victor Bockris, *Carry Out* magazine, Philadelphia, 1972. Patti really took off in this, her first great interview. And my first great interview. On West 23rd Street New York.

144. Bockris-Wylie interviews William Burroughs. "I can be jealous." *With William Burroughs: A Report from the Bunker*, Seaver Books, New York ,1981.

145-146. "Andy as a Pencil Sharpener." *Uptight: The Velvet Underground Story* by Victor Bockris and Gerard Malanga, Omnibus Press, London 1983.

146- 147. I remember this starting off well and getting better. "A Conversation between Susan Sontag and Richard Hell," *Interview* magazine, New York 1978.

149. Andy said everybody in the band was crazy the whole time they made the first album. Arguing fighting sulking. I think Andy encouraged that. *Uptight: The Velvet Underground Story* by Victor Bockris and Gerard Malanga, Omnibus Press, London 1983.

154. "Who did you shoot Bill?" "The Captain's Cocktail Party, Dinner with William Burroughs, Andy Warhol and Mick Jagger," *Index* magazine New York 2005.

155. Bowie at the Bunker. New York is the most exotic place. *Beat Punks* by Victor Bockris Da Capo New York 1998.

160. "Am I boring you?" "Lou Reed Meets William Burroughs" by Victor Bockris, Ludds Mill, Newcastle UK 1979.

162-163. "What do you write about Victor?" "Debbie Harry and Chris Stein have Dinner with William Burroughs," *New Music World*, London 1980.

163. Mapplethorpe on Time. "It's so quick!" "Robert Mapplethorpe Takes Off by Victor Bockris," *New York Rocker* 1977.

166. "I can just stop and not miss it." "Keith Richards Interview" by Victor Bockris, *High Times* New York 1978.

167. "There's going to be a new idea of what people are." "Debbie Harry Interview" by Victor Bockris, High Times New York 1996.

168. "You're crazy man!" "William Burroughs Interview" by Victor Bockris, *Interview* magazine, New York 1991.

170. "I don't know who I am." "Gregory Corso Interview" by Bockris-Wylie, *The Drummer*, Philadelphia 1973.

174. "I see Burroughs and Warhol as parallel people." *William Burroughs: The Man Within*, documentary film 2009.

177 "To write, you have to keep traveling." *With William Burroughs: A Report from The Bunker* by Victor Bockris, Seaver Books New York 1981.

181. End of the Preface, "An Interview with Allen Ginsberg" by Victor Bockris in Al Goldstein's *National Screw*, June 1977.

192. "Marcia was a smart girl and a bit of a smart aleck." Glenn O'Brien on Marcia Resnick.

195. "Bobby had a way with people." Glenn O'Brien on Bobby Grossman. Bless his heart for both these memories.

THE END